MORE REVENUE, PLEASE

500+ Ways to Grow Revenue Within 60 Days

Nader Sabry
nadersabry.com

Published by Nader Sabry
Calgary, Alberta, Canada

First Printing, 2026
Printed in the United States of America and Canada

ISBN (Paperback): 978-1-7380543-2-9
ISBN (Hardcover): 978-1-7380543-4-3
ISBN (Ebook): 978-1-7380543-3-6
ISBN (Audiobook): 978-1-7380543-5-0

Cataloguing. Published in Canada. Cataloguing in Publication (CIP) data available from Library and Archives Canada.

Nader Sabry
Royal Oak, P.O. Box 91022
Calgary, Alberta, Canada T3G 0B1

www.nadersabry.com

Contents

Part 1 — Understand the Gap 5

1.1 Introduction
1.2 How to Use This Book
1.3 The Painkiller Gap Model

Part 2 — Create Revenue 19

2.1 New Offers · 10 ideas
2.2 New Products · 15 ideas
2.3 New Monetization Models · 14 ideas
2.4 New Commercial Assets · 23 ideas
2.5 New Business Lines · 27 ideas

Part 3 — Unlock Revenue 119

3.1 Upsell & Cross-sell · 26 ideas
3.2 Repricing & Price Capture · 20 ideas
3.3 Reactivation & Recovery · 25 ideas
3.4 Underused Asset Monetization · 25 ideas
3.5 Bundling & Packaging · 20 ideas

Part 4 — Accelerate Revenue 246

4.1 Prepay & Upfront Cash · 20 ideas
4.2 Billing & Collection Speed · 28 ideas
4.3 Sales Cycle Compression · 23 ideas
4.4 Activation Speed · 19 ideas
4.5 Pull-Forward Offers · 18 ideas

Part 5 — Expand Revenue 365

5.1 New Channels · 22 ideas
5.2 New Customer Segments · 20 ideas
5.3 New Geographies · 18 ideas
5.4 Frequency Growth · 20 ideas
5.5 Customer Acquisition Growth · 25 ideas

Part 6 — Protect Revenue 481

6.1 Churn Prevention · *18 ideas*
6.2 Renewal Protection · *20 ideas*
6.3 Discount Control · *20 ideas*
6.4 Deal & Margin Protection · *20 ideas*
6.5 Delivery Reliability · *24 ideas*

Part 7 — Build Playbook & Sprint 594

7.1 Revenue Prioritization Matrix
7.2 Build Your Revenue Playbook
7.3 The 60-Day Revenue Sprint

Closing

About the Author

PART 1
Understand the Gap

Before This Business Can Fix Its Revenue, It Has to Understand Where It Is Losing It.

Most revenue problems look like sales problems. They are not. They are structural — gaps between what the business delivers and what it captures, between the value customers experience and the price they are asked to pay, between the commercial opportunity that exists and the offer built to take it.

Part 1 gives you the foundation. Three chapters. Each one builds the clarity that makes every strategy in Parts 2 through 6 more useful.

What This Part Covers

Introduction — the context behind the revenue gap and why the CFO is the right person to fix it
How to Use This Book — how to navigate 520 ideas and find the starting point that fits your business today
The Painkiller Gap Model — the single commercial framework that runs beneath every idea in this book

Where to Start

New to the book? Start with the Introduction.
Ready to identify your starting point? Go to How to Use This Book.
Want the commercial filter first? Go directly to The Painkiller Gap Model.

Introduction

You Already Know Something Is Off

You have sat in enough board meetings to feel it before anyone says a word.

The deck looks fine. The numbers hold together. Revenue is up — *just enough* to avoid the hard conversation. Margin is intact — *just about.* And everyone around the table is nodding because the story is coherent and nobody wants to be the one who pulls at the thread.

But you are pulling at it. Quietly. In the car on the way home. In the thirty minutes before the rest of the building wakes up. You are running the numbers a different way and arriving at the same uncomfortable place.

Something is being left on the table. You just cannot put your finger on exactly where.

You have seen the **pricing that has not moved in three years** — not because the market would not bear an increase, but because nobody wanted the conversation with the client. You have watched **customers go quiet** and waited for Sales to follow up, and Sales never did. You have signed off on **contract renewals that went through at exactly the same**

rate as the original deal, because the renewal landed in someone's inbox at the wrong moment and *getting it signed felt like enough of a win.*

You have delivered work that never made it onto an invoice. Absorbed costs that should have been passed on. Bundled things in for free because it felt easier than explaining the charge. None of it was a decision, exactly. ***It was just what happened.***

And what happened is that a meaningful amount of revenue — **revenue your business earned, revenue your customers would have paid** — quietly disappeared. Not to a competitor. Not to a market shift. Just into the gap between what you do and what you charge for it.

> ***That gap has a number.*** *EY research puts it at* ***1% to 5% of EBITDA, every single year.*** *On a $50 million business, that is up to* ***$2.5 million. Gone. Before you ever see it.*** *Not stolen. Not written off in a bad deal. Just never captured — slipping out through the ordinary friction of a business growing faster than its revenue controls.*

What Nobody Tells the CFO

Here is the uncomfortable truth about revenue advice. **Almost all of it is written for Sales.**

It is about pipeline, conversion rates, new logos, and closing frameworks. The entire commercial machine points outward — toward people who have never heard of you, never bought from you, and have no particular reason to trust you yet. And yes, new customers matter. They are the lifeblood of a growing business. But they are also **the most expensive revenue you will ever generate.**

> *Acquiring a new customer costs 5 to 25 times more than keeping one you already have.*
> ***— Harvard Business Review***

The probability of closing a sale with an existing customer sits at **60 to 70 percent.** With a brand new prospect, that number drops to somewhere between **5 and 20 percent.** Read those figures slowly, because they contain something important.

CHART 3 · COST OF ACQUISITION · NEW VS EXISTING CUSTOMER

5–25x

more expensive to acquire a new customer
than to retain an existing one

NEW CUSTOMER High acquisition cost	**EXISTING CUSTOMER** Low retention cost

Source: Harvard Business Review

Your existing customers are four, five, sometimes ten times more likely to buy from you — and yet the majority of commercial energy in most businesses, the budget, the headcount, and the attention of leadership, is aimed at the harder, slower, and more expensive end of the problem.

That is not a criticism of Sales. That is just where the incentives point. But **you are the CFO. You do not follow incentives. You follow the numbers.** And the numbers are pointing somewhere most businesses never look — back inside their own walls, at revenue already earned but not yet captured.

The Revenue You Are Not Seeing

Nearly half of all business leaders say **revenue leakage is a systemic problem** in their organisation. Not an occasional mistake. Not a one-off billing error. A system that reliably produces less revenue than the business actually earns — quietly, consistently, year after year.

It shows up as unbilled work that fell through the gap between delivery and invoicing. Contracts that auto-renewed at the same price while costs climbed twelve percent. Services that began as a goodwill gesture and became a permanent free expectation. Discounts applied under commercial pressure that nobody ever thought to remove from the account.

CHART 1 · REVENUE LEAKAGE · WHAT YOUR BUSINESS IS LOSING ANNUALLY

Nearly half of all business leaders say revenue leakage is a systemic problem in their organisation.

Source: EY Research, MGI Research

Gartner's research confirms that **slower top-line growth is the number one pressure CFOs are carrying right now.** When growth stalls, the instinct is to cut costs. It is the tool most finance leaders were trained to reach for, and it works — once, maybe twice. It buys a quarter. It buys goodwill with the board. And then the question comes back, harder this time: ***"Where is the growth actually coming from?"*** Cost reduction does not answer that question. **This book does.**

Because before you build new revenue — before you open new markets, launch new products, or hire another salesperson — **the smartest move is to stop the leak.** Recover what is already yours. Charge for what you are already delivering. Reprice what the market will comfortably bear. Go back to the customers who already trust you and give them a reason to buy again.

What You Will Actually Get

Most CFOs are handed a seat at the table. **This book helps you earn it in a different room.**

Not the room where you report what happened. The room where you decide what happens next. Where revenue conversations start with you — not with Sales, not with the CEO — because you walked in with the numbers, the moves, and the plan already worked out. That shift in position is the real return on reading this book. Everything else is how you get there.

In practical terms, here is what changes. You will stop watching revenue conversations happen around you and start leading them. You will bring ideas to the board that do not require a budget increase or a new headcount approval. You will find money inside the business that nobody knew was missing — and you will arrive with a clear, credible plan to capture it. You will also **protect what you already have** — the customers quietly drifting, the contracts quietly eroding, the margin quietly leaking out of a model nobody has reviewed in three years. Most businesses only see these problems after they have already cost them. **You will see them first.**

And perhaps most importantly, you will have a language. A way of talking about revenue that is specific, actionable, and grounded in numbers. Not strategy. Not vision. *Numbers* — the thing you were always supposed to own. A CFO who can find, capture, and protect revenue without adding cost is not just valuable.

They are untouchable.

CHART 7 · SALE PROBABILITY · EXISTING CUSTOMERS VS NEW PROSPECTS

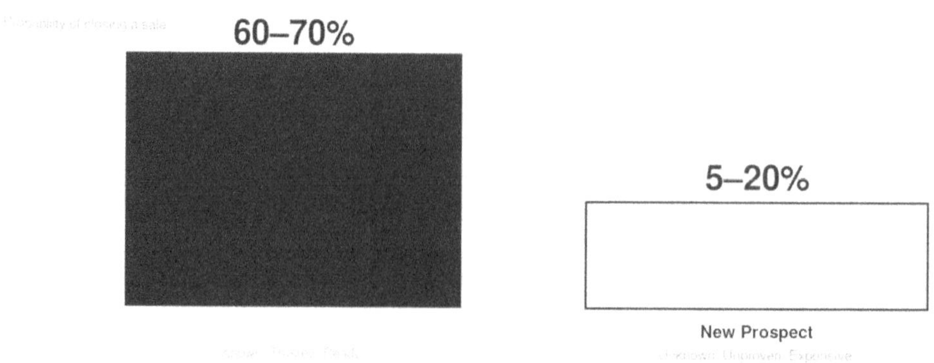

Source: Marketing Metrics, Farris et al., cited in Forbes

How This Book Works

Each chapter covers one idea. **One revenue move. Fully contained, deliberately short, and built for a CFO who does not have the luxury of time.**

You will get a clear description of what the idea is and exactly why it makes money. You will get a real-world example of a business that has executed it — not a sanitised case study, but a specific situation with a visible outcome. You will get a set of numbered steps that begin with a single, concrete action you can take this week. And you will get the ownership flow — who drives execution, who supports it, and how finance leads the process without overstepping into territory that belongs to someone else.

There is no required reading order. **If Chapter 7 is the one that makes you put the book down and pick up the phone, start there.** If you read the whole thing on a long-haul flight and land with a list of twelve things to test, that works too. The only rule is that every idea must move from the page into a conversation — because ***the most expensive revenue move is the one you found interesting and never actually did.***

One Rule

Every idea in this book passed a single test before it earned its place on the page.

Can this actually move the needle?

Not — *is this clever.* Not — *does this look good in a board deck.* Not — *could this work under the right conditions, with the right team, and a following wind.* **Can it move the needle. Now. In a real business. With real constraints and a board that wants answers on Thursday.**

That is the bar. Nothing got in without clearing it.

You are holding the map.

THE REVENUE SYSTEM · 520 IDEAS ACROSS FIVE DIMENSIONS

PART 2 **Create Revenue** *89 ideas*	PART 3 **Unlock Revenue** *116 ideas*	PART 4 **Accelerate Revenue** *108 ideas*	PART 5 **Expand Revenue** *105 ideas*	PART 6 **Protect Revenue** *102 ideas*
2.1 New Offers	3.1 Upsell & Cross-sell	4.1 Prepay & Upfront Cash	5.1 New Channels	6.1 Churn Prevention
2.2 New Products	3.2 Repricing & Price Capture	4.2 Billing & Collection Speed	5.2 New Customer Segments	6.2 Renewal Protection
2.3 New Monetization Models	3.3 Reactivation & Recovery	4.3 Sales Cycle Compression	5.3 New Geographies	6.3 Discount Control
2.4 New Commercial Assets	3.4 Underused Asset Monetizatio	4.4 Activation Speed	5.4 Frequency Growth	6.4 Deal & Margin Protection
2.5 New Business Lines	3.5 Bundling & Packaging	4.5 Pull-Forward Offers	5.5 Customer Acquisition Growth	6.5 Delivery Reliability
89 ideas	**116 ideas**	**108 ideas**	**105 ideas**	**102 ideas**

520 ideas total

Let's go and get it.

How to Use This Book

This book is not meant to be read from cover to cover in one sitting. It is meant to be used — the way a sharp operator uses any good tool. You pick it up when you have a problem, you find the right section, and you walk away with something you can act on before the week is out.

That said, read **The Painkiller Gap Model** before anything else. It is the single filter that sits behind every idea in this book. It takes ten minutes. It will change how you evaluate every revenue conversation you have from this point forward. Read it first. Everything else is ordered by where your business needs help most.

This book was written with the CFO in mind. But if you are a founder, CEO, or commercial leader without a finance title — everything here applies directly to you. The CFO lens is a way of thinking about revenue, not a job description. If you own the commercial outcomes in your business, this book is for you.

This book is not for people looking for a sales pipeline framework, a new-customer acquisition playbook, or a motivational guide to growth. It is not for businesses in their first year with no existing customer base. If you are chasing your first ten customers, start there first. This book is for the operator who already has a business running and wants to find the revenue they are already earning but not yet keeping.

Find Your Biggest Problem First

Most CFOs coming to this book are feeling pressure in one specific place. Revenue is flat and the board wants growth. Cash is tight and collection is slow. Customers are leaving and nobody has a plan. Good customers are being discounted into bad deals.

Start where the pain is. The fastest return comes from solving the problem that is already costing you money — not from working through a book in sequence.

Read the description of each part below. One of them will describe your business more accurately than the others. That is your starting point.

The Five Revenue Problems — And Where to Go

WHERE TO START

Read each situation. The one that sounds most like your business is your starting point.

YOUR SITUATION	GO TO
We have capability we can't easily sell	PART 2 Create Revenue
We deliver more value than we charge for	PART 3 Unlock Revenue
Revenue is agreed but cash arrives too slowly	PART 4 Accelerate Revenue
The offer works — not enough people are seeing it	PART 5 Expand Revenue
We are losing customers or margin we should be keeping	PART 6 Protect Revenue

If your business needs new revenue sources it does not have yet — go to Part 2.

This is the right place if your current offer set is too narrow, your market is shrinking, or you have capacity and capability that is not yet generating income. Part 2 covers new offers, new products, new monetisation models, new commercial assets, and new business lines. These moves take longer to build but create revenue that did not exist before.

If your business has revenue sitting inside it that is not being fully captured — go to Part 3.

This is the most common situation and the fastest win. You are already delivering value your customers would pay more for. You have customers who bought once and were never sold to again. You have pricing that has not moved in years. Part 3 covers upsell and cross-sell, repricing, reactivation, underused asset monetisation, and bundling. Most businesses find two or three immediately actionable ideas here within the first read.

If your revenue is real but your cash is slow — go to Part 4.

This is the right place if the problem is not the size of the number but when it arrives. Deals close but payment terms are long. Invoices go out late. The sales cycle drags for no good reason. Part 4 covers prepay and upfront cash, billing and collection speed, sales cycle compression, activation speed, and pull-forward offers. These moves do not grow the top line — **they move cash into this quarter instead of next.**

If your business is ready to grow beyond its current boundaries — go to Part 5.

This is the right place if your core model is working and the opportunity is in taking it further — into new channels, new customer segments, new geographies, or higher purchase frequency. Part 5 covers expansion moves that build on what is already proven rather than starting from scratch. These are growth plays, not recovery plays.

If your business is losing revenue it should be keeping — go to Part 6.

This is the right place if churn is climbing, renewals are slipping, discounts are being given too freely, or margin is eroding deal by deal. Revenue protection is the most overlooked lever in most businesses. A ten percent reduction in churn often delivers more than a ten percent increase in new sales — at a fraction of the cost. Part 6 covers churn prevention, renewal protection, discount control, deal and margin protection, and delivery reliability.

These Strategies Are a Starting Point, Not a Script

Every revenue move in this book is a **proven concept, not a fixed prescription.** No two businesses are the same. Your customer base, your pricing model, your team capacity, and your commercial relationships are specific to you — and the way you execute any idea here should reflect that.

Think of each chapter as a framework you pick up, examine, and then reshape to fit your business. **The structure is the guide. Your judgement is the filter.** Some ideas will work almost exactly as written. Others will need to be adapted significantly before they fit your context. A few will spark a completely different idea that is better suited to your situation than the original.

That is the right way to use this book. *Take what works. Adjust what needs adjusting. Discard what does not apply.* The goal is not to implement every idea — it is to find the three or four moves that fit your business right now and execute them with conviction.

Start Simple. Protect What Is Already Working.

Before you reach for the most ambitious revenue move on your list, **start with the simplest one that works.** This is not a counsel of caution — it is a principle of operational continuity.

Every revenue change creates some degree of disruption. A pricing move affects how Sales has conversations. A new billing structure changes how Finance processes invoices. A reactivation campaign puts pressure on a customer success team that may already be stretched. None of these are reasons not to act — but they are reasons to sequence carefully.

Simple moves first. They generate early wins, build confidence across the team, and prove the model before you scale it. They also protect the revenue you already have while you build the revenue you want. A business that chases three complex revenue moves simultaneously and executes none of them well is in a worse position than one that executes one simple move cleanly and banks the result.

Start with the idea that requires the fewest moving parts, the least cross-functional coordination, and the fastest path to a number you can put in front of the board. Build from there.

How Each Chapter Works

Every chapter in this book follows exactly the same format. Once you learn the structure, you can move through ideas quickly and make a call on each one in minutes.

What it is — a clear, plain-English description of the revenue move. No jargon. No theory. Just what it is and why it makes money.

Why it works — the commercial logic behind it. Why customers respond to it, why the numbers improve, and what makes it viable in a real business with real constraints.

Real-world example — a specific situation showing the move in action. Short, concrete, and outcome-focused. Not a case study. A reference point.

Steps — a numbered sequence starting with the first action. Each step is one thing. The sequence is designed to get from zero to revenue as directly as possible.

Who owns it — the ownership flow showing which function leads, which supports, and where finance sits in the process.

What to watch — the risks, the signals, and the numbers to monitor. Because every revenue move has a failure mode, and knowing it in advance is how you avoid it.

A Note on Speed

Every idea in this book was selected with one constraint in mind — **it has to be executable inside a normal business quarter.** Some moves will generate revenue within days. Others will take the full ninety days to show up in the numbers. None require a transformation programme, a new system, or a consultant on retainer.

Before you read a single idea, go to Chapter 7.3. Read the Sprint Mandate box on the first page. It takes ninety seconds. Then come back. Every idea you read from this point forward should be filtered through one question — could this be my first sprint priority? The reader who asks that question while reading gets three times more from this book than one who decides afterward. The Sprint is not a back-of-book bonus. It is where the ideas become money.

If you are not sure where to start, begin with Part 3. It is where most businesses find the fastest, highest-confidence wins — and where most CFOs have their first "why haven't we done this already" moment.

The revenue is there. Let's go and find it.

1.3 — The Painkiller Gap Model

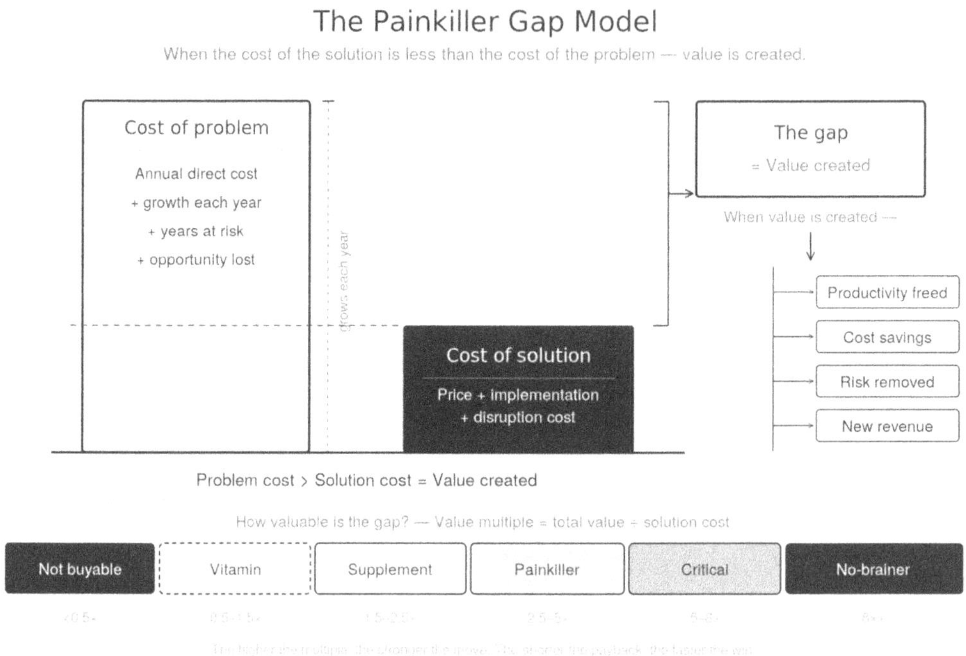

Every Business Has This Problem
Most businesses do not lose deals because their product is bad.

They lose deals because they cannot explain the value clearly enough to make the decision obvious.

The CFO or CEO on the other side of the table is not irrational. They are not being difficult. They are doing exactly what they should do — **weighing what something costs against what it is worth.** And if that calculation is not clear, the answer is always the same. Not now. Let us revisit this. We need more time.

You have heard those words. You know what they mean. The deal is not progressing because the value case was never made in a language the buyer could act on.

The Painkiller Gap Model fixes that. It gives you a single, simple framework for calculating the value you create — and for showing it to anyone who needs to make a decision. It works in a board meeting. It works in a sales conversation. And it works as an internal filter for every revenue move in this book.

The Core Idea

There are two numbers that matter in any commercial decision.

The cost of the problem. What is it costing the business to live with this situation right now — every month, every quarter, every year? Not just the direct cost. The compounding cost. What does it cost if this problem is still here in three years, growing at ten or twenty percent annually, blocking revenue, draining resource, creating risk?

The cost of the solution. What is the all-in price of fixing it? Not just the invoice. The implementation, the onboarding, the disruption, the time it takes before the fix delivers value.

When the cost of the solution is less than the cost of the problem — value is created.

That is the entire model.

Problem cost › Solution cost = Value created.

Everything else — the formulas, the calculations, the classification scale — is simply a way of making that gap visible, measurable, and undeniable.

The Model
The model has three elements. Read it left to right.

On the left sits the **problem.** It is tall because problems compound. A $500,000 annual loss growing at twenty percent does not stay at $500,000. By year three it is costing $720,000 per year — and the total damage over that period is $1.82 million. Every year without a solution is a year the problem gets more expensive.

On the right sits the **solution.** It is shorter because the cost is fixed and one-time. You pay once. The problem would have cost you indefinitely.

The gap between them is the value you create. It is not a theoretical number. It is the real, measurable difference between what the problem costs and what the solution costs. The bigger that gap, the easier the decision for the buyer. The easier the decision, the stronger the revenue move.**The Three Formulas**

The model produces three outputs. Every one of them comes from numbers already in the conversation.

- **The economic gap** is the simplest. Problem cost minus solution cost. If a problem costs a business $2 million over three years and the solution costs $400,000 — the economic gap is $1.6 million. That is the net value created in a single number. *Most people in that meeting have never seen it written down that simply.*

- **The value multiple** shows how many times bigger the value is than the price. Total value created divided by solution cost. A $1.6 million gap on a $400,000 solution is a **4x multiple.** The customer gets four dollars of value for every dollar they spend. That is not a purchase. That is an investment.

- **The payback period** shows how fast the solution pays for itself. Solution cost divided by the annual value generated. At $700,000 of annual value, a $400,000 solution pays back in **6.9 months.** By the time the first year is done, the solution has already returned its cost and delivered an additional $300,000 in net value.

These three numbers — the gap, the multiple, and the payback — are the value case. **They replace opinion with arithmetic.** They turn a conversation about price into a conversation about return. And for a CFO, that is the only conversation worth having.

What Happens When the Gap Is Real
The gap itself is only part of the story.

When a solution genuinely resolves a problem, it does not just stop the bleeding. It opens doors that the problem had been keeping shut. **This is where the value compounds beyond the direct calculation.**

A business that was spending forty hours a week managing a broken process gets those forty hours back. That is productivity freed — real, measurable, redirectable to revenue-generating work. A business carrying compliance risk that a solution removes is no longer one audit away from a significant financial event. A team that was blocked from pursuing a market opportunity because of an operational constraint can now move.

These byproducts of solving the problem — **productivity freed, cost savings, risk removed, new revenue unlocked** — all carry annual dollar values. When you add them to the direct pain resolved, the total value created grows significantly. And when total value grows, the multiple grows with it. A move that looked like a 4x multiple on direct pain alone might be a 7x or 8x multiple when the doors it opens are included.

This is why the model asks you to calculate the doors. Not because it inflates the numbers. Because it makes them honest. **The full value of solving a problem is always larger than the direct cost of the problem alone.** Most businesses only show the surface. The model shows everything.

The Classification Scale
Not every solution creates equal value. And not every revenue move is worth the same level of urgency.

The classification scale translates the value multiple into a verdict. It answers a single question: **given this gap, how strong is this move?**

1. **Not buyable** — the solution costs more than the value it creates. This is not a pricing problem. It is a value problem. The solution needs to be repositioned, repriced, or aimed at a different customer before it goes to market.

2. **Vitamin** — low pain, low urgency. The customer can live with this problem cheaply. Nice to have but easy to delay. Without a trigger event — a deadline, a regulatory change, a competitor move — this deal will not close.

3. **Supplement** — some pain, some value. The rational case exists but the urgency is low. This needs a sharper articulation of what delay costs, or a specific moment that forces a decision.

4. **Painkiller** — clear pain, strong gap. The solution costs materially less than the problem. The customer has a rational reason to act and a clear return on doing so. *This is where most good revenue moves sit.*

5. **Critical Painkiller** — high pain, high cost to ignore. The customer is losing significant money or carrying significant risk every month they do not act. The conversation shifts from *should we do this* to *when do we start.*

6. **No-Brainer** — massive pain, massive gap. At 8x or above, not buying is financially irrational. The buyer who passes on this is choosing to continue paying for a problem that could be solved for a fraction of what it costs. The conversation is not about whether. **It is about when.**

The scale is not a sales tool. It is a prioritisation filter. **Use it to decide which revenue moves to lead with, which to develop further, and which to set aside.** If a move sits below Painkiller, the value case is not yet strong enough to close. Build it first.

How a CFO Uses This Model
The Painkiller Gap Model works in three directions.

1. **Inward — evaluating your own revenue moves.** Before you bring an idea to the board, run it through the model. Does the problem cost exceed the solution cost? By how much? What is the multiple? What is the payback? If the numbers do not hold up, the idea is not ready. Build the case first.

2. **Outward — communicating value to customers.** The model gives you a structured way to build and present a value case. Start with the pain cost — not your price. Show the customer what the problem is costing them before you show them what the solution costs. *When the gap is visible, the price becomes irrelevant.* The question changes from "can we afford this" to "can we afford not to."

3. **Across the business — filtering every commercial decision.** Not every opportunity deserves the same attention. The classification scale tells you where to put energy and where to wait. A No-Brainer deserves immediate action. A Vitamin deserves a different approach or a different customer.

The model does not close deals. **It builds the conditions in which closing is inevitable** — because the numbers make the decision obvious before anyone sits down at a table.

One Rule on Using This Model
The model is only as strong as the pain estimate.

A pain cost number built on guesswork is a liability. A pain cost number built on audited data, customer-supplied figures, or direct measurement is an asset. **The difference between a weak value case and an unassailable one is almost always the quality of the pain estimate.**

Before you run the model, do the work. Talk to the customer. Ask them what the problem is costing. Most of them have never added it up — and when they do, the number is always larger than anyone expected. *That moment — when a customer calculates their own pain cost for the first time — is when a deal begins in earnest.*

The gap was always there. The model makes it visible.

Use it every time.

PART 2

Create Revenue

The Only Revenue That Didn't Exist Yesterday

Most revenue conversations start in the wrong place. They begin with the pipeline, new prospects, and outreach. All the energy points outward — toward people who do not know you yet and have no reason to trust you. That is one way to grow. It is the hardest, slowest, and most expensive.

Part 2 asks a simpler question: what can this business sell that it cannot currently sell? Not because the capability is missing — because the offer does not yet exist in a form anyone can buy. The ideas here require no new markets, customers, or technology. Only that the business asks whether what it already does can be packaged into something sellable.

In most businesses the answer is yes. Several times over.

What This Part Covers

- **New Offers** — turning delivery capability into named, packaged offers customers can buy.
- **New Products** — creating standalone products from repeatable outputs or internal tools.
- **New Monetization Models** — changing how value is charged for, not what is delivered.
- **New Commercial Assets** — turning IP, data, or capacity into revenue-generating assets.
- **New Business Lines** — building adjacent revenue streams with their own commercial logic.

Where to Start

- **Same project types appearing repeatedly?** Start with New Offers.
- **Consistent outputs with no product structure?** Start with New Products.
- **Pricing model misaligned with value created?** Start with New Monetization Models.
- **IP or assets doing internal work only?** Start with New Commercial Assets.
- **Ready to build something structurally new?** Start with New Business Lines.

2.1 — New Offers

Create new sellable solutions, services, or packages using capabilities the business can already deliver.

When These Strategies Work Best

New offer strategies deliver the fastest return when proven delivery capability exists but lacks the structure to sell it reliably.

- The same project type is quoted from scratch every time it appears
- Sales conversations stall because buyers cannot quickly understand the offer
- Delivery teams give away expertise informally before any agreement is signed
- Available capacity exists with no structured offer to fill it
- Revenue is inconsistent because every engagement is treated as a one-off

The Benefits

- Revenue growth without new customer acquisition cost
- Shorter sales cycles because buyers understand exactly what they are getting
- Improved delivery consistency through a repeatable, defined model
- A sharper value proposition Sales can communicate clearly and confidently
- A natural pipeline into higher-value work as customers experience the offer

The Risks to Manage

- **Scope creep** — offers drift back toward custom work. Define usage, access, and delivery boundaries before any commitment to launch.
- **Cannibalization** — new offers can displace higher-margin work. Use qualification criteria.
- **Underpricing** — most businesses price too low. Anchor to value, not effort.
- **Inconsistent positioning** — a standard pitch document resolves most of this.

01. Turn your best custom project into a standard offer

Convert a proven custom project into a named, repeatable offer with fixed scope, pricing, and sales language. Stop treating the same work as bespoke every time.

Why it works

Custom work hides demand. Packaging it reduces friction, speeds quoting, and captures revenue the business already delivers.

Best for

B2B services, consulting, agencies, software-enabled services.

Execution Steps

1. Review recent projects with strong margin and repeat demand
2. Select one with a clear problem and proven delivery model
3. Define scope, deliverables, exclusions, and pricing logic
4. Name it and create a one-line sales narrative
5. Pilot with three to five existing customers

Real-world example

A consulting firm launches a fixed-scope '90-Day Pricing Reset'. Same methodology, clear boundaries, higher close rate.

Risk Management

1. **Operational** · 4/5 Scope too broad, delivery reverts to custom. **Mitigation:** Tighten exclusions before launch. Brief the team.
2. **Commercial** · 3/5 Sales positions it inconsistently. **Mitigation:** Require use of one standard pitch document.
3. **Operational** · 3/5 Custom delivery workflow erodes margin. **Mitigation:** Define and enforce a fixed delivery process first.
4. **Legal** · 4/5 Former client objects to reuse of approach. **Mitigation:** Remove client elements. Review contracts.
5. **Legal** · 5/5 IP issues from methodology built on client work. **Mitigation:** Separate reusable method from client content. Legal review.

Speed	Effort	Cost	Revenue	Time to cash	Scalability
Fast (0–30 days)	**Medium**	**Low**	**High**	**Immediate**	**High**

Decision-flow: CFO → Sales → Operations

02. Package a diagnostic into a paid entry offer

Convert pre-sale discovery into a standalone paid diagnostic. The diagnostic becomes the first commercial step, not a free courtesy before the real work begins.

Why it works

Most firms do valuable early analysis without charging. A paid diagnostic captures that value, filters serious buyers, and improves downstream conversion.

Best for

Consulting, agencies, B2B services, SaaS with advisory layers.

Execution Steps

1. Identify discovery work done before larger engagements
2. Define a fixed-scope diagnostic with clear outputs
3. Set a meaningful price with credit toward larger work
4. Create a concise proposal and disciplined sales script
5. Pilot with qualified prospects before making it standard

Real-world example

An agency replaces free audits with a paid 'Conversion Leak Diagnostic'. Fee credited to full engagements. Conversion improves.

Risk Management

1. **Commercial** · 4/5 Buyers expect discovery to be free. **Mitigation:** Position as a decision tool for the buyer.
2. **Internal** · 4/5 Sales waives the fee to close faster. **Mitigation:** Floor price is policy. Exceptions require approval.
3. **Operational** · 3/5 Scope expands beyond the fixed diagnostic. **Mitigation:** Lock deliverables. Document inclusions and exclusions.
4. **Commercial** · 3/5 No follow-on sale after the diagnostic. **Mitigation:** Build a next-step offer into every diagnostic output.
5. **Financial** · 4/5 Underpricing anchors larger work too low. **Mitigation:** Set a firm floor price. Review after five completions.

Speed	Effort	Cost	Revenue	Time to cash	Scalability
Fast (0–30 days)	**Low**	**Low**	**High**	**Immediate**	**High**

Decision-flow: CFO → Sales → Operations

03. Create a 'lite' version of your core service

Design a reduced-scope version at a lower price for customers who cannot justify the full engagement. A deliberate entry point with a clear upgrade path, not a lesser product.

Why it works

Many prospects are priced out, not disinterested. A well-designed entry offer captures demand earlier and creates a structured pipeline into higher-value work.

Best for

Consulting, agencies, SaaS, B2B services, professional firms.

Execution Steps

1. Identify the service components customers value most
2. Remove complexity and non-essential elements
3. Define a clearly bounded scope and matching price
4. Position as a starter engagement, not a reduced version
5. Train Sales to introduce the upgrade path from day one

Real-world example

A consulting firm launches 'Strategy Lite' for one business unit. Same methodology, narrower scope, clear upgrade path.

Risk Management

1. **Commercial** · 4/5 Sales positions this to full-service buyers. **Mitigation:** Define and enforce a customer profile for the lite offer.
2. **Commercial** · 3/5 Perceived as inferior rather than entry point. **Mitigation:** Positioning must emphasise upgrade path and strategic intent.
3. **Commercial** · 3/5 Customers stay on lite version without upgrading. **Mitigation:** Design upgrade triggers into the delivery model.
4. **Financial** · 4/5 Margin compression when delivery cost not simplified. **Mitigation:** Redesign delivery before pricing. Scope cuts alone are not enough.
5. **Market** · 3/5 Brand diluted if perceived as a budget product. **Mitigation:** Maintain premium positioning language throughout.

Speed	Effort	Cost	Revenue	Time to cash	Scalability
Medium (1–3 months)	**Medium**	**Low**	**High**	**Medium**	**High**

Decision-flow: CFO → Product → Sales

04. Turn a repeat request into a fixed workshop offer

Convert a consistently requested client topic into a paid workshop with a fixed agenda, defined outputs, and set price. The knowledge is in your team. The workshop commercialises it.

Why it works

Repeat requests confirm demand. A workshop productises it, compresses the sales cycle, and creates a clean entry into larger engagements.

Best for

Consulting, training providers, advisory firms, agencies.

Execution Steps

1. Identify a request appearing consistently across accounts
2. Define workshop scope, outputs, and duration
3. Build standard slides, tools, and fixed agenda
4. Set a firm price and maximum participant count
5. Launch as a named standalone offer

Real-world example

An advisory firm launches a paid 'Executive Alignment Workshop'. Fixed agenda, fixed price, specific output, clear next step.

Risk Management

1. **Commercial** · 3/5 Demand weaker than expected, offer fails to convert. **Mitigation:** Validate with historical inquiry data before investing.
2. **Operational** · 3/5 Workshop scope expands during delivery. **Mitigation:** Define agenda and outputs precisely. Brief all facilitators.
3. **Internal** · 2/5 Sales unsure when to position workshop versus full engagement. **Mitigation:** Provide a pitch guide with clear qualifying criteria.
4. **Commercial** · 3/5 Perceived value low because outputs not clearly defined. **Mitigation:** Define exactly what participants leave with.
5. **Operational** · 2/5 Quality inconsistent across different facilitators. **Mitigation:** Use standardised materials for every session.

Speed	Effort	Cost	Revenue	Time to cash	Scalability
Fast (0–30 days)	**Low**	**Low**	**Medium**	**Short**	**Medium**

Decision-flow: CFO → Sales → Operations

05. Create a premium version of your best-selling product

Launch a higher-specification version of your top product at a premium price. Demand is already proven. The premium tier captures buyers willing to pay more for a better outcome.

Why it works

Your best-selling product confirms demand. A premium tier captures buyers willing to pay more without new acquisition cost or market development.

Best for

Consumer goods, e-commerce, retail, manufacturing, SaaS.

Execution Steps

1. Identify your highest-volume or most trusted product
2. Define premium enhancements with genuine buyer value
3. Set a clear price increase with a credible justification
4. Position as a distinct tier, not a replacement
5. Launch with limited volume to validate unit economics

Real-world example

A brand launches a 'Pro' version with higher quality materials. Same architecture, significantly higher margin per unit.

Risk Management

1. **Commercial** · 3/5 Upgrade demand lower than expected. **Mitigation:** Measure before scaling. Revisit differentiation if uptake is low.
2. **Product** · 3/5 Overengineering adds cost without perceived value. **Mitigation:** Build only what customers have explicitly requested.
3. **Commercial** · 4/5 Cannibalization through insufficient differentiation. **Mitigation:** Maintain sharp differentiation between tiers from launch.
4. **Financial** · 4/5 Unit economics fail if premium costs not modelled. **Mitigation:** Model unit economics.
5. **Commercial** · 3/5 Weak positioning fails to justify higher price. **Mitigation:** Emphasise specific outcome improvements. Be tangible.

Speed	Effort	Cost	Revenue	Time to cash	Scalability
Medium (1–3 months)	**Medium**	**Medium**	**High**	**Medium**	**High**

Decision-flow: CFO → Product → Sales

06. Turn installation into a paid launch package

Convert setup and deployment support into a paid launch package with defined deliverables, timeline, and go-live outcome. Work given away informally becomes a priced commercial offer.

Why it works

Product businesses treat launch support as a free extra. Packaging it generates income at point of sale, improves adoption, and establishes delivery accountability.

Best for

Manufacturing, equipment suppliers, enterprise software, B2B products.

Execution Steps

1. Identify all support currently given during launch for free
2. Define a fixed package with clear scope and timeline
3. Separate standard handoff from premium launch support
4. Price anchored to the value of a fast successful go-live
5. Pilot with new customers before making it standard

Real-world example

An equipment supplier introduces a paid 'Launch Success Package'. Previously informal. Now a priced line on every proposal.

Risk Management

1. **Commercial** · 3/5 Buyers resist paying for previously free support. **Mitigation:** Clearly separate standard handoff from premium package.
2. **Operational** · 4/5 Scope creep as fixed package becomes custom work. **Mitigation:** Define usage, access, and delivery boundaries before any commitment.
3. **Internal** · 3/5 Sales omits package from quotes to simplify. **Mitigation:** Build it into quoting flow so removal is an active decision.
4. **Operational** · 3/5 Delivery capacity strained by demand. **Mitigation:** Cap capacity.
5. **Commercial** · 3/5 Package value not visible at point of sale. **Mitigation:** Link explicitly to faster go-live and reduced disruption.

Speed	Effort	Cost	Revenue	Time to cash	Scalability
Fast (0–30 days)	**Low**	**Low**	**Medium**	**Short**	**Medium**

Decision-flow: CFO → Operations → Sales

07. *Sell a maintenance or continuity plan*

Create a paid continuity plan that keeps the customer's product or system performing after purchase. Converts a one-time transaction into an ongoing commercial relationship with recurring revenue.

Why it works

Customers invest in outcomes, not transactions. A continuity plan creates recurring revenue with predictable margin, improves retention, and competes on reliability.

Best for

Equipment suppliers, SaaS, infrastructure services, B2B products.

Execution Steps

1. Identify ongoing needs customers have after delivery
2. Define a recurring maintenance scope with clear boundaries
3. Structure into at least two tiers — standard and premium
4. Price anchored to reliability value, not delivery cost
5. Position at point of purchase, not as a later renewal

Real-world example

A machinery supplier introduces an annual maintenance contract. Sold at purchase, renewed annually. A recurring revenue line that did not previously exist.

Risk Management

1. **Commercial** · 3/5 Low adoption until a failure occurs. **Mitigation:** Bundle the first year into the initial purchase where possible.
2. **Financial** · 4/5 Underpricing by anchoring to delivery cost. **Mitigation:** Price against what it costs the customer when maintenance fails.
3. **Operational** · 3/5 Over-servicing within plan scope erodes margin **Mitigation:** Define service limits.
4. **Customer** · 3/5 Renewal drop-off when ongoing value is not visible. **Mitigation:** Track usage. Intervene proactively before the renewal window.
5. **Operational** · 3/5 Delivery capacity strained as plan scales. **Mitigation:** Model capacity before launch. Scale with take-up.

Speed	Effort	Cost	Revenue	Time to cash	Scalability
Medium (1–3 months)	**Medium**	**Low**	**High**	**Short**	**High**

Decision-flow: CFO → Operations → Customer Success

08. Create a compliance-ready version of your offer

Build a version of your offer for regulated or high-governance buyers. Adds documentation, controls, and audit structures they require — removing a procurement barrier and justifying a price premium.

Why it works

Risk-sensitive buyers pay more for certainty. A compliance-ready offer reduces procurement friction and positions the business as a lower-risk partner. Core delivery is unchanged.

Best for

Healthcare, financial services, enterprise software, regulated services.

Execution Steps

1. Identify buyer segments with elevated compliance requirements
2. Define the controls and documentation these buyers need
3. Package into a named compliance-ready variant of your offer
4. Set a premium reflecting reduced procurement risk
5. Pilot in one regulated vertical before broadening

Real-world example

A software business launches an enterprise-ready package with audit trails and approval workflows. Standard product. Governance layer on top.

Risk Management

1. **Operational** · 4/5 Compliance layer adds complexity that erodes margin. **Mitigation:** Build compliance as a fixed reusable module.
2. **Commercial** · 3/5 Demand weaker because segment is defined too broadly. **Mitigation:** Start with one regulated vertical. Financial services first.
3. **Financial** · 4/5 Cost creep not reflected in the premium from launch. **Mitigation:** Price compliance burden explicitly.
4. **Internal** · 3/5 Sales mispositioning to non-regulated buyers. **Mitigation:** Define and enforce the buyer profile and qualifying criteria.
5. **Operational** · 4/5 Delivery gaps when requirements not validated pre-launch. **Mitigation:** Audit all controls against sector requirements before launch.

Speed	Effort	Cost	Revenue	Time to cash	Scalability
Medium (1–3 months)	**Medium**	**Medium**	**High**	**Medium**	**Medium**

Decision-flow: CFO → Operations → Sales

09. Turn training into a paid customer onboarding offer

Convert informal customer training into a paid onboarding offer with fixed scope, defined format, and a measurable adoption outcome. Informal delivery that happens anyway becomes a revenue line.

Why it works

Training is the most consistently undermonetised activity in most businesses. Packaging it creates revenue, accelerates adoption, and reduces post-sale support load.

Best for

Equipment suppliers, enterprise software, service providers, installers.

Execution Steps

1. List every training activity delivered without charge
2. Define a fixed package with explicit outputs and timeframe
3. Set format, duration, and maximum participant numbers
4. Price anchored to faster adoption and fewer errors
5. Present at point of sale before assumptions of free delivery

Real-world example

A heating installer charges for a homeowner handover. A software firm sells admin onboarding workshops. Both turned informal delivery into a priced line item.

Risk Management

1. **Commercial** · 3/5 Buyers resist paying for assumed-free training. **Mitigation:** Tie to a specific adoption outcome. Benefit removes objection.
2. **Commercial** · 3/5 Low uptake when introduced after the main sale. **Mitigation:** Present during proposal stage, not post-sale.
3. **Operational** · 3/5 Scope expands as team members personalise sessions. **Mitigation:** Lock agenda and outputs. Deviation needs approval.
4. **Operational** · 2/5 Quality varies across team members. **Mitigation:** Standardise all materials. This is a product.
5. **Internal** · 2/5 Team resistance to charging for informal work. **Mitigation:** Show reduction in post-sale support load.

Speed	Effort	Cost	Revenue	Time to cash	Scalability
Fast (0–30 days)	**Low**	**Low**	**Medium**	**Immediate**	**High**

Decision-flow: CFO → Customer Success → Sales

10. Bundle outcome guarantees into a premium offer

Create a premium offer with a defined performance guarantee, backed by clear conditions and commercial accountability. The guarantee removes buyer risk and commands a meaningful price premium.

Why it works

A segment of every market pays more to eliminate risk. A well-structured guarantee shifts the conversation from cost to certainty, unlocking buyers who would not proceed without one.

Best for

Professional services, SaaS, performance-based work, specialist contractors.

Execution Steps

1. Identify outcomes you can deliver under defined conditions
2. Define measurable success criteria and tracking method
3. Set explicit qualifying conditions and customer obligations
4. Price the guarantee as a premium tier, not a closing tool
5. Pilot with a carefully selected group before any scale

Real-world example

A marketing agency offers a package with a minimum performance threshold. A contractor guarantees timelines. Both recorded higher average deal values.

Risk Management

1. **Commercial** · 5/5 Sales weakens conditions to close deals. **Mitigation:** Conditions are policy. Relaxation requires CFO sign-off.
2. **Operational** · 5/5 Delivery failure damages trust and creates liability. **Mitigation:** Pilot three to five customers under controlled conditions.
3. **Financial** · 4/5 Margin erosion if guarantee cost not accurately priced. **Mitigation:** Price to reflect delivery cost plus remediation risk.
4. **Commercial** · 4/5 Misaligned clients cannot meet guarantee obligations. **Mitigation:** Qualify every buyer rigorously before extending guarantee.
5. **Legal** · 5/5 Legal exposure if conditions not precisely defined. **Mitigation:** Legal counsel reviews all documentation before launch.

Speed	Effort	Cost	Revenue	Time to cash	Scalability
Medium (1–3 months)	**Medium**	**Low**	**High**	**Medium**	**Medium**

Decision-flow: CFO → Sales → Operations

From Ideas to Action

Ten ideas. Ten ways to package what the business already delivers into named, repeatable offers customers can buy without negotiation.

Most do not. Not because execution is difficult — most of these moves are straightforward — but because the gap between recognising an opportunity and committing to a first step is where most revenue initiatives are lost.

Before continuing, identify the single idea with the clearest commercial case in your business right now. Name the person who owns execution. Set a date by which the first step is taken.

> ***The most expensive revenue move is the one you identified, found relevant, and never acted on.***

What Comes Next

2.2 — New Products addresses businesses that produce consistent, repeatable outputs but have not yet structured those outputs as a standalone product. If your team delivers the same work repeatedly and that work lives inside a service engagement rather than on a product shelf — the next chapter is where the opportunity sits.

2.2 — New Products

Create standalone products from work the business already delivers, knowledge it already holds, or needs it already understands.

When These Strategies Work Best

New product strategies deliver the strongest return when the business already produces repeatable outputs but has not yet structured them as something a customer can buy directly.

- The same output is produced repeatedly but sold only inside a service engagement
- Customers ask for tools, templates, kits, or resources the business uses internally
- Delivery teams rebuild similar materials from scratch for every new client
- Post-sale needs go unserved because there is no product to address them
- Revenue stops when the service stops, with no recurring or passive income

The Benefits

- Revenue that scales beyond selling time or expertise directly
- New income from the installed customer base without new acquisition
- Faster sales cycles on lower-commitment, standalone purchases
- Products that create recurring purchase cycles and repeat revenue
- Reduced delivery dependency on senior or specialist team members

The Risks to Manage

- **Overbuilding** — products get too complex before they are validated. Start with version one, not the full vision.
- **Underpricing** — products priced at cost rather than value. Anchor to the service price, not the build cost.
- **IP exposure** — materials built on client work carry legal risk. Strip and clear before packaging.
- **Low distribution** — a product nobody finds generates no revenue. Plan the channel before launch.

11. Turn a repeatable service output into a sellable product

Package a repeatable service output into a standalone product — a kit, template set, tool, or digital asset customers can buy without full service delivery.

Why it works

Many services produce the same outputs repeatedly. Turning one into a product creates new revenue, reduces delivery dependency, and scales beyond selling hours.

Best for

Consulting, agencies, trades, installers, training firms, specialist operators.

Execution Steps

1. Identify one repeatable service output clients value consistently
2. Choose a product format — kit, template pack, tool, or digital asset
3. Remove client-specific elements and simplify for standalone use
4. Define what is included and excluded
5. Price it as a standalone purchase, pilot with existing customers

Real-world example

A heating installer sells a seasonal maintenance kit. A consulting firm sells a pricing model template pack built from repeat client work.

Risk Management

1. **Commercial** · 3/5 Product fit weaker than expected for this segment. **Mitigation:** Test with current customers before wider release.
2. **Product** · 4/5 Too much complexity for standalone use. **Mitigation:** Simplify sharply. Version one must work without hand-holding.
3. **Commercial** · 3/5 Low differentiation from free alternatives. **Mitigation:** Highlight unique utility customers already pay for in service.
4. **Legal** · 4/5 Client IP conflict in source materials. **Mitigation:** Remove all client-specific content before packaging.
5. **Financial** · 4/5 Underpricing relative to service value. **Mitigation:** Anchor price to what the service equivalent would cost.

Speed	Effort	Cost	Revenue	Time to cash	Scalability
Medium (1–3 months)	**Medium**	**Low**	**High**	**Medium**	**High**

Decision-flow: CFO → Product → Sales

12. Launch a starter kit for first-time buyers

Create a starter kit that helps new customers begin faster by bundling the core product with the essential items needed to use it well from day one.

Why it works

First-time buyers delay because starting feels unclear. A starter kit reduces friction, raises confidence, and creates new product revenue from convenience.

Best for

Consumer products, home services, equipment, wellness, hobby brands, software.

Execution Steps

1. Identify what first-time buyers need most to start successfully
2. Bundle the core product with essential starter items
3. Keep the kit simple and clearly named
4. Price above the base item but below separate-item total
5. Launch through current sales channels first

Real-world example

A home heater installer sells a first-season care kit. A software firm offers an admin setup pack with templates and onboarding tools.

Risk Management

1. **Commercial** · 3/5 Weak demand from first-time buyers. **Mitigation:** Test with real first-time buyers before investing in stock.
2. **Customer** · 2/5 Bundle confusion undermines confidence. **Mitigation:** Keep kit contents simple. Name them clearly.
3. **Financial** · 3/5 Margin pressure if kit economics are not controlled. **Mitigation:** Set unit economics before pricing. Track margin per kit.
4. **Commercial** · 3/5 Low differentiation from buying items separately. **Mitigation:** Stress convenience and confidence as the core benefit.
5. **Operational** · 3/5 Inventory mismatch at launch. **Mitigation:** Start with limited volume. Scale with proven demand.

Speed	Effort	Cost	Revenue	Time to cash	Scalability
Fast (0–30 days)	**Low**	**Low**	**Medium**	**Immediate**	**High**

Decision-flow: CFO → Product → Sales

13. *Create a monitoring add-on product*

Launch a product that helps customers track performance, usage, condition, or savings after the main purchase. Visibility after the sale becomes a new revenue line.

Why it works

Customers want visibility after buying. A monitoring add-on creates new product revenue, improves perceived value, and can trigger upgrades or maintenance sales.

Best for

Equipment, home systems, industrial products, SaaS, energy, logistics, facilities.

Execution Steps

1. Identify what customers most want to track after purchase
2. Define a simple monitoring product format
3. Focus on useful alerts, visibility, or reporting only
4. Price as an add-on, not a replacement
5. Train sales. to attach it to the main sale

Real-world example

A heating company offers a home performance monitor. An enterprise software firm launches a usage and savings dashboard add-on.

Risk Management

1. **Customer** · 3/5 Weak usage if it does not solve one clear need. **Mitigation:** Focus version one on the single most requested insight.
2. **Product** · 4/5 Feature bloat in version one delays launch. **Mitigation:** Ship the minimum useful version. Expand after adoption.
3. **Commercial** · 3/5 Price resistance if benefit is not visible. **Mitigation:** Tie pricing to a measurable saving or performance gain.
4. **Product** · 4/5 Technical issues undermine trust early. **Mitigation:** Pilot with one customer segment before scaling.
5. **Commercial** · 3/5 Low attach rate if not built into sales flow. **Mitigation:** Bundle into the sales conversation at point of main purchase.

Speed	Effort	Cost	Revenue	Time to cash	Scalability
Medium (1–3 months)	**Medium**	**Medium**	**High**	**Medium**	**High**

Decision-flow: CFO → Product → Sales

14. Turn consumables into a branded refill product

Create a refill, replenishment, or replacement product customers need after the initial purchase to keep the main product working. A repeat revenue line from a one-time sale.

Why it works

Businesses often sell the core item once and leave refill revenue uncaptured. A branded refill adds repeat income and increases customer lifetime value.

Best for

Home products, equipment, filters, wellness, industrial supply, maintenance-driven products.

Execution Steps

1. Identify what customers must replace, refill, or refresh regularly
2. Design a branded refill product with clear compatibility
3. Set pricing for convenience and margin
4. Position it as the recommended ongoing choice
5. Launch with reorder reminders built in

Real-world example

A water system company launches branded replacement filters. A software firm sells additional data packs tied to the main platform.

Risk Management

1. **Commercial** · 3/5 Low repeat demand if usage cycles are not validated. **Mitigation:** Confirm replacement frequency with real customers first.
2. **Commercial** · 3/5 Weak differentiation from generic alternatives. **Mitigation:** Stress compatibility, quality, and brand reliability.
3. **Financial** · 4/5 Margin pressure if unit economics are not managed. **Mitigation:** Model cost.
4. **Dependency** · 3/5 Channel resistance from resellers protecting their own supply. **Mitigation:** Align reseller incentives before launch.
5. **Operational** · 3/5 Stock shortages undermine reliability. **Mitigation:** Start with focused SKUs and proven demand before expanding.

Speed	Effort	Cost	Revenue	Time to cash	Scalability
Medium (1–3 months)	**Medium**	**Medium**	**High**	**Short**	**High**

Decision-flow: CFO → Product → Sales

15. *Create a self-service planning tool customers can buy*

Build a product that helps customers estimate, plan, size, compare, or configure a purchase before committing to the full solution. Confidence before commitment becomes a revenue line.

Why it works

Buyers want confidence before committing. A self-service planning tool creates product revenue, reduces sales friction, and improves lead quality for larger purchases.

Best for

Home improvement, equipment, software, logistics, enterprise solutions.

Execution Steps

1. Identify a buying decision customers struggle to size or compare
2. Build a simple planning, sizing, or comparison tool
3. Define outputs customers find useful enough to pay for
4. Price standalone or credit toward a larger purchase
5. Train sales. to use it as a pre-sale qualifier

Real-world example

A heating company sells a home sizing planner. An enterprise software firm offers a paid readiness assessment tool for platform selection.

Risk Management

1. **Commercial** · 3/5 Weak paid demand if free alternatives exist. **Mitigation:** Test with real buyers before investing in development.
2. **Product** · 3/5 Tool too basic to justify the price. **Mitigation:** Solve one real buying decision clearly and completely.
3. **Alignment** · 3/5 Sales team bypasses the tool. **Mitigation:** Tie the tool to the qualification process formally.
4. **Customer** · 4/5 Poor usability undermines confidence. **Mitigation:** Simplify outputs sharply. The result must be immediately usable.
5. **Commercial** · 3/5 Low conversion from tool to main purchase. **Mitigation:** Connect the tool output directly to a next-step offer.

Speed	Effort	Cost	Revenue	Time to cash	Scalability
Medium (1–3 months)	**Medium**	**Low**	**Medium**	**Medium**	**High**

Decision-flow: CFO → Product → Sales

16. Launch a retrofit upgrade product for existing customers

Create an add-on product that upgrades the performance, efficiency, or usability of something the customer already owns — without requiring full replacement.

Why it works

Customers do not always want full replacement. A retrofit product creates new revenue from the installed base with a lower-cost, lower-friction upgrade path.

Best for

Home systems, equipment, consumer products, vehicles, industrial assets, software modules.

Execution Steps

1. Identify common performance gaps in the installed customer base
2. Define one upgrade customers can adopt without replacing the core product
3. Test compatibility across current customer types
4. Price below replacement but above standard maintenance
5. Pilot with existing customers before broader release

Real-world example

A heater company sells a smart-control retrofit kit. An enterprise software firm launches an analytics upgrade module for existing users.

Risk Management

1. **Product** · 4/5 Compatibility issues with older installed base. **Mitigation:** Test against real customer configurations before launch.
2. **Commercial** · 3/5 Weak upgrade demand without clear performance pain. **Mitigation:** Target known pain points in the installed base specifically.
3. **Financial** · 3/5 Margin pressure if add-on costs are not controlled. **Mitigation:** Model add-on unit economics before pricing.
4. **Alignment** · 3/5 Sales team neglects existing customers. **Mitigation:** Use installed-base data to create upgrade trigger lists.
5. **Operational** · 3/5 High support burden from complex installation. **Mitigation:** Simplify installation guidance before launch.

Speed	Effort	Cost	Revenue	Time to cash	Scalability
Medium (1–3 months)	**Medium**	**Medium**	**High**	**Short**	**High**

Decision-flow: CFO → Product → Sales

17. *Create an emergency backup product for failure moments*

Launch a product customers can buy to keep operations running when the main system, product, or process fails. Continuity under pressure becomes a revenue line.

Why it works

Customers pay quickly when downtime hurts. A backup product protects continuity and creates revenue tied directly to the cost of disruption and loss.

Best for

Home systems, equipment, industrial supply, logistics, software, utilities, facilities.

Execution Steps

1. Identify the most painful failure or downtime scenario customers face
2. Define a backup product that keeps them running when it happens
3. Make activation simple and fast to deploy
4. Price against downtime cost, not product cost
5. Pilot with customers who already feel the pain

Real-world example

A heater company sells an emergency heat backup unit. A software firm launches a continuity module that keeps key workflows running during outages.

Risk Management

1. **Commercial** · 4/5 Weak fit if downtime pain is not significant enough. **Mitigation:** Target customers where failure has a clear, measurable cost.
2. **Operational** · 4/5 Slow activation undermines the core value proposition. **Mitigation:** Design the product for rapid deployment as the primary requirement.
3. **Commercial** · 3/5 Price resistance when failure feels unlikely. **Mitigation:** Anchor price to the cost of a single outage event.
4. **Product** · 5/5 Reliability failure during actual emergency destroys trust. **Mitigation:** Test the product under real failure conditions before any launch.
5. **Market** · 3/5 Demand overestimate in low-risk customer segments. **Mitigation:** Pilot in one segment where failure events are frequent and documented.

Speed	Effort	Cost	Revenue	Time to cash	Scalability
Medium (1–3 months)	**Medium**	**Medium**	**High**	**Immediate**	**Medium**

Decision-flow: CFO → Operations → Sales

18. Create a performance booster product around your core offer

Launch a product that helps customers get more output, speed, efficiency, or value from what they already buy or use. Better results from what already works becomes a revenue line.

Why it works

Customers buy to improve results. A performance booster creates new revenue through a clear, desirable upgrade that requires no replacement of what already works.

Best for

Home systems, equipment, consumer products, software, industrial tools, facilities.

Execution Steps

1. Identify the main result customers want more of after purchase
2. Define a simple product that measurably improves that result
3. Make the benefit easy to understand and demonstrate
4. Price below the value of the improvement delivered
5. Attach it to the main sale and post-sale customer journey

Real-world example

A heating company sells a smart efficiency controller. A software firm sells a workflow accelerator module that helps teams complete tasks faster.

Risk Management

1. **Commercial** · 4/5 Weak value proof if the gain is not measurable. **Mitigation:** Show a specific, measurable performance improvement before launch.
2. **Commercial** · 3/5 Low attach rate if not positioned at key buying moments. **Mitigation:** Build it into the sales conversation at point of main purchase.
3. **Product** · 3/5 Overdesign delays launch and adds unnecessary cost. **Mitigation:** Ship version one with the single most valuable improvement only.
4. **Commercial** · 3/5 Price resistance if benefit is not clearly communicated. **Mitigation:** Link the price explicitly to the performance gain it delivers.
5. **Market** · 3/5 Competitor copying reduces differentiation quickly. **Mitigation:** Emphasise unique advantage and move fast to build customer adoption.

Speed	Effort	Cost	Revenue	Time to cash	Scalability
Medium (1–3 months)	**Medium**	**Low**	**High**	**Short**	**High**

Decision-flow: CFO → Product → Sales

19. Create a handover product customers can keep and use

Turn the final handover into a paid product that gives customers a usable package of instructions, settings, records, and next-step guidance they can use long after delivery.

Why it works

After purchase, customers lose documents, forget settings, or misuse what they bought. A clean handover product creates lasting value and a new revenue line at point of sale.

Best for

Home installation, equipment, vehicles, healthcare, software, construction, specialist services.

Execution Steps

1. Identify the most common confusion customers face after delivery
2. Define a handover product with records, guides, settings, and next actions
3. Keep the format simple, clear, and reusable
4. Position around convenience, continuity, and control
5. Price as a paid add-on or premium closing item

Real-world example

A heater installer sells a home system handover pack. A software firm sells an admin handover kit with settings and workflows included.

Risk Management

1. **Commercial** · 4/5 Value feels too soft if time saving is not made explicit. **Mitigation:** Show the time and confusion saved versus no handover product.
2. **Alignment** · 3/5 Delivery team skips the product at close. **Mitigation:** Make it standard.
3. **Operational** · 3/5 Content becomes outdated without an owner. **Mitigation:** Assign an update owner before launch.
4. **Commercial** · 3/5 Offer devalued if free and paid are not separated. **Mitigation:** Define all terms, obligations, and conditions in writing before any agreement.
5. **Customer** · 2/5 Too much detail reduces usability. **Mitigation:** Include only what customers actually use. Keep it short.

Speed	Effort	Cost	Revenue	Time to cash	Scalability
Fast (0–30 days)	**Low**	**Low**	**Medium**	**Immediate**	**High**

Decision-flow: CFO → Operations → Sales

20. *Create a ready-to-use replacement product for urgent failures*

Launch a fast-deploy replacement product customers can buy when the original item, part, or system fails and they cannot afford delay. Speed and certainty become the product.

Why it works

Urgent replacement is highly valued. Customers pay for speed, certainty, and immediate usability when disruption is costly and waiting is not an option.

Best for

Home systems, equipment, vehicles, industrial supply, facilities, healthcare, software.

Execution Steps

1. Identify the most common urgent replacement scenario
2. Define a ready-to-use replacement product with clear scope
3. Reduce setup, fitting, or activation time as much as possible
4. Price against urgency. and downtime cost
5. Pilot where replacement pain is frequent and documented

Real-world example

A heater company offers a rapid-replacement unit for winter failures. A software firm offers a ready-deploy fallback package for critical workflows.

Risk Management

1. **Operational** · 5/5 Slow deployment undermines the core value promise. **Mitigation:** Design for rapid deployment as the primary product requirement.
2. **Operational** · 4/5 Stock shortage blocks fulfilment when needed most. **Mitigation:** Hold focused inventory for the most common failure scenarios.
3. **Commercial** · 3/5 Price resistance when failure feels unlikely in advance. **Mitigation:** Anchor price to the documented cost of a single outage.
4. **Product** · 4/5 Compatibility gaps prevent fast deployment. **Mitigation:** Standardise fit rules across the most common configurations.
5. **Market** · 3/5 Demand overestimate leads to excess stock. **Mitigation:** Start with the most common failure scenario. Expand from evidence.

Speed	Effort	Cost	Revenue	Time to cash	Scalability
Medium (1–3 months)	**Medium**	**Medium**	**High**	**Immediate**	**Medium**

Decision-flow: CFO → Operations → Sales

21. Create a seasonal readiness product bought before peak demand

Launch a product customers use before a known seasonal peak to prepare, tune, stock, or optimise what they rely on. Predictable pressure becomes a predictable revenue line.

Why it works

Seasonal pressure is predictable and costly when ignored. Customers pay in advance when preparation clearly avoids disruption, delay, waste, or poor performance.

Best for

Home services, HVAC, retail, logistics, agriculture, facilities, healthcare, software.

Execution Steps

1. Identify one seasonal pressure point customers face every year
2. Define a simple readiness product tied to that period
3. Make the outcome practical and the timing specific
4. Price against the cost of being unprepared
5. Launch before the pressure window starts each cycle

Real-world example

A heating company sells a winter-readiness pack. A software firm sells a year-end finance close-readiness module before reporting season.

Risk Management

1. **Operational** · 4/5 Timing missed — launching after the pressure window starts. **Mitigation:** Build a fixed launch calendar before peak. Launch early.
2. **Commercial** · 3/5 Weak urgency if the seasonal pain is not clearly communicated. **Mitigation:** Tie all messaging directly to the cost of being unprepared.
3. **Market** · 2/5 Low repeat demand if the cycle is not annual. **Mitigation:** Align product timing explicitly to the known annual cycle.
4. **Operational** · 3/5 Scope too broad reduces practical value. **Mitigation:** Keep the outcome tight and specific to one preparation need.
5. **Alignment** · 3/5 Sales team delays launch into the peak window. **Mitigation:** Pre-schedule campaigns and launch assets before the season begins.

Speed	Effort	Cost	Revenue	Time to cash	Scalability
Fast (0–30 days)	**Low**	**Low**	**Medium**	**Immediate**	**High**

Decision-flow: CFO → Operations → Sales

22. *Create a rapid-response product for overload periods*

Launch a product customers can buy when demand spikes, teams get stretched, or normal capacity cannot handle the pressure. A relief valve that generates revenue.

Why it works

Overload creates immediate pain. Customers pay when the alternative is missed revenue, delays, errors, or service failure during high-pressure periods.

Best for

Retail, logistics, hospitality, healthcare, field service, manufacturing, software.

Execution Steps

1. Identify a recurring overload moment customers struggle to manage
2. Define a rapid-response product that eases the pressure fast
3. Keep deployment simple and time-sensitive
4. Price against delay, failure, or lost output cost
5. Pilot in one high-pressure use case first

Real-world example

A warehouse supplier sells a peak-season overflow kit. A software firm launches a surge-support module for ticket volume spikes.

Risk Management

1. **Operational** · 5/5 Weak speed to deploy destroys the core value promise. **Mitigation:** Design for fast activation as the primary product requirement.
2. **Commercial** · 4/5 Pain not sharp enough outside proven overload periods. **Mitigation:** Target customers with documented, recurring overload events.
3. **Commercial** · 3/5 Price resistance when pressure is not currently felt. **Mitigation:** Anchor to the cost of lost output during the.
4. **Operational** · 4/5 Delivery strain if rollout is too broad too fast. **Mitigation:** Limit initial rollout. Scale from evidence.
5. **Market** · 3/5 Usage too narrow if the overload scenario is rare. **Mitigation:** Focus on repeat overload events with consistent demand patterns.

Speed	Effort	Cost	Revenue	Time to cash	Scalability
Medium (1–3 months)	**Medium**	**Medium**	**High**	**Immediate**	**Medium**

Decision-flow: CFO → Operations → Sales

23. *Create a switch-over product for unhappy competitor customers*

Launch a product that helps dissatisfied competitor customers move away faster by reducing the friction, risk, and effort of switching. Dissatisfaction becomes a revenue opportunity.

Why it works

Many customers stay with bad providers because switching feels painful. A switch-over product monetises dissatisfaction by making change easier, safer, and practical.

Best for

Home services, software, industrial supply, equipment, logistics, specialist B2B services.

Execution Steps

1. Identify where competitor dissatisfaction and switching friction are both high
2. Define a switch-over product that removes the biggest migration pain
3. Package the support, tools, setup, or credits clearly
4. Price below the perceived cost of staying with the bad provider
5. Pilot in one segment with visible dissatisfaction first

Real-world example

A heating company offers a swap-out package for unhappy competitor customers. A software firm sells a migration kit from a weak platform.

Risk Management

1. **Customer** · 4/5 Switching pain is misjudged and the product does not remove it. **Mitigation:** Map the real blockers from actual competitor customers first.
2. **Commercial** · 3/5 Product price feels higher than staying put. **Mitigation:** Price explicitly below the friction cost of staying.
3. **Operational** · 4/5 Migration delivery gets messy without standardisation. **Mitigation:** Standardise migration steps before the first customer attempt.
4. **Commercial** · 3/5 Sales targets too broadly and conversion is low. **Mitigation:** Focus on customers showing active dissatisfaction signals.
5. **Market** · 2/5 Competitor responds and closes the gap. **Mitigation:** Move fast. Build customer loyalty before the competitor adjusts.

Speed	Effort	Cost	Revenue	Time to cash	Scalability
Medium (1–3 months)	**Medium**	**Medium**	**High**	**Short**	**High**

Decision-flow: CFO → Sales → Operations

24. Create a ready-made premium bundle for urgent buyers

Launch a pre-built premium bundle that saves customers time when they need a fast, confident purchase without comparing many separate options. Urgency becomes a product.

Why it works

Urgent buyers pay for speed, simplicity, and certainty. A premium bundle creates product revenue by removing choice overload and speeding the buying decision.

Best for

Retail, e-commerce, home improvement, equipment, B2B supply, software, industrial products.

Execution Steps

1. Identify a buying situation where customers need a fast decision
2. Combine the most needed items or features into one premium bundle
3. Remove unnecessary options and make the choice easy
4. Price above standard mix-and-match buying
5. Launch first in high-urgency buying situations

Real-world example

A heater company sells a winter emergency replacement bundle. A software firm sells a rapid-launch package with core modules pre-included.

Risk Management

1. **Commercial** · 3/5 Bundle feels generic rather than purpose-built. **Mitigation:** Build around one specific, real use case. Name it clearly.
2. **Commercial** · 3/5 Price feels high without clear justification. **Mitigation:** Stress the time and decision-making effort the bundle replaces.
3. **Market** · 3/5 Weak uptake if urgency buyers are not targeted. **Mitigation:** Focus all positioning on urgent buying situations only.
4. **Financial** · 3/5 Bundle margin slips if contents are not controlled. **Mitigation:** Control bundle economics tightly before launch.
5. **Alignment** · 2/5 Sales overexplains instead of using the simple pitch. **Mitigation:** Keep the pitch to one sentence. Train for simplicity.

Speed	Effort	Cost	Revenue	Time to cash	Scalability
Fast (0–30 days)	**Low**	**Low**	**High**	**Immediate**	**High**

Decision-flow: CFO → Product → Sales

25. Create a premium experience product around everyday use

Launch a product that makes a normal customer action feel easier, better, faster, or more professional. Upgrading the ordinary becomes a new revenue line.

Why it works

Customers pay when a product improves something they already do often. It creates a fresh buying reason without relying on failure, urgency, or repair.

Best for

Consumer goods, home services, software, retail, hospitality, healthcare, B2B services.

Execution Steps

1. Identify a frequent customer action where experience falls short
2. Find where it feels slow, plain, confusing, or forgettable
3. Design a product that makes that moment clearly better
4. Price around convenience, ease, or the improved experience
5. Test with customers already paying for quality

Real-world example

A home service company sells a premium homeowner care box. A software firm sells an executive reporting interface that makes analysis easier.

Risk Management

1. **Commercial** · 4/5 Value feels soft if not tied to a frequent, specific use moment. **Mitigation:** Connect the product to a moment customers experience regularly.
2. **Market** · 3/5 Too niche if the behaviour is not common enough. **Mitigation:** Choose a behaviour that the majority of your customers share.
3. **Financial** · 3/5 Cost creep erodes margin if premium extras multiply. **Mitigation:** Define and limit what makes it premium before development.
4. **Commercial** · 3/5 Weak positioning fails to communicate the experience gain. **Mitigation:** Sell the better experience explicitly. Show before and after.
5. **Commercial** · 4/5 Low willingness to pay outside quality-sensitive segments. **Mitigation:** Target customers who already pay a premium elsewhere.

Speed	Effort	Cost	Revenue	Time to cash	Scalability
Medium (1–3 months)	**Medium**	**Medium**	**High**	**Medium**	**High**

Decision-flow: CFO → Product → Marketing

From Ideas to Action

Fifteen ideas. Fifteen ways to create standalone product revenue from repeatable work the business is already performing.

Most of these moves require no new technology and no new customer segment. They require a decision to package, price, and sell what already exists.

Before continuing, identify the single product idea with the clearest customer demand signal in your business right now. Name the person who owns it. Set a date for the first step.

> ***The most expensive product is the one you already know how to build and never launched.***

What Comes Next

2.3 — New Monetization Models addresses businesses that are already selling something well but charging for it in a way that misaligns with the value it delivers. If the pricing model feels like it is leaving money on the table — the next chapter is where the answer sits.

2.3 — New Monetization Models

Change how the business charges for what it delivers — not what it delivers — to unlock revenue that the current pricing structure cannot capture.

When These Strategies Work Best

New monetization strategies deliver the strongest return when the business already sells something well but the pricing model fails to reflect the full value it creates.

- Customers pay the same price regardless of the results or value they receive
- High-value outcomes are priced the same as low-value ones
- Price is the most common reason deals do not close
- Customers would pay more if the model felt lower-risk or more flexible
- The current model creates friction at the point of commitment

The Benefits

- Higher revenue without changing the underlying product or service
- Better alignment between price paid and value received
- New commercial access to buyers blocked by fixed pricing
- Faster decisions when risk is removed or flexibility is introduced
- A stronger value story when price is tied directly to outcomes

The Risks to Manage

- **Measurement disputes** — outcome models live or die on agreed metrics. Define them in writing before any sale.
- **Margin exposure** — performance and risk-based models carry financial uncertainty. Price for the worst case, not the average.
- **Revenue unpredictability** — usage and outcome models create variable income. Set minimums before launch.
- **Internal resistance** — new pricing models unsettle sales teams. Train and equip before the first conversation.

26. *Charge for guaranteed outcomes instead of effort*

Offer outcome-based pricing on select products or services where results are measurable. Customers pay for what they get, not how long it takes to deliver it.

Why it works

Customers care about results, not effort. Outcome pricing removes the most common objection, focuses delivery on what matters, and justifies a significant premium.

Best for

Consulting, agencies, SaaS, healthcare, construction, training, B2B services.

Execution Steps

1. Identify one measurable outcome the business reliably delivers
2. Define success metrics and boundaries clearly in writing
3. Apply model only to selected offers or segments
4. Price based on value delivered, not time spent
5. Pilot with three controlled engagements before scaling

Real-world example

A marketing firm offers outcome-based pricing for a campaign window. A SaaS firm pilots performance pricing for one product tier.

Risk Management

1. **Commercial** · 5/5 Overpromising on outcomes the business cannot control. **Mitigation:** Restrict scope tightly. Only apply where delivery is highly predictable.
2. **Operational** · 5/5 Outcome variability leads to disputes and margin loss. **Mitigation:** Control inputs rigorously. Qualify the client before committing.
3. **Financial** · 4/5 Margin risk if outcomes are not achieved consistently. **Mitigation:** Price to reflect uncertainty. Build in a floor fee.
4. **Customer** · 4/5 Wrong clients enter the model and cannot support delivery. **Mitigation:** Qualify every buyer strictly against delivery requirements.
5. **Commercial** · 4/5 Measurement disputes undermine trust and payment. **Mitigation:** Agree all metrics upfront in writing. No ambiguity at close.

Speed	Effort	Cost	Revenue	Time to cash	Scalability
Medium (1–3 months)	**Medium**	**Low**	**High**	**Medium**	**Medium**

Decision-flow: CFO → Sales → Operations

27. *Charge for priority access without degrading core service*

Introduce a paid priority tier that delivers faster outcomes through dedicated capacity, while maintaining quality for standard customers.

Why it works

Customers pay to move faster when time has a cost. Priority access works when speed is genuinely valuable and standard service is fully protected.

Best for

Healthcare, logistics, SaaS, customer support, home services, professional services.

Execution Steps

1. Identify delays in your process that carry real cost for customers
2. Define what priority means in measurable terms
3. Allocate dedicated buffered capacity for priority customers
4. Set hard limits to protect the standard service experience
5. Price based on time saved, not on effort added

Real-world example

A clinic offers same-day appointments using reserved slots. A SaaS firm provides priority support through a dedicated team.

Risk Management

1. **Customer** · 5/5 Standard service degrades as priority capacity grows. **Mitigation:** Ring-fence priority capacity.
2. **Customer** · 4/5 Standard customers perceive the tier as unfair. **Mitigation:** Keep baseline performance strong and visible.
3. **Commercial** · 4/5 Value too small to justify the premium. **Mitigation:** Ensure the time gain is real and significant before pricing.
4. **Operational** · 4/5 Overcommitment erodes the priority promise. **Mitigation:** Cap priority volume.
5. **Operational** · 3/5 Team strain from managing two service tiers. **Mitigation:** Plan workload and resourcing before launch.

Speed	Effort	Cost	Revenue	Time to cash	Scalability
Fast (0–30 days)	**Low**	**Low**	**High**	**Immediate**	**Medium**

Decision-flow: CFO → Operations → Sales

28. Charge to secure access before demand peaks

Introduce a paid access hold that lets customers secure availability, pricing, or priority before demand rises. The fee is credited toward the final purchase.

Why it works

Customers pay to avoid missing out or paying more later. Early access creates upfront revenue, improves demand forecasting, and rewards planning.

Best for

Retail, construction, logistics, software, events, education, healthcare.

Execution Steps

1. Identify where timing affects price, access, or availability
2. Define what can be secured early and for how long
3. Set a credited fee with simple, clear terms
4. Position around certainty and forward planning
5. Launch before the demand window opens

Real-world example

A home builder charges to secure a build slot. A SaaS firm lets customers lock pricing before a scheduled increase.

Risk Management

1. **Commercial** · 3/5 Feels like a deposit rather than a value-added hold. **Mitigation:** Tie the hold explicitly to a clear forward advantage.
2. **Commercial** · 3/5 Low uptake if urgency is not communicated clearly. **Mitigation:** Target time-sensitive buyers. Emphasise the cost of waiting.
3. **Customer** · 3/5 Confusion over terms reduces confidence. **Mitigation:** Keep the rules short, clear, and easy to explain.
4. **Operational** · 4/5 Overcommitment if hold volume is not capped. **Mitigation:** Limit secured volume before launch. Use a waitlist beyond it.
5. **Financial** · 3/5 Revenue recognition complexity with deferred credits. **Mitigation:** Align with finance before launch on how holds are recorded.

Speed	Effort	Cost	Revenue	Time to cash	Scalability
Fast (0–30 days)	**Low**	**Low**	**High**	**Immediate**	**High**

Decision-flow: CFO → Sales → Operations

29. Charge a membership for ongoing access to added value

Introduce a paid membership that delivers exclusive benefits not available in the standard offering, creating continuous value beyond normal transactions.

Why it works

Customers pay when they receive more than they already get. A strong membership adds visible, frequent value that justifies a recurring fee above the standard relationship.

Best for

Retail, e-commerce, SaaS, healthcare, fitness, home services, B2B supply.

Execution Steps

1. Identify value customers would pay for beyond what they already receive
2. Define exclusive benefits tied to frequent customer actions
3. Ensure benefits are used regularly, not just available
4. Price against the visible advantage the membership delivers
5. Launch with a clearly defined target segment

Real-world example

A retailer offers paid members exclusive pricing and early product access. A SaaS company provides members-only features and priority support.

Risk Management

1. **Commercial** · 5/5 No new value delivered, membership is standard offering repackaged. **Mitigation:** Add genuine exclusive benefits before launch. Nothing recycled.
2. **Customer** · 4/5 Low usage leads to churn when renewal comes. **Mitigation:** Tie membership benefits to actions customers take regularly.
3. **Customer** · 3/5 Attrition rises if value does not grow over time. **Mitigation:** Build a pipeline of new benefits before launch.
4. **Financial** · 3/5 Margin pressure if benefit cost is not modelled. **Mitigation:** Control the cost of benefits before setting the membership price.
5. **Commercial** · 3/5 Weak positioning fails to communicate the advantage clearly. **Mitigation:** Show the tangible benefit versus non-membership at every touchpoint.

Speed	Effort	Cost	Revenue	Time to cash	Scalability
Medium (1–3 months)	**Medium**	**Low**	**High**	**Immediate**	**High**

Decision-flow: CFO → Marketing → Operations

30. Charge for pay-as-you-go usage instead of fixed pricing

Introduce a usage-based model where customers pay for actual consumption or activity rather than a fixed upfront price. Alignment between cost and value unlocks new buyers.

Why it works

Pay-as-you-go reduces entry friction, aligns cost with value received, and opens the market to buyers who will not commit to fixed pricing upfront.

Best for

SaaS, utilities, logistics, equipment, infrastructure, healthcare, manufacturing.

Execution Steps

1. Identify a clear, measurable unit of consumption or activity
2. Define pricing tied directly to that unit
3. Ensure tracking is accurate and transparent to the customer
4. Set minimum threshold.s to protect baseline revenue
5. Pilot with customers sensitive to upfront commitment

Real-world example

A cloud provider charges per compute unit used. A logistics firm charges per shipment processed.

Risk Management

1. **Financial** · 4/5 Revenue volatility without minimum thresholds. **Mitigation:** Set and enforce minimum usage commitments before launch.
2. **Financial** · 4/5 Underpricing the unit destroys margin at scale. **Mitigation:** Calibrate unit pricing against full cost of delivery.
3. **Technical** · 4/5 Tracking errors create billing disputes. **Mitigation:** Test measurement accuracy extensively before customer use.
4. **Customer** · 3/5 Customer misuse or abuse of low-cost units. **Mitigation:** Define acceptable usage rules clearly in contract.
5. **Financial** · 3/5 Margin erosion as volume grows without cost control. **Mitigation:** Monitor cost per unit continuously. Build in review triggers.

Speed	Effort	Cost	Revenue	Time to cash	Scalability
Medium (1–3 months)	**Medium**	**Low**	**High**	**Medium**	**High**

Decision-flow: CFO → Product → Sales

31. Charge for results sharing instead of fixed pricing

Introduce a model where you take a percentage of the customer's upside — revenue gained, costs saved, or performance improved — instead of a fixed fee.

Why it works

Customers pay when they win. Results sharing removes upfront resistance, aligns incentives with delivery, and unlocks deals that fixed pricing would never close.

Best for

Consulting, agencies, SaaS, logistics, procurement, financial services.

Execution Steps

1. Identify a measurable customer upside the business consistently drives
2. Define the percentage share and how it is calculated
3. Agree baseline and measurement method with the client upfront
4. Include a minimum fee or hybrid structure to protect cash flow
5. Pilot in high-confidence use cases before broadening

Real-world example

A cost-reduction firm takes a share of savings achieved. A software firm charges a percentage of measured revenue uplift.

Risk Management

1. **Commercial** · 5/5 Measurement disputes destroy the commercial relationship. **Mitigation:** Define baseline, method, and audit rights in writing before signing.
2. **Financial** · 4/5 Revenue delay when results take time to materialise. **Mitigation:** Include a minimum fee component from the start.
3. **Operational** · 5/5 Outcome depends on client behaviour the business cannot control. **Mitigation:** Qualify inputs the business needs to deliver. Make them contractual.
4. **Customer** · 4/5 Client gaming of metrics reduces payout. **Mitigation:** Audit usage and results independently where possible.
5. **Financial** · 4/5 Margin uncertainty at scale. **Mitigation:** Limit exposure in early pilots. Expand after margin is confirmed.

Speed	Effort	Cost	Revenue	Time to cash	Scalability
Medium (1–3 months)	**Medium**	**Low**	**High**	**Medium**	**Medium**

Decision-flow: CFO → Sales → Finance

32. *Charge for achieved personal results, not access*

Offer pricing where customers pay when they reach a defined personal milestone — a skill level, fitness goal, financial target, or performance threshold.

Why it works

Consumers hesitate to pay upfront with no guarantee. Paying for results reduces risk, increases trust, and attracts the most committed, highest-converting customers.

Best for

Fitness, education, coaching, personal finance, wellness, career services.

Execution Steps

1. Identify one clear, measurable personal outcome
2. Define milestones that are objective and verifiable
3. Set pricing tied to milestone achievement
4. Include a minimum or hybrid fee to protect revenue
5. Pilot with high-intent customers only

Real-world example

A fitness programme charges per milestone reached. A language platform charges when users hit a defined proficiency level.

Risk Management

1. **Commercial** · 5/5 Vague outcomes create disputes at payment. **Mitigation:** Define every milestone as a measurable, objective standard.
2. **Customer** · 4/5 Customer manipulation of progress tracking. **Mitigation:** Use third-party or automated tracking where possible.
3. **Financial** · 4/5 Revenue delay when milestones take longer than expected. **Mitigation:** Include minimum fees or time-bound payment triggers.
4. **Customer** · 4/5 Low completion rates in unmotivated customer segments. **Mitigation:** Qualify customers on commitment level before enrolment.
5. **Financial** · 4/5 Margin risk if completion rates are lower than modelled. **Mitigation:** Cap exposure in pilots. Expand only after data confirms margins.

Speed	Effort	Cost	Revenue	Time to cash	Scalability
Medium (1–3 months)	**Medium**	**Low**	**High**	**Medium**	**Medium**

Decision-flow: CFO → Product → Marketing

33. Charge a one-time unlock fee for lifetime use

Offer a single upfront payment that gives the customer permanent access to a product, feature set, or service tier instead of ongoing recurring payments.

Why it works

Some customers strongly prefer certainty over recurring costs. A lifetime unlock generates immediate cash, eliminates payment friction, and rewards high-commitment buyers.

Best for

Software, digital products, education, tools, content platforms, consumer tech.

Execution Steps

1. Identify features or content customers use for the long term
2. Define the scope of lifetime access clearly
3. Price at a premium versus the equivalent recurring plan
4. Limit availability to manage long-term support obligations
5. Pilot with high-usage segments before offering broadly

Real-world example

A SaaS tool offers a lifetime deal for early users. An online platform sells lifetime access to all future content updates.

Risk Management

1. **Financial** · 5/5 Underpricing against long-term value destroys margin. **Mitigation:** Model the present value of lifetime access before setting the price.
2. **Financial** · 4/5 Revenue cannibalization of the recurring model. **Mitigation:** Offer selectively.
3. **Operational** · 4/5 Ongoing support obligations erode profitability over time. **Mitigation:** Define fair-use rules and support limits in the purchase terms.
4. **Customer** · 3/5 Overuse beyond fair-use assumptions. **Mitigation:** Include fair-use provisions in all lifetime purchase agreements.
5. **Financial** · 4/5 Missed recurring revenue if the offer is too broad. **Mitigation:** Apply only to specific segments or time windows.

Speed	Effort	Cost	Revenue	Time to cash	Scalability
Fast (0–30 days)	**Low**	**Low**	**High**	**Immediate**	**High**

Decision-flow: CFO → Product → Marketing

34. Monetize payment flexibility through embedded financing

Integrate third-party financing at the point of sale so customers pay over time while the business receives full upfront payment and earns revenue from the financing layer.

Why it works

Embedded financing removes upfront barriers, increases conversion, and creates additional revenue without the business taking on any lending risk. The partner carries it.

Best for

Retail, healthcare, education, home services, equipment, SaaS, B2B contracts.

Execution Steps

1. Identify where upfront cost blocks purchase decisions
2. Select and negotiate terms with a financing partner
3. Integrate financing cleanly into the sales or checkout flow
4. Structure pricing to capture a revenue share or margin uplift
5. Pilot across both B2C and B2B purchase types

Real-world example

A home services firm embeds financing at point of sale. A SaaS company offers multi-year financed contracts through a third-party partner.

Risk Management

1. **Financial** · 4/5 Poor partner terms erode the revenue benefit. **Mitigation:** Negotiate revenue share or margin uplift before committing.
2. **Financial** · 1/5 Customer default risk carried by the business. **Mitigation:** Offload all credit risk entirely to the financing partner.
3. **Technical** · 3/5 Integration friction disrupts the buying experience. **Mitigation:** Simplify the financing UX to one step at checkout or proposal.
4. **Financial** · 3/5 Margin leakage if pricing is not structured correctly. **Mitigation:** Model the full pricing structure including finance costs before launch.
5. **Legal** · 3/5 Regulatory exposure from financing arrangement. **Mitigation:** Use fully compliant regulated providers. Get legal sign-off.

Speed	Effort	Cost	Revenue	Time to cash	Scalability
Medium (1–3 months)	**Medium**	**Low**	**High**	**Immediate**	**High**

Decision-flow: CFO → Finance → Sales

35. Charge for transferring risk away from the customer

Offer a pricing model where the customer pays to transfer a specific business risk — cost overruns, delays, or variability — to the business. Certainty becomes the product.

Why it works

Customers pay to remove uncertainty. When the business absorbs a defined risk, pricing shifts from cost-based to confidence-based and commands a meaningful premium.

Best for

Construction, logistics, SaaS, manufacturing, healthcare, B2B services.

Execution Steps

1. Identify one risk customers consistently worry about
2. Define precisely what risk the business is absorbing
3. Set conditions, exclusions, and boundaries in writing
4. Price the risk transfer explicitly as a premium
5. Pilot with tightly controlled exposure before scaling

Real-world example

A contractor offers fixed-price builds despite cost fluctuations. A SaaS firm backs uptime with financial credits.

Risk Management

1. **Financial** · 5/5 Risk is mispriced and the business carries losses. **Mitigation:** Model the worst case fully before setting the price.
2. **Financial** · 5/5 Overexposure if too many risk transfers are active at once. **Mitigation:** Cap the number of active risk commitments at any time.
3. **Commercial** · 4/5 Scope ambiguity leads to disputes on what the transfer covers. **Mitigation:** Define every boundary of the risk transfer clearly in writing.
4. **Operational** · 5/5 Delivery failure triggers the risk commitment. **Mitigation:** Control all inputs that affect delivery before taking on risk.
5. **Customer** · 4/5 Client behaviour that increases the risk being carried. **Mitigation:** Set conditions on client obligations as part of the agreement.

Speed	Effort	Cost	Revenue	Time to cash	Scalability
Medium (1–3 months)	**Medium**	**Low**	**High**	**Medium**	**Medium**

Decision-flow: CFO → Sales → Operations

36. Charge for guaranteed improvement over current state

Offer a model where customers pay only when they are measurably better off than before, assessed against their own agreed baseline.

Why it works

Customers compare every purchase against where they are now. Charging for improvement removes hesitation completely and creates the strongest possible reason to commit.

Best for

Fitness, SaaS, consulting, education, healthcare, operations, productivity tools.

Execution Steps

1. Define the measurable before-and-after state clearly
2. Agree the baseline with the customer before work begins
3. Set pricing tied to the degree of improvement achieved
4. Include minimum thresholds to protect baseline revenue
5. Track improvement transparently throughout the engagement

Real-world example

A fitness app charges based on progress recorded. A SaaS tool charges based on efficiency gains versus an agreed starting benchmark.

Risk Management

1. **Commercial** · 5/5 Baseline disputes at payment undermine the relationship. **Mitigation:** Agree and document the baseline in writing before any work begins.
2. **Operational** · 4/5 Delivery inputs insufficient to drive the improvement promised. **Mitigation:** Control every variable that affects the outcome before committing.
3. **Financial** · 4/5 Revenue delay when improvements take longer than forecast. **Mitigation:** Include minimum fee commitments and time-bound payment milestones.
4. **Customer** · 4/5 Gaming of improvement metrics by the client. **Mitigation:** Audit all measurement independently. Define audit rights in contract.
5. **Financial** · 4/5 Margin risk if improvement rates are below model assumptions. **Mitigation:** Cap exposure in early pilots. Expand only after margins are confirmed.

Speed	Effort	Cost	Revenue	Time to cash	Scalability
Medium (1–3 months)	**Medium**	**Low**	**High**	**Medium**	**Medium**

Decision-flow: CFO → Product → Sales

37. *Charge for locking in future advantage*

Offer customers a way to pay now to secure future benefits — pricing, priority, capacity, or terms — before conditions change against them.

Why it works

Customers pay when they believe conditions will worsen. Locking advantage creates urgency, generates early cash flow, and requires no immediate service delivery.

Best for

Real estate, SaaS, manufacturing, logistics, education, energy, services.

Execution Steps

1. Identify where future conditions are likely to worsen for customers
2. Define all terms, obligations, and conditions in writing before any agreement. what can be locked in and for how long
3. Price the locked advantage relative to the expected change
4. Set time boundaries to create urgency and limit exposure
5. Launch ahead of the change signal becoming obvious

Real-world example

A SaaS company lets customers lock current pricing for future years. A builder lets buyers secure construction rates before a price increase.

Risk Management

1. **Operational** · 4/5 Overcommitment if locked volume is not capped. **Mitigation:** Set a hard cap on available locked positions before launch.
2. **Financial** · 4/5 Future costs are mispriced, eroding margin when delivered. **Mitigation:** Model the financial exposure of the locked terms carefully.
3. **Commercial** · 3/5 Low urgency if the future change is not credible. **Mitigation:** Use time-bound offers to create urgency without manufactured pressure.
4. **Customer** · 3/5 Customer confusion about what the lock actually covers. **Mitigation:** Keep the terms of the lock simple and unambiguous.
5. **Financial** · 3/5 Revenue timing complexity from deferred commitments. **Mitigation:** Align with finance on recognition treatment before launch.

Speed	Effort	Cost	Revenue	Time to cash	Scalability
Fast (0–30 days)	**Low**	**Low**	**High**	**Immediate**	**High**

Decision-flow: CFO → Sales → Finance

38. Charge for exclusivity within a defined segment

Offer customers the ability to pay for exclusive access within a defined group, territory, time window, or category so competitors cannot access the same advantage.

Why it works

Exclusivity is valuable when competition matters. Customers pay to protect position and secure advantage when being one of many is a real commercial problem.

Best for

Distribution, SaaS, events, consulting, marketplaces, healthcare, B2B services.

Execution Steps

1. Identify where exclusivity creates a genuine commercial advantage
2. Define the exclusivity boundaries — region, segment, or category
3. Limit supply intentionally to maintain the premium
4. Price based on the competitive value of the exclusivity
5. Pilot in high-competition segments first

Real-world example

A distributor grants exclusive territory rights to a partner. A SaaS firm offers category exclusivity within a defined vertical.

Risk Management

1. **Commercial** · 4/5 Over-restriction damages the broader market opportunity. **Mitigation:** Define exclusivity limits carefully. Not everything should be exclusive.
2. **Financial** · 4/5 Underpricing the exclusivity against its competitive value. **Mitigation:** Anchor price to what losing the exclusivity would cost the buyer.
3. **Market** · 3/5 Market imbalance from concentrated exclusivity. **Mitigation:** Control the number of exclusive allocations in any one market.
4. **Customer** · 3/5 Disputes over what the exclusivity actually covers. **Mitigation:** Define the terms with legal precision. Ambiguity is expensive.
5. **Financial** · 3/5 Lost broader revenue from non-exclusive buyers. **Mitigation:** Apply exclusivity selectively. Protect open access elsewhere.

Speed	Effort	Cost	Revenue	Time to cash	Scalability
Medium (1–3 months)	**Low**	**Low**	**High**	**Immediate**	**Medium**

Decision-flow: CFO → Sales → PMO

39. Charge for speed of decision, not speed of delivery

Monetize faster approvals, confirmations, or decisions within your process so customers can move forward sooner without waiting for standard-pace responses.

Why it works

Delays happen before delivery. Customers pay to accelerate decisions when timing affects their revenue, deals, or execution. Speed of yes is as valuable as speed of delivery.

Best for

Finance, approvals, procurement, SaaS, healthcare, construction, enterprise services.

Execution Steps

1. Identify where internal decisions create costly delays for customers
2. Define what a faster decision path looks like in practice
3. Allocate dedicated capacity for the premium decision route
4. Price based on the value of the time saved
5. Pilot in time-sensitive deal situations first

Real-world example

A lender charges for fast-track approval processing. A SaaS company offers rapid onboarding decisions for enterprise clients.

Risk Management

1. **Customer** · 5/5 Standard process slows down when priority capacity is drawn from it. **Mitigation:** Protect the standard process entirely. Priority runs on separate capacity.
2. **Commercial** · 4/5 Value unclear if the time gain is not significant enough. **Mitigation:** Quantify the time saving and link it to a.
3. **Operational** · 4/5 Overload if premium decision volume is not capped. **Mitigation:** Cap priority decision volume firmly before launch.
4. **Internal** · 3/5 Internal friction from teams unfamiliar with the model. **Mitigation:** Define roles..
5. **Customer** · 3/5 Fairness concerns from standard customers about the tier. **Mitigation:** Maintain strong standard service so the baseline is never questioned.

Speed	Effort	Cost	Revenue	Time to cash	Scalability
Fast (0–30 days)	**Low**	**Low**	**High**	**Immediate**	**High**

Decision-flow: CFO → Operations → Sales

From Ideas to Action

Fourteen ideas. Fourteen ways to generate more revenue from what the business already sells — by changing how it charges, not what it delivers.

Pricing model changes are among the highest-leverage moves available to any business. A single well-executed monetization shift can move revenue faster than months of new business development.

Before continuing, identify the one monetization model that best fits the commercial reality of your business right now. Name who owns the decision. Set a date for the first step.

> *The right pricing model makes the same product significantly more valuable. The wrong one makes it invisible.*

What Comes Next

2.4 — New Commercial Assets addresses the IP, data, tools, capacity, and knowledge sitting inside the business that currently generate no external revenue. If the business has built something valuable that only it uses — the next chapter is where that value gets unlocked.

2.4 — New Commercial Assets

Turn internal know-how, IP, data, audience, access, or methods into something new that can be sold.

When These Strategies Work Best

New commercial asset strategies work best when the business holds genuine knowledge, IP, tools, or operational advantages it uses only internally.

- Internal tools, frameworks, or methods are rebuilt by others at significant cost
- The business holds data, insight, or access that others in the market would pay for
- Expertise is delivered in client engagements but never packaged for external sale
- Capacity, infrastructure, or trust built over years generates no external revenue
- The business is known for a standard it has never commercialised

The Benefits

- Revenue from assets already built, with no additional delivery cost
- High-margin income from IP that compounds in value as it scales
- New revenue without new customers, new staff, or new infrastructure
- Market authority reinforced by making internal standards external
- Passive or recurring income from assets that require no active service delivery

The Risks to Manage

- **IP exposure** — assets built from client work carry legal risk. Strip and clear before selling.
- **Undervaluation** — internal assets are almost always priced below market value. Anchor to external demand.
- **Cannibalisation** — selling what you know can reduce your service premium. Position carefully.
- **Distribution gap** — a great asset nobody finds generates nothing. Plan the channel before launch.

40. Turn your internal playbook into a paid toolkit

Convert a proven internal process, checklist, calculator, script, or workflow into a paid toolkit customers can use themselves.

Why it works

Many businesses sit on practical know-how customers would pay to use. A toolkit creates new revenue from knowledge already built inside the company.

Best for

Consulting, SaaS, agencies, training, operations-heavy businesses, finance, logistics, healthcare

Execution Steps

1. Identify one internal method customers repeatedly ask about
2. Remove confidential or client-specific material
3. Turn it into templates, calculators, guides, or scripts
4. Make it easy. to use without your team
5. Price it below full-service support

Real-world example

A logistics firm sells a route-cost calculator, while a consulting firm sells a pricing reset toolkit built from its methodology.

Risk Management

1. **Legal** · 4/5 Proprietary methodology or content leaks to competitors through uncontrolled use. **Mitigation:** Separate reusable methodology from client-owned content before packaging.
2. **Customer** · 3/5 The offer is too complex for self-service use. **Mitigation:** Reduce complexity to the minimum needed for standalone customer use.
3. **Commercial** · 3/5 Willingness to pay is lower than projected for this segment. **Mitigation:** Target customers with a confirmed and urgent pain before any investment.
4. **Legal** · 5/5 Client confidentiality at risk from source materials. **Mitigation:** Strip all client-identifiable data before packaging for external use.
5. **Operational** · 3/5 Post-launch support demand is higher than planned, straining the delivery team. **Mitigation:** Include a concise usage guide so customers can self-serve.

Speed	Effort	Cost	Revenue	Time to cash	Scalability
Medium (1-3 months)	**Medium**	**Low**	**High**	**Medium**	**High**

Decision-flow: CFO → Product → Sales

41. Sell your customer data as an anonymized insight

Turn anonymized customer patterns, trends, demand signals, or usage insights into a paid report, dashboard, or briefing customers can use to make better decisions.

Why it works

Businesses often collect valuable data without monetizing it. Customers pay for insight that helps reduce uncertainty, spot demand, or make faster decisions.

Best for

Retail, e-commerce, SaaS, logistics, hospitality, healthcare, marketplaces, B2B platforms

Execution Steps

1. Identify data patterns customers would value
2. Remove personal, sensitive, or identifiable information
3. Turn insights into a simple paid format
4. Validate demand with current customers
5. Price based on decision value

Real-world example

A retailer sells category demand insights to suppliers, while a SaaS platform sells anonymized usage benchmarks to enterprise customers.

Risk Management

1. **Legal** · 5/5 Customer data privacy is at risk if access, anonymisation. **Mitigation:** Anonymize and review.
2. **Commercial** · 4/5 Insight not specific enough to justify purchase. **Mitigation:** Tie the insight directly to one high-value decision the.
3. **Product** · 4/5 Data quality is insufficient to support reliable insights or accurate predictions.. **Mitigation:** Audit and clean all data inputs before packaging as.
4. **Customer** · 4/5 Customers have concerns about how their data is being used or. **Mitigation:** Explain methodology clearly.
5. **Market** · 3/5 Repeat demand lower than projected at launch. **Mitigation:** Refresh all content, data, and offer elements on a defined schedule.

Speed	Effort	Cost	Revenue	Time to cash	Scalability
Medium (1-3 months)	**Medium**	**Low**	**High**	**Medium**	**High**

Decision-flow: CFO → IT / Data → Product

42. License your training materials to other businesses

Turn your internal training guides, onboarding content, product education, or operating manuals into a licensed asset other businesses can use with teams or customers.

Why it works

Companies often build strong training once, then use it only internally. Licensing creates revenue from existing knowledge while helping others train faster.

Best for

Retail, franchising, hospitality, healthcare, software, manufacturing, education, home services

Execution Steps

1. Identify training content with external value
2. Remove internal-only and confidential material
3. Package it into modules, videos, guides, or templates
4. Define usage rights and license terms
5. Price by user, team, location, or annual access

Real-world example

A restaurant group licenses food-safety training to franchisees, while a SaaS company licenses admin training modules to implementation partners.

Risk Management

1. **Legal** · 4/5 Licensed intellectual property is used outside agreed terms and permitted boundaries. **Mitigation:** Define permitted use cases, territories, and duration in every license.
2. **Customer** · 3/5 The content contains internal references that are unsuitable for an external audience. **Mitigation:** Remove internal context and simplify language for an external audience.
3. **Commercial** · 3/5 The buyer need is not strong or urgent enough to drive. **Mitigation:** Target training-heavy sectors.
4. **Legal** · 4/5 Non-compliance with applicable regulations or standards creates legal and financial risk. **Mitigation:** Review content legally.
5. **Operational** · 3/5 Post-launch support demand is higher than planned, straining the delivery team. **Mitigation:** Include usage boundaries.

Speed	Effort	Cost	Revenue	Time to cash	Scalability
Medium (1-3 months)	**Medium**	**Low**	**High**	**Medium**	**High**

Decision-flow: CFO → Product → Legal

43. *Sell a certification built around your standards*

Create a paid certification that validates whether people, partners, suppliers, or customers meet your method, quality standard, process, or usage requirements.

Why it works

Certification creates value when trust matters. Buyers pay for credibility, proof, status, and reduced uncertainty.

Best for

Training, healthcare, software, franchising, beauty, fitness, manufacturing, professional services

Execution Steps

1. Identify one standard others want to prove
2. Define certification criteria and assessment method
3. Create training, testing, and renewal rules
4. Price certification by person, partner, or location
5. Protect brand and usage rights

Real-world example

A software firm certifies implementation partners, while a beauty brand certifies salons trained in its treatment method.

Risk Management

1. **Commercial** · 4/5 Credibility is insufficient to justify the price premium at launch. **Mitigation:** Publish clear measurable standards before accepting certification applications.
2. **Legal** · 4/5 Brand assets are used outside of approved guidelines by partners or. **Mitigation:** Restrict badge usage to verified and current holders only.
3. **Commercial** · 3/5 Demand from the target segment is insufficient to justify full launch. **Mitigation:** Target status-driven users.
4. **Operational** · 4/5 Certification assessment criteria are too loose, reducing the credibility of the standard. **Mitigation:** Design assessments that test actual performance, not just knowledge recall.
5. **Legal** · 3/5 Legal exposure arises if obligations, claims. **Mitigation:** Define limitations clearly.

Speed	Effort	Cost	Revenue	Time to cash	Scalability
Medium (1-3 months)	**Medium**	**Low**	**High**	**Medium**	**High**

Decision-flow: CFO → Product → Legal

44. Lease underused business assets to customers or partners

Turn idle equipment, tools, vehicles, space, storage, machines, or specialist infrastructure into a paid leasing asset when not fully used internally.

Why it works

Businesses often own expensive assets that sit idle. Leasing creates revenue from sunk costs while helping customers avoid buying equipment temporarily.

Best for

Manufacturing, logistics, healthcare, events, construction, food production, retail, hospitality, home services

Execution Steps

1. Identify assets with unused capacity
2. Confirm safe external use
3. Define rental terms and access rules
4. Price by time, usage, or capacity
5. Add insurance, damage, and liability terms

Real-world example

A food producer leases cold-storage space, while a construction firm rents specialist tools to smaller contractors.

Risk Management

1. **Operational** · 4/5 Physical or digital assets are damaged through external use or mishandling.. **Mitigation:** Require a deposit and proof of insurance before releasing any asset.
2. **Operational** · 4/5 Internal teams resist sharing resources or capacity with external users. Align. **Mitigation:** Reserve internal capacity as the first priority before making.
3. **Legal** · 5/5 Liability if responsibilities are not documented. **Mitigation:** Use a written contract specifying liability, damage, and return conditions.
4. **Operational** · 3/5 Scheduling conflicts between internal and external needs. **Mitigation:** Use a booking system to prevent scheduling conflicts and.
5. **Commercial** · 3/5 Demand from the target segment is weaker than projected at launch. **Mitigation:** Launch with partners you already have a working relationship with.

Speed	Effort	Cost	Revenue	Time to cash	Scalability
Fast (0-30 days)	**Medium**	**Low**	**High**	**Immediate**	**Medium**

Decision-flow: CFO → Operations → Sales

45. Monetize your audience as a sponsored access asset

Turn your customer base, subscriber list, event audience, app users, or community into a paid sponsorship asset for relevant partners.

Why it works

Many businesses have trusted attention but do not monetize it. Relevant partners pay to reach a qualified audience when access is useful and non-intrusive.

Best for

Retail, e-commerce, apps, media, events, education, hospitality, gyms, niche communities

Execution Steps

1. Identify audience segments partners would value
2. Define sponsor-safe access formats
3. Protect customer trust and privacy
4. Price by reach, relevance, or placement
5. Target non-competing partners

Real-world example

A gym sells sponsorship access to wellness brands, while an education platform lets employers sponsor career content.

Risk Management

1. **Customer** · 5/5 Trust erodes gradually if the offer does not consistently deliver its. **Mitigation:** Accept only sponsors whose offering is directly relevant to the audience.
2. **Legal** · 5/5 Customer data privacy is at risk if access, anonymisation. **Mitigation:** Prohibit sharing identifiable customer data with any third party.
3. **Commercial** · 4/5 The sponsor profile does not align with audience expectations or brand. **Mitigation:** Screen all partners against defined brand, quality, and audience fit criteria.
4. **Customer** · 3/5 The audience becomes fatigued when communications or placements are too frequent.. **Mitigation:** Cap the frequency of outreach or placements to prevent customer fatigue.
5. **Financial** · 3/5 Low pricing power. **Mitigation:** Prove audience quality.

Speed	Effort	Cost	Revenue	Time to cash	Scalability
Fast (0-30 days)	**Low**	**Low**	**High**	**Immediate**	**High**

Decision-flow: CFO → Marketing → Partnerships / BD

46. Sell access to your buying power

Turn your negotiated supplier rates, volume discounts, or preferred vendor terms into a paid access asset for smaller customers or partners.

Why it works

Smaller buyers often pay more because they lack scale. Your stronger purchasing power can become a paid advantage through better terms or trusted suppliers.

Best for

Retail, hospitality, construction, healthcare, manufacturing, education, franchises, business communities

Execution Steps

1. Identify supplier terms that create real savings
2. Confirm suppliers allow shared or group access
3. Define who can access the buying program
4. Price as membership, admin fee, or savings share
5. Protect supplier relationships and usage limits

Real-world example

A hotel group lets boutique operators access preferred linen rates, while a construction firm creates supplier-access for smaller contractors.

Risk Management

1. **Dependency** · 5/5 Supplier restrictions. **Mitigation:** Get approval.
2. **Commercial** · 4/5 Weak savings. **Mitigation:** Prove value.
3. **Operational** · 4/5 Abuse of access. **Mitigation:** Set usage rules.
4. **Operational** · 3/5 Admin burden. **Mitigation:** Automate ordering where possible.
5. **Dependency** · 4/5 Relationship risk. **Mitigation:** Protect key suppliers.

Speed	Effort	Cost	Revenue	Time to cash	Scalability
Medium (1-3 months)	**Medium**	**Low**	**High**	**Short**	**High**

Decision-flow: CFO → Procurement → Partnerships / BD

47. Rent out your delivery or service routes

Turn existing delivery routes, service visits, field teams, or customer rounds into paid capacity for partners who need last-mile reach.

Why it works

Many businesses already travel to valuable locations daily. Selling spare route capacity creates revenue without building a new distribution network.

Best for

Logistics, food delivery, home services, healthcare, maintenance, retail, field sales, B2B supply

Execution Steps

1. Map existing routes, stops, and spare capacity
2. Identify partners needing the same reach
3. Define what can be carried, delivered, or serviced
4. Price by route, stop, delivery, or capacity
5. Protect core customer service levels

Real-world example

A pharmacy uses home-delivery routes to deliver wellness products for partners, while a maintenance company carries partner supplies.

Risk Management

1. **Operational** · 5/5 Core service disruption. **Mitigation:** Protect main routes.
2. **Legal** · 4/5 Legal liability arises if terms, access rules. **Mitigation:** Define handling rules.
3. **Customer** · 3/5 Partners do not align with the business audience, brand. **Mitigation:** Apply a written partner screening process before any agreement is signed.
4. **Operational** · 4/5 Route overload. **Mitigation:** Cap spare capacity.
5. **Customer** · 3/5 Customers are unclear on what is included, how to use it. **Mitigation:** Set clear expectations.

Speed	Effort	Cost	Revenue	Time to cash	Scalability
Medium (1-3 months)	**Medium**	**Low**	**High**	**Short**	**Medium**

Decision-flow: CFO → Operations → Partnerships / BD

48. Sell unused appointment or booking capacity to partners

Turn empty appointment slots, room time, consultation blocks, demo windows, studio hours, or service capacity into paid access for partners.

Why it works

Unused time expires. If another business needs trusted space, staff, or customer-facing capacity, you can monetize idle slots without creating a new product.

Best for

Clinics, salons, gyms, studios, training centers, hotels, event spaces, professional services

Execution Steps

1. Identify recurring unused capacity
2. Define what partners can book or use
3. Set pricing by hour, slot, room, or session
4. Protect your own customer priority
5. Create simple booking rules

Real-world example

A clinic rents unused consultation rooms to visiting specialists, while a gym rents off-peak studio hours to wellness coaches.

Risk Management

1. **Customer** · 4/5 Partner profile does not align with brand standards. **Mitigation:** Apply a written partner screening process before any agreement is signed.
2. **Customer** · 3/5 Customers are unclear on what is included, how to use it. **Mitigation:** Clarify ownership.
3. **Operational** · 4/5 Scheduling conflict. **Mitigation:** Block core demand first.
4. **Legal** · 4/5 Legal liability arises if terms, access rules. **Mitigation:** Require contracts.
5. **Commercial** · 3/5 Weak utilization. **Mitigation:** Start with peak partner need.

Speed	Effort	Cost	Revenue	Time to cash	Scalability
Fast (0-30 days)	**Low**	**Low**	**Medium**	**Immediate**	**Medium**

Decision-flow: CFO → Operations → Partnerships / BD

49. *Monetize unused production capacity*

Sell spare machine time, kitchen time, workshop time, factory slots, or production capacity to customers or partners who need output without owning infrastructure.

Why it works

Production capacity is expensive whether used or not. Selling unused capacity creates revenue from assets already paid for and helps others produce without capital investment.

Best for

Manufacturing, food production, printing, packaging, labs, workshops, bakeries, cosmetics, industrial services

Execution Steps

1. Identify predictable spare production capacity
2. Define what external work can safely fit
3. Set pricing by hour, batch, unit, or output
4. Protect priority for core production
5. Add quality, liability, and scheduling rules

Real-world example

A bakery rents off-peak kitchen production time, while a factory sells unused line capacity to smaller brands needing short runs.

Risk Management

1. **Operational** · 5/5 Core operations are disrupted when external demand competes for the same. **Mitigation:** Protect internal capacity.
2. **Operational** · 4/5 Quality standards are not maintained consistently across all deliveries. Standardize before scaling. **Mitigation:** Set production standards.
3. **Legal** · 4/5 Liability if responsibilities are not documented. **Mitigation:** Use a written contract specifying liability, damage, and return conditions.
4. **Operational** · 4/5 Scheduling conflict. **Mitigation:** Control booking windows.
5. **Commercial** · 3/5 The offer does not fit closely enough to create reliable conversion. **Mitigation:** Start with similar products.

Speed	Effort	Cost	Revenue	Time to cash	Scalability
Medium (1-3 months)	**Medium**	**Low**	**High**	**Short**	**Medium**

Decision-flow: CFO → Operations → Partnerships / BD

50. Monetize unused storage or holding space

Sell unused warehouse space, cold storage, secure rooms, parking, shelves, lockers, or holding areas to customers or partners who need temporary capacity.

Why it works

Storage space has value when customers face overflow, seasonality, or short-term pressure. Monetizing unused capacity can create attractive incremental revenue.

Best for

Warehousing, retail, food, healthcare, logistics, offices, hotels, property owners, industrial businesses

Execution Steps

1. Identify unused or underused storage capacity
2. Define what can safely be stored
3. Set pricing by space, time, temperature, or security level
4. Create access, liability, and insurance rules
5. Protect your own operational needs first

Real-world example

A restaurant monetizes spare cold-storage space, while a retail store rents unused backroom space to local brands during peak season.

Risk Management

1. **Operational** · 4/5 Damage or loss. **Mitigation:** Require clear liability terms in writing before releasing any asset.
2. **Operational** · 4/5 Security risk. **Mitigation:** Control who has access and under what conditions from day one.
3. **Operational** · 4/5 Core space conflict. **Mitigation:** Reserve internal capacity as the first priority before offering.
4. **Customer** · 3/5 Poor fit items. **Mitigation:** Define exactly what types of items can be stored.
5. **Commercial** · 3/5 Demand from the target segment is weaker than projected at launch. **Mitigation:** Target customers facing predictable overflow needs first.

Speed	Effort	Cost	Revenue	Time to cash	Scalability
Fast (0-30 days)	**Low**	**Low**	**Medium**	**Immediate**	**Medium**

Decision-flow: CFO → Operations → Partnerships / BD

51. Monetize unused staff expertise during quiet periods

Sell access to skilled staff, specialists, technicians, trainers, or operators during predictable low-demand periods when their capacity is not fully used.

Why it works

Specialist labor is expensive to keep idle. If spare time is predictable, businesses can monetize expertise already on payroll.

Best for

Healthcare, IT, engineering, home services, repair, training, hospitality, manufacturing, professional services

Execution Steps

1. Identify predictable low-demand staff capacity
2. Define which expertise can be safely sold externally
3. Set pricing by hour, session, visit, or project block
4. Protect internal service levels first
5. Create rules for scope, liability, and handoff

Real-world example

An IT team sells off-peak support blocks to small businesses, while a hotel rents chef training time to local food operators.

Risk Management

1. **Operational** · 5/5 Core service impact. **Mitigation:** Protect internal demand.
2. **Alignment** · 4/5 Staff resistance. **Mitigation:** Align team and partner incentives with the desired commercial outcome.
3. **Operational** · 4/5 Scope expands beyond agreed boundaries. **Mitigation:** Define usage, access, and delivery boundaries before any commitment.
4. **Legal** · 4/5 Legal liability arises if terms, access rules. **Mitigation:** Use specific, plain-language contract terms that eliminate ambiguity.
5. **Commercial** · 3/5 Demand from the target segment is weaker than projected at launch. **Mitigation:** Test with known buyers.

Speed	Effort	Cost	Revenue	Time to cash	Scalability
Fast (0-30 days)	**Medium**	**Low**	**High**	**Immediate**	**Medium**

Decision-flow: CFO → Operations → Sales

52. Monetize unused location visibility

Sell paid visibility on underused physical or digital spaces customers already see, such as storefronts, receipts, packaging, screens, vehicles, apps, or portals.

Why it works

Attention is an asset. If a business already has trusted customer touchpoints, relevant partners may pay to appear there.

Best for

Retail, hospitality, clinics, gyms, logistics, apps, delivery businesses, property operators

Execution Steps

1. Identify customer touchpoints with unused visibility
2. Define where partner messages can appear safely
3. Set partner-fit and brand rules
4. Price by placement, duration, or reach
5. Cap the frequency of outreach or placements to prevent customer fatigue. to protect trust

Real-world example

A gym sells screen placement to a healthy food brand, while a delivery company sells branded insert space inside customer orders.

Risk Management

1. **Customer** · 5/5 Trust erodes gradually if the offer does not consistently deliver its. **Mitigation:** Accept only partners whose offering is directly relevant to the audience.
2. **Customer** · 4/5 Partner profile does not align with brand standards. **Mitigation:** Set partner rules.
3. **Customer** · 4/5 Customer annoyance. **Mitigation:** Cap the frequency of outreach or placements to prevent customer fatigue.
4. **Legal** · 4/5 Customer data privacy is at risk if access, anonymisation. **Mitigation:** Prohibit sharing identifiable customer data with any third party.
5. **Financial** · 3/5 Weak pricing. **Mitigation:** Prove visibility value.

Speed	Effort	Cost	Revenue	Time to cash	Scalability
Fast (0-30 days)	**Low**	**Low**	**Medium**	**Immediate**	**Medium**

Decision-flow: CFO → Marketing → Partnerships / BD

53. Monetize unused testing or demonstration facilities

Sell access to demo rooms, test environments, labs, show kitchens, training floors, pilot sites, or equipment-testing spaces that are not fully used internally.

Why it works

Customers and partners often need safe places to test, demo, train, or validate before buying. Existing facilities can become a paid asset.

Best for

Manufacturing, food, healthcare, software, construction, equipment, retail, education, industrial services

Execution Steps

1. Identify underused testing or demo capacity
2. Define what external users can safely access
3. Set pricing by session, day, project, or usage
4. Create rules for supervision, safety, and liability
5. Protect internal use first

Real-world example

A food company rents its test kitchen to emerging brands, while a software firm sells access to a sandbox environment for partner testing.

Risk Management

1. **Operational** · 5/5 Safety risk. **Mitigation:** Require supervision.
2. **Legal** · 4/5 Intellectual property is exposed through unsupervised access or poor usage controls.. **Mitigation:** Restrict sensitive access.
3. **Operational** · 4/5 Core operations are disrupted when external demand competes for the same. **Mitigation:** Reserve internal capacity as the first priority before offering.
4. **Operational** · 4/5 Damage risk. **Mitigation:** Require deposits or insurance.
5. **Commercial** · 3/5 Demand from the target segment is weaker than projected at launch. **Mitigation:** Target partners needing validation.

Speed	Effort	Cost	Revenue	Time to cash	Scalability
Medium (1-3 months)	**Medium**	**Low**	**High**	**Medium**	**Medium**

Decision-flow: CFO → Operations → Partnerships / BD

54. Monetize your trusted vendor list

Turn your vetted supplier, contractor, expert, or partner list into a paid access asset for customers who need reliable providers without doing the search themselves.

Why it works

Finding trustworthy vendors is painful and risky. Customers pay for shortcuts that reduce search time and lower mistake risk.

Best for

Construction, home services, events, hospitality, healthcare, real estate, B2B services, marketplaces

Execution Steps

1. Identify vendor categories customers frequently ask about
2. Vet vendors using clear quality criteria
3. Define access format and pricing
4. Create referral, access, or introduction rules
5. Protect neutrality and trust

Real-world example

A renovation firm sells access to vetted interior suppliers, while an events company offers clients a trusted vendor directory.

Risk Management

1. **Customer** · 5/5 Vendor quality failure. **Mitigation:** Review vendors regularly.
2. **Customer** · 4/5 Customer trust damaged if delivery falls short. **Mitigation:** Disclose relationships.
3. **Commercial** · 3/5 Demand from the target segment is weaker than projected at launch. **Mitigation:** Focus on painful search areas.
4. **Legal** · 4/5 A conflict of interest between the business role and the commercial. **Mitigation:** Set transparency rules.
5. **Legal** · 4/5 Legal liability arises if terms, access rules. **Mitigation:** Define referral limits.

Speed	Effort	Cost	Revenue	Time to cash	Scalability
Fast (0-30 days)	**Low**	**Low**	**Medium**	**Immediate**	**Medium**

Decision-flow: CFO → Procurement → Partnerships / BD

55. Monetize your quality-control process

Turn your inspection, quality check, approval process, or acceptance standard into a paid review service customers or partners can use before decisions.

Why it works

Customers pay to reduce uncertainty before buying, launching, approving, or accepting work. A trusted quality process can become a sellable asset.

Best for

Manufacturing, construction, food, healthcare, software, logistics, retail, professional services

Execution Steps

1. Identify a quality check others would value
2. Define the review scope and pass/fail criteria
3. Remove internal-only or confidential methods
4. Price by inspection, review, batch, or project
5. Create clear limitations and liability terms

Real-world example

A food company sells supplier quality audits, while a software firm offers paid technical architecture reviews before implementation.

Risk Management

1. **Legal** · 5/5 Liability if responsibilities are not documented. **Mitigation:** Define scope, access, and usage limits in writing before launch.
2. **Commercial** · 4/5 Weak trust. **Mitigation:** Show review standards.
3. **Operational** · 4/5 Scope expands beyond agreed boundaries. **Mitigation:** Keep review bounded.
4. **Operational** · 3/5 Internal strain. **Mitigation:** Cap review volume.
5. **Legal** · 3/5 Conflict risk. **Mitigation:** Separate advice from approval.

Speed	Effort	Cost	Revenue	Time to cash	Scalability
Medium (1-3 months)	**Medium**	**Low**	**High**	**Medium**	**Medium**

Decision-flow: CFO → Operations → Legal

56. *Monetize your implementation templates*

Turn proven setup plans, rollout schedules, checklists, forms, SOPs, or launch templates into a paid asset customers can use to execute faster.

Why it works

Customers often know what they want but struggle with execution. Ready-made implementation assets reduce mistakes and save time.

Best for

SaaS, construction, healthcare, education, logistics, franchising, consulting, home services

Execution Steps

1. Identify repeat implementation materials customers value
2. Remove internal or confidential information
3. Package templates into a clear asset library
4. Add simple usage instructions
5. Price by download, license, or project use

Real-world example

A franchise group sells store-opening templates, while a SaaS firm sells implementation checklists and rollout plans to enterprise teams.

Risk Management

1. **Commercial** · 3/5 The offer is too generic to create meaningful value for any. **Mitigation:** Keep assets practical.
2. **Legal** · 4/5 Proprietary methodology or content leaks to competitors through uncontrolled use. **Mitigation:** License usage clearly.
3. **Customer** · 3/5 Adoption is slower than expected. **Mitigation:** Target self-implementers.
4. **Customer** · 3/5 Misuse risk. **Mitigation:** Include a concise usage guide with every deliverable at launch.
5. **Financial** · 3/5 Weak pricing. **Mitigation:** Anchor to time saved.

Speed	Effort	Cost	Revenue	Time to cash	Scalability
Fast (0-30 days)	**Low**	**Low**	**Medium**	**Immediate**	**High**

Decision-flow: CFO → Operations → Product

57. Monetize your onboarding environment

Turn your onboarding portal, welcome flow, demo environment, setup journey, or starter workspace into a paid asset other customers or partners can use.

Why it works

Good onboarding reduces confusion and speeds adoption. A strong onboarding system can become a sellable asset for partners, resellers, or customers.

Best for

SaaS, franchising, education, healthcare, hospitality, B2B services, marketplaces

Execution Steps

1. Identify onboarding assets that reduce customer friction
2. Remove internal-only content
3. Package the environment for external use
4. Define access, support, and usage rules
5. Price by user, partner, or location

Real-world example

A SaaS company licenses its onboarding portal to implementation partners, while a franchise business sells a store-launch onboarding system.

Risk Management

1. **Customer** · 3/5 Too internal. **Mitigation:** Remove internal context and simplify language for an external audience.
2. **Operational** · 4/5 Post-launch support demand is higher than planned, straining the delivery team. **Mitigation:** Limit included help.
3. **Legal** · 4/5 Proprietary methodology or content leaks to competitors through uncontrolled use. **Mitigation:** License access clearly.
4. **Customer** · 3/5 Weak usage. **Mitigation:** Include simple guidance.
5. **Customer** · 3/5 Brand inconsistency. **Mitigation:** Control customization.

Speed	Effort	Cost	Revenue	Time to cash	Scalability
Medium (1-3 months)	**Medium**	**Low**	**High**	**Medium**	**High**

Decision-flow: CFO → Product → Customer Success

58. Monetize your customer demand as a paid signal

Sell early access to real customer demand signals, such as what people are searching, requesting, or about to buy, before the transaction happens.

Why it works

Knowing demand before it converts is extremely valuable. Suppliers and partners pay to see what customers want early so they can act faster.

Best for

Marketplaces, e-commerce, retail, real estate, recruitment, SaaS platforms, services with inbound demand

Execution Steps

1. Identify where customer intent appears before purchase
2. Capture searches, inquiries, requests, or abandoned actions
3. Aggregate and anonymize. the data
4. Package signals into a paid feed, alert, or dashboard
5. Price based on decision advantage

Real-world example

A real estate platform sells early buyer inquiries to developers, while a B2B platform sells inbound demand signals to suppliers.

Risk Management

1. **Legal** · 5/5 Customer data privacy is at risk if access, anonymisation. **Mitigation:** Fully anonymize data.
2. **Customer** · 5/5 Trust erodes gradually if the offer does not consistently deliver its. **Mitigation:** Never expose individual users.
3. **Product** · 4/5 Weak signal quality. **Mitigation:** Filter noise.
4. **Market** · 3/5 Over-saturation. **Mitigation:** Limit access to the minimum level required for the commercial purpose.
5. **Legal** · 3/5 Partners use brand, content. **Mitigation:** Define usage rules.

Speed	Effort	Cost	Revenue	Time to cash	Scalability
Medium (1-3 months)	**Medium**	**Low**	**High**	**Medium**	**High**

Decision-flow: CFO → Product → Partnerships / BD

59. *Monetize your position in the customer journey*

Charge partners to plug into the exact point where your customer is about to make a decision, giving them the right to be the chosen option at that moment.

Why it works

The most valuable place is the decision moment. Businesses pay to be present exactly when a customer is choosing, not before or after.

Best for

Marketplaces, SaaS, booking platforms, healthcare pathways, home services, finance, travel, e-commerce

Execution Steps

1. Identify where customers make a final decision
2. Define the decision slot
3. Offer paid placement or preferred positioning
4. Accept only partners whose offering is directly relevant to the audience. and quality control
5. Price based on conversion advantage

Real-world example

A booking platform charges providers for preferred placement at checkout, while a healthcare pathway directs patients to paid partner providers.

Risk Management

1. **Customer** · 5/5 Trust erodes gradually if the offer does not consistently deliver its. **Mitigation:** Keep relevance strict.
2. **Legal** · 4/5 Bias perception. **Mitigation:** Communicate the commercial relationship to customers before any recommendation.
3. **Customer** · 4/5 Poor partner quality. **Mitigation:** Curate partner quality — remove any partner who degrades.
4. **Customer** · 4/5 Over-monetization. **Mitigation:** Limit placements.
5. **Customer** · 3/5 Customer backlash. **Mitigation:** Limit partner placements to a level that preserves the customer experience.

Speed	Effort	Cost	Revenue	Time to cash	Scalability
Medium (1-3 months)	**Medium**	**Low**	**High**	**Medium**	**High**

Decision-flow: CFO → Product → Partnerships / BD

60. Monetize your customer default choice

Charge to be set as the default option in your system, process, or environment where customers tend not to change the pre-selected choice.

Why it works

Default behavior is powerful. Businesses pay to become the default because it drives consistent, passive conversion when it remains relevant and trusted.

Best for

SaaS, fintech, subscriptions, platforms, marketplaces, telecom, devices, service ecosystems

Execution Steps

1. Identify where defaults exist in your flow
2. Define which default positions are valuable
3. Offer paid default positioning
4. Maintain quality thresholds
5. Price based on conversion impact

Real-world example

A payment platform charges to be the default payment option, while a SaaS system sets a preferred integration as default for new users.

Risk Management

1. **Customer** · 5/5 User trust risk. **Mitigation:** Accept only partners whose offering is directly relevant to the audience.
2. **Legal** · 4/5 Regulatory risk. **Mitigation:** Review all applicable rules and regulations and build compliance.
3. **Customer** · 4/5 Poor partner fit. **Mitigation:** Curate strictly.
4. **Customer** · 3/5 Overuse. **Mitigation:** Limit defaults.
5. **Customer** · 4/5 Experience degradation. **Mitigation:** Test with a controlled small group before any broader deployment.

Speed	Effort	Cost	Revenue	Time to cash	Scalability
Medium (1-3 months)	**Medium**	**Low**	**High**	**Medium**	**High**

Decision-flow: CFO → Product → PMO / Strategy

61. Monetize your trust layer as a paid endorsement asset

Charge approved partners to use your trusted approval, verification, or recommended-by status when selling to your customer base.

Why it works

Trust is expensive to build. If customers already trust your judgment, partners may pay to borrow that credibility to convert faster.

Best for

Marketplaces, healthcare, finance, education, hospitality, software ecosystems, professional services, retail platforms

Execution Steps

1. Define what your endorsement actually means
2. Set strict partner approval standards
3. Create usage rights and brand rules
4. Price by category, period, or partner tier
5. Monitor partner performance continuously

Real-world example

A healthcare platform charges vetted providers for approved partner status, while a SaaS company certifies selected integrations as trusted recommendations.

Risk Management

1. **Customer** · 5/5 Customer trust damaged if delivery falls short. **Mitigation:** Approve only partners with a track record that meets.
2. **Legal** · 5/5 Legal exposure arises if obligations, claims. **Mitigation:** Define exactly what the endorsement does and does not certify.
3. **Legal** · 4/5 Partners use brand, content. **Mitigation:** Control badge usage.
4. **Customer** · 4/5 Customer backlash. **Mitigation:** Communicate the commercial relationship to customers before any recommendation.
5. **Customer** · 4/5 Quality drift. **Mitigation:** Review all partner performance on a defined schedule and remove underperformers.

Speed	Effort	Cost	Revenue	Time to cash	Scalability
Medium (1-3 months)	**Medium**	**Low**	**High**	**Medium**	**Medium**

Decision-flow: CFO → Partnerships / BD → Legal

62. Monetize your operating environment as a sandbox

Sell controlled access to your real-world operating environment so partners can test, learn, validate, or improve their products before scaling.

Why it works

Real operating environments are hard to access. Partners pay to test inside a controlled setting for feedback, credibility, and faster market readiness.

Best for

Retail, healthcare, logistics, manufacturing, hospitality, education, software, smart buildings, mobility

Execution Steps

1. Identify where your operating environment has testing value
2. Define what partners can safely test
3. Set access rules, limits, and supervision
4. Price by test period, location, or use case
5. Protect customers, data, and operations

Real-world example

A hotel lets smart-room providers test products in controlled rooms, while a logistics firm offers route-testing access for delivery-tech partners.

Risk Management

1. **Operational** · 5/5 Operational disruption. **Mitigation:** Isolate the test environment from live operations to prevent customer impact.
2. **Customer** · 5/5 Customer trust risk. **Mitigation:** Keep tests controlled.
3. **Legal** · 4/5 Data exposure. **Mitigation:** Restrict access to the minimum required for the specific.
4. **Legal** · 4/5 Partners use brand, content. **Mitigation:** Set legal terms governing access, ownership, and liability before any partner engagement.
5. **Commercial** · 3/5 Weak test value. **Mitigation:** Define what success looks like before any partner or test begins.

Speed	Effort	Cost	Revenue	Time to cash	Scalability
Medium (1-3 months)	**Medium**	**Low**	**High**	**Medium**	**Medium**

Decision-flow: CFO → Operations → Partnerships / BD

From Ideas to Action

Twenty-three ideas. Twenty-three ways to turn internal IP, data, tools, capacity, and relationships into external revenue sources.

Most of these assets already exist. They are doing internal work without generating external revenue. The question is not whether the value is there. It is whether someone is willing to name it, price it, and put it in front of a buyer.

Before continuing, identify the single idea with the clearest commercial case right now. Name who owns it. Set a date for the first step. That is all that is required.

> *The most valuable asset in most businesses is the one sitting on the shelf with no price on it.*

What Comes Next

2.5 — New Business Lines addresses businesses ready to build a distinct adjacent revenue stream with its own buyer logic and commercial model. If the core business is proven and the next step is something structurally new — the next chapter is where it starts.

2.5 — New Business Lines

Create a distinct adjacent revenue line with its own buyer logic, commercial motion, or operating model.

When These Strategies Work Best

New business line strategies work best when the core business has proven something commercially and has the capacity or capability to build something structurally adjacent.

- The core business has a repeatable commercial model ready to replicate
- An adjacent customer need is clearly visible but not yet being served
- The business holds operational, brand, or distribution advantages a new line can use
- Revenue is too concentrated in one offer, segment, or channel
- Growth in the core business is slowing and adjacent revenue is the next step

The Benefits

- Revenue diversification that reduces dependence on one commercial model
- New income without abandoning what already works
- Leverage of existing assets, relationships, and operational infrastructure
- Commercial learning that can improve the core business as it grows
- Long-term compounding revenue from lines that develop their own momentum

The Risks to Manage

- **Distraction** — new lines pull attention from the core. Define a resource boundary before starting.
- **Underinvestment** — new lines fail without enough resource to reach commercial viability. Commit properly.
- **Wrong model** — building a new line before validating demand. Run a controlled pilot with three to five accounts., build after proof.
- **Brand confusion** — adjacency can blur what the business stands for. Position the new line with care.

63. Launch a done-for-you line around your core product or service

Create a new business line where you deliver the outcome for customers, instead of only selling the product, service, or tool they must use themselves.

Why it works

Some customers want results without effort, learning, staffing, or execution risk. A done-for-you line captures buyers who value convenience and outcomes more than control.

Best for

SaaS, equipment, home services, healthcare, consulting, training, manufacturing, B2B tools

Execution Steps

1. Identify customers who want the result but not the work
2. Define a narrow done-for-you scope
3. Build a small delivery capability
4. Price for convenience and outcome value
5. Position as a premium line, not a replacement

Real-world example

A software firm launches managed operations for clients, while a home equipment company offers a full-service care line around installed systems.

Risk Management

1. **Operational** · 5/5 Scope expands beyond agreed boundaries. **Mitigation:** Keep boundaries tight.
2. **Financial** · 4/5 Margin compresses if delivery cost is not controlled from the start. **Mitigation:** Price delivery effort.
3. **Commercial** · 3/5 The new offer cannibalizes existing higher-margin revenue if segmentation is not. **Mitigation:** Target different buyers.
4. **Operational** · 4/5 Scaling risk. **Mitigation:** Standardize delivery.
5. **Dependency** · 4/5 Talent dependency. **Mitigation:** Document workflows.

Speed	Effort	Cost	Revenue	Time to cash	Scalability
Medium (1-3 months)	**High**	**Medium**	**High**	**Medium**	**Medium**

Decision-flow: CFO → Operations → Sales

64. Launch a managed subscription line

Create a recurring business line where customers pay monthly or annually for ongoing management, maintenance, support, replenishment, or optimization around your core offer.

Why it works

Customers often want the outcome to keep working after the first sale. A managed subscription creates predictable revenue and reduces customer effort over time.

Best for

Home services, equipment, SaaS, healthcare, facilities, retail, logistics, professional services

Execution Steps

1. Identify ongoing customer needs after the first purchase
2. Define recurring scope and service levels
3. Price monthly or annually
4. Build delivery and renewal process
5. Sell at purchase and post-purchase moments

Real-world example

A heater installer launches a home comfort subscription, while a SaaS firm offers managed admin support for busy teams.

Risk Management

1. **Operational** · 4/5 Over-servicing. **Mitigation:** Define scope, access, and usage limits in writing before launch.
2. **Customer** · 4/5 Churn increases if the ongoing value is not clearly and regularly. **Mitigation:** Show ongoing value.
3. **Financial** · 4/5 Margin compresses if delivery cost is not controlled from the start. **Mitigation:** Monitor usage.
4. **Operational** · 3/5 Delivery capacity becomes strained as demand scales beyond the initial pilot.. **Mitigation:** Plan capacity.
5. **Commercial** · 3/5 Adoption is slower than expected. **Mitigation:** Sell at key moments.

Speed	Effort	Cost	Revenue	Time to cash	Scalability
Medium (1-3 months)	**Medium**	**Medium**	**High**	**Immediate**	**High**

Decision-flow: CFO → Operations → Customer Success

65. Launch a training and enablement business line

Create a paid business line that trains customers, partners, or teams to use your product, method, system, or category more effectively.

Why it works

Customers often need capability, not just purchase access. Training creates revenue while improving adoption, reducing misuse, and strengthening long-term success.

Best for

Software, equipment, healthcare, manufacturing, education, franchising, professional services, home services

Execution Steps

1. Identify where customers or partners need capability
2. Define paid training modules or tracks
3. Package by role, skill level, or use case
4. Price per person, team, cohort, or license
5. Build delivery materials and trainer process

Real-world example

A software firm launches admin certification training, while an equipment company offers paid operator training for safer and better use.

Risk Management

1. **Commercial** · 3/5 Willingness to pay is lower than projected for this segment. **Mitigation:** Target high-need users.
2. **Customer** · 3/5 Content too basic. **Mitigation:** Teach practical outcomes.
3. **Operational** · 3/5 Delivery quality varies across engagements, undermining customer confidence and referral rate. **Mitigation:** Standardize materials.
4. **Dependency** · 3/5 Trainer dependency. **Mitigation:** Build repeatable modules.
5. **Commercial** · 3/5 Weak uptake. **Mitigation:** Bundle with onboarding triggers.

Speed	Effort	Cost	Revenue	Time to cash	Scalability
Medium (1-3 months)	**Medium**	**Low**	**Medium**	**Medium**	**High**

Decision-flow: CFO → Product → Customer Success

66. Launch a white-label service line for other brands

Create a business line where other companies sell your product, service, process, or delivery capability under their own brand.

Why it works

Some companies have customers but lack capability. White-labeling lets them sell faster while you monetize your existing delivery engine through partner-led revenue.

Best for

Manufacturing, SaaS, agencies, food production, training, logistics, healthcare, specialist services

Execution Steps

1. Identify capabilities others could resell
2. Define white-label scope and brand rules
3. Set partner pricing and minimum volumes
4. Create delivery and quality standards
5. Build partner onboarding materials

Real-world example

A food producer manufactures private-label products for retailers, while a software company lets consultants resell its platform under their own brand.

Risk Management

1. **Customer** · 4/5 Brand confusion. **Mitigation:** Define brand boundaries.
2. **Customer** · 4/5 Inconsistent partner quality creates a variable customer experience. Certify before activation. **Mitigation:** Screen all partners against defined brand, quality, and audience fit criteria.
3. **Financial** · 3/5 Margin compresses if delivery cost is not controlled from the start. **Mitigation:** Set minimum pricing.
4. **Operational** · 4/5 Delivery capacity becomes strained as demand scales beyond the initial pilot.. **Mitigation:** Cap partner volume.
5. **Market** · 3/5 Existing channels react negatively to the new route. **Mitigation:** Separate direct and partner markets.

Speed	Effort	Cost	Revenue	Time to cash	Scalability
Medium (1-3 months)	**Medium**	**Low**	**High**	**Medium**	**High**

Decision-flow: CFO → Partnerships / BD → Operations

67. *Launch a brokerage line around customer demand*

Create a business line that connects customers to vetted third-party providers when the need sits outside your core offer.

Why it works

Customers often ask for help beyond what you sell. A brokerage line captures that demand without building full delivery capability.

Best for

Home services, healthcare, events, logistics, real estate, consulting, B2B services, hospitality

Execution Steps

1. Identify recurring customer requests outside your core offer
2. Build a vetted provider network
3. Define referral, commission, or brokerage fees
4. Set quality and service standards
5. Create a simple handoff process

Real-world example

A home renovation firm brokers interior design services, while a healthcare clinic connects patients to vetted wellness providers.

Risk Management

1. **Customer** · 5/5 Inconsistent partner quality creates a variable customer experience. Certify before activation. **Mitigation:** Vet providers.
2. **Customer** · 4/5 Customer trust damaged if delivery falls short. **Mitigation:** Disclose role clearly.
3. **Financial** · 3/5 Unit economics are weaker than projected once real delivery costs are measured. **Mitigation:** Set commission terms.
4. **Customer** · 3/5 Customers are unclear on what is included, how to use it. **Mitigation:** Explain handoff boundaries.
5. **Legal** · 4/5 Liability if responsibilities are not documented. **Mitigation:** Use referral terms.

Speed	Effort	Cost	Revenue	Time to cash	Scalability
Fast (0-30 days)	**Low**	**Low**	**Medium**	**Immediate**	**Medium**

Decision-flow: CFO → Partnerships / BD → Sales

68. Launch a certified expert marketplace around your offering

Create a marketplace where customers can hire certified experts, partners, or specialists who help them get more value from your product, service, or solution.

Why it works

Customers often need help beyond standard support. A certified expert marketplace creates partner revenue and scales help without expanding internal support teams.

Best for

SaaS, equipment, healthcare, education, professional tools, home systems, platforms, specialist B2B solutions

Execution Steps

1. Identify where customers need expert help beyond support
2. Define certification or approval standards
3. Recruit trusted experts or partner firms
4. Set marketplace fees, commissions, or listing charges
5. Create matching or booking process

Real-world example

A software company launches a certified consultant marketplace, while a medical device firm connects clinics with approved implementation specialists.

Risk Management

1. **Customer** · 5/5 Poor expert quality. **Mitigation:** Certify and review experts.
2. **Customer** · 4/5 Customer trust risk. **Mitigation:** Display ratings and quality standards prominently before any customer.
3. **Customer** · 3/5 Customers cannot clearly distinguish paid support from standard free assistance. Define. **Mitigation:** Define the scope of what experts cover versus what.
4. **Market** · 3/5 Partner imbalance. **Mitigation:** Monitor supply and demand balance to prevent quality shortfalls.
5. **Customer** · 4/5 Brand reputation is at risk if partner quality or the customer. **Mitigation:** Remove any expert who receives low ratings or fails.

Speed	Effort	Cost	Revenue	Time to cash	Scalability
Medium (1-3 months)	**Medium**	**Medium**	**High**	**Medium**	**High**

Decision-flow: CFO → Partnerships / BD → Customer Success

69. *Launch a rental line for high-cost products customers*

Create a rental business line for products customers need temporarily, occasionally, or seasonally but do not want to buy outright.

Why it works

Ownership can be expensive and unnecessary. A rental line opens revenue from customers who need access, flexibility, or short-term use without full purchase commitment.

Best for

Equipment, tools, vehicles, medical devices, event products, home systems, industrial products, consumer goods

Execution Steps

1. Identify products with high purchase friction and repeat temporary demand
2. Define rental terms, duration, deposits, and usage rules
3. Build cleaning, inspection, return, and maintenance process
4. Price by day, week, month, or usage
5. Protect against damage, loss, and misuse

Real-world example

A medical supplier rents recovery equipment to patients, while an industrial firm rents specialist tools to customers for short-term projects.

Risk Management

1. **Operational** · 4/5 Physical or digital assets are damaged through external use or mishandling.. **Mitigation:** Require deposits and inspections.
2. **Financial** · 4/5 Low utilization. **Mitigation:** Start with high-demand items
3. **Operational** · 3/5 Ongoing maintenance grows beyond the capacity planned at launch. **Mitigation:** Build a standardized quality checklist into every delivery process.
4. **Operational** · 4/5 Loss risk. **Mitigation:** Track assets carefully.
5. **Financial** · 4/5 Poor economics. **Mitigation:** Model lifetime usage.

Speed	Effort	Cost	Revenue	Time to cash	Scalability
Medium (1-3 months)	**Medium**	**Medium**	**High**	**Medium**	**Medium**

Decision-flow: CFO → Operations → Sales

70. Launch an implementation and activation business line

Create a dedicated business line that helps customers implement, configure, activate, launch, or operationalize what they buy so they get value faster.

Why it works

Customers often buy the solution but struggle to make it work in practice. Implementation support creates revenue from speed, confidence, and successful adoption.

Best for

Software, equipment, healthcare, education, home systems, industrial tools, consulting, B2B solutions

Execution Steps

1. Identify where customers struggle after purchase
2. Define standard implementation or activation packages
3. Build delivery capacity and service standards
4. Price by complexity., scope, or speed
5. Offer at point of purchase

Real-world example

A SaaS company sells implementation support, while an equipment supplier offers activation and operator setup for new customers.

Risk Management

1. **Operational** · 4/5 Scope expands beyond agreed boundaries. **Mitigation:** Define scope, access, and usage limits in writing before launch.
2. **Operational** · 4/5 Delivery quality varies across engagements, undermining customer confidence and referral rate. **Mitigation:** Build and enforce a standard process before any external deployment.
3. **Financial** · 3/5 Margin compresses if delivery cost is not controlled from the start. **Mitigation:** Price each complexity tier explicitly so margin is protected from launch.
4. **Operational** · 4/5 Capacity strain. **Mitigation:** Control bookings.
5. **Customer** · 3/5 Customer delays. **Mitigation:** Set readiness rules.

Speed	Effort	Cost	Revenue	Time to cash	Scalability
Medium (1-3 months)	**Medium**	**Medium**	**High**	**Medium**	**High**

Decision-flow: CFO → Operations → Sales

71. Launch a co-branded partner solution line

Create a joint business line with a complementary partner where both companies combine strengths into one customer-facing solution.

Why it works

Customers often need a complete solution, not separate vendors. A co-branded line combines trust, capability, reach, and delivery into one easier buying decision.

Best for

SaaS, healthcare, finance, home services, logistics, education, hospitality, manufacturing, professional services

Execution Steps

1. Identify complementary partners with shared customers
2. Define the combined customer problem
3. Build one clear co-branded solution
4. Agree pricing, margin split, and ownership
5. Create joint sales materials

Real-world example

A clinic partners with a wellness provider to launch a recovery program, while a SaaS company partners with a consultancy on transformation.

Risk Management

1. **Dependency** · 4/5 Partner misalignment. **Mitigation:** Define roles.
2. **Financial** · 4/5 Margin dispute. **Mitigation:** Agree economics upfront.
3. **Customer** · 3/5 Brand reputation is at risk if partner quality or the customer. **Mitigation:** Choose trusted partner.forc any.
4. **Commercial** · 3/5 Sales confusion. **Mitigation:** Create one simple offer.
5. **Operational** · 4/5 Delivery gaps. **Mitigation:** Set shared standards.

Speed	Effort	Cost	Revenue	Time to cash	Scalability
Medium (1-3 months)	**Medium**	**Low**	**High**	**Medium**	**High**

Decision-flow: CFO → Partnerships / BD → Sales

72. Launch a channel-as-a-service line for partners

Create a business line where partners pay to use your sales channel, customer access, distribution reach, or local market presence to sell complementary solutions.

Why it works

Many companies have good products but weak reach. If you already have trusted access, partners may pay you to become their route to market.

Best for

Retail, distribution, healthcare, hospitality, education, logistics, B2B services, platforms

Execution Steps

1. Identify partners who need your customer access
2. Define what channel support you provide
3. Set fees, commissions, or revenue share
4. Create partner qualification rules
5. Train sales. or channel teams

Real-world example

A regional distributor becomes the local sales channel for international brands, while a healthcare group helps approved providers reach its patient base.

Risk Management

1. **Customer** · 5/5 Inconsistent partner quality creates a variable customer experience. Certify before activation. **Mitigation:** Vet partners tightly.
2. **Market** · 4/5 Existing channels react negatively to the new route. **Mitigation:** Avoid direct competitors.
3. **Customer** · 4/5 Customer trust risk. **Mitigation:** Keep offers relevant.
4. **Operational** · 3/5 Sales distraction. **Mitigation:** Limit partner volume.
5. **Financial** · 3/5 Unit economics are weaker than projected once real delivery costs are measured. **Mitigation:** Define fees clearly.

Speed	Effort	Cost	Revenue	Time to cash	Scalability
Medium (1-3 months)	**Medium**	**Low**	**High**	**Medium**	**High**

Decision-flow: CFO → Partnerships / BD → Sales

73. Launch a data-enabled advisory line

Create a business line that uses your operational, customer, product, or market data to advise customers on better decisions, planning, or performance improvement.

Why it works

Customers want practical insight, not raw data. If your business sees patterns they cannot see, advisory creates revenue from intelligence already connected to operations.

Best for

Retail, SaaS, logistics, healthcare, manufacturing, hospitality, financial services, marketplaces

Execution Steps

1. Identify decisions customers struggle to make
2. Find data patterns that help answer those decisions
3. Package advice into a repeatable advisory line
4. Remove sensitive or identifiable data
5. Price by project, retainer, or subscription

Real-world example

A logistics firm advises clients on delivery network optimization, while a SaaS company helps customers improve workflows using usage-pattern insights.

Risk Management

1. **Legal** · 5/5 Data privacy. **Mitigation:** Anonymize and review.
2. **Commercial** · 4/5 Weak insight. **Mitigation:** Focus on decisions.
3. **Operational** · 3/5 Scope expands beyond agreed boundaries. **Mitigation:** Standardize advisory scope.
4. **Commercial** · 4/5 Credibility is undermined if promises made at the sale cannot be. **Mitigation:** Show method clearly.
5. **Operational** · 3/5 Low repeatability. **Mitigation:** Build reusable formats.

Speed	Effort	Cost	Revenue	Time to cash	Scalability
Medium (1-3 months)	**Medium**	**Low**	**High**	**Medium**	**High**

Decision-flow: CFO → IT / Data → Sales

74. Launch an asset-light delivery line using partner

Create a business line where partners provide capacity, people, equipment, space, or resources, while you control the customer offer, standards, pricing, and quality.

Why it works

Partner capacity lets you grow revenue without building every resource yourself. You expand faster, reduce capital needs, and still own the customer relationship.

Best for

Home services, logistics, healthcare, training, hospitality, field services, equipment support, B2B services

Execution Steps

1. Identify demand you cannot serve alone
2. Find partners with spare or scalable capacity
3. Define service standards and quality controls
4. Own pricing, customer promise, and customer relationship
5. Pay partners per job, capacity block, or outcome

Real-world example

A home services brand sells installation under its name using certified local contractors, while a training company uses approved freelance instructors.

Risk Management

1. **Customer** · 5/5 Quality failure. **Mitigation:** Certify all partners against defined quality criteria before activation.
2. **Customer** · 5/5 Brand reputation is at risk if partner quality or the customer. **Mitigation:** Control standards.
3. **Financial** · 4/5 Margin leaks if cost controls and pricing floors are not enforced. **Mitigation:** Set partner economics.
4. **Customer** · 3/5 Customers are unclear on what is included, how to use it. **Mitigation:** Keep one front door.
5. **Operational** · 4/5 Capacity gaps. **Mitigation:** Maintain backup partners.

Speed	Effort	Cost	Revenue	Time to cash	Scalability
Medium (1-3 months)	**Medium**	**Low**	**High**	**Medium**	**High**

Decision-flow: CFO → Partnerships / BD → Operations

75. Launch a pop-up business line inside partner locations

Create a business line that sells your product, service, or experience inside another company physical or digital location where target customers already gather.

Why it works

Partners already have foot traffic, trust, or audience access. A pop-up line generates revenue through borrowed reach without permanent locations.

Best for

Retail, wellness, food, education, healthcare, beauty, financial services, software, hospitality

Execution Steps

1. Identify partner locations with your target customers
2. Define the pop-up offer and operating model
3. Agree revenue share, timing, and space rules
4. Protect customer experience and brand fit
5. Launch in one location or channel first

Real-world example

A wellness brand runs pop-up recovery sessions inside gyms, while a fintech company offers advisory booths inside coworking spaces.

Risk Management

1. **Commercial** · 4/5 Poor partner fit. **Mitigation:** Choose aligned audiences.
2. **Commercial** · 3/5 Conversion from initial interest to completed purchase is lower than targeted.. **Mitigation:** Test one location first.
3. **Customer** · 4/5 Partner profile does not align with brand standards. **Mitigation:** Define and enforce presentation standards before any customer-facing activity.
4. **Operational** · 3/5 Operational friction. **Mitigation:** Reduce the setup process to the minimum steps required.
5. **Financial** · 3/5 Unit economics are weaker than projected once real delivery costs are measured. **Mitigation:** Agree revenue share upfront.

Speed	Effort	Cost	Revenue	Time to cash	Scalability
Fast (0-30 days)	**Medium**	**Low**	**High**	**Immediate**	**Medium**

Decision-flow: CFO → Partnerships / BD → Sales

76. Launch a revenue-share operator line

Create a business line where you operate a product, service, space, or capability for an asset owner and share the revenue generated.

Why it works

Some businesses own assets but lack the skill, brand, or system to monetize them well. You create revenue by becoming operator, not owner.

Best for

Hospitality, wellness, retail, real estate, education, food, events, healthcare, specialist services

Execution Steps

1. Identify asset owners with underused revenue potential
2. Define what you will operate or commercialize
3. Agree revenue-share terms and performance rules
4. Apply your brand, sales, or operating model
5. Track revenue., cost, and payout clearly

Real-world example

A wellness brand operates recovery rooms inside hotels on revenue share, while a food operator runs underused cafe space for a property owner.

Risk Management

1. **Dependency** · 4/5 Partner misalignment. **Mitigation:** Agree roles upfront.
2. **Commercial** · 4/5 Demand from the target segment is weaker than projected at launch. **Mitigation:** Validate footfall or usage.
3. **Financial** · 3/5 Margin leaks if cost controls and pricing floors are not enforced. **Mitigation:** Model revenue share carefully.
4. **Operational** · 4/5 Operational complexity increases faster than the team is resourced to manage.. **Mitigation:** Standardize playbook.
5. **Customer** · 3/5 Brand reputation is at risk if partner quality or the customer. **Mitigation:** Control customer experience.

Speed	Effort	Cost	Revenue	Time to cash	Scalability
Medium (1-3 months)	**Medium**	**Low**	**High**	**Medium**	**Medium**

Decision-flow: CFO → Partnerships / BD → Operations

77. Launch a fulfillment partner line under your brand

Create a business line where approved partners fulfill customer orders, services, or delivery under your brand standards while you own the customer relationship.

Why it works

Customers want one trusted provider. Fulfillment partners let you serve more demand, expand coverage, and generate revenue without building all delivery capacity internally.

Best for

E-commerce, home services, logistics, healthcare, equipment, food, field service, B2B supply

Execution Steps

1. Identify demand you cannot fulfill alone
2. Recruit partners with strong delivery capability
3. Define fulfillment standards and service levels
4. Keep billing and relationship under your brand
5. Pay partners per order, job, or service level

Real-world example

An e-commerce brand uses approved local installers for delivery and setup, while a healthcare supplier uses partner clinics to fulfill services.

Risk Management

1. **Customer** · 5/5 Quality failure. **Mitigation:** Certify all partners against defined quality criteria before activation.
2. **Customer** · 5/5 Brand damage. **Mitigation:** Monitor standards.
3. **Financial** 4/5 Margin leaks if cost controls and pricing floors are not enforced. **Mitigation:** Control partner rates.
4. **Customer** · 3/5 Customers are unclear on what is included, how to use it. **Mitigation:** Keep one brand front.
5. **Operational** · 4/5 Service inconsistency. **Mitigation:** Audit delivery.

Speed	Effort	Cost	Revenue	Time to cash	Scalability
Medium (1-3 months)	**Medium**	**Low**	**High**	**Medium**	**High**

Decision-flow: CFO → Operations → Partnerships / BD

78. Launch a rapid-response business line for urgent

Create a dedicated business line designed for customers who need immediate help, fast turnaround, or same-day resolution when delay is costly or stressful.

Why it works

Urgency changes buying behavior. Customers pay premium pricing for speed, certainty, and immediate action when the normal process is too slow.

Best for

Healthcare, home services, logistics, legal, IT support, equipment repair, consulting, B2B operations

Execution Steps

1. Identify situations where delay creates real pain
2. Build a dedicated rapid-response workflow
3. Define strict response and delivery standards
4. Price at premium emergency or priority rates
5. Separate this line from standard operations

Real-world example

An IT company launches critical-response support, while a home services firm offers emergency same-day repair operations.

Risk Management

1. **Commercial** · 5/5 Overpromising. **Mitigation:** Cap response volume.
2. **Alignment** · 4/5 Team burnout. **Mitigation:** Rotate staff carefully.
3. **Operational** · 4/5 Core operations are disrupted when external demand competes for the same. **Mitigation:** Separate operations.
4. **Market** · 3/5 Weak demand forecasting. **Mitigation:** Start focused.
5. **Financial** · 3/5 Margin erosion. **Mitigation:** Premium price correctly.

Speed	Effort	Cost	Revenue	Time to cash	Scalability
Fast (0-30 days)	**Medium**	**Medium**	**High**	**Immediate**	**Medium**

Decision-flow: CFO → Operations → Sales

79. *Launch a concierge business line for high-value*

Create a premium service line that gives high-value customers personalized support, coordination, planning, or problem-solving beyond the standard customer experience.

Why it works

Some customers pay for less friction and more attention. A concierge line monetizes convenience, speed, and confidence without changing the core offer.

Best for

Healthcare, travel, real estate, financial services, SaaS, luxury retail, home services, education

Execution Steps

1. Identify customers who need more coordination or support
2. Define concierge services and service limits
3. Set premium pricing or eligibility rules
4. Assign trained relationship owners
5. Protect standard service quality

Real-world example

A clinic launches a patient concierge line, while a SaaS company offers executive customer success for enterprise accounts.

Risk Management

1. **Operational** · 4/5 Scope expands beyond agreed boundaries. **Mitigation:** Define service limits.
2. **Financial** · 4/5 Cost overrun. **Mitigation:** Price support time.
3. **Customer** · 3/5 Customer dependency. **Mitigation:** Set explicit boundaries on scope and ownership before delivery begins.
4. **Operational** · 3/5 Team strain. **Mitigation:** Limit eligible customers.
5. **Customer** · 4/5 Standard service gaps. **Mitigation:** Protect the standard service baseline before adding any premium tier.

Speed	Effort	Cost	Revenue	Time to cash	Scalability
Medium (1-3 months)	**Medium**	**Medium**	**High**	**Medium**	**Medium**

Decision-flow: CFO → Customer Success → Operations

80. Launch an entry-level starter line for smaller

Create a separate business line for customers who need a lower-cost, simpler version of your expertise, delivery, or solution before they can buy the full offer.

Why it works

Entry-level buyers may have real need but lower budget, confidence, or readiness. A starter line captures them early without weakening the premium core business.

Best for

SaaS, consulting, education, home services, healthcare, equipment, financial services, B2B services

Execution Steps

1. Identify buyers who need help but cannot buy the full offer yet
2. Define a simpler, lower-scope business line
3. Separate brand, pricing, and service levels from premium offers
4. Build an upgrade path into the core business
5. Keep delivery simple and scalable

Real-world example

A consulting firm launches a small-business advisory line, while a SaaS firm creates starter implementation for smaller teams.

Risk Management

1. **Financial** · 4/5 The new offer cannibalizes existing higher-margin revenue if segmentation is not. **Mitigation:** Separate buyer segments.
2. **Financial** · 4/5 Low margins. **Mitigation:** Redesign the delivery model to reduce complexity before pricing.
3. **Customer** · 3/5 Brand dilution. **Mitigation:** Position carefully.
4. **Commercial** · 3/5 Upgrade failure. **Mitigation:** Build path upward.
5. **Operational** · 3/5 Post-launch support demand is higher than planned, straining the delivery team. **Mitigation:** Define a strict scope boundary and enforce it from.

Speed	Effort	Cost	Revenue	Time to cash	Scalability
Medium (1-3 months)	**Medium**	**Low**	**High**	**Medium**	**High**

Decision-flow: CFO → Product → Sales

81. Launch a loyalty business line for long-term customers

Create a dedicated business line for long-term customers that gives them advanced support, exclusive services, upgrades, planning, or renewal benefits.

Why it works

Long-term customers often have deeper needs and higher trust. A loyalty line creates revenue by giving them more value than first-time buyers receive.

Best for

SaaS, healthcare, home services, education, financial services, equipment, B2B services, hospitality

Execution Steps

1. Identify long-term customers with deeper recurring needs
2. Define exclusive services or benefits for them
3. Separate paid loyalty value from standard retention perks
4. Price by annual access, account level, or service tier
5. Train teams to position it as earned access

Real-world example

A home services firm launches a long-term homeowner care line, while a SaaS company offers a strategic account growth line for mature customers.

Risk Management

1. **Commercial** · 4/5 Value feels expected. **Mitigation:** Add genuinely new paid benefits before using the offer.
2. **Commercial** · 3/5 Uptake in the early period is below projections. Early signals must **Mitigation:** Prioritise accounts with the highest existing trust and relationship depth.
3. **Financial** · 3/5 Margin compresses if delivery cost is not controlled from the start. **Mitigation:** Price the offer based on the full depth of service committed.
4. **Customer** · 3/5 Confusion with retention. **Mitigation:** Define and communicate the distinction between retention perks and paid benefits.
5. **Operational** · 3/5 Delivery capacity becomes strained as demand scales beyond the initial pilot.. **Mitigation:** Define and enforce eligibility criteria consistently from day one.

Speed	Effort	Cost	Revenue	Time to cash	Scalability
Medium (1-3 months)	**Medium**	**Medium**	**High**	**Medium**	**Medium**

Decision-flow: CFO → Customer Success → Sales

82. Launch a specialist segment line for one high-value

Create a dedicated business line for one specific customer segment with unique needs, language, standards, workflows, or buying requirements.

Why it works

Specific segments often pay more when the offer feels built for them. A specialist line creates revenue by solving sharper needs than a general offer can address.

Best for

Healthcare, education, SaaS, financial services, home services, logistics, manufacturing, professional services

Execution Steps

1. Identify one segment with clear unmet needs
2. Define what makes that segment different
3. Adapt the offer, delivery, language, and pricing
4. Build segment-specific sales material
5. Launch with one focused segment first

Real-world example

A SaaS firm creates a healthcare-specific operations line, while a home services company launches a landlord-focused property care line.

Risk Management

1. **Market** · 4/5 Segment too small. **Mitigation:** Validate market size.
2. **Commercial** · 4/5 The offer lacks clear differentiation from what competitors or alternatives provide. **Mitigation:** Solve unique needs.
3. **Commercial** · 3/5 Sales confusion. **Mitigation:** Create clear positioning.
4. **Operational** · 3/5 Delivery complexity. **Mitigation:** Standardize segment workflows.
5. **Commercial** · 4/5 Willingness to pay is lower than projected for this segment. **Mitigation:** Target high-value segments.

Speed	Effort	Cost	Revenue	Time to cash	Scalability
Medium (1-3 months)	**Medium**	**Low**	**High**	**Medium**	**High**

Decision-flow: CFO → Product → Sales

83. *Launch a guided entry line for first-time buyers*

Create a business line that helps first-time buyers choose, start, use, or adopt your product or service with less confusion and lower perceived risk.

Why it works

First-time buyers hesitate because they do not know what to choose or how to start. A guided entry line makes the first purchase easier and safer.

Best for

Retail, software, healthcare, education, home services, equipment, financial services, hospitality

Execution Steps

1. Identify where first-time buyers hesitate
2. Define a simple guided entry experience
3. Create clear steps, support, and decision help
4. Price it as a beginner-friendly business line
5. Keep scope separate from premium service

Real-world example

A gym launches a beginner transformation line, while a software firm creates first-time buyer onboarding for small teams.

Risk Management

1. **Financial** · 3/5 Margin is insufficient if pricing does not cover the full cost. **Mitigation:** Redesign the delivery model to reduce complexity before pricing.
2. **Customer** · 3/5 Brand dilution. **Mitigation:** Position as guided entry.
3. **Operational** · 4/5 Support overload. **Mitigation:** Define a strict scope boundary and enforce it from.
4. **Commercial** · 3/5 Weak upgrade path. **Mitigation:** Design next step.
5. **Customer** · 3/5 Poor fit buyers. **Mitigation:** Qualify lightly.

Speed	Effort	Cost	Revenue	Time to cash	Scalability
Medium (1-3 months)	**Medium**	**Low**	**High**	**Medium**	**High**

Decision-flow: CFO → Sales → Customer Success

84. Launch a transition line for customers moving from old

Create a business line that helps customers move from an old product, system, supplier, habit, or process into a better new way with less friction.

Why it works

Customers want change but delay because transition feels messy. A transition line creates revenue by making switching easier and safer.

Best for

Software, home services, healthcare, education, equipment, financial services, logistics, professional services

Execution Steps

1. Identify where customers delay because transition feels difficult
2. Define the transition journey and support points
3. Package the line with clear stages and outcomes
4. Price around reduced friction and faster change
5. Train teams to sell against transition hesitation

Real-world example

A software firm launches migration for teams leaving spreadsheets, while a home services company helps homeowners upgrade outdated systems.

Risk Management

1. **Operational** · 4/5 Transition scope creep. **Mitigation:** Define stages clearly.
2. **Customer** · 3/5 Customer readiness gaps. **Mitigation:** Qualify before starting.
3. **Operational** · 4/5 Delivery complexity. **Mitigation:** Standardize workflow.
4. **Commercial** · 3/5 Urgency signals are insufficient to motivate prompt customer action. Build urgency. **Mitigation:** Target active change moments.
5. **Financial** · 3/5 Price pushback. **Mitigation:** Anchor to time and risk saved.

Speed	Effort	Cost	Revenue	Time to cash	Scalability
Medium (1-3 months)	**Medium**	**Low**	**High**	**Medium**	**High**

Decision-flow: CFO → Operations → Sales

85. *Launch a customer proof lab business line*

Create a business line that helps customers prove, test, or validate their claims, products, ideas, or decisions using your environment, expertise, or customer context.

Why it works

Customers often need proof before they sell, invest, launch, or scale. A proof lab creates revenue by reducing uncertainty before bigger commitments.

Best for

Manufacturing, food, healthcare, software, education, retail, logistics, professional services

Execution Steps

1. Identify where customers need proof before moving forward
2. Define what can be tested, validated, or demonstrated
3. Build a simple proof process and output format
4. Price by test, project, cohort, or validation package
5. Protect confidentiality and usage rights

Real-world example

A food company helps emerging brands test product acceptance, while a software company helps enterprise clients validate workflows before rollout.

Risk Management

1. **Commercial** · 4/5 Weak proof value. **Mitigation:** Tie to real decisions.
2. **Legal** · 5/5 Confidentiality risk. **Mitigation:** Use strict terms.
3. **Operational** · 4/5 Scope expands beyond agreed boundaries. **Mitigation:** Define test limits.
4. **Operational** · 3/5 Operational disruption. **Mitigation:** Isolate test activity.
5. **Customer** · 3/5 Misused results. **Mitigation:** Clarify limitations.

Speed	Effort	Cost	Revenue	Time to cash	Scalability
Medium (1-3 months)	**Medium**	**Medium**	**High**	**Medium**	**Medium**

Decision-flow: CFO → Operations → Product

86. Launch a customers-for-hire insight line

Create a business line where approved companies pay to learn from your customers through structured panels, feedback sessions, product reviews, or buyer interviews.

Why it works

Real customer insight is hard to access. Companies pay to understand buyer pain, language, objections, and preferences before launching or selling.

Best for

Retail, healthcare, education, SaaS, consumer goods, hospitality, finance, marketplaces

Execution Steps

1. Identify customer groups with insight value
2. Get consent and define participation rules
3. Create structured feedback formats
4. Price by panel, session, or research package
5. Screen buyers and protect customer trust

Real-world example

A fitness brand hosts paid customer panels for wellness startups, while a B2B platform sells buyer-feedback sessions to software vendors.

Risk Management

1. **Customer** · 5/5 Customer trust damaged if delivery falls short. **Mitigation:** Get clear consent.
2. **Legal** · 5/5 Customer data privacy is at risk if access, anonymisation. **Mitigation:** Protect participant data.
3. **Commercial** · 3/5 Weak insight quality. **Mitigation:** Structure sessions well.
4. **Customer** · 3/5 Customer fatigue. **Mitigation:** Cap the frequency of outreach or placements to prevent customer fatigue.
5. **Legal** · 4/5 Buyer misuse. **Mitigation:** Define usage rules.

Speed	Effort	Cost	Revenue	Time to cash	Scalability
Fast (0-30 days)	**Medium**	**Low**	**High**	**Immediate**	**Medium**

Decision-flow: CFO → Marketing → Partnerships / BD

87. Launch a micro-franchise line for your proven model

Create a smaller franchise-style business line where others can operate a simplified version of your model in defined locations, communities, or segments.

Why it works

Some operators want a proven business model without building from scratch. A micro-franchise line creates revenue from setup fees, royalties, and standards.

Best for

Food, fitness, education, home services, healthcare, beauty, retail, local services

Execution Steps

1. Identify a repeatable business model
2. Simplify it into a small operator format
3. Define territory, brand, and operating standards
4. Build training, support, and compliance rules
5. Price setup fees and royalties

Real-world example

A tutoring company launches micro-franchise learning pods, while a home services company licenses local operators to run service territories.

Risk Management

1. **Customer** · 5/5 Operator quality. **Mitigation:** Screen tightly.
2. **Customer** · 5/5 Brand damage. **Mitigation:** Enforce standards.
3. **Legal** · 4/5 Legal complexity. **Mitigation:** Structure properly.
4. **Operational** · 4/5 Post-launch support demand is higher than planned, straining the delivery team. **Mitigation:** Simplify model.
5. **Financial** · 5/5 Weak unit economics. **Mitigation:** Validate pilot numbers.

Speed	Effort	Cost	Revenue	Time to cash	Scalability
Slow (3+ months)	**High**	**Medium**	**Very High**	**Long**	**High**

Decision-flow: CFO → Operations → Legal

88. Launch a private-label line for underserved customer

Create a separate private-label business line that serves a specific customer group with a simpler, lower-cost, or specialized version of your core capability.

Why it works

Some segments want the outcome but not the full brand, price, or complexity. A private-label line opens revenue without weakening the main brand.

Best for

Food, retail, manufacturing, beauty, healthcare, education, software, B2B services

Execution Steps

1. Identify a segment your main brand does not fully serve
2. Define the private-label positioning and offer scope
3. Separate pricing, packaging, and channel strategy
4. Protect the main brand from confusion
5. Build the operating and delivery model

Real-world example

A premium food company launches a trade-only private-label line, while a SaaS firm creates a simplified partner-branded version for small businesses.

Risk Management

1. **Customer** · 4/5 Brand confusion. **Mitigation:** Separate positioning clearly.
2. **Financial** · 4/5 The new offer cannibalizes existing higher-margin revenue if segmentation is not. **Mitigation:** Target distinct segments.
3. **Financial** · 3/5 Margin compresses if delivery cost is not controlled from the start. **Mitigation:** Control cost structure.
4. **Market** · 3/5 Existing channels react negatively to the new route. **Mitigation:** Define route to market.
5. **Commercial** · 3/5 Demand from the target segment is weaker than projected at launch. **Mitigation:** Validate segment pain.

Speed	Effort	Cost	Revenue	Time to cash	Scalability
Medium (1-3 months)	**Medium**	**Medium**	**High**	**Medium**	**High**

Decision-flow: CFO → Product → Sales

89. Launch an embedded service line inside another company

Create a business line where your service becomes part of another company customer experience at the moment their customer needs your capability.

Why it works

Customers often need adjacent help during an existing journey. Embedding your service inside that flow creates revenue without owning the full acquisition process.

Best for

Finance, real estate, healthcare, travel, home services, insurance, education, software, logistics

Execution Steps

1. Identify a partner journey where your service solves the next problem
2. Define the embedded service moment
3. Agree commercial terms and customer handoff rules
4. Build a simple referral or activation flow
5. Protect service quality and brand clarity

Real-world example

A mortgage provider embeds moving services after loan approval, while a software company embeds implementation support in a partner onboarding journey.

Risk Management

1. **Commercial** · 4/5 Poor journey fit. **Mitigation:** Map customer need clearly.
2. **Dependency** · 4/5 Partner dependency. **Mitigation:** Avoid one-partner reliance.
3. **Customer** · 3/5 Customers are unclear on what is included, how to use it. **Mitigation:** Clarify who delivers what.
4. **Operational** · 4/5 Quality standards are not maintained consistently across all deliveries. Standardize before scaling. **Mitigation:** Standardize delivery.
5. **Financial** · 3/5 Unit economics are weaker than projected once real delivery costs are measured. **Mitigation:** Agree fees upfront.

Speed	Effort	Cost	Revenue	Time to cash	Scalability
Medium (1-3 months)	**Medium**	**Low**	**High**	**Medium**	**High**

Decision-flow: CFO → Partnerships / BD → Operations

From Ideas to Action

Twenty-seven ideas. Twenty-seven ways to build adjacent revenue streams using infrastructure and capability already inside the business.

A new business line does not require a new company. It requires a decision to package what the business already does into something structurally separate. That decision is usually blocked by one thing: no one owns the first step.

Before continuing, identify the single idea with the clearest commercial case right now. Name who owns it. Set a date for the first step. That is all that is required.

> *Adjacent revenue does not build itself. It needs one owner and one starting date.*

What Comes Next

Part 3 — Unlock Revenue is the next step. The business now has new offers to sell. Part 3 shows how to capture the full value of what it already delivers — through upselling, repricing, reactivation, and packaging.

PART 3
Unlock Revenue

The Revenue Already Inside the Business

The most common revenue problem is not that the business cannot find new customers. It is that it is not capturing the full value of the customers it already has.

Part 3 is about that gap. It asks a different question — not what can we sell, but what are we already delivering that we are not fully charging for? What value are we creating that buyers would pay more for if we asked? What revenue sits in our existing relationships, pipelines, and customer base, uncaptured?

In most businesses, the answer is significant. Often more significant than any new market or new product.

What This Part Covers

- **Upsell & Cross-sell** — capturing more revenue from existing customers by increasing what they buy.
- **Repricing & Price Capture** — correcting underpricing and charging properly for value already delivered.
- **Reactivation & Recovery** — recovering revenue from customers and opportunities that went inactive or were lost.
- **Underused Asset Monetization** — unlocking revenue from capacity, inventory, and assets sitting idle inside the business.
- **Bundling & Packaging** — changing how existing value is grouped and presented to improve take-up and revenue per sale.

Where to Start

- **Existing customers buying less than they could?** Start with Upsell & Cross-sell.
- **Delivering more value than the price reflects?** Start with Repricing & Price Capture.
- **Inactive customers or stalled pipeline sitting unworked?** Start with Reactivation & Recovery.
- **Capacity, inventory, or assets generating no revenue?** Start with Underused Asset Monetization.
- **Offers hard to buy or compare?** Start with Bundling & Packaging.

3.1 — Upsell & Cross-sell

Capture more revenue from existing customers by increasing what they buy.

When These Strategies Work Best

Upsell and cross-sell strategies deliver the fastest return when a base of satisfied customers exists and the business is not systematically presenting them with the next logical purchase.

- Customers regularly buy once and the commercial relationship stops there
- Post-sale conversations focus on delivery but never on the next purchase
- Customers use one product or service but have unmet needs adjacent to it
- Upgrades exist but are never presented at the right moment in the customer journey
- Revenue per customer is low relative to what those customers could be spending

The Benefits

- Immediate revenue from customers already in an active relationship
- Higher customer lifetime value without additional acquisition cost
- Deeper commercial relationships that are harder for competitors to displace
- Faster growth because existing customers convert at higher rates than new ones
- Natural product discovery for customers who do not know what else you offer

The Risks to Manage

- **Pushiness** — presenting the wrong offer at the wrong time damages trust. Timing and relevance are everything.
- **Weak offer fit** — cross-selling something unrelated creates confusion. Stay tightly adjacent.
- **Sales resistance** — teams uncomfortable with proactive selling need positioning guides, not scripts.
- **Cannibalisation** — upsells that replace existing revenue rather than adding to it. Track net uplift.

90. Offer the next logical UPGRADE at the moment of decision

Present a clear upgrade or add-on at the exact moment a customer commits, when intent is highest and the next step feels natural.

Why it works

Customers are most open to increasing spend when they have already decided to buy. A relevant next-step offer raises transaction value without creating a separate sales cycle.

Best for

Retail, e-commerce, SaaS, home services, healthcare, hospitality, B2B services

Execution Steps

1. Identify the main purchase decision moment
2. Define the most logical add-on or upgrade
3. Keep the offer simple and relevant
4. Present it immediately after commitment
5. Price it as an easy step up

Real-world example

A heater installer offers a smart thermostat upgrade at purchase, while a SaaS company offers an analytics add-on during plan selection.

Risk Management

1. **Commercial** · 4/5 Offer arrives at the wrong point in the journey. **Mitigation:** Trigger at decision point.
2. **Customer** · 4/5 Irrelevant offer. **Mitigation:** Match main purchase.
3. **Operational** · 3/5 The offer is too complex for self-service use. **Mitigation:** Keep one clear option.
4. **Financial** · 3/5 Price too high. **Mitigation:** Make it easy.
5. **Alignment** · 3/5 Sales inconsistency. **Mitigation:** Standardize trigger.

Speed	Effort	Cost	Revenue	Time to cash	Scalability
Fast (0-30 days)	**Low**	**Low**	**High**	**Immediate**	**High**

Decision-flow: CFO → Sales → Product

91. Offer the make-it-easier UPGRADE after purchase

Offer a paid add-on that makes the customer's purchase easier to use, manage, install, learn, or maintain after they have already bought.

Why it works

Customers often discover effort after the purchase. An ease-based upgrade captures extra revenue by removing friction when the need becomes clearer.

Best for

Software, equipment, home services, healthcare, education, consumer products, B2B tools

Execution Steps

1. Identify where customers struggle after buying
2. Define one upgrade that removes friction
3. Offer it after the first usage or setup moment
4. Price it against saved time and effort
5. Train support teams to spot the trigger

Real-world example

A software company offers paid setup assistance after purchase, while a furniture retailer offers assembly service after checkout.

Risk Management

1. **Customer** · 4/5 Feels like missing core value. **Mitigation:** Keep base useful.
2. **Commercial** · 3/5 Bad timing. **Mitigation:** Offer after effort appears.
3. **Commercial** · 3/5 Uptake in the early period is below projections. Early signals must. **Mitigation:** Target high-friction cases.
4. **Operational** · 3/5 Delivery capacity becomes strained as demand scales beyond the initial pilot.. **Mitigation:** Standardize service.
5. **Financial** · 3/5 Margin compresses if delivery cost is not controlled from the start. **Mitigation:** Price effort properly.

Speed	Effort	Cost	Revenue	Time to cash	Scalability
Fast (0-30 days)	**Low**	**Low**	**High**	**Immediate**	**High**

Decision-flow: CFO → Customer Success → Sales

92. *Offer the better-result UPGRADE after first use*

Offer a paid upgrade that helps customers get a stronger, faster, cleaner, safer, or more professional result after they have experienced the basic version.

Why it works

First use reveals ambition. Once customers see what is possible, many will pay more to improve the outcome, not just complete the task.

Best for

Software, fitness, education, beauty, home services, equipment, healthcare, professional tools

Execution Steps

1. Identify where customers want a better result after first use
2. Define the upgrade that improves the outcome
3. Trigger it after usage, setup, or first milestone
4. Price it against the improved result
5. Show before-and-after value. clearly

Real-world example

A design software company offers premium rendering after users create a basic design, while a salon offers a treatment upgrade after the first appointment.

Risk Management

1. **Commercial** · 4/5 Weak result gap. **Mitigation:** Target visible improvements.
2. **Commercial** · 3/5 Offer arrives at the wrong point in the journey. **Mitigation:** Offer after first use.
3. **Financial** · 3/5 Buyers push back on the price before the full value has. **Mitigation:** Show before-and-after value.
4. **Customer** · 3/5 Upgrade confusion. **Mitigation:** Keep one clear option.
5. **Customer** · 4/5 Base offer feels weak. **Mitigation:** Keep standard outcome solid.

Speed	Effort	Cost	Revenue	Time to cash	Scalability
Fast (0-30 days)	**Low**	**Low**	**High**	**Immediate**	**High**

Decision-flow: CFO → Product → Sales

93. Offer the save-time UPGRADE for busy customers

Offer a paid upgrade that reduces customer time, steps, waiting, admin, or manual work after they choose the base option.

Why it works

Time-poor customers often pay more for convenience. A time-saving upgrade captures extra revenue from customers who value speed and reduced effort.

Best for

Retail, healthcare, SaaS, home services, logistics, education, hospitality, B2B services

Execution Steps

1. Identify where customers spend unnecessary time
2. Define the upgrade that removes steps or waiting
3. Price it against time saved
4. Offer it at the friction point
5. Keep delivery simple

Real-world example

A clinic offers express check-in, while a SaaS company offers automated setup migration.

Risk Management

1. **Customer** · 3/5 The value delivered is not clearly communicated. **Mitigation:** Quantify the time saved and present it as the.
2. **Operational** · 5/5 Base service harmed. **Mitigation:** Protect the standard service baseline before adding any premium tier.
3. **Commercial** · 3/5 Uptake in the early period is below projections. Early signals must. **Mitigation:** Target busy users.
4. **Operational** · 3/5 Delivery capacity becomes strained as demand scales beyond the initial pilot.. **Mitigation:** Cap capacity.
5. **Financial** · 3/5 Price pushback. **Mitigation:** Anchor to convenience.

Speed	Effort	Cost	Revenue	Time to cash	Scalability
Fast (0-30 days)	**Low**	**Low**	**High**	**Immediate**	**High**

Decision-flow: CFO → Operations → Sales

94. *Offer the confidence UPGRADE for risk-sensitive buyers*

Offer a paid upgrade that gives customers extra assurance, review, verification, warranty, monitoring, or expert confirmation around their purchase.

Why it works

Some customers hesitate because they fear mistakes, waste, or poor outcomes. A confidence upgrade creates revenue by reducing uncertainty and making the purchase feel safer.

Best for

Healthcare, home services, equipment, education, software, construction, finance, premium retail

Execution Steps

1. Identify where customers feel risk
2. Define the assurance upgrade
3. Keep the promise clear and limited
4. Price against reduced uncertainty
5. Offer before final commitment

Real-world example

A contractor offers an expert pre-installation review, while a SaaS firm offers security validation before launch.

Risk Management

1. **Commercial** · 4/5 Promise too broad. **Mitigation:** Define scope, access, and usage limits in writing before launch.
2. **Legal** · 4/5 Legal exposure arises if obligations, claims. **Mitigation:** Submit all commercial terms to legal review before customer presentation.
3. **Customer** · 3/5 Low value perception. **Mitigation:** Quantify the specific risk or uncertainty the upgrade removes before pricing.
4. **Operational** · 3/5 Delivery quality varies across engagements, undermining customer confidence and referral rate. **Mitigation:** Build a standardized quality checklist into every delivery process.
5. **Financial** · 3/5 Margin compresses if delivery cost is not controlled from the start. **Mitigation:** Set pricing to reflect the actual time and expertise.

Speed	Effort	Cost	Revenue	Time to cash	Scalability
Fast (0-30 days)	**Low**	**Low**	**High**	**Immediate**	**High**

Decision-flow: CFO → Sales → Operations

95. Offer the personalized-fit UPGRADE

Offer a paid upgrade that adapts the product, service, setup, recommendation, or experience to the customer's specific needs.

Why it works

Customers pay more when the solution feels made for them. Personal fit increases relevance, reduces buyer doubt, and raises perceived value.

Best for

Retail, wellness, software, education, healthcare, home services, financial services, equipment

Execution Steps

1. Identify where customers differ meaningfully
2. Define personalization options
3. Reduce options to the minimum needed to serve the. to protect margin
4. Price the upgrade clearly
5. Offer after basic need is confirmed

Real-world example

A mattress retailer offers custom firmness fitting, while a software company offers role-based workflow configuration.

Risk Management

1. **Operational** · 4/5 Too many options. **Mitigation:** Reduce options to the minimum needed to serve the.
2. **Financial** · 3/5 Costs grow beyond the projected baseline. **Mitigation:** Price each complexity tier explicitly so margin is protected from launch.
3. **Operational** · 3/5 Delivery mistakes. **Mitigation:** Build standard variants into the production process before any sale.
4. **Commercial** · 3/5 Weak need. **Mitigation:** Target high-fit categories.
5. **Commercial** · 3/5 The new offer cannibalizes existing higher-margin revenue if segmentation is not. **Mitigation:** Keep base option clear.

Speed	Effort	Cost	Revenue	Time to cash	Scalability
Medium (1-3 months)	**Medium**	**Low**	**High**	**Short**	**Medium**

Decision-flow: CFO → Product → Sales

96. Sell the second use case customers discover later

Offer a cross-sell that helps customers apply what they already bought to a second problem, team, location, room, workflow, or situation.

Why it works

Customers often buy for one reason, then discover another use. Capturing that second use case expands spend without needing a new customer.

Best for

Software, home services, equipment, education, healthcare, retail, B2B tools, professional services

Execution Steps

1. Identify common second-use patterns
2. Map the trigger after initial success
3. Define the cross-sell offer
4. Position it as expanding value
5. Train teams to spot the second-use signal

Real-world example

A software tool bought by finance is cross-sold to operations, while a home security company sells additional room coverage after first installation.

Risk Management

1. **Commercial** · 3/5 Weak use case. **Mitigation:** Base cross-sell triggers on observed customer behaviour, not assumptions.
2. **Commercial** · 3/5 Offer arrives at the wrong point in the journey. **Mitigation:** Wait for first success.
3. **Customer** · 3/5 Sales pushiness. **Mitigation:** Frame the cross-sell as natural expansion, not a separate sales conversation.
4. **Operational** · 3/5 Adoption is slower than expected. **Mitigation:** Create a simple repeatable rollout process before scaling the cross-sell.
5. **Financial** · 3/5 Budget friction. **Mitigation:** Show shared value.

Speed	Effort	Cost	Revenue	Time to cash	Scalability
Fast (0-30 days)	**Low**	**Low**	**High**	**Immediate**	**High**

Decision-flow: CFO → Customer Success → Sales

97. Cross-sell the missing piece that completes the job

Offer the complementary item, service, or support customers need to fully complete what they started with the main purchase.

Why it works

Customers often buy the core piece but still need something else to finish the job. The missing piece is easier to sell because the need is already active.

Best for

Retail, construction, home services, software, equipment, education, healthcare, B2B supply

Execution Steps

1. Identify what customers commonly need after the core purchase
2. Define the most useful complementary offer
3. Attach it to the same buying journey
4. Position it as completion, not extra spending
5. Train teams to explain the full job

Real-world example

A paint retailer sells prep tools with paint, while a SaaS company cross-sells onboarding templates with its main platform.

Risk Management

1. **Commercial** · 3/5 The offer does not closely match the specific need or context. **Mitigation:** Match to the job.
2. **Customer** · 3/5 Feels pushy. **Mitigation:** Frame as completion.
3. **Commercial** · 3/5 Low attach rate. **Mitigation:** Offer at right point.
4. **Financial** · 3/5 Margin weak. **Mitigation:** Select cross-sell offers that maintain or improve overall deal margin.
5. **Alignment** · 3/5 Sales skips it. **Mitigation:** Make it standard.

Speed	Effort	Cost	Revenue	Time to cash	Scalability
Fast (0-30 days)	**Low**	**Low**	**High**	**Immediate**	**High**

Decision-flow: CFO → Sales → Operations

98. Cross-sell the person behind the product

Offer access to a specialist, advisor, technician, trainer, or expert who helps the customer use the purchase better.

Why it works

Customers do not always need more product. Sometimes they need expert help. Selling the person behind the product captures value from confidence, speed, and better usage.

Best for

Software, equipment, healthcare, education, home services, beauty, fitness, industrial products

Execution Steps

1. Identify where expert guidance improves results
2. Define advisor or technician access clearly
3. Price by session, block, or package
4. Offer after purchase or during setup
5. Keep scope limited

Real-world example

A software firm sells expert admin sessions, while an equipment supplier sells technician guidance for advanced use.

Risk Management

1. **Operational** · 4/5 Scope expands beyond agreed boundaries. **Mitigation:** Limit session scope.
2. **Operational** · 4/5 Expert shortage. **Mitigation:** Cap availability to protect quality and prevent over-commitment
3. **Commercial** · 3/5 Uptake in the early period is below projections. Early signals must. **Mitigation:** Target complex purchases.
4. **Financial** · 3/5 Margin compresses if delivery cost is not controlled from the start. **Mitigation:** Price expert time.
5. **Customer** · 3/5 Customers cannot clearly distinguish paid support from standard free assistance. Define. **Mitigation:** Separate from free support.

Speed	Effort	Cost	Revenue	Time to cash	Scalability
Fast (0-30 days)	**Medium**	**Low**	**High**	**Immediate**	**Medium**

Decision-flow: CFO → Customer Success → Sales

99. *Cross-sell the next location, seat, room, or site*

Offer expansion to another user, room, branch, site, department, vehicle, device, or location after the first one works.

Why it works

Once customers prove value in one place, expansion becomes easier. The second unit is lower-friction because trust and usage already exist.

Best for

SaaS, home services, security, equipment, education, healthcare, facilities, logistics

Execution Steps

1. Identify offers that naturally expand by unit
2. Track first-location or first-user success
3. Trigger the expansion offer after proof
4. Price the second unit attractively but profitably
5. Make rollout easy

Real-world example

A security company expands from one room to the full home, while a SaaS firm expands from one team to multiple departments.

Risk Management

1. **Customer** · 4/5 First value not proven. **Mitigation:** Wait for success signal.
2. **Financial** · 3/5 Budget friction. **Mitigation:** Present the ROI from the first result before initiating.
3. **Operational** · 3/5 Rollout complexity. **Mitigation:** Standardize deployment.
4. **Customer** · 3/5 Low usage. **Mitigation:** Restrict upgrade outreach to customers actively using the core product.
5. **Commercial** · 2/5 Sales delay. **Mitigation:** Use usage data to trigger the expansion offer automatically.

Speed	Effort	Cost	Revenue	Time to cash	Scalability
Fast (0-30 days)	**Low**	**Low**	**Very High**	**Immediate**	**High**

Decision-flow: CFO → Customer Success → Sales

100. Cross-sell the team version after individual adoption

Offer a team, family, department, group, or multi-user version after one person has already adopted the product or service.

Why it works

Individual adoption can reveal wider group value. This expands revenue by moving from one user to a shared-use model with stronger retention and higher spend.

Best for

Software, education, healthcare, fitness, financial tools, consumer subscriptions, professional services

Execution Steps

1. Identify individual users with group potential
2. Define the team or family version
3. Trigger after usage or satisfaction signals
4. Price for shared value
5. Make migration easy

Real-world example

A language app offers family plans, while a SaaS tool converts one power user into a team account.

Risk Management

1. **Commercial** · 3/5 Weak group fit. **Mitigation:** Target shared-use cases.
2. **Financial** · 3/5 Buyers push back on the price before the full value has. **Mitigation:** Show the per-seat cost saving of the group version.
3. **Operational** · 3/5 Migration friction. **Mitigation:** Build a one-click migration path from individual to team.
4. **Customer** · 2/5 Admin confusion. **Mitigation:** Reduce the setup process to the minimum steps required.
5. **Customer** · 3/5 Adoption is slower than expected. **Mitigation:** Use active-user triggers.

Speed	Effort	Cost	Revenue	Time to cash	Scalability
Fast (0-30 days)	**Low**	**Low**	**High**	**Immediate**	**High**

Decision-flow: CFO → Product → Sales

101. Cross-sell the maintenance customers forget until it fails

Offer recurring or one-time maintenance products or services customers typically delay, overlook, or forget until failure happens.

Why it works

Customers often focus on buying, not upkeep. Preventive maintenance is easier to sell once the customer already owns and depends on the product or service.

Best for

Home services, equipment, healthcare, vehicles, software, industrial tools, facilities

Execution Steps

1. Identify maintenance customers commonly delay
2. Define the maintenance offer clearly
3. Trigger after purchase or usage milestone
4. Price against avoided disruption
5. Make scheduling easy

Real-world example

A HVAC company cross-sells annual servicing, while a SaaS company offers paid system health reviews for active customers.

Risk Management

1. **Commercial** · 3/5 Urgency signals are insufficient to motivate prompt customer action. Build urgency. **Mitigation:** Link the maintenance offer directly to the quantified cost of failure.
2. **Customer** · 3/5 Feels optional. **Mitigation:** Show customers the ongoing maintenance responsibility before the sale completes.
3. **Operational** · 3/5 Scheduling gaps. **Mitigation:** Use reminder workflows.
4. **Financial** · 3/5 Margin compresses if delivery cost is not controlled from the start. **Mitigation:** Define the time commitment per maintenance event and track.
5. **Customer** · 3/5 Low repeat use. **Mitigation:** Use lifecycle stage data to time maintenance offers at.

Speed	Effort	Cost	Revenue	Time to cash	Scalability
Fast (0-30 days)	**Low**	**Low**	**High**	**Immediate**	**High**

Decision-flow: CFO → Customer Success → Operations

102. Upsell customers from reactive buying to planned buying

Move customers from one-off purchases into scheduled replenishment, recurring ordering, or planned usage programs that increase consistency and spend.

Why it works

Planned buying increases predictability and wallet share. Customers buy more consistently when the process becomes structured instead of reactive.

Best for

Retail, healthcare, food, industrial supply, SaaS, beauty, hospitality, office products

Execution Steps

1. Identify repeat-purchase patterns
2. Define the planned-buying program
3. Set cadence, volume, and rules
4. Position around convenience and reliability
5. Trigger from past purchase behavior

Real-world example

A coffee supplier moves offices from ad-hoc orders to scheduled replenishment, while a beauty retailer moves customers to planned product cycles.

Risk Management

1. **Commercial** · 3/5 Customer commitment low. **Mitigation:** Start with a flexible cadence option to lower the.
2. **Operational** · 3/5 Fulfillment strain. **Mitigation:** Plan inventory levels based on conservative demand projections before launch.
3. **Financial** · 3/5 Weak margin. **Mitigation:** Define minimum order thresholds before the program is launched.
4. **Customer** · 3/5 Feels restrictive. **Mitigation:** Build in easy adjustment options so customers feel in.
5. **Commercial** · 3/5 Offer arrives at the wrong point in the journey. **Mitigation:** Use actual purchase history data to time the planned buying conversation.

Speed	Effort	Cost	Revenue	Time to cash	Scalability
Medium (1-3 months)	**Medium**	**Low**	**Very High**	**Short**	**High**

Decision-flow: CFO → Sales → Operations

103. Cross-sell the professional version after customer maturity increases

Offer a more advanced, capable, or higher-performance version once customers become more experienced, sophisticated, or dependent on the core offer.

Why it works

Customer sophistication grows over time. As usage deepens, willingness to pay for professional capability increases naturally.

Best for

Software, fitness, education, equipment, creator tools, healthcare, financial tools

Execution Steps

1. Identify maturity signals
2. Define professional-version triggers
3. Position as next-level capability
4. Price against advanced value
5. Offer after usage depth increases

Real-world example

A creator tool cross-sells pro features to active users, while a fitness brand offers advanced equipment to experienced customers.

Risk Management

1. **Commercial** · 3/5 Maturity misread. **Mitigation:** Use actual usage data rather than time alone to.
2. **Customer** · 3/5 Upgrade feels premature. **Mitigation:** Wait for clear maturity signals in usage data before presenting upgrades.
3. **Financial** · 3/5 Buyers push back on the price before the full value has. **Mitigation:** Demonstrate specific capability improvements that justify the premium price.
4. **Product** · 3/5 Feature confusion. **Mitigation:** List specific benefits of the professional version before any upgrade conversation.
5. **Commercial** · 3/5 Low migration. **Mitigation:** Restrict upgrade outreach to customers actively using the core product.

Speed	Effort	Cost	Revenue	Time to cash	Scalability
Fast (0-30 days)	**Low**	**Low**	**High**	**Immediate**	**High**

Decision-flow: CFO → Product → Customer Success

104. Cross-sell the done-with-you layer to self-service

Offer guided help, reviews, checkpoints, or assisted execution to customers currently using the self-service version on their own.

Why it works

Some customers want support without fully outsourcing. This captures extra revenue between self-service and fully managed service.

Best for

Software, education, consulting, fitness, healthcare, home improvement, financial services

Execution Steps

1. Identify self-service customers showing friction
2. Define guided support checkpoints
3. Price by session or package
4. Offer before drop-off occurs
5. Keep scope clear

Real-world example

An online course sells review calls to learners, while a SaaS company offers assisted workflow reviews to self-service teams.

Risk Management

1. **Operational** · 4/5 Scope expands beyond agreed boundaries. **Mitigation:** Define support blocks with a fixed duration and fixed.
2. **Customer** · 3/5 Confusion with support. **Mitigation:** Draw a clear visible line between paid support and.
3. **Commercial** · 3/5 Uptake in the early period is below projections. Early signals must. **Mitigation:** Use friction signals — failed tasks.
4. **Financial** · 3/5 Margin compresses if delivery cost is not controlled from the start. **Mitigation:** Price guidance time.
5. **Operational** · 3/5 Capacity strain. **Mitigation:** Cap the total sessions per customer to protect delivery capacity.

Speed	Effort	Cost	Revenue	Time to cash	Scalability
Fast (0-30 days)	**Low**	**Low**	**High**	**Immediate**	**Medium**

Decision-flow: CFO → Customer Success → Sales

105. Upsell customers into a higher usage tier

Move existing customers into a higher tier when their usage, volume, activity, or dependency has clearly increased.

Why it works

Usage growth signals value. When customers are already using more, a higher tier feels like a natural next step rather than a forced sale.

Best for

SaaS, utilities, logistics, telecom, healthcare, education, memberships, equipment services

Execution Steps

1. Define usage thresholds
2. Track customers near limits
3. Create tier-migration message
4. Show value of higher tier
5. Make upgrade simple

Real-world example

A SaaS company moves high-usage accounts into a higher plan, while a logistics provider upgrades customers to higher-volume service levels.

Risk Management

1. **Customer** · 4/5 Feels forced. **Mitigation:** Present actual usage data when initiating any tier upgrade conversation.
2. **Commercial** · 3/5 Poor threshold. **Mitigation:** Set tier limits at levels that feel fair to.
3. **Financial** · 3/5 Underpriced tier. **Mitigation:** Review economics.
4. **Product** · 3/5 Upgrade confusion. **Mitigation:** Clarify tier value.
5. **Customer** · 3/5 Churn increases if the ongoing value is not clearly and regularly. **Mitigation:** Offer a short migration session to remove friction from tier upgrades.

Speed	Effort	Cost	Revenue	Time to cash	Scalability
Fast (0-30 days)	**Low**	**Low**	**Very High**	**Immediate**	**High**

Decision-flow: CFO → Product → Sales

106. Cross-sell the specialist add-on for advanced needs

Offer a related specialist product or service when customers move beyond basic needs and require more capability, precision, or support.

Why it works

Advanced customers often need more than the standard offer. Specialist add-ons increase wallet share by matching deeper needs already emerging inside the account.

Best for

Healthcare, software, equipment, education, fitness, financial services, industrial tools

Execution Steps

1. Identify advanced-use signals
2. Define the specialist add-on
3. Match add-on to deeper need
4. Price against capability gained
5. Offer after readiness appears

Real-world example

A healthcare provider cross-sells specialist screening to existing patients, while an industrial tool supplier cross-sells precision accessories to advanced users.

Risk Management

1. **Commercial** · 3/5 Need too narrow. **Mitigation:** Identify advanced users through behaviour data before add-on conversations.
2. **Customer** · 3/5 Buyers push back on the price before the full value has. **Mitigation:** Quantify the specific capability gain the add-on delivers before pricing.
3. **Operational** · 3/5 Delivery complexity. **Mitigation:** Standardize add-on delivery so quality is consistent at scale.
4. **Product** · 4/5 The offer does not closely match the specific need or context. **Mitigation:** Match each add-on offer to a specific confirmed customer use case.
5. **Commercial** · 3/5 Low awareness. **Mitigation:** Train the sales team on the exact signals that.

Speed	Effort	Cost	Revenue	Time to cash	Scalability
Medium (1-3 months)	**Medium**	**Low**	**High**	**Short**	**Medium**

Decision-flow: CFO → Product → Sales

107. Cross-sell the adjacent need already connected to the purchase

Offer a related product or service that naturally follows from the customer's existing purchase, problem, or goal.

Why it works

Customers rarely have one isolated need. A relevant adjacent cross-sell captures more wallet share by solving the next connected problem.

Best for

Home services, retail, healthcare, software, hospitality, education, construction, B2B services

Execution Steps

1. Map the next connected need
2. Define the adjacent offer
3. Trigger after the main purchase
4. Position as natural next step
5. Keep the cross-sell relevant

Real-world example

A dental clinic cross-sells whitening after treatment, while a software vendor cross-sells reporting after workflow adoption.

Risk Management

1. **Commercial** · 4/5 Weak connection. **Mitigation:** Only cross-sell when the adjacent need directly follows from the purchase.
2. **Customer** · 3/5 Feels salesy. **Mitigation:** Frame the cross-sell as the obvious next step.
3. **Operational** · 3/5 Offer complexity. **Mitigation:** Keep version one as simple as possible and add.
4. **Financial** · 3/5 Margin is insufficient if pricing does not cover the full cost. **Mitigation:** Choose profitable adjacent offers.
5. **Alignment** · 3/5 Sales misses trigger. **Mitigation:** Build a structured prompt into the sales process so.

Speed	Effort	Cost	Revenue	Time to cash	Scalability
Fast (0-30 days)	**Low**	**Low**	**High**	**Immediate**	**High**

Decision-flow: CFO → Sales → Operations

108. Upsell customers into the expert-reviewed version

Offer a higher-value version where an expert reviews, checks, validates, or improves the customer's selected product, setup, plan, or output.

Why it works

Customers pay more when expert review reduces doubt and improves confidence. This increases spend without changing the core purchase.

Best for

Software, education, healthcare, home improvement, financial services, design, consulting, equipment

Execution Steps

1. Identify where expert review increases confidence
2. Define review scope and limits
3. Price by review or package
4. Offer at high-doubt moments
5. Standardize review output

Real-world example

A financial planning tool sells expert portfolio review, while a home improvement company sells expert design review before final purchase.

Risk Management

1. **Operational** · 4/5 Expert bottleneck. **Mitigation:** Cap volume.
2. **Legal** · 4/5 Legal liability arises if terms, access rules. **Mitigation:** Specify exactly what the review covers and what is.
3. **Customer** · 3/5 The value delivered is not clearly communicated. **Mitigation:** Explain the specific uncertainty removed by the expert review before pricing.
4. **Financial** · 3/5 Margin compresses if delivery cost is not controlled from the start. **Mitigation:** Price expert time.
5. **Operational** · 3/5 Inconsistent review. **Mitigation:** Use standard output.

Speed	Effort	Cost	Revenue	Time to cash	Scalability
Fast (0-30 days)	**Low**	**Low**	**High**	**Immediate**	**Medium**

Decision-flow: CFO → Customer Success → Sales

109. Cross-sell the renewal companion before the next

Offer a related product or service that prepares the customer for their next renewal, reorder, replacement, upgrade, or usage cycle.

Why it works

Existing customers are easier to expand before the next buying cycle. A companion offer keeps them engaged and increases spend before competitors re-enter the conversation.

Best for

SaaS, equipment, subscriptions, healthcare, home services, education, beauty, industrial supply

Execution Steps

1. Identify next cycle timing
2. Define the companion offer
3. Trigger before renewal or reorder window
4. Position around preparation and continuity
5. Make purchase easy

Real-world example

A SaaS firm offers a pre-renewal optimization session, while a beauty brand cross-sells prep products before the next treatment cycle.

Risk Management

1. **Commercial** · 4/5 Wrong timing. **Mitigation:** Use lifecycle data to time offers at the highest-relevance moments.
2. **Customer** · 3/5 Feels unnecessary. **Mitigation:** Frame the companion offer as preparation for the upcoming.
3. **Financial** · 3/5 Budget friction. **Mitigation:** Time the companion offer to land before the customer.
4. **Operational** · 3/5 Delivery capacity becomes strained as demand scales beyond the initial pilot.. **Mitigation:** Standardize the companion offer so all salespeople present it consistently.
5. **Commercial** · 3/5 Conversion from initial interest to completed purchase is lower than targeted.. **Mitigation:** Test different trigger timings to identify the highest-conversion window.

Speed	Effort	Cost	Revenue	Time to cash	Scalability
Fast (0-30 days)	**Low**	**Low**	**High**	**Short**	**High**

Decision-flow: CFO → Customer Success → Sales

110. *Cross-sell customer-to-customer knowledge access*

Offer paying customers direct access to experienced customers who already solved similar problems, workflows, setups, or growth challenges using your product or service.

Why it works

Customers often trust experienced users more than vendors. This creates new value by turning proven customer experience into a premium peer-learning layer.

Best for

SaaS, healthcare, education, investing, fitness, professional tools, B2B platforms, home systems

Execution Steps

1. Identify experienced customers willing to help
2. Define peer-access formats
3. Set participation rules and rewards
4. Price access by session or tier
5. Match customers by problem

Real-world example

A SaaS company sells access to expert customer panels, while a fitness brand connects beginners to advanced users who solved similar goals.

Risk Management

1. **Customer** · 5/5 Customer trust damaged if delivery falls short. **Mitigation:** Vet participants.
2. **Legal** · 5/5 Customer data privacy is at risk if access, anonymisation. **Mitigation:** Get consent and protect data.
3. **Operational** · 4/5 Weak match quality. **Mitigation:** Use clear matching criteria.
4. **Customer** · 3/5 Participant fatigue. **Mitigation:** Limit sessions.
5. **Commercial** · 3/5 Willingness to pay is lower than projected for this segment. **Mitigation:** Target high-stakes use cases.

Speed	Effort	Cost	Revenue	Time to cash	Scalability
Medium (1-3 months)	**Medium**	**Low**	**High**	**Medium**	**Medium**

Decision-flow: CFO → Customer Success → Marketing

111. Upsell the future-proof version before customer regret

Offer an upgraded version designed to protect customers from becoming outdated, incompatible, underpowered, or limited as their needs grow.

Why it works

Customers fear buying the wrong thing long-term. A future-proof upsell captures more spend by selling confidence in tomorrow, not just functionality today.

Best for

Technology, home systems, healthcare, education, vehicles, industrial equipment, software, financial products

Execution Steps

1. Identify where customers risk outgrowing the base option
2. Define future-ready features or capacity
3. Position around avoiding regret
4. Price against replacement pain
5. Offer before final decision

Real-world example

A solar company upsells battery readiness, while a software company sells a scalable architecture tier to growing teams.

Risk Management

1. **Commercial** · 3/5 Future need unclear. **Mitigation:** Use growth signals.
2. **Customer** · 3/5 Overbuying concern. **Mitigation:** Show upgrade logic.
3. **Financial** · 3/5 Price pushback. **Mitigation:** Anchor to replacement cost.
4. **Product** · 4/5 The offer lacks clear differentiation from what competitors or alternatives provide. **Mitigation:** Make future benefit visible.
5. **Commercial** · 3/5 The new offer cannibalizes existing higher-margin revenue if segmentation is not. **Mitigation:** Separate customer profiles.

Speed	Effort	Cost	Revenue	Time to cash	Scalability
Fast (0-30 days)	**Low**	**Low**	**Very High**	**Immediate**	**High**

Decision-flow: CFO → Product → Sales

112. Cross-sell the decision shortcut customers normally

Offer customers pre-made recommendations, presets, configurations, workflows, routines, or proven combinations so they avoid researching and deciding everything manually.

Why it works

Decision fatigue is expensive. Customers will pay for trusted shortcuts that reduce uncertainty, setup time, and mental effort.

Best for

Software, retail, healthcare, fitness, education, finance, home improvement, B2B operations

Execution Steps

1. Identify decisions customers repeatedly struggle with
2. Create trusted shortcuts or presets
3. Package them as a paid cross-sell
4. Explain the time and doubt removed
5. Offer at decision-heavy moments

Real-world example

A finance app sells model portfolios, while a software platform sells pre-built workflows for common business processes.

Risk Management

1. **Customer** · 4/5 Shortcut lacks trust. **Mitigation:** Explain the recommendation logic so customers can trust the shortcut.
2. **Commercial** · 3/5 Value feels soft. **Mitigation:** Quantify the time saved by using the shortcut versus deciding independently.
3. **Product** · 3/5 The offer is too generic to create meaningful value for any. **Mitigation:** Build around real use cases.
4. **Financial** · 3/5 Low price ceiling. **Mitigation:** Bundle with high-value moments.
5. **Customer** · 4/5 Misfit recommendations. **Mitigation:** Offer clear choice paths.

Speed	Effort	Cost	Revenue	Time to cash	Scalability
Fast (0-30 days)	**Low**	**Low**	**High**	**Immediate**	**High**

Decision-flow: CFO → Product → Customer Success

113. Cross-sell the silent monitor customers never knew they needed

Offer a lightweight monitoring layer that quietly tracks risk, performance, usage, mistakes, waste, or deterioration and alerts the customer before problems become expensive.

Why it works

Customers often react too late because problems stay invisible until damage appears. Silent monitoring creates wallet expansion by turning hidden problems into visible action.

Best for

Healthcare, SaaS, home systems, finance, logistics, equipment, industrial operations, fitness

Execution Steps

1. Identify hidden problems customers miss
2. Define what the monitor will track
3. Set simple alerts or reports
4. Price against avoided cost
5. Offer to active users or owners

Real-world example

A home system company cross-sells sensor monitoring, while a SaaS firm offers silent workflow-risk alerts for active accounts.

Risk Management

1. **Customer** · 4/5 Value invisible. **Mitigation:** Use real examples.
2. **Product** · 4/5 Tracking errors. **Mitigation:** Validate monitoring accuracy against a historical dataset before launch.
3. **Customer** · 3/5 Alert fatigue. **Mitigation:** Cap alert frequency to a level that drives action.
4. **Legal** · 4/5 Data sensitivity. **Mitigation:** Apply strict data governance before monitoring any customer-sensitive data.
5. **Commercial** · 3/5 Low attach rate. **Mitigation:** Focus on customers with the highest dependency on the core product.

Speed	Effort	Cost	Revenue	Time to cash	Scalability
Medium (1-3 months)	**Medium**	**Low**	**Very High**	**Short**	**High**

Decision-flow: CFO → Product → Customer Success

114. Upsell the auto-pilot version customers stop managing

Offer a higher-tier version where repetitive customer decisions, settings, scheduling, optimization, or management tasks become automated.

Why it works

Customers eventually get tired of manual effort. Automation upgrades increase spend by replacing ongoing mental load with convenience and consistency.

Best for

Software, finance, logistics, home systems, healthcare, marketing, industrial tools, education

Execution Steps

1. Identify repeated customer tasks
2. Define what can be automated safely
3. Create the auto-pilot version
4. Price against effort removed
5. Offer to frequent users

Real-world example

A marketing platform upsells campaign automation, while a home system provider upsells automated climate optimization.

Risk Management

1. **Product** · 5/5 Automation failure. **Mitigation:** Test the automation under realistic failure conditions before customer use.
2. **Customer** · 4/5 Trust barrier. **Mitigation:** Always include a manual override option so customers retain control.
3. **Operational** · 3/5 Complex setup. **Mitigation:** Simplify onboarding.
4. **Financial** · 3/5 Costs grow beyond the projected baseline. **Mitigation:** Monitor usage. cost
5. **Customer** · 3/5 Adoption is slower than expected. **Mitigation:** Target customers performing the automated task most frequently.

Speed	Effort	Cost	Revenue	Time to cash	Scalability
Medium (1-3 months)	**Medium**	**Medium**	**Very High**	**Short**	**High**

Decision-flow: CFO → Product → Operations

115. Cross-sell the reputation protection layer around the customer

Offer products or services that help customers avoid embarrassment, public mistakes, visible failure, bad reviews, compliance problems, or professional credibility loss.

Why it works

People pay aggressively to avoid visible failure. Reputation protection increases wallet share by reducing social, professional, or customer-facing risk.

Best for

Healthcare, finance, SaaS, hospitality, education, legal, beauty, home services, professional services

Execution Steps

1. Identify visible failure points customers fear
2. Define the protection layer
3. Price against credibility risk
4. Offer before public-facing moments
5. Set clear scope. and limits

Real-world example

A hospitality tech company cross-sells review-risk monitoring, while a beauty clinic offers post-treatment care to avoid visible customer dissatisfaction.

Risk Management

1. **Customer** · 4/5 Fear-selling concern. **Mitigation:** Frame reputation protection as proactive risk management, not reactive damage control.
2. **Legal** · 4/5 Compliance exposure. **Mitigation:** Review scope.
3. **Operational** · 3/5 Delivery quality varies across engagements, undermining customer confidence and referral rate. **Mitigation:** Build a standardized quality checklist into every delivery process.
4. **Commercial** · 3/5 Value too abstract. **Mitigation:** Use clear examples.
5. **Financial** · 3/5 Margin compresses if delivery cost is not controlled from the start. **Mitigation:** Price support time.

Speed	Effort	Cost	Revenue	Time to cash	Scalability
Fast (0-30 days)	**Low**	**Low**	**High**	**Immediate**	**Medium**

Decision-flow: CFO → Sales → Customer Success

From Ideas to Action

Twenty-six ideas. Twenty-six ways to increase revenue from customers already buying — without acquiring a single new one.

Every customer in this chapter is already inside the business. The revenue is not hidden — it is sitting in relationships that have not been deepened. The only thing required is a deliberate reason to go back.

Before continuing, identify the single idea with the clearest commercial case right now. Name who owns it. Set a date for the first step. That is all that is required.

> *The customer who bought once is the easiest customer you will ever sell to. Most businesses never return.*

What Comes Next

3.2 — Repricing & Price Capture addresses businesses that are already delivering clear value but pricing below what that value is worth. If the commercial model has not kept pace with what the business actually delivers — the next chapter closes the gap.

3.2 — Repricing & Price Capture

Unlock revenue by correcting underpricing or charging properly for value already being delivered.

When These Strategies Work Best

Repricing strategies deliver the fastest return when the business is delivering clear value but not charging in proportion to what that value is worth.

- Prices have not changed despite costs, demand, or value delivered increasing
- Features or services added over time are being given away without charge
- Certain customers or segments are paying less than others for the same outcome
- The business hesitates to charge for scope it knows it delivers beyond the agreement
- Competitors charge more for an equivalent or inferior offer

The Benefits

- Immediate margin improvement with no change to delivery or customer base
- Revenue recovery from work already being done but not fully billed
- A cleaner commercial model where price reflects the value the customer receives
- Higher average deal value without increasing sales volume or effort
- Reduced internal resentment when teams are paid for work they actually do

The Risks to Manage

- **Customer pushback** — price increases require a clear value story. Lead with what changed, not just the new number.
- **Churn from price-sensitive segments** — some customers will leave. Model the net revenue impact before acting.
- **Inconsistency** — repricing some customers and not others creates friction. Apply systematically.
- **Underdone communication** — price changes with no context feel arbitrary. Frame every increase with a reason.

116. Charge for work you keep doing for free

List the extra work your team repeatedly does for customers without charging, then turn the most valuable items into clear paid line items.

Why it works

Small unpaid tasks add up. When customers regularly ask for extra help, changes, checks, or support, pricing those items captures revenue already being created.

Best for

Professional services, agencies, construction, logistics, healthcare, SaaS support, equipment services, B2B services

Execution Steps

1. Identify repeated unpaid work
2. Rank by effort and customer value
3. Convert common extras into priced line items
4. Communicate what is included vs charged
5. Train sales. and delivery teams

Real-world example

An agency starts charging for extra revision rounds, while a SaaS support team prices repeated custom reporting requests.

Risk Management

1. **Customer** · 3/5 Buyer pushback. **Mitigation:** Explain what remains included.
2. **Alignment** · 4/5 Team giving it away. **Mitigation:** Require approval. for exceptions.
3. **Operational** · 3/5 Tracking gaps. **Mitigation:** Log unpaid requests first.
4. **Commercial** · 3/5 Low perceived value. **Mitigation:** Name the benefit clearly.
5. **Financial** · 4/5 Underpricing extras. **Mitigation:** Review effort and margin monthly.

Speed	Effort	Cost	Revenue	Time to cash	Scalability
Fast (0-30 days)	**Low**	**Low**	**High**	**Immediate**	**High**

Decision-flow: CFO → Sales → Operations

117. Price the annoying edge cases customers keep creating

Create clear charges for non-standard requests, exceptions, rush clarifications, unusual formats, special handling, or repeated changes that currently get absorbed for free.

Why it works

Edge cases quietly drain margin. Charging for them protects the standard offer while making customers pay when they create extra complexity.

Best for

Manufacturing, logistics, agencies, consulting, software support, healthcare, construction, printing, custom products

Execution Steps

1. List recurring exceptions
2. Define standard vs non-standard work
3. Create exception pricing rules
4. Add rules to quotes and contracts
5. Train teams to flag exceptions

Real-world example

A printer charges for unusual file formats, while a logistics firm adds fees for special handling beyond standard delivery.

Risk Management

1. **Customer** · 3/5 Customers dislike new fees. **Mitigation:** Frame as non-standard work.
2. **Operational** · 3/5 Teams misclassify exceptions. **Mitigation:** Create clear examples.
3. **Commercial** · 3/5 Sales avoids the charge. **Mitigation:** Make it part of quoting.
4. **Legal** · 3/5 Unclear terms create disputes and undermine trust in the commercial relationship.. **Mitigation:** Add contract language.
5. **Financial** · 2/5 Fees too small. **Mitigation:** Review margin impact.

Speed	Effort	Cost	Revenue	Time to cash	Scalability
Fast (0-30 days)	**Low**	**Low**	**High**	**Immediate**	**High**

Decision-flow: CFO → Operations → Sales

118. Raise prices where customers would feel more pain

Find products, services, or accounts where switching cost, dependency, trust, or operational reliance is high, then adjust pricing to better reflect that embedded value.

Why it works

Some customers stay because the offer has become critical. Pricing should reflect dependency and value, not just original acquisition assumptions.

Best for

SaaS, healthcare, logistics, B2B services, equipment maintenance, financial services, enterprise tools

Execution Steps

1. Identify high-dependency customers
2. Map switching pain and value delivered
3. Segment accounts by pricing headroom
4. Design a careful price adjustment
5. Communicate value before increase

Real-world example

A mission-critical software provider adjusts pricing for deeply embedded enterprise accounts, while a maintenance provider reprices critical support contracts.

Risk Management

1. **Customer** · 4/5 Churn increases if the ongoing value is not clearly and regularly. **Mitigation:** Target high-value dependency carefully.
2. **Commercial** · 4/5 Poor communication. **Mitigation:** Explain value clearly.
3. **Financial** · 3/5 Underestimating price headroom. **Mitigation:** Use customer-level analysis.
4. **Alignment** · 3/5 Sales resistance. **Mitigation:** Give clear account logic.
5. **Market** · 3/5 Competitor reaction. **Mitigation:** Monitor alternatives.

Speed	Effort	Cost	Revenue	Time to cash	Scalability
Medium (1-3 months)	**Medium**	**Low**	**Very High**	**Short**	**High**

Decision-flow: CFO → Finance → Sales

119. Stop giving premium response times at standard prices

Separate standard delivery from priority handling and charge customers who want faster turnaround, quicker replies, or accelerated execution.

Why it works

Many businesses quietly deliver urgency for free. Customers who value speed are often willing to pay more when faster response is clearly defined.

Best for

Healthcare, logistics, agencies, SaaS support, legal, consulting, construction, professional services

Execution Steps

1. Define standard response times
2. Identify faster response requests
3. Set premium response pricing
4. Protect the standard service baseline before adding any premium tier. levels
5. Add priority terms to quotes

Real-world example

A law firm charges for expedited review, while a SaaS support team prices premium response windows separately from standard support.

Risk Management

1. **Operational** · 4/5 Base service suffers. **Mitigation:** Ring-fence priority capacity.
2. **Customer** · 3/5 Unfairness perception. **Mitigation:** Keep standard service clear.
3. **Commercial** · 3/5 The value delivered is not clearly communicated. **Mitigation:** Quantify the time saved and present it as the.
4. **Alignment** · 4/5 Team overcommits. **Mitigation:** Cap priority volume.
5. **Financial** · 3/5 Pricing is set too low to adequately cover the real cost. **Mitigation:** Anchor to urgency value.

Speed	Effort	Cost	Revenue	Time to cash	Scalability
Fast (0-30 days)	**Low**	**Low**	**High**	**Immediate**	**High**

Decision-flow: CFO → Operations → Sales

120. Raise prices on products customers compare the least

Increase pricing selectively on products or services where customers focus more on trust, convenience, urgency, or outcomes than direct price comparison.

Why it works

Not all purchases are equally price-sensitive. Businesses often undercharge where customers care more about confidence and speed than saving money.

Best for

Healthcare, emergency services, luxury services, B2B support, hospitality, legal, specialist products

Execution Steps

1. Identify low-comparison purchase areas
2. Check customer decision drivers
3. Test selective price increases
4. Communicate value and trust factors
5. Monitor volume and objections

Real-world example

A specialist clinic raises pricing for hard-to-compare procedures, while a legal firm reprices urgent expert opinions.

Risk Management

1. **Commercial** · 4/5 Demand drops. **Mitigation:** Test selectively first.
2. **Customer** · 3/5 Price shock. **Mitigation:** Communicate value clearly.
3. **Market** · 3/5 Competitor visibility. **Mitigation:** Monitor alternatives.
4. **Financial** · 4/5 Wrong elasticity assumption. **Mitigation:** Use pilot cohorts.
5. **Alignment** · 3/5 Sales discomfort. **Mitigation:** Prepare talk tracks.

Speed	Effort	Cost	Revenue	Time to cash	Scalability
Medium (1-3 months)	**Medium**	**Low**	**Very High**	**Short**	**High**

Decision-flow: CFO → Finance → Sales

121. Charge separately for customer-caused delays

Add pricing for delays caused by slow approvals, missing information, repeated revisions, rescheduling, or late responses from the customer side.

Why it works

Customer delays create hidden operational costs and lost capacity. Charging for delay-related disruption protects margin and encourages faster customer action.

Best for

Construction, agencies, consulting, logistics, software implementation, manufacturing, healthcare, legal services

Execution Steps

1. Identify common customer delay points
2. Define delay fees or reset charges
3. Add clear deadlines and grace periods
4. Include terms. in contracts
5. Train teams to document delays

Real-world example

A construction firm charges for client-caused rescheduling, while an implementation team bills for repeated delays due to missing customer inputs.

Risk Management

1. **Customer** · 4/5 Fee frustration. **Mitigation:** Use clear deadlines upfront.
2. **Legal** · 4/5 Contract disputes. **Mitigation:** Write terms clearly.
3. **Operational** · 3/5 Poor documentation. **Mitigation:** Log delay evidence.
4. **Commercial** · 3/5 Sales waives fees. **Mitigation:** Require approval.
5. **Financial** · 3/5 Fee too punitive. **Mitigation:** Keep charges fair.

Speed	Effort	Cost	Revenue	Time to cash	Scalability
Fast (0-30 days)	**Low**	**Low**	**High**	**Immediate**	**High**

Decision-flow: CFO → Operations → Legal

122. *Charge for senior-level attention, not just delivery*

Separate standard delivery from senior expert involvement, and charge more when customers want leadership review, senior judgment, or executive-level input.

Why it works

Senior attention is scarce and valuable. Many businesses give it away to win or retain customers, even when customers would pay for the added confidence.

Best for

Consulting, agencies, legal, healthcare, construction, finance, software implementation, professional services

Execution Steps

1. Identify senior involvement currently given free
2. Define when senior review is included
3. Create senior-attention pricing
4. Add options to proposals
5. Protect senior capacity

Real-world example

A consulting firm charges for partner-led review, while a healthcare provider prices specialist oversight separately from standard appointments.

Risk Management

1. **Customer** · 3/5 Customers expect access. **Mitigation:** Clarify standard vs senior support.
2. **Operational** · 4/5 Senior capacity strain. **Mitigation:** Cap availability to protect quality and prevent over-commitment.
3. **Commercial** · 3/5 Sales overpromises. **Mitigation:** Use approval rules.
4. **Financial** · 3/5 Underpriced expertise. **Mitigation:** Anchor to senior value.
5. **Alignment** · 2/5 Leadership resistance. **Mitigation:** Show revenue impact.

Speed	Effort	Cost	Revenue	Time to cash	Scalability
Fast (0-30 days)	**Low**	**Low**	**High**	**Immediate**	**High**

Decision-flow: CFO → Sales → Operations

123. Price for usage intensity, not just access

Raise prices for customers whose usage, support needs, service requests, or operational load are materially higher than average.

Why it works

Heavy users often consume more resources while paying the same as light users. Pricing intensity captures value and protects margin without changing the core offer.

Best for

SaaS, healthcare, logistics, support services, facilities, equipment rental, education, B2B services

Execution Steps

1. Measure usage intensity by customer
2. Identify high-load accounts
3. Define fair intensity thresholds
4. Communicate pricing logic clearly
5. Add higher-use pricing bands

Real-world example

A SaaS company reprices heavy support users, while a logistics firm charges more for accounts with complex handling loads.

Risk Management

1. **Customer** · 4/5 Fairness concerns. **Mitigation:** Use transparent thresholds.
2. **Financial** · 4/5 Thresholds set poorly. **Mitigation:** Model cost.
3. **Operational** · 3/5 Measurement gaps. **Mitigation:** Track usage accurately.
4. **Commercial** · 4/5 Account pushback. **Mitigation:** Prepare value rationale.
5. **Alignment** · 3/5 Sales exceptions. **Mitigation:** Control approvals.

Speed	Effort	Cost	Revenue	Time to cash	Scalability
Medium (1-3 months)	**Medium**	**Low**	**Very High**	**Short**	**High**

Decision-flow: CFO → Finance → Operations

124. *Charge for special formats customers keep requesting*

Add clear pricing for special reports, custom files, extra documentation, alternative formats, translated materials, or non-standard outputs customers repeatedly request.

Why it works

Special formats look small but consume time. Pricing them turns repeated hidden work into clean revenue while keeping the standard offer protected.

Best for

Agencies, SaaS, logistics, healthcare, education, manufacturing, legal, professional services

Execution Steps

1. List repeated special format requests
2. Define what standard output includes
3. Price non-standard formats separately
4. Update quotes and terms
5. Train teams to flag requests

Real-world example

A software company charges for custom export formats, while a logistics provider prices non-standard compliance documents separately.

Risk Management

1. **Customer** · 3/5 Feels nickel-and-dimed. **Mitigation:** Explain standard includes enough.
2. **Operational** · 3/5 Request tracking weak. **Mitigation:** Log format requests.
3. **Commercial** · 3/5 Sales waives charges. **Mitigation:** Standardize quote lines.
4. **Financial** · 2/5 Low fee value. **Mitigation:** Group requests into tiers.
5. **Legal** · 3/5 Document risk. **Mitigation:** Review regulated outputs.

Speed	Effort	Cost	Revenue	Time to cash	Scalability
Fast (0-30 days)	**Low**	**Low**	**Medium**	**Immediate**	**High**

Decision-flow: CFO → Operations → Sales

125. Stop undercharging for small orders that cost big

Raise prices or add minimum charges for small orders, low-volume jobs, or tiny accounts that require nearly the same effort as larger customers.

Why it works

Small orders can quietly destroy margin. Minimum pricing captures the real cost of service and encourages customers to buy at more efficient levels.

Best for

Manufacturing, logistics, wholesale, printing, catering, agencies, healthcare, B2B services

Execution Steps

1. Identify small orders with poor economics
2. Calculate minimum service cost
3. Set minimum charges or order floors
4. Communicate efficiently
5. Offer larger-order alternatives

Real-world example

A printer adds minimum job charges, while a distributor sets minimum order values for low-volume customers.

Risk Management

1. **Customer** · 3/5 Small customers leave. **Mitigation:** Target unprofitable orders first.
2. **Commercial** · 3/5 Pushback on minimums. **Mitigation:** Explain cost to serve.
3. **Financial** · 4/5 Floor too low. **Mitigation:** Model actual costs.
4. **Operational** · 3/5 Process unchanged. **Mitigation:** Automate small orders where possible.
5. **Alignment** · 3/5 Sales exceptions. **Mitigation:** Control approvals.

Speed	Effort	Cost	Revenue	Time to cash	Scalability
Fast (0-30 days)	**Low**	**Low**	**High**	**Immediate**	**High**

Decision-flow: CFO → Finance → Sales

126. Charge more for high-risk customer requests

Increase pricing for customer requests that create higher risk, complexity, uncertainty, liability, or operational exposure than standard work.

Why it works

Risk should be priced, not absorbed. Customers asking for higher-risk work should pay more because the business carries more exposure and operational burden.

Best for

Construction, healthcare, logistics, legal, consulting, manufacturing, events, software implementation

Execution Steps

1. Identify high-risk request patterns
2. Define risk factors and thresholds
3. Set risk-adjusted pricing rules
4. Add legal and operational conditions
5. Train teams to identify risk early

Real-world example

A construction firm charges more for high-complexity site work, while a cybersecurity firm reprices sensitive incident work with higher exposure.

Risk Management

1. **Legal** · 5/5 Liability if responsibilities are not documented. **Mitigation:** Use specific, plain-language contract terms that eliminate ambiguity.
2. **Financial** · 4/5 Risk underpriced. **Mitigation:** Model downside cases.
3. **Customer** · 3/5 Buyers push back on the price before the full value has. **Mitigation:** Explain exposure clearly.
4. **Operational** · 3/5 Risk misclassification. **Mitigation:** Create criteria.
5. **Alignment** · 3/5 Approval bypass. **Mitigation:** Require risk review.

Speed	Effort	Cost	Revenue	Time to cash	Scalability
Medium (1-3 months)	**Medium**	**Low**	**High**	**Short**	**Medium**

Decision-flow: CFO → Operations → Legal

127. Price by decision-maker value, not user value

Raise prices where the buyer or decision-maker gets strategic, financial, compliance, or risk-reduction value beyond what the end user sees.

Why it works

End users value function, but decision-makers often value control, savings, risk reduction, or visibility. Pricing should reflect the higher-level value actually driving approval.

Best for

SaaS, healthcare, education, B2B services, compliance, logistics, financial services, enterprise tools

Execution Steps

1. Map user value vs decision-maker value
2. Identify executive or financial benefits
3. Reframe pricing around buyer outcomes
4. Update sales materials
5. Train sales. to sell to the buyer

Real-world example

A compliance software firm prices around executive risk visibility, while a healthcare solution prices around administrator control rather than only user convenience.

Risk Management

1. **Commercial** · 4/5 Wrong buyer framing. **Mitigation:** Map decision roles.
2. **Customer** · 3/5 User value mismatch. **Mitigation:** Keep user benefits clear.
3. **Financial** · 3/5 Price jump too large. **Mitigation:** Test in one controlled segment before expanding to the broader market.
4. **Alignment** · 3/5 Sales sells too low. **Mitigation:** Train buyer-level messaging.
5. **Market** · 3/5 Competitor anchors. **Mitigation:** Differentiate buyer value.

Speed	Effort	Cost	Revenue	Time to cash	Scalability
Medium (1-3 months)	**Medium**	**Low**	**Very High**	**Short**	**High**

Decision-flow: CFO → Sales → Product

128. Price the customer's alternative, not your cost

Raise prices where the customer's real alternative is slower, riskier, harder, or more expensive than staying with you.

Why it works

Customers do not compare against your cost. They compare against their next-best option. Pricing against the avoided alternative captures value already created but underpriced.

Best for

SaaS, logistics, healthcare, specialist services, equipment support, legal, B2B operations

Execution Steps

1. Identify the customer's true alternative
2. Estimate cost, time, and risk of switching
3. Compare against your current price
4. Adjust pricing where value gap is clear
5. Communicate avoided alternative cost

Real-world example

A logistics provider reprices where internal delivery would cost clients more, while a SaaS firm prices against manual work replacement.

Risk Management

1. **Commercial** · 4/5 Alternative misunderstood. **Mitigation:** Validate with customer interviews.
2. **Customer** · 3/5 Price sensitivity. **Mitigation:** Use selective rollout.
3. **Financial** · 4/5 Overestimating value gap. **Mitigation:** Model conservatively.
4. **Alignment** 3/5 Sales underuses rationale. **Mitigation:** Provide talk tracks.
5. **Market** · 3/5 Alternative changes. **Mitigation:** Review annually.

Speed	Effort	Cost	Revenue	Time to cash	Scalability
Medium (1-3 months)	**Medium**	**Low**	**Very High**	**Short**	**High**

Decision-flow: CFO → Finance → Sales

129. Charge more where your mistake would cost them more

Increase prices for work where customer risk, exposure, or consequence is high if the job is done poorly.

Why it works

High-stakes work deserves high-stakes pricing. Customers pay more when accuracy, safety, compliance, or reliability matters more than the cheapest option.

Best for

Healthcare, construction, finance, legal, cybersecurity, logistics, engineering, enterprise software

Execution Steps

1. Identify high-consequence work
2. Define consequence levels
3. Create premium pricing for higher stakes
4. Add quality and review controls
5. Communicate risk-reduction value

Real-world example

A medical testing provider charges more for high-risk specialty testing, while an engineering firm prices critical safety reviews at a premium.

Risk Management

1. **Legal** · 5/5 Legal liability arises if terms, access rules. **Mitigation:** Submit all commercial terms to legal review before customer presentation.
2. **Customer** · 3/5 Price objections. **Mitigation:** Anchor to consequence avoided.
3. **Operational** · 4/5 Quality control burden. **Mitigation:** Standardize reviews.
4. **Financial** · 4/5 Underpricing exposure. **Mitigation:** Model downside cost.
5. **Commercial** · 3/5 Scope ambiguity. **Mitigation:** Define work clearly.

Speed	Effort	Cost	Revenue	Time to cash	Scalability
Medium (1-3 months)	**Medium**	**Low**	**High**	**Short**	**Medium**

Decision-flow: CFO → Operations → Legal

130. Raise prices where customers ask for just one more

Track repeated small extras customers request after agreement, then price those extras instead of absorbing them inside the original scope.

Why it works

Small extras look harmless but compound into unpaid work. Pricing them forces scope clarity and captures revenue from value already being delivered.

Best for

Agencies, consulting, construction, software implementation, healthcare, logistics, legal, professional services

Execution Steps

1. Track post-agreement extra requests
2. Identify frequent micro-scope items
3. Create a menu of priced extras
4. Add change language to proposals
5. Train teams to price extras early

Real-world example

A consultant charges for added analysis beyond scope, while a contractor prices extra site changes after the original agreement.

Risk Management

1. **Operational** · 3/5 Teams miss extras. **Mitigation:** Track requests visibly.
2. **Customer** · 3/5 Client pushback. **Mitigation:** Set expectations in writing before any engagement or commitment begins.
3. **Commercial** · 3/5 Sales avoids conflict. **Mitigation:** Use standard change language.
4. **Financial** · 3/5 Extras priced too low. **Mitigation:** Review actual effort.
5. **Alignment** · 4/5 Delivery gives away work. **Mitigation:** Require approval.

Speed	Effort	Cost	Revenue	Time to cash	Scalability
Fast (0-30 days)	**Low**	**Low**	**High**	**Immediate**	**High**

Decision-flow: CFO → Operations → Sales

131. *Price the value lift customers can clearly see*

Raise prices where your product or service creates a visible improvement customers can measure, feel, or show to others.

Why it works

Customers resist price increases when value is vague. When the improvement is obvious, pricing can move closer to the value created instead of the work performed.

Best for

Beauty, healthcare, SaaS, fitness, home improvement, education, design, professional services

Execution Steps

1. Identify visible customer improvements
2. Collect proof of before/after value
3. Segment offers with clear value lift
4. Raise prices where proof is strongest
5. Update messaging around improvement

Real-world example

A design firm reprices premium transformations, while a healthcare provider prices visible outcome services above routine appointments.

Risk Management

1. **Commercial** · 4/5 Value proof weak. **Mitigation:** Use clear examples.
2. **Customer** · 3/5 Buyers push back on the price before the full value has. **Mitigation:** Show visible lift.
3. **Financial** · 3/5 Increase too aggressive. **Mitigation:** Run a controlled pilot with three to five accounts.
4. **Market** · 3/5 Competitor anchoring. **Mitigation:** Differentiate results.
5. **Alignment** · 3/5 Sales lacks confidence. **Mitigation:** Train around proof.

Speed	Effort	Cost	Revenue	Time to cash	Scalability
Medium (1-3 months)	**Medium**	**Low**	**High**	**Short**	**High**

Decision-flow: CFO → Sales → Product

132. Charge for the business value hidden inside the service

Reprice services that create measurable financial value for the customer, such as cost savings, risk reduction, faster work, better conversion, or higher productivity.

Why it works

Many services are priced by effort even when they create financial upside. Value-added pricing captures a fair share of the impact customers already receive.

Best for

Consulting, SaaS, logistics, procurement, marketing, finance, legal, B2B services

Execution Steps

1. Identify financial value created
2. Estimate customer impact
3. Compare value against current price
4. Reposition price around financial gain
5. Train sales. to quantify value

Real-world example

A procurement advisor reprices around savings created, while a marketing agency raises fees where conversion lift is measurable.

Risk Management

1. **Financial** · 4/5 Value overstated. **Mitigation:** Use conservative estimates.
2. **Customer** · 4/5 Buyer challenges math. **Mitigation:** Show calculation logic.
3. **Commercial** · 3/5 Sales cannot quantify. **Mitigation:** Create value calculator.
4. **Market** · 3/5 Competitor lower price. **Mitigation:** Sell impact not hours.
5. **Alignment** · 3/5 Finance lacks data. **Mitigation:** Track proof points.

Speed	Effort	Cost	Revenue	Time to cash	Scalability
Medium (1-3 months)	**Medium**	**Low**	**Very High**	**Short**	**High**

Decision-flow: CFO → Finance → Sales

133. Price the confidence premium customers already feel

Raise prices where customers choose you because they trust your reliability, judgment, brand, expertise, or reduced-risk delivery.

Why it works

Trust is economic value. If customers pick you because they feel safer buying from you, pricing should reflect the confidence premium you already create.

Best for

Healthcare, legal, finance, home services, luxury services, enterprise software, construction, specialist B2B services

Execution Steps

1. Identify where trust drives selection
2. Collect proof of reliability and preference
3. Raise prices selectively in trust-led categories
4. Update messaging around confidence
5. Train sales. to defend premium

Real-world example

A trusted contractor raises prices for high-stakes projects, while a legal firm prices specialist advice at a confidence premium.

Risk Management

1. **Customer** · 4/5 Trust not strong enough. **Mitigation:** Validate with customers.
2. **Commercial** · 3/5 Sales discounts trust away. **Mitigation:** Use proof points.
3. **Financial** · 3/5 Price increase too broad. **Mitigation:** Deploy the approach only in the highest-confidence accounts at launch.
4. **Market** · 3/5 Cheaper alternatives. **Mitigation:** Differentiate trust value.
5. **Alignment** · 3/5 Weak messaging. **Mitigation:** Build trust narrative.

Speed	Effort	Cost	Revenue	Time to cash	Scalability
Fast (0-30 days)	**Low**	**Low**	**High**	**Immediate**	**High**

Decision-flow: CFO → Sales → Marketing

134. Price the boardroom value your offer creates

Raise prices where your product or service helps customers make better executive decisions, defend budgets, justify investments, or report stronger outcomes internally.

Why it works

Some offers create value beyond daily users. When your work helps leaders look informed, reduce risk, or make better decisions, pricing should reflect that higher-level value.

Best for

SaaS, consulting, data, healthcare, finance, logistics, compliance, B2B services

Execution Steps

1. Identify executive-level value delivered
2. Map how leaders use your output
3. Reframe pricing around decision support
4. Add proof for budget and reporting value
5. Train sales. to sell above user level

Real-world example

A data platform reprices around executive reporting value, while a consulting firm prices board-ready decision support above standard analysis.

Risk Management

1. **Commercial** · 3/5 Value seen as reporting only. **Mitigation:** Tie to decisions.
2. **Customer** · 4/5 Buyer level mismatch. **Mitigation:** Sell to senior sponsors.
3. **Financial** · 3/5 Value hard to quantify. **Mitigation:** Use decision examples.
4. **Alignment** · 3/5 Sales stays user-level. **Mitigation:** Train executive narrative.
5. **Market** · 3/5 Commodity comparison. **Mitigation:** Position against strategic value.

Speed	Effort	Cost	Revenue	Time to cash	Scalability
Medium (1-3 months)	**Medium**	**Low**	**Very High**	**Short**	**High**

Decision-flow: CFO → Sales → Product

135. Charge for the decision certainty customers get from your expertise

Raise prices where your expertise helps customers choose correctly, avoid regret, reduce doubt, or move forward with confidence.

Why it works

Customers pay more when uncertainty is expensive. If your offer reduces hesitation, bad decisions, or internal debate, that certainty is value already delivered but often underpriced.

Best for

Healthcare, legal, financial services, education, consulting, home improvement, enterprise software, specialist retail

Execution Steps

1. Identify decisions customers fear getting wrong
2. Define how your offer creates certainty
3. Capture proof of reduced doubt or regret
4. Raise prices where certainty is valued
5. Position around decision confidence

Real-world example

A specialist retailer prices expert selection support into premium products, while a consulting firm reprices recommendations that reduce executive decision risk.

Risk Management

1. **Customer** · 4/5 Certainty feels vague. **Mitigation:** Use clear decision examples.
2. **Commercial** · 4/5 Buyer expects advice free. **Mitigation:** Make expert judgment visible.
3. **Financial** · 3/5 Price increase too large. **Mitigation:** Pilot carefully.
4. **Alignment** · 3/5 Sales underexplains value. **Mitigation:** Give language and proof.
5. **Legal** · 3/5 Advice liability. **Mitigation:** Clarify limits.

Speed	Effort	Cost	Revenue	Time to cash	Scalability
Fast (0-30 days)	**Low**	**Low**	**High**	**Immediate**	**High**

Decision-flow: CFO → Sales → Marketing

From Ideas to Action

Twenty ideas. Twenty ways to charge correctly for the value the business already delivers — and stop leaving margin behind.

Repricing conversations feel uncomfortable until the numbers make them inevitable. Run the calculation first. What is this customer paying today versus what they would pay if the account were opened fresh? That gap is the starting point.

Before continuing, identify the single idea with the clearest commercial case right now. Name who owns it. Set a date for the first step. That is all that is required.

> *Underpricing is a decision. So is fixing it. One of them is costing you money every month.*

What Comes Next

3.3 — Reactivation & Recovery addresses the revenue sitting in former customers, stalled deals, and lapsed relationships that were never systematically worked. If the business has a base of people who bought before and stopped — the next chapter is where that revenue gets recovered.

3.3 — Reactivation & Recovery

Recover revenue from customers, leads, or opportunities that already existed but went inactive, stalled, or were lost.

When These Strategies Work Best

Reactivation strategies deliver the fastest return when the business has a meaningful base of former customers, stalled deals, or lapsed contacts that have not been systematically worked.

- Former customers who left have not been contacted since their last purchase
- Pipeline opportunities stalled months ago and were never formally closed or reopened
- Customers who stopped buying were never asked why or offered a path back
- Lapsed accounts sit in the CRM with no scheduled re-engagement activity
- Acquisition cost is rising while a recoverable base sits untouched

The Benefits

- Revenue from relationships that required no new acquisition cost to build
- Higher conversion rates than cold outreach because trust already exists
- Faster sales cycles because the buying journey does not start from zero
- Insight into why customers left that improves retention across the whole business
- A systematic commercial motion that turns a passive asset into active revenue

The Risks to Manage

- **Wrong message** — contacting lapsed customers as if nothing happened destroys the opportunity. Acknowledge the gap.
- **Undifferentiated outreach** — the same message to all lapsed customers underperforms. Segment by reason for leaving.
- **No reason to return** — reactivation without a changed offer or reason gives customers nothing new to say yes to.
- **Volume over quality** — mass reactivation without prioritisation wastes effort on low-probability contacts.

136. Recover customers who left because they were

Bring back customers who stopped using, buying, or engaging because the product, process, setup, or onboarding felt too complicated or heavy.

Why it works

Many customers do not leave because the offer is bad. They leave because it became mentally exhausting. Simplifying the return path unlocks hidden revenue.

Best for

SaaS, fitness, education, healthcare, financial tools, B2B software, subscriptions, professional services

Execution Steps

1. Identify customers who dropped during complexity-heavy stages
2. Find the most confusing step
3. Create a simpler return path
4. Remove unnecessary setup or decisions
5. Message the easier version clearly

Real-world example

A SaaS firm reactivates users with a simplified workspace, while a fitness program brings back members through a simple restart plan.

Risk Management

1. **Customer** · 4/5 Return still feels hard. **Mitigation:** Remove steps aggressively.
2. **Product** · 3/5 Simplification not enough. **Mitigation:** Test with inactive users.
3. **Commercial** · 3/5 Message too generic. **Mitigation:** Speak to overwhelm dircctly.
4. **Operational** · 3/5 Support spike. **Mitigation:** Prepare guided resources.
5. **Financial** · 3/5 Low recovery yield. **Mitigation:** Prioritize high-value accounts.

Speed	Effort	Cost	Revenue	Time to cash	Scalability
Fast (0-30 days)	**Medium**	**Low**	**High**	**Short**	**High**

Decision-flow: CFO › Customer Success → Product

137. Reopen almost-bought deals that died from timing, not fit

Target stalled opportunities where the buyer liked the offer but paused because priorities, budgets, leadership attention, or timing shifted temporarily.

Why it works

Many dead deals are not true losses. They are delayed decisions. Revisiting them at the right moment can unlock revenue with lower acquisition effort.

Best for

B2B services, SaaS, construction, healthcare, consulting, enterprise sales, industrial products

Execution Steps

1. Pull stalled deals with positive past signals
2. Identify the original pause reason
3. Look for new timing triggers
4. Reopen with a relevant message
5. Offer a simple next step

Real-world example

A consulting firm reopens paused proposals after budget season, while a SaaS company restarts demos after a leadership change.

Risk Management

1. **Commercial** · 3/5 Buyer has moved on. **Mitigation:** Check current relevance.
2. **Customer** · 3/5 Message feels stale. **Mitigation:** Reference original need.
3. **Alignment** · 3/5 Sales ignores old pipeline. **Mitigation:** Create recovery targets.
4. **Market** · 2/5 Timing still wrong. **Mitigation:** Use trigger-based timing.
5. **Financial** · 3/5 Low deal quality. **Mitigation:** Prioritize high-intent deals.

Speed	Effort	Cost	Revenue	Time to cash	Scalability
Fast (0-30 days)	**Low**	**Low**	**Very High**	**Immediate**	**High**

Decision-flow: CFO → Sales → Marketing

138. Recover customers who downgraded themselves emotionally

Reconnect with customers who quietly reduced spending because they felt guilty, uncertain, embarrassed, intimidated, or no longer good enough for the brand.

Why it works

Some customers disengage emotionally before they disengage financially. Rebuilding comfort and belonging can reactivate customers competitors ignore.

Best for

Luxury services, education, fitness, wellness, finance, memberships, coaching, premium retail

Execution Steps

1. Identify segments showing emotional withdrawal
2. Understand the confidence barrier
3. Create a warm re-entry message
4. Avoid blame, pressure, or judgment
5. Offer a safe next step

Real-world example

A premium fitness brand invites lapsed members back through a confidence-building restart, while an education platform helps learners resume without shame.

Risk Management

1. **Customer** · 4/5 Tone feels patronizing. **Mitigation:** Use respectful language.
2. **Commercial** · 4/5 Pain is misread. **Mitigation:** Conduct buyer interviews to validate demand before launch investment.
3. **Market** · 3/5 Not broad enough. **Mitigation:** Target relevant categories
4. **Alignment** · 3/5 Team over-sells. **Mitigation:** Use gentle scripts.
5. **Financial** · 3/5 Lower conversion. **Mitigation:** Test cohorts first.

Speed	Effort	Cost	Revenue	Time to cash	Scalability
Medium (1-3 months)	**Medium**	**Low**	**High**	**Medium**	**Medium**

Decision-flow: CFO → Marketing → Customer Success

139. Recover abandoned customers with a restart from where they stopped

Allow inactive customers to resume from their last stage, progress point, setup, or milestone instead of forcing them to restart completely.

Why it works

Restart friction kills recovery. Customers are more likely to return when progress already made is respected and preserved.

Best for

Education, SaaS, fitness, healthcare, subscriptions, onboarding-heavy services, financial tools

Execution Steps

1. Identify abandoned progress points
2. Preserve prior data or milestones
3. Build a resume-from-here path
4. Message saved progress clearly
5. Offer a simple continuation action

Real-world example

An online course lets learners resume from their last module, while a SaaS platform restores unfinished setup progress.

Risk Management

1. **Product** · 4/5 Progress data missing. **Mitigation:** Preserve key milestones.
2. **Customer** · 3/5 Customer forgot context. **Mitigation:** Summarize last state.
3. **Operational** · 3/5 Complex restart logic. **Mitigation:** Start with simple cases.
4. **Commercial** · 3/5 Return message unclear. **Mitigation:** Show exact next step.
5. **Financial** · 3/5 Cost to build. **Mitigation:** Prioritize high-value journeys.

Speed	Effort	Cost	Revenue	Time to cash	Scalability
Medium (1-3 months)	**Medium**	**Medium**	**High**	**Short**	**High**

Decision-flow: CFO → Product → Customer Success

140. *Recover silent customers before competitors wake them*

Identify customers who stopped engaging, slowed activity, or became unusually quiet before they fully leave, then proactively reconnect with them.

Why it works

Silence is often an early warning sign. Recovering customers before they actively shop alternatives is cheaper and easier than winning them back later.

Best for

SaaS, healthcare, B2B services, memberships, logistics, subscriptions, agencies, financial services

Execution Steps

1. Define silence signals
2. Build an inactive-risk list
3. Prioritize high-value customers.
4. Reach out with useful context
5. Offer a low-friction next action

Real-world example

A SaaS firm contacts accounts with usage drop-offs, while a healthcare provider reconnects patients who missed follow-up cycles.

Risk Management

1. **Customer** · 3/5 Outreach feels intrusive. **Mitigation:** Use helpful tone.
2. **Commercial** · 3/5 Signal is false positive. **Mitigation:** Use multiple indicators.
3. **Alignment** · 3/5 Teams do not act. **Mitigation:** Assign a named owner to every action item before.
4. **Operational** · 3/5 Manual follow-up load. **Mitigation:** Use usage data to trigger the expansion offer automatically.s
5. **Financial** · 2/5 Low-value accounts dilute effort. **Mitigation:** Prioritize by value.

Speed	Effort	Cost	Revenue	Time to cash	Scalability
Fast (0-30 days)	**Low**	**Low**	**Very High**	**Immediate**	**High**

Decision-flow: CFO → Customer Success → Sales

141. Recover customers by removing the shame of coming back

Create a frictionless return path that avoids making inactive customers explain why they left, failed, paused, or disappeared.

Why it works

Many customers avoid returning because re-engagement feels socially uncomfortable. Removing emotional friction can reactivate customers without discounts or aggressive selling.

Best for

Fitness, education, SaaS, healthcare, memberships, coaching, finance, communities

Execution Steps

1. Identify moments where return feels awkward
2. Remove explanation requirements
3. Create no-questions-asked re-entry
4. Use welcoming return messaging
5. Offer one simple restart action

Real-world example

A gym lets members restart without discussing missed months, while an education platform invites learners back with a clean reset option.

Risk Management

1. **Customer** · 3/5 Message feels manipulative. **Mitigation:** Keep it genuine.
2. **Commercial** · 3/5 Offer too soft. **Mitigation:** Pair with clear action.
3. **Operational** · 3/5 Process still asks questions. **Mitigation:** Remove return blockers.
4. **Alignment** · 3/5 Staff adds friction. **Mitigation:** Train front-line teams.
5. **Financial** · 2/5 Low monetization. **Mitigation:** Target high-lifetime-value customers.

Speed	Effort	Cost	Revenue	Time to cash	Scalability
Fast (0-30 days)	**Low**	**Low**	**High**	**Immediate**	**High**

Decision-flow: CFO → Marketing → Customer Success

142. *Recover customers through a smaller bridge-back version*

Offer inactive customers a lighter, simpler, lower-commitment way to re-engage before asking them to return to the full experience.

Why it works

Customers who disappeared often cannot psychologically or financially jump straight back into the full offer. A bridge-back path lowers return resistance.

Best for

SaaS, education, healthcare, fitness, subscriptions, consulting, financial services, memberships

Execution Steps

1. Identify the full-return barrier
2. Define a lighter re-entry version
3. Keep it clearly temporary or transitional
4. Price or position it carefully
5. Create upgrade path back to full use

Real-world example

A coaching program offers a short restart sprint, while a SaaS firm offers a limited reactivation workspace before full renewal.

Risk Management

1. **Commercial** · 3/5 Bridge cannibalizes full return. **Mitigation:** Make it temporary.
2. **Customer** · 3/5 Value feels too small. **Mitigation:** Show clear next step.
3. **Product** · 3/5 Scope expands beyond agreed boundaries. **Mitigation:** Keep bridge narrow.
4. **Financial** · 3/5 Margin is insufficient if pricing does not cover the full cost. **Mitigation:** Redesign the delivery model to reduce complexity before pricing.
5. **Alignment** · 3/5 Sales mispositions it. **Mitigation:** Use clear criteria.

Speed	Effort	Cost	Revenue	Time to cash	Scalability
Medium (1-3 months)	**Medium**	**Low**	**High**	**Short**	**High**

Decision-flow: CFO → Product → Customer Success

143. Recover lost customers by showing what changed since

Reconnect with inactive customers using meaningful improvements, fixes, upgrades, simplifications, or outcomes added after they stopped engaging.

Why it works

Customers often leave based on an old perception. Showing what is now different creates a reason to reconsider without relying on price cuts.

Best for

Software, healthcare, logistics, education, memberships, B2B services, retail, hospitality

Execution Steps

1. Identify meaningful changes since churn
2. Match changes to churn reasons
3. Create a what-changed message
4. Target relevant inactive customers
5. Offer a simple return path

Real-world example

A SaaS platform invites lost users back after simplifying features, while a clinic recontacts patients after adding easier booking.

Risk Management

1. **Commercial** · 4/5 Changes are not meaningful. **Mitigation:** Use real improvements only.
2. **Customer** · 3/5 Old perception remains. **Mitigation:** Show proof.
3. **Product** · 3/5 Wrong changes highlighted. **Mitigation:** Map to churn reasons.
4. **Operational** · 3/5 Return path still weak. **Mitigation:** Simplify re-entry.
5. **Financial** · 3/5 The urgency is not strong enough to drive timely purchasing decisions.. **Mitigation:** Add timely trigger.

Speed	Effort	Cost	Revenue	Time to cash	Scalability
Fast (0-30 days)	**Low**	**Low**	**Very High**	**Immediate**	**High**

Decision-flow: CFO → Marketing → Product

144. *Recover customers by solving the problem that happened*

Identify downstream problems customers faced after buying from you, then help solve those problems to reopen the relationship and restore value.

Why it works

Customers sometimes disengage because of issues adjacent to your product, not the product itself. Solving the downstream pain rebuilds trust and spending.

Best for

Home services, software, healthcare, finance, logistics, construction, education, B2B services

Execution Steps

1. Identify common post-purchase downstream problems
2. Separate your issue from adjacent blockers
3. Create a recovery support path
4. Position it as restoring value
5. Reconnect customers affected by the blocker

Real-world example

A home service company helps customers solve follow-on maintenance issues, while a SaaS firm helps users fix internal workflow blockers after purchase.

Risk Management

1. **Operational** · 4/5 Problem outside control. **Mitigation:** Define solvable boundaries.
2. **Customer** · 4/5 Customer blames you. **Mitigation:** Acknowledge without overaccepting blame.
3. **Financial** · 3/5 Support cost too high. **Mitigation:** Define a strict scope boundary and enforce it from.
4. **Commercial** · 3/5 The value delivered is not clearly communicated. **Mitigation:** Tie to restored outcome.
5. **Alignment** · 3/5 Teams resist extra work. **Mitigation:** Target high-value accounts.

Speed	Effort	Cost	Revenue	Time to cash	Scalability
Medium (1-3 months)	**Medium**	**Medium**	**High**	**Medium**	**Medium**

Decision-flow: CFO → Customer Success → Operations

145. Recover customers by turning old unused value back on for them

Reconnect with inactive customers by resurfacing credits, unused features, dormant balances, unfinished setups, saved progress, or overlooked value they already paid for.

Why it works

People hate wasting value they already own. Reactivating forgotten value creates a powerful reason to return without needing a discount.

Best for

SaaS, memberships, gaming, education, healthcare, loyalty programs, subscriptions, finance

Execution Steps

1. Identify unused paid value
2. Segment inactive customers by unused asset
3. Create a reminder message
4. Make access immediate
5. Link to next paid action

Real-world example

A SaaS firm reminds users of unused premium features, while a loyalty program shows dormant points that can unlock a paid return journey.

Risk Management

1. **Customer** · 3/5 Reminder feels weak. **Mitigation:** Show specific unused value.
2. **Product** · 4/5 Access issues. **Mitigation:** Make redemption simple.
3. **Financial** · 3/5 No next revenue step. **Mitigation:** Link to paid action.
4. **Commercial** · 3/5 The urgency is not strong enough to drive timely purchasing decisions.. **Mitigation:** Set useful window.
5. **Legal** · 3/5 Credit rules unclear. **Mitigation:** Check terms.

Speed	Effort	Cost	Revenue	Time to cash	Scalability
Fast (0-30 days)	**Low**	**Low**	**Very High**	**Immediate**	**High**

Decision-flow: CFO → Customer Success → Product

146. Recover customers with a one-click return path

Make it extremely easy for inactive customers to restart, reorder, reactivate, or resume without repeating forms, setup, onboarding, or old steps.

Why it works

Return friction kills reactivation. Customers are more likely to come back when the next action feels effortless and familiar.

Best for

SaaS, subscriptions, e-commerce, healthcare, education, fitness, home services, financial tools

Execution Steps

1. Identify steps returning customers repeat
2. Remove duplicate forms or setup
3. Create a one-click return action
4. Pre-fill known information
5. Confirm the next step simply

Real-world example

An e-commerce brand offers one-click reorder for lapsed buyers, while a SaaS product lets dormant users reactivate their workspace instantly.

Risk Management

1. **Product** · 4/5 Flow fails. **Mitigation:** Test before launch.
2. **Customer** · 3/5 Trust concern. **Mitigation:** Confirm clearly before activation.
3. **Operational** · 3/5 Back-end mismatch. **Mitigation:** Align systems.
4. **Commercial** · 3/5 Wrong offer shown. **Mitigation:** Personalize return path.
5. **Legal** · 3/5 Consent issues. **Mitigation:** Respect permissions.

Speed	Effort	Cost	Revenue	Time to cash	Scalability
Fast (0-30 days)	**Low**	**Low**	**High**	**Immediate**	**High**

Decision-flow: CFO → Product → Customer Success

147. Recover abandoned buyers with their original intent

Remind inactive leads or customers of the specific problem, goal, cart, quote, plan, or decision they originally came for.

Why it works

Generic win-back messages are weak. Original intent reactivates the reason they cared in the first place, making recovery more relevant and easier to convert.

Best for

E-commerce, SaaS, healthcare, education, travel, real estate, financial services, B2B sales

Execution Steps

1. Capture original intent signals
2. Segment by goal, cart, quote, or inquiry
3. Write intent-specific messages
4. Link directly back to the original path
5. Add one clear next step

Real-world example

A travel site reminds users of a saved trip, while a B2B provider reopens a quote around the original business problem.

Risk Management

1. **Commercial** · 3/5 Intent data missing. **Mitigation:** Use available signals.
2. **Customer** · 4/5 Message feels creepy. **Mitigation:** Keep tone helpful.
3. **Product** · 3/5 Link path broken. **Mitigation:** Test recovery links.
4. **Financial** · 2/5 Low-value abandoned items. **Mitigation:** Prioritize value.
5. **Market** · 3/5 Need changed. **Mitigation:** Include update option.

Speed	Effort	Cost	Revenue	Time to cash	Scalability
Fast (0-30 days)	**Low**	**Low**	**High**	**Immediate**	**High**

Decision-flow: CFO → Marketing → Sales

148. Recover customers when their situation changes

Reconnect with inactive customers when a trigger suggests they may need you again, such as renewal dates, season changes, growth, relocation, hiring, funding, or life events.

Why it works

Timing creates relevance. Customers who ignored you before may become active buyers when their situation changes and the need becomes real again.

Best for

Healthcare, home services, SaaS, education, finance, insurance, real estate, B2B services

Execution Steps

1. Identify meaningful change triggers
2. Connect triggers to inactive customers
3. Build relevant reactivation messages
4. Time outreach around the trigger
5. Offer a simple next action

Real-world example

A home services firm reconnects after seasonal changes, while a SaaS firm reopens accounts after hiring or funding signals.

Risk Management

1. **Market** · 3/5 Trigger inaccurate. **Mitigation:** Use multiple signals.
2. **Customer** · 3/5 Timing feels intrusive. **Mitigation:** Keep message relevant.
3. **Commercial** · 4/5 Wrong trigger-offer fit. **Mitigation:** Map triggers to needs.
4. **Product** · 3/5 Data gaps. **Mitigation:** Start with reliable signals.
5. **Financial** · 3/5 Conversion from initial interest to completed purchase is lower than targeted.. **Mitigation:** Prioritize high-value triggers.

Speed	Effort	Cost	Revenue	Time to cash	Scalability
Medium (1-3 months)	**Medium**	**Low**	**Very High**	**Short**	**High**

Decision-flow: CFO → Marketing → Sales

149. Recover too-expensive customers with proof of missed

Re-engage customers who paused over price by showing the cost, waste, risk, or lost upside of not solving the problem.

Why it works

Some buyers leave because price feels high, not because value is low. Showing the cost of delay reframes the original decision and reopens demand.

Best for

B2B services, healthcare, consulting, home improvement, software, logistics, financial services, education

Execution Steps

1. Identify price-paused customers
2. Calculate cost of inaction
3. Build simple proof examples
4. Reframe the original decision
5. Offer a next step without discounting

Real-world example

A consulting firm shows the cost of delayed process fixes, while a healthcare provider shows the cost of postponing preventive care.

Risk Management

1. **Customer** · 4/5 Cost proof disputed. **Mitigation:** Use conservative numbers.
2. **Commercial** · 3/5 Message feels fear-based. **Mitigation:** Keep tone practical.
3. **Financial** · 3/5 Value hard to quantify. **Mitigation:** Use ranges.
4. **Alignment** · 3/5 Sales defaults to discounts. **Mitigation:** Train value framing.
5. **Market** · 3/5 Buyer has cheaper workaround. **Mitigation:** Compare trade-offs.

Speed	Effort	Cost	Revenue	Time to cash	Scalability
Fast (0-30 days)	**Low**	**Low**	**High**	**Immediate**	**High**

Decision-flow: CFO → Sales → Marketing

150. Recover customers through a you were right to pause

Re-engage inactive customers by acknowledging that pausing may have made sense before, then showing why the timing, offer, or context is now better.

Why it works

Customers dislike feeling pressured or wrong. Validating their pause lowers resistance and makes the return feel smart rather than awkward.

Best for

Consulting, healthcare, finance, education, SaaS, home services, professional services, subscriptions

Execution Steps

1. Identify customers who paused intentionally
2. Acknowledge their earlier choice
3. Explain what changed now
4. Offer a low-pressure next step
5. Avoid blame or urgency pressure

Real-world example

A financial advisor validates a client's pause during uncertainty, while a SaaS firm invites delayed buyers back after better timing.

Risk Management

1. **Commercial** · 3/5 Message too soft. **Mitigation:** Still include clear action.
2. **Customer** · 3/5 Feels insincere. **Mitigation:** Use truthful context.
3. **Market** · 4/5 Nothing changed. **Mitigation:** Only use when timing changed.
4. **Alignment** · 3/5 Sales pushes too hard. **Mitigation:** Use gentle scripts.
5. **Financial** · 3/5 Slow conversion. **Mitigation:** Use with high-fit accounts.

Speed	Effort	Cost	Revenue	Time to cash	Scalability
Fast (0-30 days)	**Low**	**Low**	**High**	**Immediate**	**High**

Decision-flow: CFO → Marketing → Sales

151. Recover customers by making the first win happen faster

Bring back inactive customers by simplifying the path to the first visible result, outcome, saving, improvement, or success moment.

Why it works

Many customers disengage before experiencing meaningful value. Accelerating the first win rebuilds momentum and reopens spending.

Best for

SaaS, education, healthcare, fitness, subscriptions, home services, financial tools, B2B services

Execution Steps

1. Identify the first meaningful win
2. Remove steps before that win
3. Create a fast-win reactivation path
4. Message the visible result clearly
5. Guide customers to complete it

Real-world example

A fitness app reactivates users with a 7-day first-win challenge, while a SaaS platform guides dormant users to one immediate business result.

Risk Management

1. **Customer** · 4/5 Win not meaningful. **Mitigation:** Choose visible outcomes.
2. **Product** · 3/5 Too many steps remain. **Mitigation:** Simplify aggressively.
3. **Operational** · 3/5 Support load rises. **Mitigation:** Use guided automation.
4. **Commercial** · 3/5 Message overpromises. **Mitigation:** Keep claims realistic.
5. **Financial** · 2/5 Cost to deliver. **Mitigation:** Start with scalable wins.

Speed	Effort	Cost	Revenue	Time to cash	Scalability
Medium (1-3 months)	**Medium**	**Low**	**Very High**	**Short**	**High**

Decision-flow: CFO → Product → Customer Success

152. Recover customers by reducing the size of the next

Re-engage inactive customers with a smaller next step instead of asking them to fully recommit immediately.

Why it works

Large commitments create hesitation. Smaller re-entry decisions reduce psychological resistance and restart customer movement.

Best for

Consulting, SaaS, healthcare, education, fitness, financial services, home services, B2B sales

Execution Steps

1. Identify the large recommitment barrier
2. Define a smaller paid or engagement step
3. Make the next action easy
4. Avoid discounting the core offer
5. Build path back to full spend

Real-world example

A consultant offers a short restart session, while a SaaS company offers a small reactivation package before annual renewal.

Risk Management

1. **Commercial** · 3/5 Small step becomes the end. **Mitigation:** Create clear progression.
2. **Financial** · 3/5 Low revenue per return. **Mitigation:** Focus on high-LTV customers.
3. **Customer** · 3/5 Still feels too much. **Mitigation:** Reduce friction further.
4. **Alignment** · 3/5 Sales skips small steps. **Mitigation:** Use clear triggers.
5. **Product** · 3/5 Offer unclear. **Mitigation:** Define scope tightly.

Speed	Effort	Cost	Revenue	Time to cash	Scalability
Fast (0-30 days)	**Low**	**Low**	**High**	**Immediate**	**High**

Decision-flow: CFO → Sales → Customer Success

153. Recover customers by helping them restart after failure

Reconnect with customers who stopped engaging after a failed attempt, bad experience, poor outcome, or unfinished implementation.

Why it works

Customers often abandon solutions after feeling they failed. Helping them restart safely rebuilds trust and unlocks revenue competitors ignore.

Best for

Fitness, education, SaaS, healthcare, consulting, coaching, finance, home improvement

Execution Steps

1. Identify failure-related drop-offs
2. Understand what went wrong
3. Create a safe restart pathway
4. Remove blame from messaging
5. Provide focused support

Real-world example

An education provider helps learners restart after failed exams, while a SaaS firm helps stalled users complete their setup.

Risk Management

1. **Customer** · 4/5 Customer feels blamed. **Mitigation:** Use supportive language.
2. **Operational** · 3/5 Root cause unclear. **Mitigation:** Diagnose before outreach.
3. **Commercial** · 4/5 Trust in the offer is too low to drive adoption without. **Mitigation:** Offer proof and support.
4. **Financial** · 3/5 Support cost. **Mitigation:** Define a strict scope boundary and enforce it from.
5. **Product** · 4/5 Same failure repeats. **Mitigation:** Fix known blockers first.

Speed	Effort	Cost	Revenue	Time to cash	Scalability
Medium (1-3 months)	**Medium**	**Low**	**High**	**Short**	**Medium**

Decision-flow: CFO → Customer Success → Operations

154. Recover customers by translating complexity into plain

Re-engage inactive customers by simplifying confusing terms, reports, instructions, pricing, workflows, or technical language that previously overwhelmed them.

Why it works

Confusion quietly kills engagement. Simplicity restores confidence and reduces the mental burden that caused customers to disengage.

Best for

Healthcare, SaaS, finance, logistics, education, legal, insurance, B2B services

Execution Steps

1. Identify confusing language or workflows
2. Rewrite in plain language
3. Create a simple return explanation
4. Remove jargon from reactivation messages
5. Test clarity with inactive customers

Real-world example

An insurer rewrites complex policy explanations, while a SaaS firm simplifies technical setup instructions for dormant users.

Risk Management

1. **Customer** · 3/5 Still confusing. **Mitigation:** Test with real users.
2. **Alignment** · 3/5 Experts resist simplification. **Mitigation:** Set clarity standard.
3. **Commercial** · 3/5 Value not obvious. **Mitigation:** Connect clarity to action.
4. **Legal /** · 3/5 Oversimplification risk. This creates legal or compliance exposure that must be resolved before launch. **Mitigation:** Review regulated language.
5. **Financial** · 2/5 Low immediate revenue. **Mitigation:** Target large inactive pool.

Speed	Effort	Cost	Revenue	Time to cash	Scalability
Fast (0-30 days)	**Low**	**Low**	**High**	**Immediate**	**High**

Decision-flow: CFO → Product → Marketing

155. Recover customers by reconnecting them to their original goal

Re-engage inactive customers by reminding them what they originally wanted to achieve before distractions, delays, or competing priorities took over.

Why it works

Customers often abandon goals before abandoning desire. Reconnecting them emotionally to the original outcome reactivates motivation and buying intent.

Best for

Fitness, education, healthcare, SaaS, finance, coaching, subscriptions, professional services

Execution Steps

1. Identify the original goal
2. Segment customers by goal type
3. Create goal-based return messages
4. Show the next step toward that goal
5. Remove pressure from the tone

Real-world example

A fitness program reminds users of their original health goal, while a SaaS firm reconnects buyers to the business outcome they first pursued.

Risk Management

1. **Customer** · 3/5 Goal no longer matters. **Mitigation:** Allow goal update.
2. **Commercial** · 3/5 Message too emotional. **Mitigation:** Balance emotion with action.
3. **Product** · 3/5 Next step unclear. **Mitigation:** Provide a clear path.
4. **Financial** · 2/5 Low intent segment. **Mitigation:** Prioritize recent inactivity.
5. **Alignment** · 3/5 Generic messaging. **Mitigation:** Use customer goal data.

Speed	Effort	Cost	Revenue	Time to cash	Scalability
Fast (0-30 days)	**Low**	**Low**	**High**	**Immediate**	**High**

Decision-flow: CFO → Marketing → Customer Success

156. Recover customers by showing them how close they

Reconnect with inactive customers by highlighting how much progress, setup, learning, implementation, or investment they already completed before stopping.

Why it works

People hate wasting effort already invested. Showing customers how close they were creates momentum and reduces restart resistance.

Best for

Education, SaaS, fitness, healthcare, onboarding-heavy services, financial tools, subscriptions

Execution Steps

1. Identify completed progress before drop-off
2. Calculate remaining effort
3. Message how close they are
4. Offer the next small action
5. Preserve their prior work

Real-world example

An online course tells learners they are 80% complete, while a SaaS implementation team shows customers only two setup steps remain.

Risk Management

1. **Product** · 3/5 Progress tracking missing. **Mitigation:** Track key milestones.
2. **Customer** · 3/5 Progress does not feel valuable. **Mitigation:** Show outcome tied to progress.
3. **Commercial** · 3/5 Message feels generic. **Mitigation:** Personalize with specifics.
4. **Operational** · 3/5 Return path hard. **Mitigation:** Link directly to next step.
5. **Financial** · 2/5 Low-value accounts. **Mitigation:** Prioritize high-potential users.

Speed	Effort	Cost	Revenue	Time to cash	Scalability
Fast (0-30 days)	**Low**	**Low**	**High**	**Immediate**	**High**

Decision-flow: CFO → Product → Customer Success

157. Recover customers by making the return feel exclusive

Invite inactive customers back through limited-access return windows, priority re-entry, insider reactivation groups, or early-access restart opportunities.

Why it works

Exclusivity increases perceived value and emotional pull. Customers are more likely to return when re-engagement feels special instead of desperate.

Best for

Memberships, SaaS, luxury services, fitness, education, subscriptions, communities, hospitality

Execution Steps

1. Identify inactive high-value customers
2. Design an exclusive return window
3. Define limited access clearly
4. Message the invite personally
5. Provide a simple re-entry action

Real-world example

A premium club invites lapsed members into a priority return window, while a SaaS product offers inactive users early access to new features.

Risk Management

1. **Customer** · 4/5 Exclusivity feels fake. **Mitigation:** Make the limit real.
2. **Commercial** · 3/5 Wrong customers targeted. **Mitigation:** Use high-value segments.
3. **Financial** · 3/5 The urgency is not strong enough to drive timely purchasing decisions.. **Mitigation:** Set clear deadline.
4. **Market** · 3/5 Desperation signal. **Mitigation:** Position as invitation.
5. **Operational** · 3/5 Capacity pressure. **Mitigation:** Cap volume.

Speed	Effort	Cost	Revenue	Time to cash	Scalability
Fast (0-30 days)	**Low**	**Low**	**High**	**Immediate**	**High**

Decision-flow: CFO → Marketing → Customer Success

158. Recover customers by solving the hidden blocker they

Identify the silent operational, emotional, financial, technical, or organizational reason customers stopped engaging, then remove that blocker directly.

Why it works

Customers rarely explain the true reason they disengaged. Solving the hidden blocker unlocks recovery competitors never address.

Best for

SaaS, healthcare, consulting, education, finance, B2B services, logistics, subscriptions

Execution Steps

1. Analyze drop-off patterns
2. Interview a sample of inactive customers
3. Identify hidden blockers
4. Build blocker-specific return paths
5. Prioritize high-value segments

Real-world example

A SaaS firm discovers inactive accounts lacked internal ownership, while a clinic finds patients stopped because scheduling was too hard.

Risk Management

1. **Customer** · 4/5 Wrong blocker identified. **Mitigation:** Conduct buyer interviews to validate demand before launch investment.
2. **Operational** · 3/5 Fix too broad. **Mitigation:** Start with one blocker.
3. **Commercial** · 3/5 Message misses pain. **Mitigation:** Personalize by blocker.
4. **Product** · 3/5 Data unavailable. **Mitigation:** Combino data and calls.
5. **Financial** · 3/5 Recovery cost too high. **Mitigation:** Focus on high-value accounts.

Speed	Effort	Cost	Revenue	Time to cash	Scalability
Medium (1-3 months)	**Medium**	**Low**	**Very High**	**Short**	**Medium**

Decision-flow: CFO → Customer Success → Operations

159. Recover customers by letting them skip the parts they

Allow returning customers to bypass frustrating steps, unnecessary setup, repeated approvals, or painful workflows that previously caused disengagement.

Why it works

Customers often leave because of one painful section of the experience, not the entire offer. Removing the hated step dramatically lowers re-entry friction.

Best for

Healthcare, SaaS, logistics, education, subscriptions, finance, home services, enterprise tools

Execution Steps

1. Identify the most hated step
2. Confirm it caused drop-off
3. Create a bypass or shortcut
4. Keep core quality protected
5. Message the easier return

Real-world example

A healthcare provider lets returning patients skip repeated intake forms, while a SaaS firm bypasses setup steps for dormant accounts.

Risk Management

1. **Operational** · 4/5 Bypass creates risk. **Mitigation:** Keep essential controls.
2. **Product** · 3/5 Shortcut hard to build. **Mitigation:** Start with manual bypass.
3. **Customer** · 3/5 Wrong step removed. **Mitigation:** Validate with real customers before any significant investment is committed.
4. **Legal** · 4/5 Compliance issue. **Mitigation:** Review regulated steps.
5. **Financial** · 3/5 Cost to maintain shortcut. **Mitigation:** Limit to recovery cases.

Speed	Effort	Cost	Revenue	Time to cash	Scalability
Medium (1-3 months)	**Medium**	**Medium**	**High**	**Short**	**High**

Decision-flow: CFO → Product → Operations

160. Recover customers by reminding them what they already

Reconnect with inactive customers by reminding them of the important decision, data, project, health issue, investment, or responsibility they previously trusted you to handle.

Why it works

Trust already existed once. Reawakening that emotional memory reduces skepticism and shortens the path back to engagement.

Best for

Healthcare, finance, legal, SaaS, consulting, home services, education, professional services

Execution Steps

1. Identify trust-based past relationships
2. Find the original responsibility handled
3. Create a respectful reminder message
4. Link the past trust to today's need
5. Offer a low-friction return action

Real-world example

A financial advisor reminds former clients of prior planning work, while a home services provider reconnects homeowners around previously trusted repairs.

Risk Management

1. **Customer** · 4/5 Feels too personal. **Mitigation:** Use respectful tone.
2. **Legal** · 4/5 Privacy sensitivity. **Mitigation:** Avoid exposing sensitive details.
3. **Commercial** · 3/5 Trust memory weak. **Mitigation:** Use only strong histories.
4. **Market** · 3/5 Customer has moved on. **Mitigation:** Check current relevance.
5. **Alignment** · 3/5 Message generic. **Mitigation:** Personalize carefully.

Speed	Effort	Cost	Revenue	Time to cash	Scalability
Fast (0-30 days)	**Low**	**Low**	**High**	**Immediate**	**High**

Decision-flow: CFO → Marketing → Sales

From Ideas to Action

Twenty-five ideas. Twenty-five ways to recover revenue from lapsed customers, stalled deals, and relationships that went quiet.

Lapsed customers already know the business. They do not need to be convinced from zero. They need a reason to return that acknowledges the gap and makes the first step back feel easy, not awkward.

Before continuing, identify the single idea with the clearest commercial case right now. Name who owns it. Set a date for the first step. That is all that is required.

> *The customer who left is not lost. They are waiting for the right reason to come back.*

What Comes Next

3.4 — Underused Asset Monetization addresses the capacity, inventory, space, tools, and operational assets sitting inside the business generating no external revenue. If something the business already owns is going unused — the next chapter shows how to make it pay.

3.4 — Underused Asset Monetization

Unlock revenue from underused assets, capacity, inventory, capabilities, or commercial advantages already inside the business.

When These Strategies Work Best

Underused asset strategies deliver the fastest return when the business holds real capacity, infrastructure, or commercial advantages it is not currently monetising.

- Equipment, space, or infrastructure sits idle for predictable periods
- Staff expertise or time is available beyond what current demand requires
- Inventory, licences, or operational assets exceed current utilisation rates
- Commercial advantages such as buying power, relationships, or access are not sold
- The business carries the cost of an asset that generates no external revenue

The Benefits

- New revenue from costs already being paid regardless of whether they generate income
- Improved asset efficiency that reduces the effective unit cost of existing operations
- Fast implementation because the asset or capacity already exists
- No new investment required to generate the first dollar of new revenue
- Commercial relationships formed around underused assets that grow into larger deals

The Risks to Manage

- **Core business interference** — monetising spare capacity must not affect primary delivery. Ring-fence clearly.
- **Underpricing** — spare assets are routinely undervalued. Price against market rate, not against your sunk cost.
- **Reliability commitment** — selling access to capacity creates a delivery obligation. Only commit what you can guarantee.
- **Regulatory exposure** — some assets carry licensing or compliance implications when monetised. Check before launch.

161. Sell your empty-time capacity before it disappears

Turn unused staff time, operational downtime, appointment gaps, production slack, or idle service windows into revenue before that capacity is permanently lost.

Why it works

Unused capacity expires every day. Monetizing even part of it creates high-margin revenue from resources the business already pays for.

Best for

Healthcare, logistics, consulting, agencies, manufacturing, fitness, hospitality, professional services

Execution Steps

1. Identify recurring unused time or capacity
2. Define what can be safely sold
3. Set clear rules and communicate them before any access. for access and priority
4. Price by time, slot, or output
5. Protect core customers first

Real-world example

A clinic sells unused appointment blocks, while a manufacturer sells spare production windows to smaller buyers.

Risk Management

1. **Operational** · 5/5 Core work disrupted. **Mitigation:** Protect internal priority.
2. **Customer** · 3/5 Demand from the target segment is insufficient to justify full launch. **Mitigation:** Target urgent capacity buyers.
3. **Commercial** · 3/5 Pricing is set too low to adequately cover the real cost. **Mitigation:** Anchor to access value.
4. **Legal** · 4/5 Legal liability arises if terms, access rules. **Mitigation:** Use specific, plain-language contract terms that eliminate ambiguity.
5. **Alignment** · 3/5 Teams resist extra work. **Mitigation:** Align team and partner incentives with the desired commercial outcome.

Speed	Effort	Cost	Revenue	Time to cash	Scalability
Fast (0-30 days)	**Low**	**Low**	**Very High**	**Immediate**	**High**

Decision-flow: CFO → Operations → Sales

162. Turn internal tools into external revenue

Commercialize internal calculators, dashboards, workflows, templates, systems, scripts, or operational tools already built for internal use.

Why it works

Many businesses accidentally build valuable tools while solving their own problems. External buyers often want the same shortcut without building it themselves.

Best for

SaaS, consulting, logistics, finance, agencies, operations-heavy businesses, healthcare, education

Execution Steps

1. Identify internal tools with external value
2. Remove confidential data
3. Package for customer use
4. Define access and usage rules
5. Price below custom build cost

Real-world example

A logistics firm sells a route-cost calculator, while a finance team licenses an internal planning template to clients.

Risk Management

1. **Product** · 3/5 Tool too internal. **Mitigation:** Simplify for outside users.
2. **Legal** · 4/5 Intellectual property is exposed through unsupervised access or poor usage controls.. **Mitigation:** License usage clearly.
3. **Customer** · 3/5 Low perceived value. **Mitigation:** Quantify the time saved and present it as the.
4. **Operational** · 3/5 Post-launch support demand is higher than planned, straining the delivery team. **Mitigation:** Include a concise usage guide with every deliverable at launch.
5. **Financial** · 3/5 The offer is underpriced relative to the value it creates. **Mitigation:** Benchmark against alternatives.

Speed	Effort	Cost	Revenue	Time to cash	Scalability
Medium (1-3 months)	**Medium**	**Low**	**High**	**Medium**	**High**

Decision-flow: CFO → Product → Operations

163. Monetize customer waiting time

Turn customer wait periods into revenue opportunities through premium upgrades, add-on services, educational moments, convenience offers, or partner monetization.

Why it works

Waiting time is trapped attention. Businesses often ignore monetizable moments customers are already forced to spend inside the experience.

Best for

Healthcare, automotive, hospitality, logistics, airports, salons, education, service businesses

Execution Steps

1. Map where customers wait
2. Identify useful offers during the wait
3. Keep offers relevant. and low-friction
4. Protect the customer experience
5. Price via add-on or partner fee

Real-world example

A clinic offers paid wellness add-ons during waiting time, while an airport service monetizes waiting with premium convenience offers.

Risk Management

1. **Customer** · 4/5 Feels intrusive. **Mitigation:** Keep offers useful.
2. **Market** · 4/5 Trust erodes gradually if the offer does not consistently deliver its. **Mitigation:** Limit low-quality offers.
3. **Commercial** · 3/5 Conversion from initial interest to completed purchase is lower than targeted.. **Mitigation:** Use relevant timing.
4. **Operational** · 3/5 Workflow distraction. **Mitigation:** Keep execution simple.
5. **Legal** · 4/5 Privacy concerns. **Mitigation:** Avoid sensitive targeting.

Speed	Effort	Cost	Revenue	Time to cash	Scalability
Fast (0-30 days)	**Low**	**Low**	**High**	**Immediate**	**Medium**

Decision-flow: CFO → Operations → Partnerships / BD

164. Rent out the expertise sitting idle inside your business

Offer temporary access to specialized staff, operators, analysts, technicians, advisors, or experts during periods where their capacity is underused internally.

Why it works

Many businesses have expensive expertise that is not fully utilized year-round. Externalizing spare expertise creates revenue without major new investment.

Best for

Engineering, healthcare, finance, SaaS, consulting, manufacturing, legal, logistics

Execution Steps

1. Identify underused specialist capacity
2. Define what expertise can be sold externally
3. Set scope and pricing
4. Protect internal priorities
5. Create liability and quality rules

Real-world example

An engineering firm sells expert review hours during quiet periods, while an IT team offers spare support capacity to small firms.

Risk Management

1. **Operational** · 5/5 Internal work impacted. **Mitigation:** Reserve internal capacity as the first priority before offering.
2. **Alignment** · 4/5 Staff resistance. **Mitigation:** Align team and partner incentives with the desired commercial outcome.
3. **Legal** · 4/5 Liability if responsibilities are not documented. **Mitigation:** Use contracts.
4. **Commercial** · 3/5 Demand from the target segment is weaker than projected at launch. **Mitigation:** Target known buyers.
5. **Financial** · 3/5 Margin unclear. **Mitigation:** Price by expertise level.

Speed	Effort	Cost	Revenue	Time to cash	Scalability
Medium (1-3 months)	**Medium**	**Low**	**Very High**	**Short**	**Medium**

Decision-flow: CFO → Operations → HR / People

165. Monetize the trust your business already earned

Generate revenue from the customer trust, credibility, access, or attention your business already has without needing to acquire a new audience.

Why it works

Trust is a commercial asset. Businesses often spend years building attention and credibility but monetize only the core transaction.

Best for

Healthcare, SaaS, finance, education, memberships, retail, hospitality, communities

Execution Steps

1. Identify where customers already trust your recommendations
2. Define safe monetization formats
3. Select relevant partners or offers
4. Set strict quality rules
5. Price access or endorsement carefully

Real-world example

A healthcare platform monetizes trusted recommendations, while a membership group charges relevant partners for approved access.

Risk Management

1. **Market** · 5/5 Customer trust damaged if delivery falls short. **Mitigation:** Only approve high-fit partners.
2. **Legal** · 4/5 Failure to disclose relationships or terms creates a trust and compliance. **Mitigation:** Communicate the basis for all decisions and relationships clearly upfront.
3. **Customer** · 4/5 Perceived selling out. **Mitigation:** Cap the frequency of outreach or placements to prevent customer fatigue.
4. **Commercial** · 3/5 Weak partner fit. **Mitigation:** Screen tightly.
5. **Financial** · 3/5 Underpricing trust. **Mitigation:** Price by conversion value.

Speed	Effort	Cost	Revenue	Time to cash	Scalability
Medium (1-3 months)	**Medium**	**Low**	**Very High**	**Short**	**High**

Decision-flow: CFO → Marketing → Partnerships / BD

166. Sell the unused certainty already inside your process

Turn internal predictability, forecasting accuracy, operational visibility, benchmarking, or planning confidence into something customers can pay to access.

Why it works

Businesses often create valuable certainty internally without realizing customers would pay to reduce their own uncertainty using the same insights.

Best for

Logistics, SaaS, healthcare, manufacturing, finance, construction, retail, operations-heavy businesses

Execution Steps

1. Identify where internal certainty exists
2. Confirm customer uncertainty pain
3. Package visibility or forecasts simply
4. Price based on planning value
5. Protect sensitive information

Real-world example

A logistics firm sells delivery certainty insights, while a manufacturer offers planning visibility to key customers.

Risk Management

1. **Customer** · 3/5 Certainty not valued. **Mitigation:** Target planning-heavy buyers.
2. **Product** · 4/5 Forecast errors. **Mitigation:** Show confidence ranges.
3. **Legal** · 4/5 Sensitive data risk. **Mitigation:** Remove confidential details.
4. **Commercial** · 3/5 Message too abstract. **Mitigation:** Tie to customer decisions.
5. **Financial** · 3/5 Low pricing power. **Mitigation:** Anchor to avoided uncertainty.

Speed	Effort	Cost	Revenue	Time to cash	Scalability
Medium (1-3 months)	**Medium**	**Low**	**Very High**	**Medium**	**High**

Decision-flow: CFO → Operations → Product

167. Turn your operational leftovers into sellable value

Monetize excess outputs, spare materials, partial inventory, abandoned work, unused data, or side-products already created during normal operations.

Why it works

Many businesses accidentally create valuable by-products they ignore because the main business is focused elsewhere. Hidden leftovers can become profitable revenue streams.

Best for

Manufacturing, food, SaaS, healthcare, logistics, retail, construction, agriculture

Execution Steps

1. Identify operational leftovers
2. Check if they have customer value
3. Define safe sale conditions
4. Price below primary output but above disposal value
5. Create simple sales channel

Real-world example

A food producer sells by-products to ingredient buyers, while a SaaS firm repurposes anonymized unused logs into operational insights.

Risk Management

1. **Operational** · 3/5 Quality inconsistency. **Mitigation:** Set standards.
2. **Legal** · 4/5 Usage restrictions. **Mitigation:** Review saleability.
3. **Customer** · 3/5 Demand from the target segment is weaker than projected at launch. **Mitigation:** Test niche buyers.
4. **Market** · 3/5 Perceived low quality. **Mitigation:** Position carefully.
5. **Financial** · 2/5 Margin is insufficient if pricing does not cover the full cost. **Mitigation:** Keep cost minimal.

Speed	Effort	Cost	Revenue	Time to cash	Scalability
Fast (0-30 days)	**Low**	**Low**	**High**	**Immediate**	**Medium**

Decision-flow: CFO → Operations → Operations

168. Monetize the customer traffic you already paid to generate

Generate additional revenue from existing customer traffic, visits, logins, bookings, appointments, deliveries, or interactions already happening inside the business.

Why it works

Most businesses monetize only the primary transaction while ignoring additional value opportunities inside existing customer movement.

Best for

Retail, SaaS, healthcare, hospitality, logistics, memberships, education, e-commerce

Execution Steps

1. Map high-traffic customer moments
2. Identify relevant monetization opportunities
3. Avoid disrupting the main transaction
4. Price by placement, referral, or conversion
5. Test one moment first

Real-world example

A retailer monetizes checkout traffic with relevant services, while a SaaS app surfaces paid partner tools inside active user flows.

Risk Management

1. **Customer** · 4/5 Experience disruption. **Mitigation:** Keep offers relevant.
2. **Market** · 4/5 Trust erodes gradually if the offer does not consistently deliver its. **Mitigation:** Screen offers.
3. **Commercial** · 3/5 Conversion from initial interest to completed purchase is lower than targeted.. **Mitigation:** Use high-intent moments.
4. **Legal** · 4/5 Customer data privacy is at risk if access, anonymisation. **Mitigation:** Avoid data misuse.
5. **Operational** · 3/5 Execution clutter. **Mitigation:** Start with one touchpoint.

Speed	Effort	Cost	Revenue	Time to cash	Scalability
Fast (0-30 days)	**Low**	**Low**	**Very High**	**Immediate**	**High**

Decision-flow: CFO → Marketing → Partnerships / BD

169. Turn your operational downtime into premium access

Use low-demand periods, quiet seasons, unused shifts, or spare operational windows to offer unique access, experiences, production runs, or customer opportunities.

Why it works

Downtime is usually treated as dead time. Reframing it as exclusive availability creates revenue from capacity already sitting idle.

Best for

Manufacturing, hospitality, healthcare, fitness, education, entertainment, logistics, SaaS infrastructure

Execution Steps

1. Identify recurring downtime
2. Define what access can be sold
3. Package downtime as opportunity
4. Price for availability or exclusivity
5. Protect core operating windows

Real-world example

A hotel sells quiet-season corporate retreats, while a manufacturer offers off-peak short production runs.

Risk Management

1. **Commercial** · 3/5 Downtime seen as low value. **Mitigation:** Frame as exclusive access.
2. **Operational** · 4/5 Core scheduling conflict. **Mitigation:** Reserve priority windows.
3. **Customer** · 3/5 Demand from the target segment is weaker than projected at launch. **Mitigation:** Target flexible buyers.
4. **Financial** · 3/5 The offer is underpriced relative to the value it creates. **Mitigation:** Price against access value.
5. **Market** · 3/5 Looks like discounting. **Mitigation:** Avoid cheap positioning.

Speed	Effort	Cost	Revenue	Time to cash	Scalability
Fast (0-30 days)	**Medium**	**Low**	**High**	**Immediate**	**Medium**

Decision-flow: CFO → Operations → Sales

170. Monetize the problems your customers repeatedly ask

Track the recurring questions, frustrations, fixes, shortcuts, or operational challenges customers constantly ask your team to help solve informally.

Why it works

Repeated customer questions signal hidden demand. Businesses often provide valuable guidance for free without realizing customers would pay for structured help.

Best for

SaaS, healthcare, finance, logistics, education, retail, consulting, home services

Execution Steps

1. Collect repeated customer questions
2. Identify which questions signal paid demand
3. Turn answers into structured paid help
4. Keep scope focused
5. Offer to existing customers first

Real-world example

A SaaS firm monetizes repeated workflow questions, while a home services company sells guidance around common homeowner issues.

Risk Management

1. **Customer** · 3/5 Customers expect free answers. **Mitigation:** Separate basic vs advanced help.
2. **Commercial** · 3/5 Demand too scattered. **Mitigation:** Focus on repeated pain.
3. **Operational** · 3/5 Support team overloaded. **Mitigation:** Use structured formats.
4. **Financial** · 3/5 Pricing is set too low to adequately cover the real cost. **Mitigation:** Anchor to time saved.
5. **Product** · 3/5 Solution too generic. **Mitigation:** Build around real questions.

Speed	Effort	Cost	Revenue	Time to cash	Scalability
Medium (1-3 months)	**Medium**	**Low**	**Very High**	**Short**	**High**

Decision-flow: CFO → Customer Success → Product

171. Sell the implementation shortcuts your team already

Turn internal shortcuts, workarounds, best practices, checklists, accelerators, or execution patterns into paid customer-facing assets or services.

Why it works

Experienced teams quietly develop faster ways of getting results. Customers will often pay to skip trial-and-error and reduce implementation friction.

Best for

SaaS, consulting, healthcare, logistics, manufacturing, finance, education, construction

Execution Steps

1. Identify repeat shortcuts used internally
2. Remove sensitive details
3. Package as an accelerator
4. Define use cases and limits
5. Price against time saved.

Real-world example

A SaaS company sells setup accelerators, while a construction firm packages proven project-start shortcuts for clients.

Risk Management

1. **Legal** · 4/5 Intellectual property is exposed through unsupervised access or poor usage controls.. **Mitigation:** Protect proprietary method.
2. **Customer** · 3/5 Shortcut not trusted. **Mitigation:** Show proof.
3. **Operational** · 3/5 Post-launch support demand is higher than planned, straining the delivery team. **Mitigation:** Include a concise usage guide with every deliverable at launch.
4. **Commercial** · 3/5 Too similar to service. **Mitigation:** Define it as asset or accelerator.
5. **Financial** · 3/5 The offer is underpriced relative to the value it creates. **Mitigation:** Price against avoided delay.

Speed	Effort	Cost	Revenue	Time to cash	Scalability
Medium (1-3 months)	**Medium**	**Low**	**Very High**	**Short**	**High**

Decision-flow: CFO → Operations → Product

172. Monetize the unused buying power inside your business

Leverage your purchasing scale, supplier relationships, negotiated rates, or procurement advantages to create customer-facing value or revenue opportunities.

Why it works

Many businesses negotiate better pricing than smaller players ever could. That unused leverage can become a monetizable commercial advantage.

Best for

Retail, hospitality, healthcare, manufacturing, logistics, construction, franchises, multi-site businesses

Execution Steps

1. Identify procurement advantages
2. Confirm supplier permissions
3. Define who can access the advantage
4. Set fees, savings share, or admin charges
5. Protect supplier relationships

Real-world example

A hotel group gives smaller operators paid access to preferred supplier terms, while a contractor monetizes negotiated material rates.

Risk Management

1. **Legal** · 5/5 Supplier restrictions. **Mitigation:** Get approval.
2. **Commercial** · 3/5 Savings too small. **Mitigation:** Prove value.
3. **Operational** · 3/5 Admin burden. **Mitigation:** Simplify ordering.
4. **Market** · 4/5 Relationship risk. **Mitigation:** Protect key suppliers.
5. **Financial** · 3/5 Margin leaks if cost controls and pricing floors are not enforced. **Mitigation:** Set clear fees.

Speed	Effort	Cost	Revenue	Time to cash	Scalability
Medium (1-3 months)	**Medium**	**Low**	**High**	**Short**	**High**

Decision-flow: CFO → Procurement → Partnerships / BD

173. Turn your customer success stories into operational

Reuse successful customer transformations, workflows, setups, playbooks, or before-and-after journeys as monetizable frameworks customers can adopt faster.

Why it works

Businesses repeatedly solve similar problems but rarely package the operational learning. Proven pathways reduce customer uncertainty and speed adoption.

Best for

SaaS, healthcare, consulting, education, fitness, finance, agencies, B2B services

Execution Steps

1. Identify repeated success patterns
2. Remove customer-identifiable details
3. Convert patterns into frameworks
4. Validate with similar customers
5. Price against speed and certainty

Real-world example

A SaaS firm sells a proven workflow path, while a healthcare provider shares paid implementation patterns from successful clinics.

Risk Management

1. **Legal** · 5/5 Confidentiality risk. **Mitigation:** Anonymize fully.
2. **Customer** · 3/5 Framework feels generic. **Mitigation:** Use specific use cases.
3. **Commercial** · 3/5 Willingness to pay is lower than projected for this segment. **Mitigation:** Target high-pain buyers.
4. **Operational** · 3/5 Hard to maintain. **Mitigation:** Update periodically.
5. **Market** · 3/5 Overclaiming success. **Mitigation:** State limits clearly.

Speed	Effort	Cost	Revenue	Time to cash	Scalability
Medium (1-3 months)	**Medium**	**Low**	**High**	**Short**	**High**

Decision-flow: CFO → Customer Success → Marketing

174. Monetize the unused influence of your operational

Generate revenue from the network of suppliers, vendors, installers, partners, operators, or specialists already interacting around your business ecosystem.

Why it works

Businesses often sit at the center of valuable commercial ecosystems without monetizing the coordination power or trusted access they already control.

Best for

Construction, healthcare, logistics, SaaS, retail, hospitality, manufacturing, marketplaces

Execution Steps

1. Map ecosystem participants
2. Identify who wants access to whom
3. Define monetizable connection points
4. Set clear rules and communicate them before any access. and fees
5. Protect neutrality and trust

Real-world example

A construction platform monetizes access between suppliers and contractors, while a healthcare network connects approved specialists to providers.

Risk Management

1. **Market** · 5/5 Customer trust damaged if delivery falls short. **Mitigation:** Curate carefully.
2. **Legal** · 4/5 Conflict risk. **Mitigation:** Disclose relationships.
3. **Commercial** · 3/5 Unit economics are weaker than projected once real delivery costs are measured. **Mitigation:** Set clear fees.
4. **Operational** · 3/5 Coordination burden. **Mitigation:** Start with one tightly defined use case and expand.
5. **Customer** · 4/5 Poor match quality. **Mitigation:** Use standards.

Speed	Effort	Cost	Revenue	Time to cash	Scalability
Medium (1-3 months)	**Medium**	**Low**	**Very High**	**Medium**	**High**

Decision-flow: CFO → Partnerships / BD → Operations

175. Sell access to your spare operational readiness

Monetize underused preparedness, standby capability, backup systems, reserve inventory, emergency responsiveness, or excess operational resilience already maintained internally.

Why it works

Many businesses pay to stay ready for peak demand or risk events. Customers may pay for access to that preparedness without major new investment.

Best for

Healthcare, logistics, cloud infrastructure, manufacturing, security, construction, facilities management, enterprise services

Execution Steps

1. Identify spare readiness capacity
2. Define what customers can access
3. Set limits. and response conditions
4. Price against risk. avoided
5. Protect your own resilience first

Real-world example

A logistics firm sells reserve delivery capability, while a cloud provider monetizes spare resilience capacity for critical clients.

Risk Management

1. **Operational** · 5/5 Core resilience reduced. **Mitigation:** Reserve internal needs first.
2. **Legal** · 4/5 Promise exposure. **Mitigation:** Define conditions.
3. **Commercial** · 3/5 Low perceived need. **Mitigation:** Target high-risk buyers.
4. **Financial** · 4/5 Underpricing readiness. **Mitigation:** Price against risk.
5. **Operational** · 5/5 Overcommitment. **Mitigation:** Cap access.

Speed	Effort	Cost	Revenue	Time to cash	Scalability
Medium (1-3 months)	**Medium**	**Low**	**Very High**	**Medium**	**Medium**

Decision-flow: CFO → Operations → Sales

176. Monetize unused customer access moments

Turn underused moments where customers already interact with you—check-ins, confirmations, reminders, receipts, dashboards, visits, or support touchpoints—into revenue opportunities.

Why it works

Customer access is expensive to create. If customers already pay attention at certain touchpoints, those moments can carry useful offers, partner value, or paid convenience.

Best for

Healthcare, retail, SaaS, hospitality, logistics, education, finance, home services

Execution Steps

1. Map recurring customer access moments
2. Identify underused touchpoints
3. Choose useful monetization formats
4. Protect customer experience
5. Test one moment first

Real-world example

A clinic monetizes appointment reminders with relevant services, while a SaaS dashboard offers paid convenience prompts at active-use moments.

Risk Management

1. **Customer** · 4/5 Feels spammy. **Mitigation:** Use only relevant offers.
2. **Market** · 4/5 Trust erodes gradually if the offer does not consistently deliver its. **Mitigation:** Cap the frequency of outreach or placements to prevent customer fatigue.
3. **Commercial** · 3/5 Weak uptake. **Mitigation:** Test high-intent moments.
4. **Legal** · 4/5 Consent issue. **Mitigation:** Follow permissions.
5. **Operational** · 3/5 Touchpoint clutter. **Mitigation:** Keep version one as simple as possible and add.

Speed	Effort	Cost	Revenue	Time to cash	Scalability
Fast (0-30 days)	**Low**	**Low**	**High**	**Immediate**	**High**

Decision-flow: CFO → Marketing → Operations

177. Turn unused internal benchmarks into customer value

Monetize internal performance benchmarks, cost comparisons, usage averages, timing standards, or operating norms that customers can use to assess themselves.

Why it works

Businesses often know what good looks like internally. Customers will pay for benchmarks that help them see gaps, justify action, or improve decisions.

Best for

SaaS, logistics, healthcare, finance, manufacturing, education, consulting, B2B services

Execution Steps

1. Identify useful internal benchmarks
2. Remove sensitive details
3. Package benchmarks around decisions
4. Explain method clearly
5. Price based on decision value

Real-world example

A logistics company sells delivery benchmarks, while a SaaS platform monetizes workflow-performance norms for enterprise teams.

Risk Management

1. **Product** · 4/5 Benchmark quality weak. **Mitigation:** Clean methodology.
2. **Legal** · 5/5 Customer data privacy is at risk if access, anonymisation. **Mitigation:** Anonymize fully.
3. **Customer** · 3/5 The value delivered is not clearly communicated. **Mitigation:** Tie to decisions.
4. **Commercial** · 3/5 Repeat demand lower than projected at launch. **Mitigation:** Refresh all content, data, and offer elements on a defined schedule.
5. **Market** · 3/5 Method challenged. **Mitigation:** Explain limits.

Speed	Effort	Cost	Revenue	Time to cash	Scalability
Medium (1-3 months)	**Medium**	**Low**	**High**	**Medium**	**High**

Decision-flow: CFO → Operations → Product

178. *Monetize unused supplier attention*

Turn the attention and interest of suppliers, vendors, or partners who want access to your customer base, operations, or purchasing decisions into paid commercial opportunities.

Why it works

Suppliers often want influence and visibility, not just contracts. If your business controls trusted access to buyers or decision points, that attention has monetizable value.

Best for

Retail, hospitality, healthcare, construction, manufacturing, education, logistics, marketplaces

Execution Steps

1. Identify suppliers seeking access
2. Define safe paid access formats
3. Set quality and relevance rules
4. Price by placement, event, or access
5. Protect procurement integrity

Real-world example

A retailer charges suppliers for approved buyer events, while a healthcare group monetizes vetted supplier access to procurement forums.

Risk Management

1. **Legal** · 5/5 A conflict of interest between the business role and the commercial. **Mitigation:** Set transparency rules.
2. **Market** · 4/5 Customer trust damaged if delivery falls short. **Mitigation:** Screen suppliers.
3. **Operational** · 3/5 Supplier pressure. **Mitigation:** Control access.
4. **Customer** · 3/5 Irrelevant offers. **Mitigation:** Keep relevance high.
5. **Financial** · 2/5 Low price. **Mitigation:** Prove access value.

Speed	Effort	Cost	Revenue	Time to cash	Scalability
Fast (0-30 days)	**Low**	**Low**	**High**	**Immediate**	**Medium**

Decision-flow: CFO → Procurement → Partnerships / BD

179. Turn underused service data into customer alerts

Use existing service history, maintenance records, usage patterns, or issue logs to create paid alerts that help customers act before problems or opportunities are missed.

Why it works

The business already holds signals customers cannot easily see. Turning those signals into timely alerts creates value from information already being collected.

Best for

Home services, equipment, SaaS, healthcare, logistics, finance, facilities, industrial services

Execution Steps

1. Identify useful signals in service data
2. Define alert triggers
3. Remove sensitive details
4. Package alerts simply
5. Price against action value

Real-world example

A facilities provider alerts clients to service patterns, while a SaaS firm monetizes usage signals that indicate workflow risk.

Risk Management

1. **Product** · 4/5 False alerts. **Mitigation:** Tune signal thresholds regularly using real performance data.
2. **Customer** · 3/5 Alert fatigue. **Mitigation:** Cap alert frequency to a level that drives action.
3. **Legal** · 4/5 Data sensitivity. **Mitigation:** Protect privacy.
4. **Commercial** · 3/5 The value delivered is not clearly communicated. **Mitigation:** Show use cases.
5. **Product** · 3/5 Data gaps. **Mitigation:** Start with reliable signals.

Speed	Effort	Cost	Revenue	Time to cash	Scalability
Medium (1-3 months)	**Medium**	**Low**	**High**	**Short**	**High**

Decision-flow: CFO → Product → Customer Success

180. Monetize unused brand permission

Generate revenue from the trust and brand permission you already have by allowing carefully selected partners to appear in customer-safe contexts.

Why it works

Not every business can borrow your customer's trust. If customers already accept your recommendations, relevant partner placement can become valuable without new acquisition spend.

Best for

Healthcare, education, finance, retail, hospitality, fitness, memberships, professional services

Execution Steps

1. Identify where brand permission exists
2. Define acceptable partner contexts
3. Set partner standards and approval rules
4. Price trusted placement
5. Cap the frequency of outreach or placements to prevent customer fatigue.

Real-world example

A university allows vetted career partners into student channels, while a health brand permits relevant wellness partners in trusted communications.

Risk Management

1. **Market** · 5/5 Trust erodes gradually if the offer does not consistently deliver its. **Mitigation:** Select partners carefully.
2. **Legal** · 4/5 Disclosure issue. **Mitigation:** Communicate the basis for all decisions and relationships clearly upfront.
3. **Customer** · 4/5 Partners do not align with the business audience, brand. **Mitigation:** Keep high relevance.
4. **Commercial** · 3/5 Underpriced access. **Mitigation:** Price by trust value.
5. **Operational** · 3/5 Too many partners. **Mitigation:** Cap volume.

Speed	Effort	Cost	Revenue	Time to cash	Scalability
Medium (1-3 months)	**Medium**	**Low**	**High**	**Short**	**Medium**

Decision-flow: CFO → Marketing → Partnerships / BD

181. Turn your business into the control tower of your ecosystem

Monetize the operational visibility, coordination power, and decision influence your business already has across suppliers, customers, vendors, partners, and workflows.

Why it works

Businesses sitting at the center of fragmented ecosystems often control more information and coordination than they realize. Becoming the operational control layer creates massive monetization power.

Best for

Logistics, healthcare, construction, SaaS, manufacturing, finance, procurement, infrastructure

Execution Steps

1. Map the ecosystem around your operations
2. Identify coordination pain points
3. Define what visibility or coordination you control
4. Create paid access or coordination rules
5. Protect neutrality and data

Real-world example

A logistics platform sells coordination visibility across carriers, while a construction operator monetizes supplier and project coordination.

Risk Management

1. **Legal** · 4/5 Neutrality concerns. **Mitigation:** Set governance rules.
2. **Product** · 5/5 Sensitive information. **Mitigation:** Restrict data access.
3. **Operational** · 4/5 Coordination complexity. **Mitigation:** Start with narrow scope.
4. **Commercial** · 3/5 Value hard to explain. **Mitigation:** Tie to delays avoided.
5. **Market** · 4/5 Trust risk. **Mitigation:** Communicate the basis for all decisions and relationships clearly upfront.

Speed	Effort	Cost	Revenue	Time to cash	Scalability
Medium (1-3 months)	**High**	**Medium**	**Very High**	**Medium**	**High**

Decision-flow: CFO → Operations → Partnerships / BD

182. *Monetize the decisions customers already ask you to make*

Identify where customers already rely on your recommendations, judgment, rankings, approvals, shortlists, or operational preferences, then commercialize that influence carefully.

Why it works

Many businesses already shape customer decisions informally. Formalizing trusted influence turns invisible commercial power into measurable revenue.

Best for

Healthcare, SaaS, finance, construction, education, logistics, procurement-heavy industries, professional services

Execution Steps

1. Identify decision-influence points
2. Define ethical monetization boundaries
3. Set partner quality rules
4. Price influence access carefully
5. Disclose relationships. where needed

Real-world example

A procurement advisor monetizes approved supplier shortlists, while a software platform charges partners for vetted recommendation positions.

Risk Management

1. **Legal** · 5/5 A conflict of interest between the business role and the commercial. **Mitigation:** Use disclosure and rules.
2. **Market** · 5/5 Customer trust damaged if delivery falls short. **Mitigation:** Protect customer interest.
3. **Commercial** · 4/5 Partners use brand, content. **Mitigation:** Set usage limits.
4. **Customer** · 4/5 Perceived bias. **Mitigation:** Maintain relevance.
5. **Operational** · 3/5 Review burden. **Mitigation:** Cap partners.

Speed	Effort	Cost	Revenue	Time to cash	Scalability
Fast (0-30 days)	**Medium**	**Low**	**Very High**	**Immediate**	**Medium**

Decision-flow: CFO → Sales → Partnerships / BD

183. Turn operational waste into a premium customer

Convert excess inventory, spare production runs, canceled capacity, dormant resources, or underused operational assets into high-value customer opportunities instead of internal waste.

Why it works

Operational waste is often trapped value. Reframing waste as exclusive customer advantage can unlock large revenue with minimal new investment.

Best for

Manufacturing, hospitality, healthcare, logistics, retail, cloud infrastructure, food, education

Execution Steps

1. Identify waste with potential customer value
2. Reframe it as exclusive access or advantage
3. Define scope, access, and usage limits in writing before launch. and availability
4. Price above liquidation value
5. Promote to relevant customers

Real-world example

A hotel sells canceled premium room blocks as corporate retreat windows, while a manufacturer sells spare run capacity as limited custom access.

Risk Management

1. **Market** · 3/5 Looks like dumping. **Mitigation:** Position as exclusive opportunity.
2. **Customer** · 3/5 Weak perceived value. **Mitigation:** Target right users.
3. **Operational** · 4/5 Core operations are disrupted when external demand competes for the same. **Mitigation:** Protect normal operations.
4. **Financial** · 3/5 The offer is underpriced relative to the value it creates. **Mitigation:** Avoid clearance mindset.
5. **Commercial** · 3/5 Demand inconsistent. **Mitigation:** Use time-bound offers to create urgency without manufactured pressure.

Speed	Effort	Cost	Revenue	Time to cash	Scalability
Fast (0-30 days)	**Medium**	**Low**	**Very High**	**Immediate**	**Medium**

Decision-flow: CFO → Operations → Sales

184. Monetize the operational speed competitors cannot match

Generate premium revenue from faster execution, response, deployment, turnaround, fulfillment, onboarding, or recovery capability already built into the business.

Why it works

Speed is an underpriced asset. Customers often pay far more to remove delays than businesses realize, especially in high-friction industries.

Best for

Healthcare, logistics, SaaS, manufacturing, finance, legal, construction, enterprise services

Execution Steps

1. Identify speed advantages already built
2. Define what customers can buy faster
3. Set premium price for speed
4. Protect standard delivery quality
5. Cap fast-track capacity

Real-world example

A logistics firm monetizes same-day routing advantage, while a SaaS company charges for accelerated deployment capability already available internally.

Risk Management

1. **Operational** · 5/5 Core service suffers. **Mitigation:** Allocate a defined capacity block and do not allow.
2. **Customer** · 3/5 Speed value unclear. **Mitigation:** Show delay cost.
3. **Commercial** · 4/5 Overpromising. **Mitigation:** Cap volume.
4. **Financial** · 3/5 Underpricing speed. **Mitigation:** Price against urgency.
5. **Market** · 3/5 Fairness concern. **Mitigation:** Maintain baseline.

Speed	Effort	Cost	Revenue	Time to cash	Scalability
Fast (0-30 days)	**Low**	**Low**	**Very High**	**Immediate**	**High**

Decision-flow: CFO → Operations → Sales

185. Turn your installed customer base into infrastructure

Use your existing customer network, installed footprint, operational presence, or deployed systems as a monetizable platform others can plug into.

Why it works

Large installed bases create hidden infrastructure value. Businesses often own distribution, visibility, trust, and operational reach they never fully monetize.

Best for

SaaS, logistics, healthcare, telecom, retail, industrial services, finance, enterprise platforms

Execution Steps

1. Map the installed base or footprint
2. Identify who would pay to access it
3. Define safe plug-in options
4. Set commercial and quality rules
5. Protect customer trust and operations

Real-world example

A telecom provider monetizes its installed network footprint, while a SaaS platform lets partners plug into its enterprise customer base under strict rules.

Risk Management

1. **Market** · 5/5 Customer trust risk. This reduces confidence and increases the likelihood of churn. **Mitigation:** Approve only high-fit access.
2. **Legal** · 5/5 Data and consent risk. **Mitigation:** Set strict boundaries.
3. **Operational** · 4/5 Platform strain. **Mitigation:** Limit early pilots.
4. **Commercial** · 4/5 Partners do not align with the business audience, brand. **Mitigation:** Screen carefully.
5. **Financial** · 3/5 Underpricing infrastructure. **Mitigation:** Price by strategic value.

Speed	Effort	Cost	Revenue	Time to cash	Scalability
Medium (1-3 months)	**High**	**Medium**	**Very High**	**Medium**	**High**

Decision-flow: CFO → PMO / Strategy → Partnerships / BD

From Ideas to Action

Twenty-five ideas. Twenty-five ways to turn idle capacity, unused inventory, and operational assets into active revenue.

Every asset on this list is already paid for. The cost is sunk. Revenue from unused capacity is pure margin — there is no acquisition cost, no new customer to find, no product to build. There is only the decision to ask whether someone else can use what sits idle.

Before continuing, identify the single idea with the clearest commercial case right now. Name who owns it. Set a date for the first step. That is all that is required.

> ***Idle capacity is a cost. Used capacity is revenue. The gap between them is a decision.***

What Comes Next

3.5 — Bundling & Packaging addresses businesses whose offers are solid but whose packaging creates friction, confusion, or missed revenue. If the way value is grouped and presented is holding back what customers buy — the next chapter is where the structure gets fixed.

3.5 — Bundling & Packaging

Unlock revenue by changing how existing value is grouped, framed, simplified, or presented for purchase.

When These Strategies Work Best

Bundling and packaging strategies work best when the business already has strong individual offers but the way they are presented creates friction, confusion, or missed revenue.

- Customers regularly buy only one item from a range they would benefit from using together
- The buying decision involves too many separate choices that slow or stop commitment
- The same components are sold piecemeal when most customers need most of them
- Revenue per transaction is consistently lower than the value the customer actually receives
- Competitors with simpler packaging win deals that the business should be closing

The Benefits

- Higher average transaction value without new products or new customers
- Faster buying decisions through reduced choice complexity
- Better customer outcomes when the full solution is bought rather than partial components
- Improved margin through value-anchored bundle pricing versus item-by-item comparison
- A cleaner commercial conversation when the offer structure is clear and easy to explain

The Risks to Manage

- **Forced bundling** — customers who only need one item resent paying for more. Keep unbundled options available.
- **Margin dilution** — bundles priced below the sum of parts can erode revenue. Model carefully before launch.
- **Complexity creep** — bundles that try to solve everything solve nothing. Keep the structure simple and purposeful.
- **Cannibalisation** — bundles should add revenue, not redirect existing purchases. Track net impact from launch.

186. Turn many small painful decisions into one easy yes

Combine fragmented products, services, approvals, steps, or purchases into one packaged decision customers can buy quickly with lower mental friction.

Why it works

Customers often delay because buying feels complicated. Simpler packaged decisions increase conversion, speed, and total spend without changing the underlying value.

Best for

Healthcare, SaaS, consulting, retail, logistics, education, hospitality, home services

Execution Steps

1. Identify where customers face too many decisions
2. Group the required items or steps
3. Remove unnecessary options
4. Name the package clearly
5. Price for simplicity and total value

Real-world example

A clinic packages consultation, tests, and follow-up into one decision, while a SaaS firm packages setup steps into one launch package.

Risk Management

1. **Customer** · 4/5 Package still feels complex. **Mitigation:** Cut options aggressively.
2. **Commercial** · 3/5 Weak perceived value. **Mitigation:** Show decision time saved.
3. **Operational** · 4/5 Missing required components. **Mitigation:** Map the full journey.
4. **Financial** · 3/5 Underpriced package. **Mitigation:** Price against complete outcome.
5. **Alignment** · 3/5 Sales explains it inconsistently. **Mitigation:** Use one clear pitch.

Speed	Effort	Cost	Revenue	Time to cash	Scalability
Fast (0-30 days)	**Low**	**Low**	**Very High**	**Immediate**	**High**

Decision-flow: CFO → Sales → Product

187. Package the full outcome instead of selling the pieces

Bundle all required components, services, tools, support, or steps into one packaged outcome customers can achieve faster and more confidently.

Why it works

Customers buy outcomes, not internal company components. Packaging the complete result removes uncertainty and increases willingness to buy.

Best for

Healthcare, SaaS, construction, consulting, fitness, education, home improvement, finance

Execution Steps

1. Define the complete customer outcome
2. List every component needed
3. Remove unnecessary line-item decisions
4. Create one outcome package
5. Price around result value

Real-world example

A home improvement firm packages inspection, materials, installation, and support, while a SaaS firm packages all launch essentials.

Risk Management

1. **Operational** · 4/5 Scope gaps. **Mitigation:** Map outcome thoroughly.
2. **Financial** · 4/5 Margin leaks if cost controls and pricing floors are not enforced. **Mitigation:** Model full delivery cost.
3. **Customer** · 3/5 Outcome promise unclear. **Mitigation:** Define deliverables clearly.
4. **Commercial** · 3/5 Package feels expensive. **Mitigation:** Anchor to complete result.
5. **Alignment** · 3/5 Teams protect silos. **Mitigation:** Align owners upfront.

Speed	Effort	Cost	Revenue	Time to cash	Scalability
Medium (1-3 months)	**Medium**	**Low**	**Very High**	**Short**	**High**

Decision-flow: CFO → Product → Operations

188. Turn customer confusion into premium packaged clarity

Bundle complexity, choices, comparisons, setup, prioritization, or planning into a simplified package that removes customer overwhelm.

Why it works

Confused customers delay purchases. Packaging clarity itself becomes valuable because it reduces stress, time, and fear of making the wrong decision.

Best for

Finance, SaaS, healthcare, education, insurance, retail, consulting, legal services

Execution Steps

1. Identify confusing buying moments
2. Group decisions into a clear path
3. Remove jargon and complexity
4. Package clarity as the value
5. Train teams to sell simplicity

Real-world example

An insurer packages plan selection into a clear buyer path, while a software firm packages confusing setup choices into one recommendation path.

Risk Management

1. **Customer** · 3/5 Clarity not strong enough. **Mitigation:** Test with confused buyers.
2. **Commercial** · 3/5 Seems like free advice. **Mitigation:** Attach to purchase value.
3. **Operational** · 3/5 Package lacks structure. **Mitigation:** Create a fixed flow.
4. **Legal** · 3/5 Oversimplification risk. **Mitigation:** Review regulated wording.
5. **Financial** · 2/5 Low price ceiling. **Mitigation:** Tie to decision speed.

Speed	Effort	Cost	Revenue	Time to cash	Scalability
Fast (0-30 days)	**Low**	**Low**	**High**	**Immediate**	**High**

Decision-flow: CFO → Marketing → Customer Success

189. Bundle speed, certainty, and convenience into one

Combine faster delivery, easier execution, reduced coordination, and lower customer effort into one high-value premium packaged offer.

Why it works

Customers often pay more to reduce friction than to gain extra features. Convenience and certainty are highly monetizable when packaged together.

Best for

Healthcare, logistics, SaaS, legal, finance, hospitality, enterprise services, construction

Execution Steps

1. Identify friction customers hate
2. Combine speed, certainty, and convenience elements
3. Define service boundaries
4. Price as a premium package
5. Protect standard delivery

Real-world example

A legal firm packages faster review, fewer handoffs, and status updates, while a logistics firm packages faster delivery with proactive visibility.

Risk Management

1. **Operational** · 5/5 Core service disruption. **Mitigation:** Allocate a defined capacity block and do not allow.
2. **Commercial** · 3/5 Premium value unclear. **Mitigation:** Show friction removed.
3. **Customer** · 3/5 Fairness concerns. **Mitigation:** Protect the standard service baseline before adding any premium tier.
4. **Financial** · 3/5 Underpricing convenience. **Mitigation:** Price against time saved.
5. **Alignment** · 4/5 Teams overpromise. **Mitigation:** Set delivery limits.

Speed	Effort	Cost	Revenue	Time to cash	Scalability
Fast (0-30 days)	**Medium**	**Low**	**Very High**	**Immediate**	**High**

Decision-flow: CFO → Operations → Sales

190. Turn fragmented customer spending into one larger

Combine multiple smaller recurring purchases, approvals, vendors, or service interactions into one integrated packaged relationship.

Why it works

Fragmented spending hides the true value customers already consume. Packaging it together increases visibility, stickiness, and total commercial size.

Best for

B2B services, healthcare, SaaS, logistics, facilities, education, hospitality, finance

Execution Steps

1. Identify fragmented spend patterns
2. Group related purchases into one package
3. Create one price and relationship owner
4. Show total value consumed
5. Move customers into packaged commitment

Real-world example

A facilities firm consolidates recurring small jobs into one package, while a SaaS firm combines repeated service requests into one account package.

Risk Management

1. **Customer** · 3/5 Commitment feels too large. **Mitigation:** Show existing spend baseline.
2. **Financial** · 3/5 Package discount pressure. **Mitigation:** Protect margin floors.
3. **Commercial** · 4/5 Stakeholders fragmented. **Mitigation:** Map all buyers.
4. **Operational** · 3/5 Delivery coordination. **Mitigation:** Assign one owner.
5. **Alignment** · 3/5 Sales misclassifies accounts. **Mitigation:** Use spend data.

Speed	Effort	Cost	Revenue	Time to cash	Scalability
Medium (1-3 months)	**Medium**	**Low**	**Very High**	**Short**	**High**

Decision-flow: CFO → Sales → Customer Success

191. Bundle risk reduction into the offer itself

Package guarantees, safeguards, support, monitoring, backup options, recovery paths, or contingency planning directly into the buying experience.

Why it works

Customers hesitate when risk feels unclear. Packaging reassurance directly into the offer increases confidence and accelerates purchase decisions.

Best for

Healthcare, SaaS, finance, logistics, construction, consulting, enterprise services, home services

Execution Steps

1. Identify risk points in the buying journey
2. Choose practical safeguards
3. Bundle them into the offer
4. Define scope, access, and usage limits in writing before launch. and exclusions
5. Communicate reassurance clearly

Real-world example

A construction firm packages contingency planning into projects, while a SaaS vendor packages backup and support into launch offers.

Risk Management

1. **Legal** · 5/5 Promise too broad. **Mitigation:** Define exclusions clearly.
2. **Financial** · 4/5 Safeguards underpriced. **Mitigation:** Model expected cost.
3. **Customer** · 3/5 Risk still unclear. **Mitigation:** Explain protections simply.
4. **Operational** · 3/5 Delivery burden. **Mitigation:** Standardize safeguards.
5. **Commercial** · 3/5 Looks like insurance. **Mitigation:** Position as confidence.

Speed	Effort	Cost	Revenue	Time to cash	Scalability
Fast (0-30 days)	**Medium**	**Low**	**Very High**	**Immediate**	**High**

Decision-flow: CFO → Operations → Sales

192. Turn do-it-yourself customers into packaged guided

Bundle guidance, templates, shortcuts, checkpoints, reviews, or operational support around customers already trying to solve the problem themselves.

Why it works

Many customers want progress without fully outsourcing. Guided packaging creates higher-value purchases without requiring full-service delivery.

Best for

Education, SaaS, finance, fitness, healthcare, legal, consulting, home improvement

Execution Steps

1. Identify DIY customers who get stuck
2. Add guidance and checkpoints
3. Package support without full delivery
4. Price below full-service alternatives
5. Make the path easy to follow

Real-world example

A fitness brand packages self-training with expert check-ins, while a SaaS firm packages self-setup with review checkpoints.

Risk Management

1. **Customer** · 3/5 Customers expect free help. **Mitigation:** Define paid guidance clearly.
2. **Operational** · 3/5 Support scope creeps. **Mitigation:** Limit checkpoints.
3. **Commercial** · 3/5 The offer lacks clear differentiation from what competitors or alternatives provide. **Mitigation:** Show faster progress.
4. **Financial** · 3/5 Too cheap. **Mitigation:** Anchor below full service.
5. **Product** · 3/5 Templates too generic. **Mitigation:** Customize by use case.

Speed	Effort	Cost	Revenue	Time to cash	Scalability
Medium (1-3 months)	**Low**	**Low**	**High**	**Short**	**High**

Decision-flow: CFO → Product → Customer Success

193. Package the first 90% so customers stop getting stuck

Bundle the most difficult early setup, implementation, planning, onboarding, or activation stages into one simplified package customers can complete quickly.

Why it works

Most customers fail early, not late. Packaging the hardest starting stages dramatically improves adoption and purchase confidence.

Best for

SaaS, healthcare, education, finance, logistics, fitness, enterprise software, construction

Execution Steps

1. Identify where customers get stuck early
2. Package the critical starting steps
3. Remove non-essential tasks
4. Create a fast activation path
5. Price for reduced failure risk

Real-world example

A software firm packages the first setup milestones, while a healthcare provider packages intake, testing, and first plan into one start package.

Risk Management

1. **Product** · 4/5 Wrong starting steps. **Mitigation:** Use drop-off data.
2. **Operational** · 3/5 Delivery capacity becomes strained as demand scales beyond the initial pilot.. **Mitigation:** Standardize the path.
3. **Customer** · 3/5 Early package still heavy. **Mitigation:** Simplify further.
4. **Commercial** · 3/5 Value not obvious. **Mitigation:** Show success rate improvement.
5. **Financial** · 3/5 Margin risk. **Mitigation:** Model support cost.

Speed	Effort	Cost	Revenue	Time to cash	Scalability
Medium (1-3 months)	**Medium**	**Low**	**Very High**	**Short**	**High**

Decision-flow: CFO → Product → Operations

194. Turn scattered expertise into one packaged command

Bundle multiple fragmented experts, departments, vendors, or service layers into one coordinated customer-facing experience.

Why it works

Customers hate managing fragmentation themselves. Packaging coordination creates major value because it reduces stress, delay, and operational complexity.

Best for

Healthcare, construction, finance, enterprise services, logistics, legal, consulting, facilities management

Execution Steps

1. Identify fragmented expertise customers manage
2. Define one command-center experience
3. Assign coordination ownership
4. Set communication and escalation rules
5. Price for coordination value

Real-world example

A hospital packages multiple specialists into one care coordination package, while a construction firm packages vendor coordination into one client layer.

Risk Management

1. **Operational** · 5/5 Coordination complexity. **Mitigation:** Start with narrow use cases.
2. **Financial** · 4/5 Cost overrun. **Mitigation:** Price for coordination load.
3. **Customer** · 3/5 Role confusion. **Mitigation:** Define one front door.
4. **Alignment** · 4/5 Teams resist coordination. **Mitigation:** Assign clear owner.
5. **Legal** · 3/5 Vendor liability. **Mitigation:** Set explicit boundaries on scope and ownership before delivery begins.

Speed	Effort	Cost	Revenue	Time to cash	Scalability
Medium (1-3 months)	**High**	**Medium**	**Very High**	**Medium**	**Medium**

Decision-flow: CFO → Operations → Customer Success

195. Bundle recurring customer problems into one peace-of-mind package

Combine multiple recurring frustrations, maintenance tasks, operational headaches, or customer concerns into one simplified recurring package.

Why it works

Customers often pay more to stop worrying than to gain features. Packaging ongoing relief creates sticky, high-value customer relationships.

Best for

Home services, SaaS, healthcare, logistics, finance, IT services, facilities, automotive

Execution Steps

1. Identify recurring customer worries
2. Group related relief items
3. Define package frequency and scope
4. Price for peace of mind
5. Sell after repeated issues

Real-world example

A home services firm packages seasonal checks and reminders, while an IT provider packages recurring security and maintenance tasks.

Risk Management

1. **Customer** · 3/5 Value feels vague. **Mitigation:** Name the worries removed.
2. **Operational** · 4/5 Over-servicing. **Mitigation:** Set limits.
3. **Financial** · 3/5 Margin leaks if cost controls and pricing floors are not enforced. **Mitigation:** Monitor usage.
4. **Commercial** · 3/5 Looks like warranty. **Mitigation:** Position as relief package.
5. **Alignment** · 3/5 Support teams overdeliver. **Mitigation:** Use service rules.

Speed	Effort	Cost	Revenue	Time to cash	Scalability
Fast (0-30 days)	**Medium**	**Low**	**Very High**	**Immediate**	**High**

Decision-flow: CFO → Customer Success → Operations

196. Package decision fatigue removal as the premium offer

Bundle selection, prioritization, sequencing, coordination, and execution choices into one simplified package where the customer no longer has to figure everything out alone.

Why it works

Customers are overwhelmed by constant decisions. Removing mental load itself becomes highly valuable and increases conversion speed.

Best for

Healthcare, SaaS, finance, consulting, education, logistics, legal, home services

Execution Steps

1. Identify decision-heavy journeys
2. Choose what decisions to remove
3. Package recommended paths
4. Make the choice architecture simple
5. Price for mental load removed

Real-world example

A legal firm packages recommended next steps, while an education provider packages course selection into one guided path.

Risk Management

1. **Customer** · 3/5 Customer wants control. **Mitigation:** Allow limited choices.
2. **Commercial** · 3/5 Value hard to explain. **Mitigation:** Use time and stress framing.
3. **Product** · 4/5 Recommendations weak. **Mitigation:** Use proven paths.
4. **Operational** · 3/5 Hard to personalize. **Mitigation:** Start with common profiles.
5. **Financial** · 3/5 Willingness to pay is lower than projected for this segment. **Mitigation:** Target overwhelmed buyers.

Speed	Effort	Cost	Revenue	Time to cash	Scalability
Fast (0-30 days)	**Medium**	**Low**	**Very High**	**Immediate**	**High**

Decision-flow: CFO → Product → Customer Success

197. Turn optional extras into a complete packaged standard

Bundle the most commonly selected add-ons, support layers, accessories, or operational extras into a new default package customers naturally choose.

Why it works

Customers repeatedly buying the same extras signals hidden package demand. Pre-grouping them increases average order size and simplifies buying.

Best for

Retail, SaaS, automotive, healthcare, hospitality, construction, electronics, B2B services

Execution Steps

1. Identify the most common extras
2. Group high-fit extras into one package
3. Make it the recommended option
4. Protect the base offer
5. Train teams to present the standard

Real-world example

An electronics retailer packages device, case, setup, and support, while a SaaS firm packages common add-ons into a standard business tier.

Risk Management

1. **Customer** · 3/5 Package feels inflated. **Mitigation:** Include only common extras.
2. **Financial** · 3/5 Margin leaks if cost controls and pricing floors are not enforced. **Mitigation:** Model each component.
3. **Commercial** · 3/5 The new offer cannibalizes existing higher-margin revenue if segmentation is not. **Mitigation:** Keep base available.
4. **Operational** · 3/5 Fulfillment complexity. **Mitigation:** Standardize contents.
5. **Product** · 3/5 Wrong extras included. **Mitigation:** Use purchase data.

Speed	Effort	Cost	Revenue	Time to cash	Scalability
Fast (0-30 days)	**Low**	**Low**	**Very High**	**Immediate**	**High**

Decision-flow: CFO → Sales → Product

198. Bundle implementation failure prevention into the purchase

Package setup guidance, accountability, checkpoints, reviews, reminders, operational oversight, or recovery support directly into the initial purchase experience.

Why it works

Many customers fail not because the solution is bad, but because execution collapses. Packaging success support increases completion and customer confidence.

Best for

SaaS, healthcare, fitness, education, consulting, finance, enterprise services, construction

Execution Steps

1. Identify why customers fail after purchase
2. Package preventive checkpoints
3. Add automated reminders at key milestones to prevent drop-off. and accountability
4. Define support limits
5. Price into the purchase package

Real-world example

A course provider packages accountability checkpoints, while a SaaS firm packages launch reviews and milestone reminders.

Risk Management

1. **Operational** · 4/5 Support burden grows. **Mitigation:** Limit touchpoints.
2. **Customer** · 3/5 Feels like extra cost. **Mitigation:** Show failure avoided.
3. **Product** · 4/5 Wrong failure points. **Mitigation:** Use drop-off data.
4. **Financial** · 3/5 Underpriced support. **Mitigation:** Model service effort.
5. **Alignment** · 3/5 Teams treat it as free support. **Mitigation:** Clarify scope.

Speed	Effort	Cost	Revenue	Time to cash	Scalability
Medium (1-3 months)	**Medium**	**Low**	**Very High**	**Short**	**High**

Decision-flow: CFO → Customer Success → Operations

199. Turn fragmented vendor coordination into one packaged

Bundle communication, scheduling, tracking, approvals, coordination, and issue management across multiple providers into one simplified customer-facing package.

Why it works

Customers hate acting as the project manager between vendors. Packaging coordination creates massive perceived value without necessarily changing the core services.

Best for

Construction, healthcare, logistics, legal, enterprise services, events, facilities, IT services

Execution Steps

1. Identify vendor coordination pain
2. Define what coordination includes
3. Create one customer-facing package
4. Set vendor communication rules
5. Price for coordination burden removed

Real-world example

An events firm packages vendor coordination, while a facilities provider bundles scheduling and issue management across contractors.

Risk Management

1. **Operational** · 5/5 Vendor complexity. **Mitigation:** Start with limited vendor set.
2. **Legal** · 4/5 Liability ambiguity. **Mitigation:** Define responsibility boundaries.
3. **Customer** · 4/5 Expectations too high. **Mitigation:** Set coordination scope.
4. **Financial** · 4/5 Cost overrun. **Mitigation:** Price by complexity.
5. **Alignment** · 3/5 Unclear owner. **Mitigation:** Assign coordinator role.

Speed	Effort	Cost	Revenue	Time to cash	Scalability
Medium (1-3 months)	**High**	**Medium**	**Very High**	**Medium**	**Medium**

Decision-flow: CFO → Operations → Partnerships / BD

200. Package certainty of outcome instead of quantity of deliverables

Bundle operational confidence, execution assurance, oversight, guidance, quality control, and progress visibility into one outcome-focused package.

Why it works

Customers often care less about features than confidence the result will actually happen. Packaging certainty changes how value is perceived.

Best for

Healthcare, SaaS, consulting, finance, logistics, legal, education, enterprise services

Execution Steps

1. Define the outcome customers want
2. Identify certainty-building components
3. Package oversight and visibility
4. Avoid feature-led selling
5. Price for confidence created

Real-world example

A consulting firm packages progress visibility and quality review, while a SaaS provider packages success oversight instead of more features.

Risk Management

1. **Customer** · 4/5 Certainty promise vague. **Mitigation:** Define what certainty means.
2. **Legal** · 4/5 Overpromise risk. **Mitigation:** Avoid guarantees unless controlled.
3. **Operational** · 3/5 Oversight burden. **Mitigation:** Set review cadence.
4. **Commercial** · 3/5 Sales reverts to features. **Mitigation:** Train outcome messaging.
5. **Financial** · 3/5 Underpricing confidence. **Mitigation:** Anchor to outcome value.

Speed	Effort	Cost	Revenue	Time to cash	Scalability
Medium (1-3 months)	**Medium**	**Low**	**Very High**	**Short**	**High**

Decision-flow: CFO → Sales → Customer Success

201. Bundle nothing gets forgotten into the customer

Package reminders, tracking, follow-through, deadlines, approvals, renewals, checkpoints, and operational follow-up into one reliability-focused customer package.

Why it works

Customers lose money, time, and trust when things slip through cracks. Packaging operational memory creates massive perceived reliability and relief.

Best for

Healthcare, finance, legal, SaaS, logistics, education, construction, enterprise services

Execution Steps

1. Identify customer follow-up failures
2. Bundle reminders and tracking
3. Assign responsibility for follow-through
4. Package reliability as the value
5. Add simple visibility for customers

Real-world example

A legal firm packages deadline tracking, while a healthcare provider packages appointment, test, and follow-up reminders.

Risk Management

1. **Operational** · 5/5 Follow-through fails. **Mitigation:** Use clear owners.
2. **Customer** · 3/5 Seems basic. **Mitigation:** Show consequences avoided.
3. **Product** · 3/5 Tracking gaps. **Mitigation:** Use simple tools first.
4. **Financial** · 3/5 Underpriced reliability. **Mitigation:** Price against avoided misses.
5. **Alignment** · 3/5 Teams ignore process. **Mitigation:** Add accountability.

Speed	Effort	Cost	Revenue	Time to cash	Scalability
Fast (0-30 days)	**Medium**	**Low**	**Very High**	**Immediate**	**High**

Decision-flow: CFO → Operations → Customer Success

202. Turn figuring it out into a packaged shortcut

Bundle proven pathways, recommended sequences, implementation order, operational logic, and simplified execution into one packaged shortcut customers can immediately follow.

Why it works

Customers waste huge amounts of energy trying to determine the right path. Packaging proven direction dramatically reduces hesitation and failure.

Best for

Education, SaaS, finance, consulting, healthcare, construction, logistics, fitness

Execution Steps

1. Identify where customers struggle to choose a path
2. Create proven sequences
3. Package the shortcut clearly
4. Add simple instructions
5. Price for time and error avoided

Real-world example

A construction firm packages project sequencing, while an education provider packages the best learning pathway for common goals.

Risk Management

1. **Customer** · 3/5 Path not trusted. **Mitigation:** Show proof. and logic
2. **Product** · 3/5 The offer is too generic to create meaningful value for any. **Mitigation:** Build by use case.
3. **Operational** · 2/5 Hard to maintain. **Mitigation:** Review periodically.
4. **Commercial** · 3/5 Value understated. **Mitigation:** Show mistakes avoided.
5. **Financial** · 2/5 Low price ceiling. **Mitigation:** Attach to bigger purchase.

Speed	Effort	Cost	Revenue	Time to cash	Scalability
Medium (1-3 months)	**Low**	**Low**	**High**	**Short**	**High**

Decision-flow: CFO → Product → Customer Success

203. Package operational calm as the premium experience

Bundle proactive communication, visibility, predictability, issue prevention, coordination, and reduced customer stress into one premium operational package.

Why it works

Customers often pay more to avoid chaos than to gain more features. Calm itself becomes valuable in high-friction industries.

Best for

Logistics, healthcare, enterprise services, finance, SaaS, legal, hospitality, construction

Execution Steps

1. Identify where customers feel operational chaos
2. Bundle visibility and coordination
3. Add proactive updates
4. Define escalation rules
5. Price for reduced stress and delay

Real-world example

A logistics firm packages proactive updates and issue prevention, while a construction firm packages calm project coordination.

Risk Management

1. **Operational** · 4/5 Updates inconsistent. **Mitigation:** Set cadence and owners.
2. **Customer** · 3/5 Calm feels intangible. **Mitigation:** Show chaos avoided.
3. **Financial** · 3/5 Costs grow beyond the projected baseline. **Mitigation:** Limit service scope.
4. **Commercial** · 3/5 Hard to sell. **Mitigation:** Use pain stories.
5. **Alignment** · 3/5 Teams overcommit. **Mitigation:** Define usage, access, and delivery boundaries before any commitment.

Speed	Effort	Cost	Revenue	Time to cash	Scalability
Medium (1-3 months)	**Medium**	**Low**	**Very High**	**Short**	**High**

Decision-flow: CFO → Operations → Customer Success

204. Bundle fragmented customer data into one actionable

Combine scattered reports, updates, operational signals, service history, usage information, or customer metrics into one simplified decision-ready package.

Why it works

Customers are overwhelmed by fragmented information. Packaging clarity and actionability creates strong decision-making value.

Best for

SaaS, healthcare, finance, logistics, education, facilities, enterprise services, manufacturing

Execution Steps

1. Identify fragmented customer information
2. Group it into decision categories
3. Remove noise
4. Add simple recommended actions
5. Package as decision-ready output

Real-world example

A SaaS firm packages scattered reports into an executive action view, while a healthcare provider packages patient history into one decision-ready summary.

Risk Management

1. **Product** · 4/5 Data quality is insufficient to support reliable insights or accurate predictions.. **Mitigation:** Clean inputs.
2. **Legal** · 5/5 Customer data privacy is at risk if access, anonymisation. **Mitigation:** Control access.
3. **Customer** · 3/5 Too much information. **Mitigation:** Keep action-oriented.
4. **Product** · 3/5 Integration effort. **Mitigation:** Start manually if needed.
5. **Commercial** · 3/5 Value not clear. **Mitigation:** Tie to decisions.

Speed	Effort	Cost	Revenue	Time to cash	Scalability
Medium (1-3 months)	**Medium**	**Low**	**Very High**	**Short**	**High**

Decision-flow: CFO → Product → Operations

205. Turn operational complexity into one done-for-you experience

Bundle coordination, structure, guidance, checkpoints, tools, and simplified execution into a near-done-for-you experience without fully taking over operations.

Why it works

Customers want simplicity but many businesses cannot scale full-service delivery profitably. This creates high perceived support without full operational burden.

Best for

SaaS, education, healthcare, finance, legal, logistics, consulting, home services

Execution Steps

1. Identify complexity customers want removed
2. Define what you will not fully own
3. Bundle guidance, structure, and checkpoints
4. Price below full service
5. Set customer responsibilities clearly

Real-world example

A SaaS firm packages guided implementation without managing the whole operation, while a legal firm packages structured document completion support.

Risk Management

1. **Operational** · 5/5 Scope expands beyond agreed boundaries. **Mitigation:** Define responsibilities.
2. **Customer** · 4/5 Expects full service. **Mitigation:** Set clear boundaries.
3. **Financial** · 4/5 Underpriced effort. **Mitigation:** Model support time.
4. **Commercial** · 3/5 Value confusing. **Mitigation:** Explain near-done-for-you clearly.
5. **Alignment** · 3/5 Teams overdeliver. **Mitigation:** Train scope discipline.

Speed	Effort	Cost	Revenue	Time to cash	Scalability
Medium (1-3 months)	**Medium**	**Low**	**Very High**	**Short**	**High**

Decision-flow: CFO → Product → Operations

From Ideas to Action

Twenty ideas. Twenty ways to repackage what the business already sells so customers pay more, commit sooner, and buy more per transaction.

None of these moves change the product. They change how it is seen. A customer who would not buy three items separately will often buy them together without hesitation. Packaging is not a sales trick. It is a clarity decision.

Before continuing, identify the single idea with the clearest commercial case right now. Name who owns it. Set a date for the first step. That is all that is required.

> ***The same product at the same price sells differently when it is presented differently. Packaging is a revenue lever.***

What Comes Next

Part 4 — Accelerate Revenue follows. The business is now capturing its full value. Part 4 focuses on timing — getting that revenue to land faster, in cash, at the pace the business needs.

PART 4
Accelerate Revenue

The Revenue Already Agreed That Has Not Arrived Yet

Parts 2 and 3 were about creating and unlocking revenue — finding what could be sold, and capturing more from what was already being sold. Part 4 is different.

Part 4 is about time. It asks a different question — not what can we sell or what are we leaving on the table, but why does revenue that has already been agreed take so long to arrive? What decisions could close faster? What customers could pay earlier? What implementations could deliver value sooner?

In most businesses, significant revenue is already committed but delayed. Accelerating it does not require new customers or new products. It requires removing the friction that sits between agreement and cash.

What This Part Covers

- **Prepay & Upfront Cash** — bringing revenue forward by getting customers to pay earlier or more upfront.
- **Billing & Collection Speed** — accelerating cash by improving invoicing, payment terms, and collection.
- **Sales Cycle Compression** — reducing the time from opportunity to closed deal.
- **Activation Speed** — getting customers to first value faster after the deal is signed.
- **Pull-Forward Offers** — using time-based offers to shift demand and commitment earlier.

Where to Start

- **Cash arriving late despite deals being closed?** Start with Billing & Collection Speed.
- **Customers willing to pay earlier in the right structure?** Start with Prepay & Upfront Cash.
- **Long sales cycles despite strong product-market fit?** Start with Sales Cycle Compression.
- **Customers slow to get value after signing?** Start with Activation Speed.
- **Revenue consistently landing late in the quarter?** Start with Pull-Forward Offers.

4.1 — Prepay & Upfront Cash

Bring revenue forward by getting customers to pay earlier or more upfront.

When These Strategies Work Best

Prepay strategies work best when customers have a reason to commit earlier and the business has not yet structured a clear incentive or mechanism to capture that commitment.

- Customers would pay upfront in exchange for a clear advantage or certainty
- Annual or multi-year pricing exists but most customers are still on monthly billing
- Cash flow is inconsistent despite strong underlying demand and delivery
- Customers delay final payment without a compelling reason to pay sooner
- Deposits or advance payments are not currently part of the commercial model

The Benefits

- Immediate improvement in cash position without changing delivery or pricing
- Stronger customer commitment that reduces late-stage churn and deal drop-off
- Reduced collection effort when cash arrives before delivery rather than after
- Better financial forecasting when income is committed and dated in advance
- Competitive advantage when upfront terms fund delivery others cannot match

The Risks to Manage

- **Buyer resistance** — prepay requires a clear value exchange. Discounts alone are the wrong incentive. Offer certainty.
- **Refund exposure** — collecting upfront creates an obligation. Ensure delivery can be guaranteed before the ask.
- **Wrong customer targeting** — not every customer is a prepay candidate. Focus on those with the motivation and the means.
- **Over-incentivising** — discounts that are too deep reduce the revenue benefit. Model net cash impact before launch.

206. Get paid before the work starts

Require an upfront deposit before committing resources, scheduling delivery, ordering materials, or starting client work.

Why it works

Many businesses begin delivery before cash is secured. Deposits reduce risk, improve cash flow, and confirm buyer seriousness.

Best for

Consulting, agencies, construction, logistics, manufacturing, healthcare, home services, B2B services

Execution Steps

1. Identify work that starts before cash is received
2. Define deposit amount and trigger
3. Add deposit language to proposals and checkout
4. Require payment before scheduling or resource allocation
5. Train sales. to explain commitment value

Real-world example

A contractor collects a deposit before ordering materials, while a consulting firm requires an upfront start fee before assigning the project team.

Risk Management

1. **Customer** · 3/5 Buyer resists upfront payment. **Mitigation:** Explain it secures resources and start date.
2. **Commercial** · 4/5 Sales waives deposit. **Mitigation:** Make deposit non-optional without approval.
3. **Legal** · 3/5 Unclear terms create disputes and undermine trust in the commercial relationship.. **Mitigation:** Add clear refund and cancellation rules.
4. **Operational** · 4/5 Work starts before payment. **Mitigation:** Block scheduling until payment clears.
5. **Financial** · 3/5 Deposit too low. **Mitigation:** Set deposit against real upfront cost.

Speed	Effort	Cost	Revenue	Time to cash	Scalability
Fast (0-30 days)	**Low**	**Low**	**High**	**Immediate**	**High**

Decision-flow: CFO → Sales → Operations

207. Turn annual commitment into upfront cash

Offer customers a clear reason to pay annually upfront instead of monthly, quarterly, or after usage.

Why it works

Annual prepay pulls cash forward, improves forecasting, and reduces churn risk while giving customers budgeting simplicity.

Best for

SaaS, subscriptions, education, maintenance, healthcare, memberships, B2B services, software-enabled services

Execution Steps

1. Identify recurring customers paying monthly or quarterly
2. Define annual prepay terms
3. Offer budgeting, simplicity, or continuity benefit
4. Update renewal and sales scripts
5. Target customers with stable usage first

Real-world example

A SaaS firm moves monthly users to annual prepay, while a maintenance provider collects annual service plan cash upfront.

Risk Management

1. **Customer** · 3/5 Customer prefers flexibility. **Mitigation:** Target stable customers first.
2. **Financial** · 3/5 Cash benefit offset by concessions. **Mitigation:** Limit any incentive.
3. **Commercial** · 3/5 Uptake in the early period is below projections. Early signals must. **Mitigation:** Position budgeting certainty.
4. **Operational** · 2/5 Service delivery not ready. **Mitigation:** Ensure annual service capacity.
5. **Legal** · 3/5 Cancellation ambiguity. **Mitigation:** Clarify annual terms.

Speed	Effort	Cost	Revenue	Time to cash	Scalability
Fast (0-30 days)	**Low**	**Low**	**Very High**	**Immediate**	**High**

Decision-flow: CFO → Sales → Finance

208. Charge milestone payments before each delivery stage

Break projects into payment gates where customers pay before the next major phase begins.

Why it works

Milestone billing prevents the business from financing the customer's project. Cash arrives before resources are consumed.

Best for

Construction, consulting, agencies, software implementation, manufacturing, events, legal, enterprise services

Execution Steps

1. Break delivery into clear stages
2. Define payment required before each stage
3. Add gates to contracts and project plans
4. Stop work until each payment is received
5. Communicate milestones clearly upfront

Real-world example

A software implementation charges before configuration begins, while a construction firm requires payment before each build phase.

Risk Management

1. **Customer** · 3/5 Customer dislikes gated payments. **Mitigation:** Link each gate to clear deliverables.
2. **Operational** · 4/5 Teams continue without payment. **Mitigation:** Use project controls.
3. **Legal** · 3/5 Contract gaps. **Mitigation:** Document payment gates.
4. **Financial** · 3/5 Milestones poorly sized. **Mitigation:** Align payment with cost exposure.
5. **Commercial** · 3/5 Deal friction. **Mitigation:** Explain cash-risk logic early.

Speed	Effort	Cost	Revenue	Time to cash	Scalability
Medium (1-3 months)	**Medium**	**Low**	**High**	**Short**	**High**

Decision-flow: CFO → Operations → Finance

209. *Sell prepaid credits customers spend later*

Let customers buy prepaid credit balances that can be used later for services, products, support, capacity, or future purchases.

Why it works

Prepaid credits create immediate cash while giving customers flexibility. The business gets funded before delivery.

Best for

SaaS, agencies, healthcare, consulting, retail, logistics, education, professional services

Execution Steps

1. Identify repeat purchases or variable usage
2. Create prepaid credit packages
3. Define expiry, usage, and refund rules
4. Make balances easy to track
5. Sell to customers with predictable future needs

Real-world example

An agency sells prepaid design credits, while a healthcare provider sells prepaid visit credits for future appointments.

Risk Management

1. **Legal** · 4/5 Credit terms unclear. **Mitigation:** Set clear usage and expiry rules.
2. **Customer** · 3/5 Customer forgets credits. **Mitigation:** Provide balance reminders.
3. **Financial** · 4/5 Liability management issue. **Mitigation:** Track deferred revenue properly.
4. **Commercial** · 3/5 Adoption is slower than expected. **Mitigation:** Target repeat buyers.
5. **Operational** · 3/5 Redemption overload. **Mitigation:** Monitor capacity.

Speed	Effort	Cost	Revenue	Time to cash	Scalability
Fast (0-30 days)	**Low**	**Low**	**High**	**Immediate**	**High**

Decision-flow: CFO → Sales → Finance

210. Use customer-funded inventory before ordering stock

Ask customers to prepay for reserved stock, custom inventory, limited runs, or materials before the business commits cash.

Why it works

Inventory ties up cash. Customer-funded purchasing reduces working capital pressure and validates demand before stock is bought.

Best for

Retail, manufacturing, food, construction, wholesale, equipment, consumer products, custom goods

Execution Steps

1. Identify inventory that creates cash strain
2. Define what customers can pre-fund
3. Set minimum order or prepay thresholds
4. Communicate timing and delivery rules
5. Order only after payment threshold is reached

Real-world example

A furniture maker takes prepayment before ordering custom materials, while a food brand pre-sells limited production runs before buying ingredients.

Risk Management

1. **Operational** · 4/5 Supplier delays. **Mitigation:** Set realistic delivery windows.
2. **Customer** · 4/5 Customer worries about delivery. **Mitigation:** Provide clear timeline.fore any.
3. **Financial** · 3/5 Refund exposure. **Mitigation:** Set terms.
4. **Commercial** · 3/5 Demand from the target segment is weaker than projected at launch. **Mitigation:** Validate before launch.
5. **Legal** · 3/5 Consumer protection issues. **Mitigation:** Submit all commercial terms to legal review before customer presentation.

Speed	Effort	Cost	Revenue	Time to cash	Scalability
Medium (1-3 months)	**Medium**	**Low**	**Very High**	**Short**	**Medium**

Decision-flow: CFO → Operations → Operations

211. Turn waiting lists into paid reservation cash

Convert serious demand into paid reservation fees for future access, delivery, production, or service slots.

Why it works

Free waiting lists create weak intent. Paid reservations pull cash forward and reveal real demand.

Best for

Healthcare, hospitality, education, manufacturing, home services, events, retail, specialist services

Execution Steps

1. Identify waiting lists or future demand queues
2. Define a paid reservation amount
3. Clarify what the payment secures
4. Set expiry, transfer, and refund rules
5. Offer to high-intent customers first

Real-world example

A clinic charges a small reservation fee for future specialist appointments, while a manufacturer takes paid reservations for limited production capacity.

Risk Management

1. **Customer** · 3/5 Fee feels unnecessary. **Mitigation:** Credit it toward final purchase.
2. **Commercial** · 2/5 Weak intent still persists. **Mitigation:** Use meaningful payment amount.
3. **Operational** · 4/5 Overbooking risk. **Mitigation:** Cap reservations.
4. **Legal** · 3/5 Refund disputes. **Mitigation:** Define rules.
5. **Financial** · 2/5 Small cash impact. **Mitigation:** Apply to high-value demand.

Speed	Effort	Cost	Revenue	Time to cash	Scalability
Fast (0-30 days)	**Low**	**Low**	**High**	**Immediate**	**High**

Decision-flow: CFO → Sales → Operations

212. Get paid upfront for setup-heavy work

Charge setup, onboarding, mobilization, configuration, or preparation fees before delivery begins.

Why it works

Setup work consumes resources before customers see the final outcome. Charging upfront protects cash and recovers early effort.

Best for

SaaS, consulting, logistics, healthcare, agencies, enterprise services, manufacturing, education

Execution Steps

1. Identify setup work currently absorbed
2. Define the setup fee and scope
3. Charge before onboarding or mobilization starts
4. Explain what preparation includes
5. Separate setup from ongoing delivery

Real-world example

A SaaS company charges onboarding setup upfront, while a logistics provider charges mobilization before launching a new client operation.

Risk Management

1. **Customer** · 3/5 Setup fee pushback. **Mitigation:** Show required preparation work.
2. **Commercial** · 3/5 Sales hides the fee. **Mitigation:** Include in standard proposal.
3. **Operational** · 4/5 Setup scope expands. **Mitigation:** Define scope, access, and usage limits in writing before launch.
4. **Financial** · 3/5 Fee too low. **Mitigation:** Map real setup cost.
5. **Legal** · 3/5 Scope ambiguity. **Mitigation:** Include terms.

Speed	Effort	Cost	Revenue	Time to cash	Scalability
Fast (0-30 days)	**Low**	**Low**	**High**	**Immediate**	**High**

Decision-flow: CFO → Customer Success → Operations

213. *Sell prepaid service blocks*

Offer customers prepaid blocks of hours, visits, sessions, support, maintenance, or advisory time they can draw down later.

Why it works

Service blocks convert future usage into immediate cash while locking in repeat demand.

Best for

Consulting, agencies, healthcare, legal, coaching, IT support, maintenance, education, home services

Execution Steps

1. Identify repeat service usage
2. Create prepaid block sizes
3. Define drawdown and expiry rules
4. Sell blocks before work is used
5. Track balance and utilization

Real-world example

A legal firm sells prepaid advisory hours, while a home services company sells prepaid maintenance visit blocks.

Risk Management

1. **Customer** · 3/5 Unused balance frustration. **Mitigation:** Send usage reminders.
2. **Financial** · 4/5 Deferred revenue tracking. **Mitigation:** Track liability correctly.
3. **Operational** · 3/5 Capacity spikes. **Mitigation:** Limit redemption windows.
4. **Commercial** · 3/5 Uptake in the early period is below projections. Early signals must. **Mitigation:** Target repeat customers.
5. **Legal** · 3/5 Expiry disputes. **Mitigation:** Use specific, plain-language contract terms that eliminate ambiguity.

Speed	Effort	Cost	Revenue	Time to cash	Scalability
Fast (0-30 days)	**Low**	**Low**	**High**	**Immediate**	**High**

Decision-flow: CFO → Sales → Operations

214. Pull renewal cash forward before the renewal date

Invite customers to renew early with a clear operational, budget, or continuity benefit before the formal renewal cycle begins.

Why it works

Renewals often wait until the last moment. Early renewal pulls cash forward and reduces future uncertainty.

Best for

SaaS, subscriptions, maintenance, education, healthcare, B2B services, memberships, software

Execution Steps

1. Identify renewal dates 60-120 days ahead
2. Define early-renewal benefit
3. Prioritize healthy accounts
4. Ask before the formal renewal window
5. Collect payment upfront

Real-world example

A SaaS firm asks strong customers to renew early for continuity planning, while a maintenance company collects next-year service plan cash before year-end.

Risk Management

1. **Customer** · 3/5 Customer delays decision. **Mitigation:** Use budget timing triggers.
2. **Commercial** · 3/5 Looks like desperation. **Mitigation:** Position around planning.
3. **Financial** · 3/5 Benefit too costly. **Mitigation:** Limit concessions.
4. **Alignment** · 3/5 CS waits too long. **Mitigation:** Set outreach calendar.
5. **Legal** · 3/5 Term confusion. **Mitigation:** Clarify renewal dates.

Speed	Effort	Cost	Revenue	Time to cash	Scalability
Fast (0-30 days)	**Low**	**Low**	**Very High**	**Immediate**	**High**

Decision-flow: CFO → Customer Success → Sales

215. Ask customers to pre-fund limited capacity

Require upfront payment to secure scarce production, delivery, expert, support, installation, or service capacity before it is allocated.

Why it works

Scarce capacity should not be held for free. Pre-funding turns demand into cash, confirms buyer seriousness, and prevents weak commitments from blocking valuable slots.

Best for

Manufacturing, healthcare, consulting, logistics, home services, SaaS support, installation, agencies

Execution Steps

1. Identify scarce capacity that customers want held
2. Define pre-funding amount and rules
3. Require payment before allocation
4. Cap capacity. commitments
5. Release unpaid holds quickly

Real-world example

A specialist installer requires payment to secure installation capacity, while a manufacturer pre-funds scarce production slots before allocation.

Risk Management

1. **Operational** · 5/5 Overcommitment. **Mitigation:** Cap allocations.
2. **Customer** · 3/5 Customer sees it as unfair. **Mitigation:** Explain scarcity and commitment.
3. **Operational** · 4/5 Core customers displaced. **Mitigation:** Protect priority capacity.
4. **Financial** · 3/5 Payment too small. **Mitigation:** Set meaningful amount.
5. **Legal** · 3/5 Refund disputes. **Mitigation:** Define rules.

Speed	Effort	Cost	Revenue	Time to cash	Scalability
Fast (0-30 days)	**Low**	**Low**	**Very High**	**Immediate**	**High**

Decision-flow: CFO → Operations → Sales

216. Turn customer indecision into paid commitment deposits

Allow hesitant customers to place a small paid commitment deposit that locks pricing, inventory, access, timing, or future delivery before they fully decide.

Why it works

Many buyers want to move forward emotionally before they are operationally ready. Commitment deposits convert hesitation into immediate cash while preserving momentum.

Best for

Retail, SaaS, healthcare, automotive, construction, hospitality, consulting, manufacturing

Execution Steps

1. Identify high-intent hesitant buyers
2. Define what deposit secures
3. Keep payment small but meaningful
4. Set deadline and conversion rules
5. Credit deposit toward purchase

Real-world example

A car dealer lets buyers place a paid commitment deposit, while a consulting firm lets prospects hold start dates with a credited deposit.

Risk Management

1. **Customer** · 3/5 Customers are unclear on what is included, how to use it. **Mitigation:** Clarify it is a commitment deposit.
2. **Commercial** · 3/5 Low conversion after deposit. **Mitigation:** Set clear expiry.
3. **Financial** · 2/5 Deposit too small. **Mitigation:** Make amount meaningful.
4. **Legal** · 3/5 Refund ambiguity. **Mitigation:** Define terms.
5. **Operational** · 3/5 Held resources wasted. **Mitigation:** Use short hold windows.

Speed	Effort	Cost	Revenue	Time to cash	Scalability
Fast (0-30 days)	**Low**	**Low**	**High**	**Immediate**	**High**

Decision-flow: CFO → Sales → Operations

217. Get customers to fund future innovation before you

Offer customers early paid access to future improvements, upcoming releases, enhanced versions, or planned capabilities before development begins.

Why it works

Customers already paying for the problem are often willing to fund the next solution if it solves meaningful pain faster.

Best for

SaaS, manufacturing, healthcare, consumer products, education, enterprise services, hardware, logistics

Execution Steps

1. Identify future capability customers strongly want
2. Define what early payment secures
3. Set delivery expectations and limits
4. Pre-sell to high-pain customers
5. Use funds to support development

Real-world example

A SaaS firm pre-sells an advanced module to enterprise clients, while a hardware company pre-sells an upgraded version before production.

Risk Management

1. **Product** · 5/5 Development delay. **Mitigation:** Set realistic timeline.
2. **Customer** · 4/5 Expectation mismatch. **Mitigation:** Define scope clearly.
3. **Financial** · 4/5 Refund exposure. **Mitigation:** Use terms and staged commitments.
4. **Commercial** · 3/5 Demand from the target segment is weaker than projected at launch. **Mitigation:** Validate with paid interest.
5. **Legal** · 4/5 Promise risk. **Mitigation:** Review customer commitments.

Speed	Effort	Cost	Revenue	Time to cash	Scalability
Medium (1-3 months)	**Medium**	**Low**	**Very High**	**Short**	**High**

Decision-flow: CFO → Product → Sales

218. Pre-sell urgent execution before capacity is assigned

Ask customers to prepay for urgent execution before the business allocates production, delivery, expert time, installation, or deployment capacity.

Why it works

Urgent demand is often operationally disruptive. Prepayment ensures the business receives cash before committing scarce fast-response capacity.

Best for

Healthcare, logistics, SaaS, manufacturing, legal, finance, home services, consulting

Execution Steps

1. Identify urgent execution requests
2. Define the urgent capacity commitment
3. Require prepayment before allocation
4. Set clear timing and delivery rules
5. Cap urgent capacity

Real-world example

A logistics company requires prepayment for urgent rerouting, while a SaaS firm pre-sells rapid deployment slots before assigning implementation capacity.

Risk Management

1. **Operational** · 4/5 Urgent work disrupts core delivery. **Mitigation:** Allocate a defined capacity block and do not allow.
2. **Customer** · 4/5 Promise expectations too high. **Mitigation:** Set timing clearly.
3. **Commercial** · 4/5 Sales overpromises. **Mitigation:** Require operations approval.
4. **Financial** · 3/5 Price does not match disruption. **Mitigation:** Anchor to urgency cost.
5. **Legal** · 3/5 Delivery disputes. **Mitigation:** Document terms.

Speed	Effort	Cost	Revenue	Time to cash	Scalability
Fast (0-30 days)	**Low**	**Low**	**Very High**	**Immediate**	**High**

Decision-flow: CFO → Operations → Sales

219. Use a limited prepaid customer pool to fund a specific

Invite customers to prepay into a time-bound access pool that funds a specific future benefit, such as a launch, drop, upgrade, event, capacity block, or new availability window.

Why it works

Customers often want early participation in valuable future opportunities. Prepaid pools create upfront cash while validating future demand.

Best for

Retail, SaaS, hospitality, education, fitness, gaming, premium consumer brands, memberships

Execution Steps

1. Define the specific future benefit
2. Set pool size and payment amount
3. Clarify what customers receive
4. Make the pool time-bound
5. Collect payment before delivery

Real-world example

A premium brand funds a limited product drop through prepaid access, while a SaaS company funds a customer-requested feature pool.

Risk Management

1. **Customer** · 3/5 Feels like membership. **Mitigation:** Make it one-time and specific.
2. **Financial** · 4/5 Delivery obligation risk. **Mitigation:** Track liabilities.
3. **Commercial** · 3/5 Demand from the target segment is weaker than projected at launch. **Mitigation:** Limit pool size.
4. **Legal** · 3/5 Unclear terms create disputes and undermine trust in the commercial relationship.. **Mitigation:** Define benefit and refund rules.
5. **Market** · 3/5 Overuse reduces trust. **Mitigation:** Use sparingly.

Speed	Effort	Cost	Revenue	Time to cash	Scalability
Medium (1-3 months)	**Medium**	**Low**	**Very High**	**Short**	**High**

Decision-flow: CFO → Marketing → Operations

220. Pre-sell operational capacity before hiring or scaling

Secure customer prepayments for future production, support, implementation, staffing, or operational expansion before increasing fixed costs internally.

Why it works

Many businesses scale too early and carry the risk alone. Pre-selling demand allows customers to help finance growth capacity.

Best for

Agencies, SaaS, manufacturing, logistics, consulting, healthcare, construction, education

Execution Steps

1. Identify demand that requires added capacity
2. Define what customers can pre-buy
3. Secure commitments before hiring or scaling
4. Set minimum prepayment threshold
5. Scale only after cash is secured

Real-world example

An agency pre-sells delivery capacity before hiring specialists, while a manufacturer pre-sells production volume before adding a shift.

Risk Management

1. **Operational** · 4/5 Capacity not ready in time. **Mitigation:** Use realistic ramp plans.
2. **Financial** · 4/5 Threshold too low. **Mitigation:** Set minimum funding level.
3. **Customer** · 3/5 Customer worries about delivery. **Mitigation:** Provide clear timeline.
4. **Commercial** · 4/5 Demand overstated. **Mitigation:** Use paid commitments only.
5. **Alignment** · 3/5 Hiring risk. **Mitigation:** Scale in stages.

Speed	Effort	Cost	Revenue	Time to cash	Scalability
Medium (1-3 months)	**Medium**	**Low**	**Very High**	**Short**	**High**

Decision-flow: CFO → Operations → Sales

221. Turn customer forecasting into upfront cash commitments

Ask customers to financially commit upfront against future usage, inventory, demand, service needs, or operational allocation they already expect to consume.

Why it works

Customers often know future demand internally before the supplier does. Converting forecast confidence into cash improves planning and liquidity.

Best for

Manufacturing, logistics, SaaS, healthcare, retail, wholesale, construction, enterprise services

Execution Steps

1. Ask customers for expected future demand
2. Identify forecasted demand they trust
3. Convert forecast into prepaid commitment
4. Offer allocation or planning benefit
5. Track usage against commitment

Real-world example

A distributor turns customer demand forecasts into prepaid purchase commitments, while a SaaS firm converts expected seat growth into upfront allocation cash.

Risk Management

1. **Customer** · 4/5 Forecast changes. **Mitigation:** Allow defined adjustment windows.
2. **Financial** · 3/5 Commitment too weak. **Mitigation:** Require meaningful propayment.
3. **Operational** · 3/5 Mismatch with supply plan. **Mitigation:** Align with operations.
4. **Commercial** · 3/5 Buyer hesitates. **Mitigation:** Show planning benefit.
5. **Legal** · 3/5 Unclear terms create disputes and undermine trust in the commercial relationship.. **Mitigation:** Document commitment rules.

Speed	Effort	Cost	Revenue	Time to cash	Scalability
Medium (1-3 months)	**Medium**	**Low**	**Very High**	**Short**	**High**

Decision-flow: CFO → Sales → Operations

222. *Turn customer onboarding into a paid activation phase*

Structure onboarding, preparation, implementation, migration, setup, or mobilization as a prepaid activation stage before the main delivery begins.

Why it works

Businesses often absorb onboarding cost for free even though it consumes heavy operational resources before revenue fully materializes.

Best for

SaaS, healthcare, consulting, finance, logistics, enterprise services, agencies, education

Execution Steps

1. Identify activation work before full delivery
2. Define the paid activation phase
3. Charge before onboarding begins
4. Clarify what activation includes
5. Separate activation from ongoing service

Real-world example

A SaaS company charges a prepaid activation phase before go-live, while a logistics firm charges mobilization before operations begin.

Risk Management

1. **Customer** · 3/5 Buyer expects free onboarding. **Mitigation:** Explain activation work clearly.
2. **Commercial** · 4/5 Sales waives charge. **Mitigation:** Make it standard.
3. **Operational** · 4/5 Scope expands beyond agreed boundaries. **Mitigation:** Define activation boundaries.
4. **Financial** · 3/5 Fee too low. **Mitigation:** Map actual effort.
5. **Legal** · 3/5 Deliverable ambiguity. **Mitigation:** Add specific, unambiguous terms before any customer-facing agreement is signed.

Speed	Effort	Cost	Revenue	Time to cash	Scalability
Fast (0-30 days)	**Low**	**Low**	**High**	**Immediate**	**High**

Decision-flow: CFO → Customer Success → Operations

223. Sell prepaid access windows for future demand periods

Let customers prepay for a defined future access window during known busy periods, seasonal peaks, launches, high-demand cycles, or limited operating periods.

Why it works

Customers pay earlier when future access certainty matters. The business stabilizes future cash flow before operational pressure arrives.

Best for

Hospitality, logistics, healthcare, SaaS infrastructure, education, events, manufacturing, travel

Execution Steps

1. Identify predictable future demand periods
2. Define access windows customers can prepay for
3. Set capacity limits
4. Collect payment before peak demand
5. Communicate access rules clearly

Real-world example

A hotel sells prepaid access windows for peak season, while a manufacturer sells prepaid production windows before seasonal demand spikes.

Risk Management

1. **Operational** · 4/5 Overbooking risk. **Mitigation:** Cap windows tightly.
2. **Customer** · 3/5 Access terms misunderstood. **Mitigation:** Clarify what is secured.
3. **Financial** · 3/5 Revenue recognition complexity. **Mitigation:** Review accounting treatment.
4. **Commercial** · 3/5 The urgency is not strong enough to drive timely purchasing decisions.. **Mitigation:** Launch before demand peaks.
5. **Legal** · 3/5 Refund disputes. **Mitigation:** Set written terms.

Speed	Effort	Cost	Revenue	Time to cash	Scalability
Fast (0-30 days)	**Low**	**Low**	**Very High**	**Immediate**	**High**

Decision-flow: CFO → Operations → Sales

224. Turn repeat customer behavior into automatic prepaid

Convert highly predictable repeat purchases into prepaid operational cycles customers fund upfront for simplicity and continuity.

Why it works

Many repeat purchases are operationally predictable. Prepay cycles improve cash flow while reducing reorder friction for customers.

Best for

Healthcare, retail, SaaS, facilities, logistics, maintenance, hospitality, professional services

Execution Steps

1. Identify predictable repeat purchasing patterns
2. Group them into prepaid cycles
3. Define cycle length and usage rules
4. Sell simplicity and continuity
5. Collect payment before the cycle starts

Real-world example

A facilities company sells prepaid quarterly service cycles, while a healthcare provider sells prepaid recurring care cycles.

Risk Management

1. **Customer** · 3/5 Customer fears overcommitment. **Mitigation:** Start with short cycles.
2. **Financial** · 3/5 Unused balance liability. **Mitigation:** Track usage carefully.
3. **Operational** · 3/5 Demand varies. **Mitigation:** Use flexible allowances.
4. **Commercial** · 3/5 Adoption is slower than expected. **Mitigation:** Target predictable buyers.
5. **Legal** · 3/5 Cycle rules unclear. **Mitigation:** Document terms.

Speed	Effort	Cost	Revenue	Time to cash	Scalability
Medium (1-3 months)	**Medium**	**Low**	**Very High**	**Short**	**High**

Decision-flow: CFO → Customer Success → Sales

225. Use customer co-investment to finance premium delivery

Invite customers to pre-fund enhanced production, technology, staffing, equipment, infrastructure, or operational upgrades tied directly to their future benefit.

Why it works

Customers often want better capability faster. Shared funding accelerates business upgrades while reducing internal capital strain.

Best for

Manufacturing, logistics, SaaS, healthcare, infrastructure, enterprise services, construction, industrial businesses

Execution Steps

1. Identify capability customers want improved
2. Link investment to direct customer benefit
3. Define customer pre-funding structure
4. Set delivery milestones and rights
5. Collect funds before upgrade spending

Real-world example

A manufacturer asks major customers to co-fund a faster production line, while a SaaS provider pre-funds enterprise-grade capability with anchor customers.

Risk Management

1. **Financial** · 4/5 Funding not enough. **Mitigation:** Set minimum threshold.
2. **Customer** · 4/5 Customer expects ownership rights. **Mitigation:** Clarify no equity unless intended.
3. **Operational** · 4/5 Capability delivery delay. **Mitigation:** Use milestones.
4. **Legal** · 4/5 Contract complexity. **Mitigation:** Use clear agreements.
5. **Commercial** · 3/5 Benefit too narrow. **Mitigation:** Target anchor customers.

Speed	Effort	Cost	Revenue	Time to cash	Scalability
Medium (1-3 months)	**High**	**Medium**	**Very High**	**Medium**	**High**

Decision-flow: CFO → PMO / Strategy → Operations

From Ideas to Action

Twenty ideas. Twenty ways to move cash forward — converting future revenue into money the business holds today.

Cash in hand today is worth more than the same amount arriving in ninety days. Every idea here moves that timeline forward without changing the deal size. The revenue is already agreed. The only question is when it arrives.

Before continuing, identify the single idea with the clearest commercial case right now. Name who owns it. Set a date for the first step. That is all that is required.

> ***Revenue that is agreed but not yet collected is not revenue. It is a promise. Move the cash forward.***

What Comes Next

4.2 — Billing & Collection Speed addresses businesses where revenue is real and agreed but cash is delayed by late invoicing, long payment terms, or collection processes that lack structure. If the money is owed but arriving slowly — the next chapter closes the gap.

4.2 — Billing & Collection Speed

Accelerate cash realisation by improving invoicing, payment terms, and collection mechanics.

When These Strategies Work Best

Billing and collection strategies work best when revenue is real but cash is delayed — through late invoicing, long payment terms, or collection processes that lack discipline or structure.

- Invoices are sent days or weeks after delivery rather than immediately
- Payment terms are longer than what customers actually require to pay
- Late invoices sit unpursued for weeks before any follow-up action is taken
- Collection is treated as a finance task rather than a commercial one
- Cash conversion cycles are significantly longer than the sales cycle that created the revenue

The Benefits

- Immediate cash improvement with no change to price, product, or customer base
- Reduced debtor days across the customer portfolio
- Lower bad debt exposure when collection is structured and systematic
- Better working capital that reduces reliance on external funding
- Cleaner financial signals that improve forecasting and operational decision-making

The Risks to Manage

- **Customer relationship friction** — aggressive collection damages trust. Speed and professionalism must go together.
- **Internal resistance** — sales teams often deprioritise collection. Ownership and accountability must be explicit.
- **System gaps** — manual billing processes cannot scale. Automation is required for sustained improvement.
- **Terms misalignment** — tightening terms with existing customers requires communication and transition time.

226. *Invoice the moment value is accepted, not at month-end*

Trigger invoices immediately when delivery, approval, usage, shipment, milestone, or customer acceptance happens instead of waiting for the next billing cycle.

Why it works

Month-end batching delays cash for no strategic reason. Event-based invoicing shortens the cash gap without changing price, product, or terms.

Best for

SaaS, logistics, consulting, agencies, manufacturing, construction, healthcare, B2B services

Execution Steps

1. Identify events that prove value was delivered
2. Define invoice trigger rules
3. Connect operations to finance alerts
4. Send invoice immediately after acceptance
5. Remove month-end batching where possible

Real-world example

A logistics firm invoices on delivery confirmation, while a consulting firm invoices once a milestone is approved.

Risk Management

1. **Operational** · 3/5 Acceptance trigger unclear. **Mitigation:** Define trigger rules.
2. **Product** · 4/5 Systems not connected. **Mitigation:** Add simple handoff alerts.
3. **Customer** · 3/5 Invoice surprise. **Mitigation:** Communicate billing timing upfront.
4. **Alignment** · 3/5 Finance still batches invoices. **Mitigation:** Set daily invoicing rhythm.
5. **Financial** · 2/5 Small invoices increase workload. **Mitigation:** Automate frequent billing.

Speed	Effort	Cost	Revenue	Time to cash	Scalability
Fast (0-30 days)	**Low**	**Low**	**Very High**	**Immediate**	**High**

Decision-flow: CFO → Finance → Operations

227. *Remove the approval maze before the invoice is sent*

Pre-agree invoice requirements, PO numbers, approvers, formats, tax details, and documentation before delivery is completed.

Why it works

Many invoices are delayed because billing details are fixed after the fact. Pre-clearing invoice requirements prevents avoidable payment friction.

Best for

B2B services, logistics, consulting, manufacturing, healthcare, construction, enterprise software, agencies

Execution Steps

1. Identify common invoice rejection reasons
2. Collect PO, tax, format, and approver details before delivery
3. Add billing requirements to the sales handoff
4. Confirm details before invoice issue
5. Escalate missing information early

Real-world example

An agency confirms PO and approver details before project completion, while a manufacturer confirms invoice format before shipment.

Risk Management

1. **Customer** · 3/5 Customer delays providing details. **Mitigation:** Request before work starts.
2. **Operational** · 3/5 Sales skips billing intake. **Mitigation:** Make it mandatory.
3. **Financial** · 3/5 Invoices still rejected. **Mitigation:** Track rejection reason codes.
4. **Alignment** · 3/5 Ownership unclear. **Mitigation:** Assign finance-sales owner.
5. **Product** · 3/5 Format mismatch. **Mitigation:** Store customer billing profiles.

Speed	Effort	Cost	Revenue	Time to cash	Scalability
Fast (0-30 days)	**Low**	**Low**	**High**	**Immediate**	**High**

Decision-flow: CFO → Finance → Sales

228. Turn every invoice into a payment-ready checkout

Add direct payment links, saved payment methods, wallet options, card payment, bank transfer instructions, and instant confirmation to every invoice.

Why it works

Customers often delay because paying requires effort. Making every invoice immediately payable reduces friction and speeds cash collection.

Best for

Healthcare, education, SaaS, retail services, professional services, subscriptions, agencies, home services

Execution Steps

1. Review how customers currently pay
2. Add payment links to invoices
3. Provide clear transfer instructions
4. Enable saved or repeat payment options
5. Confirm payment instantly

Real-world example

A clinic adds card links to invoices, while a professional services firm adds one-click payment to statements.

Risk Management

1. **Product** · 4/5 Payment link failure. **Mitigation:** Test links before sending.
2. **Financial** · 3/5 Processing fees. **Mitigation:** Price or route appropriately.
3. **Customer** · 3/5 Payment method mismatch. **Mitigation:** Offer several options.
4. **Legal** · 4/5 Security concern. **Mitigation:** Use trusted providers.
5. **Operational** · 3/5 Reconciliation issues. **Mitigation:** Connect payment references.

Speed	Effort	Cost	Revenue	Time to cash	Scalability
Fast (0-30 days)	**Low**	**Low**	**High**	**Immediate**	**High**

Decision-flow: CFO → Finance → IT / Data

229. *Fix invoice disputes before they become payment excuses*

Create a pre-invoice review step for high-value customers or complex work to confirm scope, quantities, rates, and documentation before invoice issue.

Why it works

Disputes often delay the entire invoice. Resolving mismatch before billing keeps payment moving and reduces collection drag.

Best for

Construction, logistics, consulting, agencies, manufacturing, healthcare, legal, enterprise services

Execution Steps

1. Identify invoices often disputed
2. Add pre-invoice confirmation for complex work
3. Confirm quantities, rates, and scope
4. Resolve mismatches before invoice issue
5. Send clean invoice immediately

Real-world example

A construction firm confirms approved quantities before invoicing, while a logistics firm validates accessorial charges before billing.

Risk Management

1. **Operational** · 3/5 Review slows invoicing. **Mitigation:** Limit to high-risk invoices.
2. **Customer** · 3/5 Customer ignores review. **Mitigation:** Set response deadline.
3. **Financial** · 3/5 Disputes still occur. **Mitigation:** Capture evidence early.
4. **Alignment** · 4/5 Operations data incomplete. **Mitigation:** Standardize delivery records
5. **Commercial** · 3/5 Scope arguments reopen. **Mitigation:** Use signed confirmations.

Speed	Effort	Cost	Revenue	Time to cash	Scalability
Medium (1-3 months)	**Medium**	**Low**	**Very High**	**Immediate**	**High**

Decision-flow: CFO → Finance → Operations

230. Create a no-invoice-left-behind cash desk

Create a daily operating rhythm where every invoice has an owner, next action, due date, blocker status, and escalation path.

Why it works

Receivables age because no one owns the next move. A cash desk turns collection from passive waiting into active cash execution.

Best for

B2B services, SaaS, logistics, construction, healthcare, manufacturing, agencies, wholesale

Execution Steps

1. List all open invoices
2. Assign an owner to each invoice
3. Record next action and blocker
4. Review the list daily or weekly
5. Escalate stuck invoices quickly

Real-world example

A wholesale firm runs a daily cash desk, while a SaaS company assigns every overdue invoice to a named owner.

Risk Management

1. **Alignment** · 4/5 No clear ownership. **Mitigation:** Assign invoice owners.
2. **Operational** · 3/5 Review becomes admin burden. **Mitigation:** Focus on material invoices.
3. **Customer** · 3/5 Follow-up feels excessive. **Mitigation:** Use professional cadence.
4. **Financial** · 3/5 Old debt remains stuck. **Mitigation:** Prioritize by value. and age
5. **Commercial** · 3/5 Sales resists involvement. **Mitigation:** Tie to cash outcome.

Speed	Effort	Cost	Revenue	Time to cash	Scalability
Fast (0-30 days)	**Medium**	**Low**	**Very High**	**Immediate**	**High**

Decision-flow: CFO → Finance → Sales

231. Segment collections by customer behavior, not invoice

Classify customers by payment behavior, dispute pattern, approval complexity, and payment reliability, then tailor follow-up paths accordingly.

Why it works

Aging reports are too blunt. Behavior-based collection improves speed because each customer receives the right action before delay becomes serious.

Best for

B2B services, SaaS, logistics, manufacturing, healthcare, agencies, wholesale, enterprise sales

Execution Steps

1. Analyze payment patterns
2. Create behavior segments
3. Define collection path per segment
4. Use proactive outreach for slow patterns
5. Escalate chronic blockers earlier

Real-world example

A manufacturer uses different follow-up paths for approval-heavy accounts versus chronic dispute accounts.

Risk Management

1. **Product** · 3/5 Behavior data incomplete. **Mitigation:** Start with payment history.
2. **Customer** · 3/5 Wrong segment treatment. **Mitigation:** Review exceptions.
3. **Operational** · 3/5 Too many segments. **Mitigation:** Keep 3-5 groups.
4. **Alignment** · 3/5 Teams use old aging only. **Mitigation:** Train on behavior logic.
5. **Financial** · 3/5 No speed improvement. **Mitigation:** Track DSO by segment.

Speed	Effort	Cost	Revenue	Time to cash	Scalability
Medium (1-3 months)	**Medium**	**Low**	**Very High**	**Immediate**	**High**

Decision-flow: CFO → Finance → Sales

232. Give sales ownership of payment speed after the deal

Make sales partly accountable for payment readiness, customer approvals, PO accuracy, and unresolved invoice blockers after closing the deal.

Why it works

Sales often closes revenue that finance later struggles to collect. Shared ownership prevents sold-but-stuck cash from becoming a finance-only problem.

Best for

B2B services, SaaS, consulting, construction, manufacturing, logistics, enterprise products

Execution Steps

1. Define sales role after close
2. Add payment-readiness items to handoff
3. Require PO and approver confirmation
4. Escalate blockers to account owners
5. Review cash status in sales meetings

Real-world example

A SaaS sales team confirms customer AP details before handoff, while a contractor makes account managers own approval blockers.

Risk Management

1. **Alignment** · 4/5 Sales resists collection ownership. **Mitigation:** Frame as revenue realization.
2. **Commercial** · 3/5 Customer relationship tension. **Mitigation:** Use support role not pressure.
3. **Operational** · 3/5 Handoff gaps. **Mitigation:** Use a pre-delivery checklist to catch quality issues before customer contact.
4. **Financial** · 3/5 Commission conflict. **Mitigation:** Link to collectible revenue logic.
5. **Customer** · 3/5 Mixed messages. **Mitigation:** Coordinate finance-sales contact.

Speed	Effort	Cost	Revenue	Time to cash	Scalability
Fast (0-30 days)	**Medium**	**Low**	**Very High**	**Immediate**	**High**

Decision-flow: CFO → Sales → Finance

233. Replace polite reminders with blocker-based follow-up conversations

Stop sending generic payment reminders and instead ask directly which blocker is preventing payment: approval, PO, dispute, cash timing, missing document, or process issue.

Why it works

Generic reminders are easy to ignore. Blocker-based follow-up diagnoses the real delay and moves payment forward faster.

Best for

B2B services, agencies, healthcare, logistics, construction, manufacturing, SaaS, professional services

Execution Steps

1. List common payment blockers
2. Replace generic reminder templates
3. Ask the customer to identify the blocker
4. Route each blocker to the right owner
5. Resolve blockers quickly

Real-world example

An agency asks if the delay is approval, PO, dispute, or missing documentation instead of sending another reminder.

Risk Management

1. **Customer** · 3/5 Tone feels blunt. **Mitigation:** Keep wording helpful.
2. **Operational** · 3/5 Blockers not resolved. **Mitigation:** Create routing rules.
3. **Alignment** · 3/5 Finance lacks authority. **Mitigation:** Assign blocker owners.
4. **Financial** · 3/5 Chronic cash timing remains. **Mitigation:** Escalate risk signals early — do not wait for.
5. **Commercial** · 2/5 Sales not informed. **Mitigation:** Share account notes.

Speed	Effort	Cost	Revenue	Time to cash	Scalability
Fast (0-30 days)	**Low**	**Low**	**High**	**Immediate**	**High**

Decision-flow: CFO → Finance → Customer Success

234. Make payment terms visible before customers say yes

Put payment terms, due dates, late consequences, required documents, and approval responsibilities clearly inside proposals, quotes, and order confirmations.

Why it works

Customers delay payment when expectations are vague. Making payment rules visible before agreement reduces later confusion and payment friction.

Best for

Consulting, agencies, healthcare, construction, logistics, manufacturing, SaaS, B2B services

Execution Steps

1. Review where terms are currently hidden
2. Add terms to proposals and quotes
3. Highlight approval responsibilities
4. Confirm acceptance before work starts
5. Repeat terms in order confirmation

Real-world example

A consulting firm puts invoice due dates and required approvers in proposals, while a manufacturer lists payment requirements in order confirmations.

Risk Management

1. **Customer** · 3/5 Terms ignored. **Mitigation:** Make them visible and plain.
2. **Commercial** · 3/5 Sales hides terms. **Mitigation:** Standardize proposal language.
3. **Legal** · 3/5 Terms incomplete. **Mitigation:** Review standard wording.
4. **Operational** · 3/5 Approvers not captured. **Mitigation:** Add required fields.
5. **Financial** · 3/5 Late payment continues. **Mitigation:** Pair with follow-up cadence.

Speed	Effort	Cost	Revenue	Time to cash	Scalability
Fast (0-30 days)	**Low**	**Low**	**High**	**Immediate**	**High**

Decision-flow: CFO → Sales → Finance

235. *Create a fast-pay lane for customers who want clean*

Offer customers a simplified payment path with saved details, automatic approvals, predictable invoice timing, and fewer admin steps.

Why it works

Some customers want operational ease as much as you want faster cash. A fast-pay lane aligns both sides around less admin and quicker settlement.

Best for

SaaS, healthcare, logistics, B2B services, education, agencies, wholesale, subscriptions

Execution Steps

1. Identify customers open to smoother billing
2. Build a simplified payment flow
3. Save billing details and preferences
4. Automate confirmations where possible
5. Offer the lane to reliable payers first

Real-world example

A healthcare provider sets up saved payment approvals, while a SaaS firm offers consolidated predictable billing for clean accounts.

Risk Management

1. **Product** · 4/5 Automation errors. **Mitigation:** Run a controlled pilot with three to five accounts.
2. **Customer** · 3/5 Low enrollment. **Mitigation:** Target admin-heavy customers.
3. **Financial** · 3/5 Fees or processing cost. **Mitigation:** Model savings.
4. **Legal** · 4/5 Authorization risk. **Mitigation:** Use clear consent
5. **Operational** · 3/5 Exception handling. **Mitigation:** Define rules.

Speed	Effort	Cost	Revenue	Time to cash	Scalability
Medium (1-3 months)	**Medium**	**Low**	**Very High**	**Immediate**	**High**

Decision-flow: CFO → Finance → Customer Success

236. Create an A++ customer payment scorecard

Score customers based on payment speed, clean approvals, dispute behavior, document readiness, and payment reliability, then show them their status.

Why it works

Customers respond to status. A visible scorecard turns payment behavior into reputation, making faster payment feel like good customer performance.

Best for

B2B services, SaaS, logistics, manufacturing, healthcare, wholesale, agencies, enterprise accounts

Execution Steps

1. Define payment health criteria
2. Score customers on payment behavior
3. Create simple A++ to C status levels
4. Share status with customers professionally
5. Link status to operational benefits

Real-world example

A supplier gives A++ status to customers with clean approvals and fast payments, creating a visible incentive to maintain payment discipline.

Risk Management

1. **Customer** · 4/5 Score feels punitive. **Mitigation:** Frame as partnership health.
2. **Product** · 4/5 Score inaccurate. **Mitigation:** Use transparent criteria.
3. **Commercial** · 3/5 Large customers resist. **Mitigation:** Pilot with willing accounts.
4. **Legal** · 3/5 Credit implication concern. **Mitigation:** Avoid formal credit language.
5. **Alignment** · 3/5 Teams ignore status. **Mitigation:** Tie to account handling.

Speed	Effort	Cost	Revenue	Time to cash	Scalability
Medium (1-3 months)	**Medium**	**Low**	**Very High**	**Immediate**	**High**

Decision-flow: CFO → Finance → Customer Success

237. Reward fast payers with operational credits, not discounts

Give customers small credits, priority admin support, service credits, bonus usage, or convenience benefits when they consistently pay quickly.

Why it works

Discounts reduce margin. Operational credits reward good payment behavior while keeping customers inside your ecosystem.

Best for

SaaS, healthcare, logistics, education, B2B services, subscriptions, agencies, wholesale

Execution Steps

1. Define fast-payment behavior
2. Choose non-cash rewards
3. Set clear eligibility rules
4. Communicate reward path
5. Apply credits automatically

Real-world example

A SaaS firm gives bonus usage credits for consistent on-time payment, while a logistics firm offers faster admin handling to reliable payers.

Risk Management

1. **Financial** · 3/5 Reward cost too high. **Mitigation:** Use low-cost operational perks — admin support.
2. **Customer** · 3/5 Reward not valued. **Mitigation:** Test options.
3. **Commercial** · 3/5 Seen as discount substitute. **Mitigation:** Position as operational benefit.
4. **Operational** · 3/5 Tracking complexity. **Mitigation:** Automate rules.
5. **Legal** · 2/5 Unclear terms create disputes and undermine trust in the commercial relationship.. **Mitigation:** Document eligibility.

Speed	Effort	Cost	Revenue	Time to cash	Scalability
Fast (0-30 days)	**Low**	**Low**	**High**	**Immediate**	**High**

Decision-flow: CFO → Finance → Customer Success

238. Turn payment speed into customer privilege

Give fast-paying customers access to easier approvals, smoother ordering, cleaner account handling, faster documentation, or lower admin friction.

Why it works

Customers value convenience. When good payment behavior unlocks smoother operations, finance improvement becomes a customer experience benefit.

Best for

B2B services, SaaS, healthcare, logistics, wholesale, agencies, manufacturing, enterprise accounts

Execution Steps

1. Identify privileges customers value
2. Link privileges to payment behavior
3. Define eligibility. and review periods
4. Communicate benefits clearly
5. Deliver privileges consistently

Real-world example

A supplier gives clean payers simplified order approvals, while a SaaS firm gives reliable accounts smoother billing administration.

Risk Management

1. **Customer** · 3/5 Fairness concern. **Mitigation:** Keep baseline service strong.
2. **Operational** · 3/5 Privilege delivery inconsistent. **Mitigation:** Standardize perks.
3. **Financial** · 3/5 Weak cash impact. **Mitigation:** Track days-to-cash.
4. **Commercial** · 3/5 Customer does not care. **Mitigation:** Use valued benefits.
5. **Legal** · 2/5 Discriminatory treatment concern. **Mitigation:** Use objective criteria.

Speed	Effort	Cost	Revenue	Time to cash	Scalability
Medium (1-3 months)	**Medium**	**Low**	**Very High**	**Immediate**	**High**

Decision-flow: CFO → Finance → Operations

239. *Create a clean account badge customers want to keep*

Give customers a visible clean-account status when they have no overdue invoices, no unresolved disputes, and clean billing behavior.

Why it works

Customers dislike losing status once it exists. A clean-account badge uses reputation psychology to encourage faster resolution and better payment discipline.

Best for

B2B services, healthcare, SaaS, logistics, memberships, education, wholesale, professional services

Execution Steps

1. Define clean-account criteria
2. Identify eligible customers
3. Show badge or status in account communications
4. Explain how to maintain it
5. Remind customers before status is lost

Real-world example

A B2B platform shows customers their clean account status and warns before unresolved invoices risk losing it.

Risk Management

1. **Customer** · 3/5 Badge feels childish. **Mitigation:** Keep tone professional.
2. **Product** · 4/5 Status inaccurate. **Mitigation:** Use reliable invoice data.
3. **Commercial** · 3/5 Low motivation. **Mitigation:** Link to useful benefits.
4. **Operational** · 3/5 Manual updates. **Mitigation:** Automate status.
5. **Legal** · 2/5 Credit wording risk. **Mitigation:** Avoid credit-rating claims.

Speed	Effort	Cost	Revenue	Time to cash	Scalability
Fast (0-30 days)	**Low**	**Low**	**High**	**Immediate**	**High**

Decision-flow: CFO → Finance → Customer Success

240. Use payment behavior to unlock better commercial access

Let strong payment behavior unlock access to smoother ordering, higher capacity allocation, simpler approvals, or preferred commercial treatment.

Why it works

Customers often care about access more than small discounts. Linking payment behavior to commercial ease encourages faster cash without cutting price.

Best for

Manufacturing, logistics, SaaS, wholesale, healthcare, distribution, B2B services, facilities

Execution Steps

1. Define access benefits
2. Set payment behavior thresholds
3. Link clean payment to access rules
4. Communicate the path clearly
5. Review access periodically

Real-world example

A manufacturer gives better allocation access to clean-paying customers, while a logistics firm offers smoother booking access to reliable payers.

Risk Management

1. **Customer** · 4/5 Feels punitive to others. **Mitigation:** Use positive framing.
2. **Operational** · 4/5 Capacity overpromised. **Mitigation:** Cap benefits.
3. **Commercial** · 3/5 Strategic accounts push back. **Mitigation:** Use exceptions carefully.
4. **Financial** · 3/5 Risk not reduced. **Mitigation:** Track overdue behavior.
5. **Legal** · 3/5 Unclear terms create disputes and undermine trust in the commercial relationship.. **Mitigation:** Document criteria.

Speed	Effort	Cost	Revenue	Time to cash	Scalability
Medium (1-3 months)	**Medium**	**Low**	**Very High**	**Immediate**	**High**

Decision-flow: CFO → Finance → Sales

241. *Create a customer payment health report*

Send customers a simple quarterly view of their payment performance, dispute rate, approval delays, overdue days, and operational friction created.

Why it works

Many customers do not realize they are difficult to collect from. Showing the operational impact turns hidden friction into a visible business issue.

Best for

B2B services, SaaS, logistics, manufacturing, healthcare, wholesale, agencies, enterprise accounts

Execution Steps

1. Collect payment performance data
2. Create a simple payment health report
3. Show delays, disputes, and blockers
4. Share with customer stakeholders
5. Agree improvement actions

Real-world example

A supplier shows an enterprise customer how late approvals and disputes added 18 days to settlement time.

Risk Management

1. **Customer** · 4/5 Report feels accusatory. **Mitigation:** Use neutral operational tone.
2. **Product** · 4/5 Data disputed. **Mitigation:** Show source details.
3. **Commercial** · 3/5 Relationship tension. **Mitigation:** Share with account context.
4. **Operational** · 3/5 Report too complex. **Mitigation:** Keep it simple.
5. **Financial** · 3/5 No behavior change. **Mitigation:** Agree next actions.

Speed	Effort	Cost	Revenue	Time to cash	Scalability
Medium (1-3 months)	**Medium**	**Low**	**High**	**Immediate**	**High**

Decision-flow: CFO → Finance → Customer Success

242. *Make late payment visible as operational cost, not just debt*

Show customers how late payment creates delays, admin work, capacity uncertainty, delivery risk, or service friction instead of simply asking them to pay.

Why it works

Customers respond better to operational consequences than blame. Framing payment as workflow health improves cooperation and reduces defensiveness.

Best for

B2B services, logistics, manufacturing, healthcare, construction, SaaS, agencies, professional services

Execution Steps

1. Identify operational impact of late payment
2. Translate it into simple business language
3. Replace blame-based reminders
4. Explain specific blockers created
5. Ask for practical resolution

Real-world example

A supplier explains that late payment delays capacity planning rather than accusing the customer of bad behavior.

Risk Management

1. **Customer** · 3/5 Still feels like blame. **Mitigation:** Use factual tone.
2. **Commercial** · 3/5 Impact not credible. **Mitigation:** Use real examples.
3. **Alignment** · 3/5 Finance uses old templates. **Mitigation:** Replace scripts.
4. **Operational** · 3/5 No escalation path. **Mitigation:** Add a single next action to every outreach to.
5. **Financial** · 3/5 Weak response. **Mitigation:** Pair with blocker follow-up.

Speed	Effort	Cost	Revenue	Time to cash	Scalability
Fast (0-30 days)	**Low**	**Low**	**High**	**Immediate**	**High**

Decision-flow: CFO → Finance → Customer Success

243. Offer a zero-friction billing upgrade for good payers

For reliable customers, offer automated invoicing, saved approvals, recurring payment permissions, consolidated statements, or one-click payment workflows.

Why it works

Good payers often want less admin too. Making payment easier for the right customers speeds cash while improving customer experience.

Best for

SaaS, healthcare, logistics, wholesale, B2B services, subscriptions, education, agencies

Execution Steps

1. Identify reliable payers
2. Offer automated billing options
3. Capture approvals and permissions
4. Consolidate statements where useful
5. Make payment one-click where possible

Real-world example

A SaaS company offers auto-approved billing for clean payers, while a healthcare provider simplifies recurring payment workflows.

Risk Management

1. **Product** · 4/5 Automation failure. **Mitigation:** Pilot and test.
2. **Legal** · 4/5 Authorization issue. **Mitigation:** Get clear consent.
3. **Customer** · 3/5 Customer fears loss of control. **Mitigation:** Allow alerts and review.
4. **Financial** · 3/5 Processing fees. **Mitigation:** Model cost.
5. **Operational** · 3/5 Exception handling. **Mitigation:** Define manual fallback.

Speed	Effort	Cost	Revenue	Time to cash	Scalability
Medium (1-3 months)	**Medium**	**Low**	**Very High**	**Immediate**	**High**

Decision-flow: CFO → Finance → IT / Data

244. Create a payment concierge for strategic accounts

Assign a finance contact who works directly with the customer's AP, procurement, and approvers to prevent invoices from getting stuck.

Why it works

Large accounts often pay slowly because of internal complexity, not unwillingness. A finance-side concierge removes blockers before they age.

Best for

Enterprise services, SaaS, logistics, healthcare, manufacturing, construction, agencies, B2B services

Execution Steps

1. Identify strategic slow-paying accounts
2. Assign finance contact
3. Map customer AP and approval process
4. Resolve blockers before due date
5. Coordinate with account owner

Real-world example

A manufacturer assigns a finance contact to a large account's AP team to prevent invoices from getting stuck in approval.

Risk Management

1. **Financial** · 3/5 Cost too high. **Mitigation:** Limit to strategic accounts.
2. **Customer** · 3/5 Too much contact. **Mitigation:** Agree cadence.
3. **Alignment** · 3/5 Sales and finance conflict. **Mitigation:** Define roles.
4. **Operational** · 3/5 No customer AP access. **Mitigation:** Get intro from account owner.
5. **Commercial** · 3/5 Weak impact. **Mitigation:** Track cash improvement.

Speed	Effort	Cost	Revenue	Time to cash	Scalability
Medium (1-3 months)	**Medium**	**Low**	**Very High**	**Immediate**	**High**

Decision-flow: CFO → Finance → Customer Success

245. *Turn invoice settlement into a customer success*

Treat payment completion as part of successful delivery, with confirmation, closure, documentation, and next-step readiness built into the customer journey.

Why it works

Payment often feels separate from value delivery. Making settlement part of project completion normalizes faster payment and reduces awkward collection cycles.

Best for

Consulting, agencies, construction, healthcare, SaaS, education, logistics, professional services

Execution Steps

1. Define payment completion as closure step
2. Link settlement to delivery confirmation
3. Include documentation and next-step readiness
4. Communicate professionally
5. Close projects only when billing is clean

Real-world example

An agency treats final invoice settlement as part of project closeout, including confirmation and next-step planning.

Risk Management

1. **Customer** · 3/5 Payment feels forced. **Mitigation:** Position as clean closure.
2. **Operational** · 3/5 Teams skip closure step. **Mitigation:** Add to project checklist.
3. **Financial** · 3/5 Late invoices remain. **Mitigation:** Track closure status.
4. **Alignment** · 3/5 Customer success avoids finance. **Mitigation:** Align roles.
5. **Commercial** · 2/5 Future work delayed. **Mitigation:** Separate unresolved issues.

Speed	Effort	Cost	Revenue	Time to cash	Scalability
Fast (0-30 days)	**Low**	**Low**	**High**	**Immediate**	**High**

Decision-flow: CFO → Customer Success → Finance

246. Increase credit limits for customers who pay cleanly

Give customers larger order limits, higher account credit, or smoother purchasing authority only after they prove strong payment behavior.

Why it works

Good payers get growth room. The business increases sales potential while protecting cash risk through earned credit access.

Best for

Wholesale, manufacturing, logistics, SaaS, healthcare, distribution, B2B services, retail supply

Execution Steps

1. Define clean payment criteria
2. Identify customers eligible for more credit
3. Set increased limits carefully
4. Communicate earned access
5. Monitor utilization and payment behavior

Real-world example

A distributor increases order limits for customers with six months of clean payment history.

Risk Management

1. **Financial** · 5/5 Credit exposure rises. **Mitigation:** Set limit caps.
2. **Customer** · 3/5 Customers expect automatic increases. **Mitigation:** Use criteria.
3. **Product** · 3/5 Payment history incomplete. **Mitigation:** Verify records.
4. **Commercial** · 4/5 Sales pushes unsafe limits. **Mitigation:** Require finance approval.
5. **Legal** · 3/5 Credit terms unclear. **Mitigation:** Document changes.

Speed	Effort	Cost	Revenue	Time to cash	Scalability
Medium (1-3 months)	**Medium**	**Low**	**Very High**	**Immediate**	**High**

Decision-flow: CFO → Finance → Sales

247. Create a payment health ladder customers can climb

Build visible customer levels such as Standard, Preferred, Gold, and A++ based on payment speed, dispute quality, and billing cooperation.

Why it works

Gamified progression makes payment behavior feel like status improvement. Customers can see what unlocks better treatment.

Best for

B2B services, wholesale, SaaS, healthcare, logistics, manufacturing, education, enterprise services

Execution Steps

1. Define payment health levels
2. Set clear criteria. for each level
3. Link levels to operational benefits
4. Show customers how to improve
5. Review movement periodically

Real-world example

A supplier creates Standard, Preferred, and A++ payment tiers tied to approval cleanliness and payment timing.

Risk Management

1. **Customer** · 3/5 Gamification feels unserious. **Mitigation:** Use professional naming.
2. **Product** · 4/5 Scores disputed. **Mitigation:** Share criteria.
3. **Commercial** · 3/5 Benefits not compelling. **Mitigation:** Use valued operational perks.
4. **Alignment** · 3/5 Teams ignore levels. **Mitigation:** Embed in account process.
5. **Legal** · 2/5 Credit language risk. **Mitigation:** Avoid formal rating claims.

Speed	Effort	Cost	Revenue	Time to cash	Scalability
Medium (1-3 months)	**Medium**	**Low**	**High**	**Immediate**	**High**

Decision-flow: CFO → Finance → Customer Success

248. Shrink credit access for bad payers automatically

Reduce order limits, payment terms, service access, or delivery flexibility for customers with repeated overdue invoices or unresolved payment friction.

Why it works

Bad payment behavior should create consequences. Automatic tightening protects cash and forces customers to earn flexibility back.

Best for

Wholesale, logistics, manufacturing, B2B services, healthcare, SaaS, distribution, construction

Execution Steps

1. Define bad-payer triggers
2. Set automatic tightening rules
3. Communicate rules before enforcement
4. Apply reductions consistently
5. Provide path to regain flexibility

Real-world example

A distributor reduces order limits for chronic late payers until they restore clean payment behavior.

Risk Management

1. **Customer** · 4/5 Relationship damage. **Mitigation:** Communicate path to recovery.
2. **Commercial** · 4/5 Sales exceptions. **Mitigation:** Require CFO approval.
3. **Financial** · 3/5 Lost revenue. **Mitigation:** Focus on risky revenue.
4. **Legal** · 3/5 Terms challenge. **Mitigation:** Document all rules and exceptions before the first live engagement.
5. **Operational** · 3/5 Inconsistent enforcement. **Mitigation:** Use usage data to trigger the expansion offer automatically.s

Speed	Effort	Cost	Revenue	Time to cash	Scalability
Medium (1-3 months)	**Medium**	**Low**	**Very High**	**Immediate**	**High**

Decision-flow: CFO → Finance → Sales

249. Require bad payers to move onto clean-payment terms

Shift customers with poor payment history to upfront payment, shorter terms, card-on-file, deposits, or payment-before-delivery until behavior improves.

Why it works

Some customers should not receive flexible terms. Clean-payment terms protect cash while keeping the relationship alive.

Best for

B2B services, wholesale, logistics, healthcare, construction, SaaS, manufacturing, professional services

Execution Steps

1. Identify repeated poor payers
2. Define clean-payment terms
3. Communicate the reset clearly
4. Apply to new orders or renewals
5. Create path back to standard terms

Real-world example

A supplier moves chronic late payers to payment-before-shipment until they rebuild payment reliability.

Risk Management

1. **Customer** · 4/5 Customer leaves. **Mitigation:** Apply to high-risk accounts.
2. **Commercial** · 4/5 Sales resistance. **Mitigation:** Show cash risk.
3. **Legal** · 4/5 Contract conflict. **Mitigation:** Submit all commercial terms to legal review before customer presentation.
4. **Financial** · 3/5 Short-term volume loss. **Mitigation:** Prioritize cash quality.
5. **Operational** · 3/5 Manual enforcement. **Mitigation:** Update order controls.

Speed	Effort	Cost	Revenue	Time to cash	Scalability
Fast (0-30 days)	**Low**	**Low**	**Very High**	**Immediate**	**High**

Decision-flow: CFO → Finance → Sales

250. Reward perfect payment streaks with operational perks

Give customers small non-discount perks after consecutive on-time payments, such as faster admin handling, simplified approvals, bonus service credits, or priority documentation.

Why it works

Streaks create motivation. Customers often protect a clean record once the business makes it visible and valuable.

Best for

SaaS, healthcare, education, logistics, B2B services, wholesale, subscriptions, agencies

Execution Steps

1. Define streak length
2. Choose non-discount perks
3. Track on-time payment streaks
4. Notify customers of progress
5. Award perks automatically

Real-world example

A SaaS firm gives priority documentation after three clean payments, while a supplier grants smoother admin handling after a clean streak.

Risk Management

1. **Financial** · 3/5 Perks cost too much. **Mitigation:** Use low-cost benefits.
2. **Customer** · 3/5 Streak not motivating. **Mitigation:** Show progress clearly.
3. **Operational** · 3/5 Tracking burden. **Mitigation:** Automate status.
4. **Commercial** · 2/5 Perks confuse sales. **Mitigation:** Document all rules and exceptions before the first live engagement.
5. **Legal** · 2/5 Unclear terms create disputes and undermine trust in the commercial relationship.. **Mitigation:** Publish criteria.

Speed	Effort	Cost	Revenue	Time to cash	Scalability
Fast (0-30 days)	**Low**	**Low**	**High**	**Immediate**	**High**

Decision-flow: CFO → Finance → Customer Success

251. Use a payment-splitting partner to remove cash-flow

Integrate a third-party payment provider that lets customers split large invoices into smaller payments while your business receives faster or guaranteed settlement.

Why it works

Customers may want to pay but face short-term cash pressure. A payment-splitting partner reduces friction without turning your business into the lender.

Best for

Healthcare, education, home services, B2B services, retail services, SaaS, events, professional services

Execution Steps

1. Identify invoices where size delays payment
2. Select a payment-splitting provider
3. Confirm settlement timing and fees
4. Add option to invoices or checkout
5. Communicate affordability clearly

Real-world example

A healthcare provider lets patients split bills through a payment partner while receiving faster settlement.

Risk Management

1. **Financial** · 3/5 Provider fees reduce margin. **Mitigation:** Model net cash benefit.
2. **Customer** · 3/5 Customer distrusts provider. **Mitigation:** Use reputable partner.
3. **Legal** · 4/5 Regulatory terms. **Mitigation:** Review agreements.
4. **Operational** · 3/5 Integration friction. **Mitigation:** Start manually if needed.
5. **Commercial** · 3/5 Uptake in the early period is below projections. Early signals must. **Mitigation:** Target large invoices.

Speed	Effort	Cost	Revenue	Time to cash	Scalability
Medium (1-3 months)	**Medium**	**Low**	**Very High**	**Immediate**	**High**

Decision-flow: CFO → Finance → Partnerships / BD

252. Offer bank-backed payment plans at checkout or proposal stage

Partner with a bank or finance provider to offer structured payment plans directly inside quotes, invoices, checkout, or customer payment flows.

Why it works

Customers are more likely to pay when affordability is built into the payment process. The business improves collection speed while shifting credit risk to a financial partner.

Best for

Retail, healthcare, education, equipment, B2B services, home services, SaaS, manufacturing

Execution Steps

1. Identify high-ticket invoices or purchases
2. Select bank or finance partner
3. Integrate payment-plan option
4. Clarify approval and settlement rules
5. Train teams to offer the option

Real-world example

An equipment seller embeds bank-backed payment plans in quotes, while a clinic offers structured plans through a finance partner.

Risk Management

1. **Legal** · 5/5 Financing disclosure risk. **Mitigation:** Use compliant partner terms.
2. **Financial** · 4/5 Settlement timing unclear. **Mitigation:** Confirm payout rules.
3. **Customer** · 3/5 Approval friction. **Mitigation:** Simplify process.
4. **Market** · 4/5 Partner experience poor. **Mitigation:** Choose strong partner.
5. **Commercial** · 3/5 Usage low. **Mitigation:** Target affordability-sensitive buyers.

Speed	Effort	Cost	Revenue	Time to cash	Scalability
Medium (1-3 months)	**Medium**	**Low**	**Very High**	**Immediate**	**High**

Decision-flow: CFO → Finance → Partnerships / BD

253. Turn unpaid invoices into financed receivables

Use invoice financing, factoring, or receivables funding partners to convert approved unpaid invoices into faster cash for the business.

Why it works

Some customers will always pay slowly. Financing approved receivables turns delayed cash into usable cash without waiting for customer payment cycles.

Best for

B2B services, logistics, manufacturing, wholesale, construction, healthcare, agencies, enterprise suppliers

Execution Steps

1. Identify slow but collectible invoices
2. Select receivables funding partner
3. Define eligible invoice criteria
4. Compare fees against cash need
5. Fund approved invoices selectively

Real-world example

A manufacturer finances approved enterprise invoices to access cash faster instead of waiting through long customer payment cycles.

Risk Management

1. **Financial** · 4/5 Funding fees too high. **Mitigation:** Deploy only in high-confidence accounts before broadening the approach.
2. **Customer** · 3/5 Customer notified awkwardly. **Mitigation:** Understand disclosure model.
3. **Legal** · 4/5 Contract restrictions. **Mitigation:** Review receivable assignment rights.
4. **Operational** · 3/5 Eligibility mismatch. **Mitigation:** Set clear criteria.
5. **Commercial** · 4/5 Overdependence on factoring. **Mitigation:** Use as cash tool not crutch.

Speed	Effort	Cost	Revenue	Time to cash	Scalability
Medium (1-3 months)	**Medium**	**Medium**	**Very High**	**Immediate**	**High**

Decision-flow: CFO → Finance → Partnerships / BD

From Ideas to Action

Twenty-eight ideas. Twenty-eight ways to close the gap between revenue agreed and cash collected.

Most billing problems are process problems. The invoice goes out late. The follow-up is polite when it should be direct. The escalation path does not exist. These are not customer problems. They are internal decisions that have never been made.

Before continuing, identify the single idea with the clearest commercial case right now. Name who owns it. Set a date for the first step. That is all that is required.

> ***The money is already owed. The only thing standing between agreement and cash is process.***

What Comes Next

4.3 — Sales Cycle Compression addresses businesses where deals are consistently good but slow — where the friction is internal process, buyer uncertainty, or approval complexity rather than genuine commercial objection. If qualified deals take longer than they should — the next chapter compresses the timeline.

4.3 — Sales Cycle Compression

Bring revenue forward by reducing the time it takes to move from opportunity to closed deal.

When These Strategies Work Best

Sales cycle compression works best when deals are consistently good but slow — where the friction is internal process, buyer uncertainty, or approval complexity rather than genuine commercial objection.

- Qualified deals regularly take months longer than the complexity of the decision warrants
- Proposals are customised from scratch for every deal regardless of similarity
- Buyers lack the internal tools to move approvals forward without external support
- Negotiation cycles repeat the same objections that could be resolved structurally
- Revenue forecasts are consistently pushed right because close dates keep slipping

The Benefits

- More revenue in the same period without adding new opportunities to the pipeline
- Lower cost of sale when fewer cycles are needed to reach a decision
- Better forecasting accuracy when close dates become more predictable
- Stronger buyer experience when the process feels responsive and clear
- Earlier cash flow from deals that were always good but previously delayed

The Risks to Manage

- **Pressure tactics** — forcing speed without removing friction erodes trust. The goal is to make deciding easier, not faster artificially.
- **Skipping qualification** — compressing cycles on poor-fit deals accelerates waste. Speed should apply to good deals only.
- **Underprepared buyers** — buyers rushed to a decision without the right information will stall later. Prepare them, do not push them.
- **Sales team resistance** — compressed cycles require new habits. Train and equip before expecting behaviour change.

254. Turn proposals into one-decision offers

Collapse multiple choices, configurations, approval paths, or pricing permutations into one highly recommended decision-ready offer.

Why it works

Too many choices slow commitment. Simplified offers reduce internal customer debate and accelerate executive approval.

Best for

SaaS, consulting, healthcare, logistics, agencies, manufacturing, enterprise services, construction

Execution Steps

1. Review proposals with too many options
2. Identify the strongest recommended path
3. Remove unnecessary choices
4. Present one clear decision-ready offer
5. Keep optional details in an appendix

Real-world example

A SaaS company replaces a complex pricing matrix with one recommended enterprise package for faster approval.

Risk Management

1. **Commercial** · 3/5 Offer feels too limited. **Mitigation:** Keep backup options available.
2. **Customer** · 3/5 Stakeholders want customization. **Mitigation:** Use appendix options.
3. **Alignment** · 3/5 Sales adds choices back. **Mitigation:** Standardize proposal rules.
4. **Financial** · 4/5 Wrong option recommended. **Mitigation:** Use qualification criteria.
5. **Operational** · 3/5 Delivery scope unclear. **Mitigation:** Define included scope.

Speed	Effort	Cost	Revenue	Time to cash	Scalability
Fast (0-30 days)	**Low**	**Low**	**Very High**	**Immediate**	**High**

Decision-flow: CFO → Sales → Product

255. Pre-build legal and procurement approval paths before closing

Map customer procurement, legal, compliance, security, and approval requirements during early sales stages instead of after commercial agreement.

Why it works

Many deals stall after verbal agreement because operational approval work begins too late. Early preparation compresses closing time dramatically.

Best for

Enterprise SaaS, healthcare, logistics, finance, consulting, cybersecurity, manufacturing, B2B services

Execution Steps

1. Ask approval-process questions early
2. Collect legal, procurement, and compliance requirements
3. Prepare standard documents in advance
4. Identify approval owners
5. Start non-commercial reviews before final agreement

Real-world example

A cybersecurity vendor starts security review while commercial discussions are still active, avoiding weeks of delay after verbal approval.

Risk Management

1. **Customer** · 3/5 Buyer resists early process questions. **Mitigation:** Explain time savings.
2. **Alignment** · 4/5 Legal joins too late. **Mitigation:** Create early trigger.
3. **Operational** · 3/5 Requirements missed. **Mitigation:** Use a pre-delivery checklist to catch quality issues before customer contact.
4. **Commercial** · 3/5 Deal not qualified enough. **Mitigation:** Apply to serious opportunities.
5. **Legal** · 3/5 Wrong document version. **Mitigation:** Maintain approved templates.

Speed	Effort	Cost	Revenue	Time to cash	Scalability
Medium (1-3 months)	**Medium**	**Low**	**Very High**	**Immediate**	**High**

Decision-flow: CFO → Sales → Legal

256. Turn customer hesitation into a reversible decision

Create a low-risk decision step such as conditional approval, pilot authorization, internal go-ahead, or decision reservation that moves the deal forward without requiring full final commitment.

Why it works

Customers often delay because final commitment feels psychologically heavy. Smaller reversible decisions reduce resistance while preserving deal momentum.

Best for

Healthcare, SaaS, consulting, construction, manufacturing, logistics, agencies, education

Execution Steps

1. Identify where final commitment feels too heavy
2. Define a reversible decision step
3. Make the step non-financial or low-risk
4. Clarify what it does and does not commit
5. Use it to keep approvals moving

Real-world example

A consulting firm asks for internal go-ahead to prepare approval documents before final contract signature.

Risk Management

1. **Customer** · 4/5 Step feels like hidden commitment. **Mitigation:** Clarify reversibility.
2. **Commercial** · 3/5 Sales treats it as closed. **Mitigation:** Define stage rules.
3. **Operational** · 3/5 Too much work before close. **Mitigation:** Limit effort.
4. **Legal** · 4/5 Ambiguous obligation. **Mitigation:** Use clear wording.
5. **Financial** · 3/5 Low conversion after step. **Mitigation:** Use only on qualified deals.

Speed	Effort	Cost	Revenue	Time to cash	Scalability
Fast (0-30 days)	**Low**	**Low**	**Very High**	**Immediate**	**High**

Decision-flow: CFO → Sales → Customer Success

257. *Create a decision-ready proposal format for executives*

Build proposals specifically for executive approval with short business cases, ROI clarity, implementation confidence, and approval-ready summaries.

Why it works

Most proposals are written for evaluation, not executive decisions. Executive-ready formatting reduces internal customer translation work.

Best for

Enterprise SaaS, consulting, healthcare, logistics, manufacturing, finance, construction, B2B services

Execution Steps

1. Identify what executives need to approve
2. Add business case, risk, ROI, and timing summary
3. Remove unnecessary technical detail from the main view
4. Create a one-page approval summary
5. Add appendix details for evaluators

Real-world example

A logistics provider replaces technical proposals with decision-ready summaries showing cost, risk, timing, and operational impact.

Risk Management

1. **Customer** · 2/5 Executive needs more detail. **Mitigation:** Include appendix.
2. **Commercial** · 4/5 ROI unsupported. **Mitigation:** Use defensible assumptions.
3. **Alignment** · 3/5 Sales keeps old format. **Mitigation:** Make template mandatory.
4. **Financial** · 3/5 Weak business case. **Mitigation:** Qualify value before proposal.
5. **Operational** · 3/5 Implementation confidence vague. **Mitigation:** Add a specific delivery plan with dates and owners before committing.

Speed	Effort	Cost	Revenue	Time to cash	Scalability
Fast (0-30 days)	**Medium**	**Low**	**Very High**	**Immediate**	**High**

Decision-flow: CFO → Sales → PMO / Strategy

258. Remove silent delays with mandatory next-step

Never end customer meetings without scheduling the next approval step, review meeting, decision date, or commercial checkpoint.

Why it works

Deals often die in silence because no next action exists. Mandatory forward scheduling keeps momentum alive and shortens idle time between stages.

Best for

SaaS, consulting, agencies, healthcare, logistics, manufacturing, enterprise sales, professional services

Execution Steps

1. Define required next-step types
2. Train sales. to schedule before meetings end
3. Add next-step field to CRM
4. Escalate deals without next action
5. Review silent gaps weekly

Real-world example

A consulting firm requires every proposal meeting to end with a decision-date or approval-review meeting scheduled.

Risk Management

1. **Customer** · 3/5 Customer refuses scheduling. **Mitigation:** Offer two simple options.
2. **Commercial** · 3/5 Next step is weak. **Mitigation:** Define meaningful actions.
3. **Alignment** · 3/5 Sales forgets. **Mitigation:** Make it CRM-required.
4. **Operational** · 2/5 Too many low-value meetings. **Mitigation:** Use only qualified steps.
5. **Financial** · 3/5 No close-rate lift. **Mitigation:** Track stage velocity.

Speed	Effort	Cost	Revenue	Time to cash	Scalability
Fast (0-30 days)	**Low**	**Low**	**Very High**	**Immediate**	**High**

Decision-flow: CFO → Sales → Customer Success

259. *Use a micro-yes ladder before the final close*

Break the deal into small sequential approvals where the customer says yes to individual pieces before the final commercial commitment.

Why it works

Large decisions feel risky. Smaller progressive commitments reduce psychological resistance and accelerate overall decision momentum.

Best for

Enterprise SaaS, consulting, healthcare, logistics, manufacturing, finance, agencies, construction

Execution Steps

1. Map the final decision into smaller approvals
2. Define each micro-yes
3. Sequence them logically
4. Confirm each yes in writing
5. Use progress to reduce final decision friction

Real-world example

A SaaS vendor gets agreement on problem, scope, stakeholders, risk plan, and timing before asking for final contract approval.

Risk Management

1. **Commercial** · 3/5 Too many steps slow deal. **Mitigation:** Keep ladder short.
2. **Customer** · 3/5 Feels manipulative. **Mitigation:** Communicate the basis for all decisions and relationships clearly upfront.
3. **Alignment** · 3/5 Sales skips sequence. **Mitigation:** Use stage checklist.
4. **Operational** · 3/5 Micro-yes lacks meaning. **Mitigation:** Tie to real approval.
5. **Financial** · 3/5 No final close. **Mitigation:** Qualify intent early.

Speed	Effort	Cost	Revenue	Time to cash	Scalability
Medium (1-3 months)	**Medium**	**Low**	**Very High**	**Immediate**	**High**

Decision-flow: CFO → Sales → Customer Success

260. Build a buying champion kit customers can use

Give internal champions ready-made slides, ROI summaries, FAQ responses, risk answers, approval memos, and executive talking points.

Why it works

Many deals slow because internal champions must resell the solution internally themselves. A champion kit accelerates internal alignment dramatically.

Best for

Enterprise SaaS, consulting, healthcare, logistics, manufacturing, finance, cybersecurity, B2B services

Execution Steps

1. Identify what champions need internally
2. Build approval slides and ROI summary
3. Add FAQ and objection answers
4. Include risk and implementation notes
5. Make it easy. to forward

Real-world example

A cybersecurity company gives its buyer a ready-to-forward risk and ROI pack for internal committee approval.

Risk Management

1. **Customer** · 3/5 Champion does not use kit. **Mitigation:** Make it easy. to edit
2. **Commercial** · 4/5 Kit too salesy. **Mitigation:** Write in buyer language.
3. **Financial** · 4/5 ROI challenged. **Mitigation:** Use conservative numbers.
4. **Alignment** · 3/5 Marketing creates generic material. **Mitigation:** Base on sales objections.
5. **Legal** · 3/5 Claims too strong. **Mitigation:** Review statements.

Speed	Effort	Cost	Revenue	Time to cash	Scalability
Fast (0-30 days)	**Medium**	**Low**	**Very High**	**Immediate**	**High**

Decision-flow: CFO → Sales → Marketing

261. Turn waiting for approval into active deal progression

While approvals are pending, continue advancing technical reviews, implementation planning, security checks, training prep, or operational alignment.

Why it works

Most companies pause while waiting for approval. Parallel progression removes dead time and compresses total deal duration.

Best for

Enterprise SaaS, healthcare, logistics, consulting, manufacturing, finance, construction, B2B services

Execution Steps

1. Identify work that can progress before signature
2. Separate low-risk prep from delivery
3. Get customer permission to proceed
4. Run approval and prep in parallel
5. Avoid irreversible commitments

Real-world example

A SaaS company completes security review and implementation planning while procurement finalizes contract approval.

Risk Management

1. **Operational** · 4/5 Too much unpaid work. **Mitigation:** Limit prep effort.
2. **Legal** · 4/5 Work starts before contract. **Mitigation:** Use non-binding prep only.
3. **Customer** · 3/5 Confusion about commitment. **Mitigation:** Clarify status.
4. **Alignment** · 3/5 Teams over-invest. **Mitigation:** Set effort caps.
5. **Financial** · 3/5 Deal still fails. **Mitigation:** Use only high-probability deals.

Speed	Effort	Cost	Revenue	Time to cash	Scalability
Medium (1-3 months)	**Medium**	**Low**	**Very High**	**Immediate**	**High**

Decision-flow: CFO → Sales → Operations

262. Use decision deadlines tied to operational reality,

Anchor decision timing to real operational constraints such as implementation windows, production planning, staffing allocation, seasonal cycles, or capacity scheduling.

Why it works

Fake urgency damages trust. Real operational deadlines create legitimate momentum and help customers prioritize decisions faster.

Best for

Manufacturing, SaaS, healthcare, logistics, consulting, construction, education, enterprise services

Execution Steps

1. Identify real operational timing constraints
2. Link decision timing to those constraints
3. Explain the impact of delay clearly
4. Avoid fake scarcity language
5. Put the decision date in writing

Real-world example

A manufacturer ties approval timing to production planning windows instead of using artificial end-of-month pressure.

Risk Management

1. **Customer** · 4/5 Deadline feels fake. **Mitigation:** Use only real constraints.
2. **Commercial** · 4/5 Sales abuses urgency. **Mitigation:** Set clear rules and communicate them before any access.
3. **Operational** · 3/5 Constraint changes. **Mitigation:** Update customer quickly.
4. **Financial** · 3/5 Deadline missed. **Mitigation:** Define next window.
5. **Market** · 4/5 Customer trust damaged if delivery falls short. **Mitigation:** Communicate the commercial relationship to customers before any recommendation.

Speed	Effort	Cost	Revenue	Time to cash	Scalability
Fast (0-30 days)	**Low**	**Low**	**Very High**	**Immediate**	**High**

Decision-flow: CFO → Sales → Operations

263. Create a decision simulation customers can mentally

Show customers exactly what happens after approval step-by-step, including implementation flow, stakeholder actions, timelines, risks removed, and expected outcomes.

Why it works

Customers delay decisions when the future feels unclear. Mental simulation reduces uncertainty and increases decision confidence.

Best for

Healthcare, SaaS, consulting, finance, logistics, manufacturing, education, construction

Execution Steps

1. Map the post-approval journey
2. Show stakeholder actions and timing
3. Highlight risks removed
4. Explain first outcomes clearly
5. Share simulation before final approval

Real-world example

A healthcare technology provider shows the buyer the exact first 30 days after approval so internal stakeholders can visualize execution.

Risk Management

1. **Customer** · 3/5 Simulation feels too complex. **Mitigation:** Keep it visual and simple.
2. **Operational** · 4/5 Future flow inaccurate. **Mitigation:** Use real delivery inputs.
3. **Commercial** · 3/5 Raises new objections. **Mitigation:** Prepare answers.
4. **Alignment** · 3/5 Customer success not involved. **Mitigation:** Co-create with delivery.
5. **Financial** · 3/5 No decision impact. **Mitigation:** Use with uncertain buyers.

Speed	Effort	Cost	Revenue	Time to cash	Scalability
Medium (1-3 months)	**Medium**	**Low**	**Very High**	**Immediate**	**High**

Decision-flow: CFO → Sales → Customer Success

264. Build an automated deal momentum engine

Use automation to trigger reminders, approvals, next steps, stakeholder nudges, document requests, and follow-up actions automatically as deals progress.

Why it works

Deals slow when momentum depends entirely on manual sales follow-up. Automation keeps decision energy alive between meetings.

Best for

SaaS, consulting, logistics, healthcare, manufacturing, finance, agencies, enterprise sales

Execution Steps

1. Map deal stages and required actions
2. Define automatic nudges and reminders
3. Connect triggers to CRM stages
4. Assign a named owner to every action item before. for each action
5. Test with live deals

Real-world example

A RevOps team automates document reminders and stakeholder nudges when deals sit too long in approval stage.

Risk Management

1. **Product** · 3/5 Automation misfires. **Mitigation:** Test rules.
2. **Customer** · 3/5 Messages feel robotic. **Mitigation:** Personalize templates.
3. **Alignment** · 3/5 Sales ignores alerts. **Mitigation:** Assign a named owner to every action item before.
4. **Operational** · 3/5 Too many notifications. **Mitigation:** Limit triggers.
5. **Financial** · 3/5 No cycle impact. **Mitigation:** Measure stage velocity.

Speed	Effort	Cost	Revenue	Time to cash	Scalability
Medium (1-3 months)	**Medium**	**Low**	**Very High**	**Immediate**	**High**

Decision-flow: CFO → Sales → Revenue Operations

265. Automatically detect stalled deals before they die

Use automation rules to flag silent deals based on inactivity, missing approvals, delayed replies, document gaps, or abnormal stage duration.

Why it works

Most deals do not formally die — they silently decay. Early automated detection allows intervention before momentum collapses.

Best for

Enterprise SaaS, B2B services, consulting, healthcare, logistics, finance, manufacturing, agencies

Execution Steps

1. Define stall signals
2. Set inactivity and stage-age thresholds
3. Create automated alerts
4. Assign intervention actions
5. Review flagged deals weekly

Real-world example

A SaaS company flags deals with no stakeholder reply for 10 days and triggers a manager review before the deal goes cold.

Risk Management

1. **Product** · 3/5 Too many false alerts. **Mitigation:** Tune signal thresholds regularly using real performance data.
2. **Alignment** · 3/5 Alerts ignored. **Mitigation:** Assign review owner.
3. **Commercial** · 3/5 Wrong intervention. **Mitigation:** Use playbooks.
4. **Operational** · 4/5 CRM data poor. **Mitigation:** Improve stage hygiene.
5. **Financial** · 3/5 Low recovery rate. **Mitigation:** Focus on high-value deals.

Speed	Effort	Cost	Revenue	Time to cash	Scalability
Fast (0-30 days)	**Low**	**Low**	**Very High**	**Immediate**	**High**

Decision-flow: CFO → Revenue Operations → Sales

266. Use automated proposal generation to compress

Automatically generate proposals, pricing summaries, ROI cases, legal terms, and approval-ready documents directly from CRM or deal inputs.

Why it works

Manual proposal creation creates unnecessary delay and inconsistency. Automated proposal assembly dramatically reduces sales-cycle friction.

Best for

SaaS, consulting, healthcare, logistics, manufacturing, agencies, finance, enterprise services

Execution Steps

1. Identify repetitive proposal components
2. Build approved templates
3. Connect CRM deal fields
4. Generate proposal drafts automatically
5. Add review controls

Real-world example

A consulting firm automatically generates proposal drafts from CRM scope fields and approved pricing logic.

Risk Management

1. **Product** · 4/5 Incorrect proposal data. **Mitigation:** Use validation checks.
2. **Legal** · 4/5 Wrong terms inserted. **Mitigation:** Lock approved clauses.
3. **Commercial** · 3/5 Proposal feels generic. **Mitigation:** Allow controlled customization.
4. **Alignment** · 3/5 Sales bypasses tool. **Mitigation:** Make it faster than manual.
5. **Financial** · 3/5 Implementation cost. **Mitigation:** Start with top proposal types.

Speed	Effort	Cost	Revenue	Time to cash	Scalability
Medium (1-3 months)	**Medium**	**Medium**	**Very High**	**Immediate**	**High**

Decision-flow: CFO → Sales → IT / Data

267. Create automated stakeholder follow-up paths

Automatically send role-specific follow-ups to procurement, finance, legal, security, executives, or operational stakeholders during the deal cycle.

Why it works

Different stakeholders delay deals for different reasons. Automated targeted communication keeps each approval path moving simultaneously.

Best for

Enterprise SaaS, cybersecurity, healthcare, logistics, consulting, finance, manufacturing, B2B services

Execution Steps

1. Map common stakeholder roles
2. Define each role's concerns
3. Build role-specific follow-up messages
4. Trigger messages by deal stage
5. Coordinate with the account owner

Real-world example

A cybersecurity vendor sends security, procurement, and executive stakeholders different approval-support messages during the same deal cycle.

Risk Management

1. **Customer** · 4/5 Messages feel spammy. **Mitigation:** Use low frequency.
2. **Legal** · 3/5 Wrong recipient. **Mitigation:** Confirm stakeholders.
3. **Commercial** · 3/5 Misaligned messaging. **Mitigation:** Coordinate with sales.
4. **Product** · 3/5 Automation errors. **Mitigation:** Test workflows.
5. **Market** · 3/5 Too much automation. **Mitigation:** Use human review for large deals.

Speed	Effort	Cost	Revenue	Time to cash	Scalability
Medium (1-3 months)	**Medium**	**Low**	**Very High**	**Immediate**	**High**

Decision-flow: CFO → Sales → IT / Data

268. Use AI to predict which deals need executive

Analyze deal behavior, stakeholder activity, delays, objections, approval patterns, and engagement signals to identify deals likely to stall without leadership involvement.

Why it works

Executives often join deals too late. AI-assisted escalation identifies high-risk opportunities before momentum breaks down.

Best for

Enterprise SaaS, consulting, healthcare, logistics, finance, manufacturing, cybersecurity, B2B services

Execution Steps

1. Identify signals of deal stall risk
2. Feed CRM and engagement data into model or scoring logic
3. Flag deals needing executive intervention
4. Define intervention playbooks
5. Review predictions weekly

Real-world example

A B2B company flags enterprise deals where legal delay, executive silence, and low engagement indicate the need for senior intervention.

Risk Management

1. **Product** · 4/5 Poor prediction quality. **Mitigation:** Start with simple rules.
2. **Alignment** · 4/5 Executives overused. **Mitigation:** Define a minimum performance threshold before committing to scale.
3. **Commercial** · 3/5 Intervention feels heavy-handed. **Mitigation:** Use appropriate tone.
4. **Product** · 4/5 Data quality weak. **Mitigation:** Improve CRM hygiene.
5. **Financial** · 3/5 Tool cost. **Mitigation:** Pilot manually first.

Speed	Effort	Cost	Revenue	Time to cash	Scalability
Medium (1-3 months)	**High**	**Medium**	**Very High**	**Immediate**	**High**

Decision-flow: CFO → Revenue Operations → Cross-functional

269. Offer an approval-completion bonus for finishing the process early

Give customers a useful non-discount bonus when they complete the internal approval process by an agreed date, such as extra setup help, admin support, training, or documentation.

Why it works

Customers often delay because the decision is not internally prioritized. A practical operational incentive helps move the approval process forward faster.

Best for

SaaS, consulting, manufacturing, healthcare, logistics, agencies, construction, enterprise services

Execution Steps

1. Identify deals stuck in approval
2. Choose a low-cost non-discount bonus
3. Tie the bonus to approval completion
4. Set an agreed decision date
5. Communicate the operational value

Real-world example

A SaaS vendor offers extra admin setup support if the buyer completes internal approval by the agreed decision date.

Risk Management

1. **Financial** · 3/5 Bonus costs too much. **Mitigation:** Use low-cost operational support.
2. **Customer** · 3/5 Looks like pressure. **Mitigation:** Frame as planning benefit.
3. **Commercial** · 3/5 Sales uses it too broadly. **Mitigation:** Limit to qualified deals.
4. **Operational** · 3/5 Bonus delivery burden. **Mitigation:** Standardize bonus options.
5. **Market** · 2/5 Feels like discounting. **Mitigation:** Avoid price concessions.

Speed	Effort	Cost	Revenue	Time to cash	Scalability
Fast (0-30 days)	**Low**	**Low**	**High**	**Immediate**	**High**

Decision-flow: CFO → Sales → Customer Success

270. Give buyers a fast approval pack for their boss

Provide a ready-to-forward approval pack with one-page business case, cost, risk, timeline, expected result, and decision recommendation.

Why it works

Deals slow when buyers must explain the decision internally. Removing that work helps them get approval faster.

Best for

SaaS, consulting, healthcare, logistics, manufacturing, finance, agencies, enterprise services

Execution Steps

1. Identify boss-level approval questions
2. Build one-page approval pack
3. Include cost, risk, timeline, and outcome
4. Make it easy. to forward
5. Customize for the opportunity

Real-world example

A manufacturing supplier gives the buyer a one-page approval pack to forward to the CFO and operations leader.

Risk Management

1. **Customer** · 3/5 Pack misses key concern. **Mitigation:** Ask buyer what boss needs.
2. **Commercial** · 3/5 Too salesy. **Mitigation:** Use executive language.
3. **Financial** · 4/5 Weak ROI. **Mitigation:** Use realistic numbers.
4. **Alignment** · 3/5 Sales does not customize. **Mitigation:** Provide template fields.
5. **Legal** · 3/5 Claims unsupported. **Mitigation:** Review claims.

Speed	Effort	Cost	Revenue	Time to cash	Scalability
Fast (0-30 days)	**Low**	**Low**	**Very High**	**Immediate**	**High**

Decision-flow: CFO → Sales → Marketing

271. Run a 15-minute deal unblocker call

Offer a short structured call focused only on identifying the one thing preventing the customer from deciding and resolving the next action.

Why it works

Long sales cycles often hide one unresolved blocker. A short unblocker call creates clarity and gets the deal moving quickly.

Best for

SaaS, consulting, agencies, healthcare, logistics, manufacturing, finance, professional services

Execution Steps

1. Identify stalled qualified deals
2. Invite buyer to a 15-minute unblocker call
3. Ask what blocks the decision
4. Agree one next action
5. Assign owner. and date

Real-world example

A consulting firm uses a short unblocker call to discover that procurement needs one missing insurance document.

Risk Management

1. **Customer** · 3/5 Buyer declines call. **Mitigation:** Keep invitation specific.
2. **Commercial** · 2/5 Call becomes full sales meeting. **Mitigation:** Use strict agenda.
3. **Alignment** · 3/5 No follow-through. **Mitigation:** Assign next action.
4. **Operational** · 3/5 Wrong people attend. **Mitigation:** Invite blocker owner.
5. **Financial** · 3/5 No movement. **Mitigation:** Use on real opportunities.

Speed	Effort	Cost	Revenue	Time to cash	Scalability
Fast (0-30 days)	**Low**	**Low**	**High**	**Immediate**	**High**

Decision-flow: CFO → Sales → Customer Success

272. Offer a decision concierge for complex buyers

Assign one person to help the buyer coordinate internal approvals, documents, stakeholder questions, and next steps until the deal is signed.

Why it works

Complex deals stall because the buyer becomes the internal project manager. Helping them coordinate speeds commitment.

Best for

Enterprise SaaS, consulting, healthcare, logistics, construction, finance, manufacturing, B2B services

Execution Steps

1. Identify complex approval deals
2. Assign a decision concierge
3. Map required stakeholders and documents
4. Track approvals and next steps
5. Remove blockers with the buyer

Real-world example

A SaaS company assigns a deal concierge to help the buyer coordinate legal, security, finance, and executive approvals.

Risk Management

1. **Operational** · 3/5 Too much handholding. **Mitigation:** Limit to strategic deals.
2. **Customer** · 3/5 Feels intrusive. **Mitigation:** Ask permission.
3. **Commercial** · 3/5 Role confused with customer success. **Mitigation:** Define pre-signature scope.
4. **Alignment** · 3/5 No owner availability. **Mitigation:** Assign specific capacity.
5. **Financial** · 3/5 Cost exceeds benefit. **Mitigation:** Use on high-value deals.

Speed	Effort	Cost	Revenue	Time to cash	Scalability
Medium (1-3 months)	**Medium**	**Low**	**Very High**	**Immediate**	**High**

Decision-flow: CFO → Sales → Customer Success

273. Use a decision-date rule for holding commercial terms

Hold pricing, scope, delivery timing, or implementation capacity only when the buyer agrees to a clear decision date.

Why it works

Open-ended commercial holds let deals drift indefinitely. Decision-date discipline protects operational planning while encouraging customers to prioritize decisions.

Best for

SaaS, consulting, manufacturing, logistics, construction, healthcare, agencies, enterprise services

Execution Steps

1. Define which commercial terms can be held
2. Require an agreed decision date
3. Communicate the reason clearly
4. Record the date in the opportunity
5. Release holds when no decision is made

Real-world example

A manufacturer holds production timing only when the buyer agrees to a decision date tied to planning cutoffs.

Risk Management

1. **Customer** · 3/5 Feels like pressure. **Mitigation:** Explain operational reason.
2. **Commercial** · 3/5 Sales misuses rule. **Mitigation:** Set policy.
3. **Operational** · 3/5 Capacity still held too long. **Mitigation:** Release automatically.
4. **Financial** · 2/5 Lost late deals. **Mitigation:** Use for qualified opportunities.
5. **Market** · 3/5 Looks like fake urgency. **Mitigation:** Use real constraints.

Speed	Effort	Cost	Revenue	Time to cash	Scalability
Fast (0-30 days)	**Low**	**Low**	**High**	**Immediate**	**High**

Decision-flow: CFO → Sales → Operations

274. Create a board-ready decision memo automatically from the proposal

Automatically convert the proposal into a board-ready or executive-ready approval memo with ROI, risks, implementation impact, budget logic, and recommendation already prepared.

Why it works

Large deals often stall because internal teams must rebuild the business case for leadership. Removing that translation layer dramatically accelerates approvals.

Best for

Enterprise SaaS, healthcare, manufacturing, logistics, finance, consulting, infrastructure, B2B services

Execution Steps

1. Identify board or executive approval needs
2. Define memo structure
3. Pull deal facts from proposal or CRM
4. Add ROI, risks, timing, and recommendation
5. Review for accuracy

Real-world example

A consulting firm automatically turns its proposal into a board-ready decision memo for the buyer's executive team.

Risk Management

1. **Financial** · 4/5 ROI challenged. **Mitigation:** Use transparent assumptions.
2. **Legal** · 3/5 Claims overstate value. **Mitigation:** Review memo language.
3. **Customer** · 3/5 Memo not in buyer style. **Mitigation:** Allow editing.
4. **Product** · 4/5 Automation pulls wrong data. **Mitigation:** Validate fields.
5. **Commercial** · 2/5 Too much detail. **Mitigation:** Keep concise.

Speed	Effort	Cost	Revenue	Time to cash	Scalability
Medium (1-3 months)	**Medium**	**Low**	**Very High**	**Immediate**	**High**

Decision-flow: CFO → Sales → PMO / Strategy

275. *Use a decision war room for high-value stuck deals*

Create a short cross-functional rapid-response team that temporarily attacks one stalled strategic deal until blockers, approvals, risks, and stakeholder objections are resolved.

Why it works

Big deals often die because no coordinated push exists. A focused decision war room compresses weeks of fragmented movement into days.

Best for

Enterprise SaaS, construction, manufacturing, healthcare, consulting, finance, logistics, infrastructure

Execution Steps

1. Identify a high-value stuck deal
2. Assemble sales, finance, legal, operations, and executive owners
3. Map every blocker
4. Assign rapid actions
5. Meet briefly until blockers clear

Real-world example

A manufacturing supplier creates a one-week war room to clear legal, procurement, and operations blockers on a strategic contract.

Risk Management

1. **Alignment** · 3/5 Too many people involved. **Mitigation:** Keep team small.
2. **Commercial** · 3/5 Customer feels pressured. **Mitigation:** Coordinate carefully.
3. **Operational** · 3/5 War room distracts teams. **Mitigation:** Use only for strategic deals
4. **Financial** · 3/5 Deal still fails. **Mitigation:** Qualify value first.
5. **Alignment** · 3/5 Leadership overused. **Mitigation:** Define a minimum performance threshold before committing to scale.

Speed	Effort	Cost	Revenue	Time to cash	Scalability
Fast (0-30 days)	**Medium**	**Low**	**Very High**	**Immediate**	**High**

Decision-flow: CFO → Sales → Cross-functional

276. Turn implementation fear into a signed risk-removal

Before contract signature, give the customer a clear written roadmap showing risks, mitigation steps, support structure, fallback plans, and operational protections.

Why it works

Many buyers delay because they fear failure after signing. Reducing implementation anxiety accelerates commitment without lowering price.

Best for

Healthcare, SaaS, logistics, manufacturing, finance, consulting, construction, enterprise services

Execution Steps

1. Identify customer fears before signing
2. Build a risk-removal roadmap
3. Show mitigation steps and fallback plans
4. Clarify support structure
5. Share roadmap before final approval

Real-world example

A SaaS company gives the buyer a signed risk-removal roadmap showing migration risks, mitigation actions, and support coverage before contract approval.

Risk Management

1. **Customer** · 3/5 Roadmap raises new concerns. **Mitigation:** Frame risks with mitigations.
2. **Legal** · 4/5 Creates implied guarantees. **Mitigation:** Review wording.
3. **Operational** · 4/5 Delivery team cannot support promises. **Mitigation:** Co-create with operations.
4. **Commercial** · 3/5 Too much pre-sale effort. **Mitigation:** Use for high-value deals.
5. **Financial** · 3/5 No cycle reduction. **Mitigation:** Track objection clearance.

Speed	Effort	Cost	Revenue	Time to cash	Scalability
Medium (1-3 months)	**Medium**	**Low**	**Very High**	**Immediate**	**High**

Decision-flow: CFO → Sales → Operations

From Ideas to Action

Twenty-three ideas. Twenty-three ways to shorten the distance between a qualified prospect and a signed agreement.

A long sales cycle is rarely caused by a difficult customer. It is caused by friction the business built into its own process — unclear proposals, unresolved objections, approvals that were never mapped, decisions left open too long. Remove the friction. The cycle compresses.

Before continuing, identify the single idea with the clearest commercial case right now. Name who owns it. Set a date for the first step. That is all that is required.

> ***Every week a deal stays open is a week the business financed the customer for free.***

What Comes Next

4.4 — Activation Speed addresses businesses where customers buy but are slow to start, use, or expand their purchase. If the gap between signed deal and first real value is wider than it should be — the next chapter closes it.

4.4 — Activation Speed

Accelerate revenue by getting customers to first value, first use, or first expansion faster after the sale.

When These Strategies Work Best

Activation speed strategies work best when customers buy but are slow to use, derive value from, or expand their purchase — creating a gap between contracted revenue and realised commercial impact.

- Onboarding takes weeks or months when the product could deliver value in days
- Customers who bought have not used the product within the first 30 days
- Expansion and upsell depend on adoption that is not happening fast enough
- Support load is high in the first 90 days because customers do not know how to start
- Churn correlates strongly with customers who never fully activated after purchase

The Benefits

- Faster time to first value that directly reduces early churn
- Earlier expansion and upsell triggers that compound lifetime value
- Reduced support cost when customers reach self-sufficiency faster
- Stronger references and social proof from customers who succeed quickly
- Higher renewal rates because activated customers have more to protect at renewal

The Risks to Manage

- **Activation theatre** — measuring completion of steps rather than actual value received. Define activation as an outcome, not a checklist.
- **One-size onboarding** — different customers need different activation paths. Segment and personalise where it matters.
- **Handoff gaps** — the transition from sales to delivery is where customers get lost. Own the handoff completely.
- **Speed over quality** — activating customers into a bad first experience accelerates churn. Quality and speed must be designed together.

277. Get customers to their first win in the first session

Design onboarding so every customer achieves one visible result, useful setup, completed action, or meaningful progress point in the first session.

Why it works

Customers trust the purchase faster when they feel value immediately. A first-session win builds momentum and reduces buyer regret.

Best for

SaaS, education, healthcare, fitness, consulting, financial tools, professional services, home services

Execution Steps

1. Define the smallest meaningful first win
2. Rebuild the first session around that win
3. Remove all non-essential steps
4. Prepare customer inputs in advance
5. Confirm the win before the session ends

Real-world example

A SaaS company helps users build one useful dashboard in the first session, while a fitness program completes a first personalized plan immediately.

Risk Management

1. **Customer** · 4/5 First win not meaningful. **Mitigation:** Choose visible value.
2. **Operational** · 3/5 Session too long. **Mitigation:** Cut non-essential steps.
3. **Product** · 4/5 Setup blockers. **Mitigation:** Prepare inputs early.
4. **Alignment** · 3/5 Teams define value differently. **Mitigation:** Use one standard outcome.
5. **Financial** · 3/5 No downstream impact. **Mitigation:** Track activation-to-retention.

Speed	Effort	Cost	Revenue	Time to cash	Scalability
Fast (0-30 days)	**Medium**	**Low**	**Very High**	**Immediate**	**High**

Decision-flow: CFO → Customer Success → Product

278. Remove every activation step that does not create value

Cut unnecessary forms, setup tasks, approvals, training modules, configuration steps, or internal handoffs that delay the customer from using the offer.

Why it works

Activation often slows because businesses confuse process completion with customer value. Removing low-value steps shortens time-to-use.

Best for

SaaS, healthcare, logistics, education, finance, memberships, B2B services, home services

Execution Steps

1. Map every activation step
2. Label each step as value-creating or not
3. Remove, delay, or automate low-value steps
4. Simplify customer inputs
5. Test the shorter path

Real-world example

A healthcare provider removes duplicate intake questions, while a SaaS company delays advanced configuration until after first use.

Risk Management

1. **Operational** · 4/5 Important control removed. **Mitigation:** Review risk-critical steps.
2. **Customer** · 3/5 Customer lacks context. **Mitigation:** Keep essential guidance.
3. **Product** · 4/5 Hidden dependency breaks. **Mitigation:** Test end-to-end.
4. **Legal** · 4/5 Required step removed. **Mitigation:** Review regulated steps.
5. **Financial** · 2/5 Limited impact. **Mitigation:** Prioritize high-friction paths.

Speed	Effort	Cost	Revenue	Time to cash	Scalability
Fast (0-30 days)	**Medium**	**Low**	**High**	**Immediate**	**High**

Decision-flow: CFO → Operations → Product

279. Create a day-one activation path for every offer

Define the exact actions, assets, instructions, support, and checkpoints needed for a customer to start using the product or service on day one.

Why it works

Customers lose momentum when the first step is unclear. A day-one path turns purchase energy into immediate usage.

Best for

SaaS, education, healthcare, consulting, logistics, finance, fitness, professional services

Execution Steps

1. Define what day-one usage means
2. List required customer actions
3. Prepare instructions and assets
4. Assign support owner
5. Send the path immediately after sale

Real-world example

A consulting firm sends a day-one action path after signature, while a SaaS firm gives users an immediate setup sequence.

Risk Management

1. **Customer** · 3/5 Customer ignores path. **Mitigation:** Send at peak purchase momentum.
2. **Operational** · 3/5 Instructions unclear. **Mitigation:** Use plain language.
3. **Alignment** · 3/5 Owner missing. **Mitigation:** Assign activation lead.
4. **Product** · 4/5 Access delay. **Mitigation:** Provision immediately.
5. **Financial** · 3/5 Low usage lift. **Mitigation:** Measure day-one completion.

Speed	Effort	Cost	Revenue	Time to cash	Scalability
Fast (0-30 days)	**Low**	**Low**	**High**	**Immediate**	**High**

Decision-flow: CFO → Customer Success → Operations

280. Turn onboarding into a guided checklist customers

Replace vague onboarding with a short guided checklist that shows customers what to do, why it matters, who owns it, and when it should be completed.

Why it works

Customers stall when onboarding feels open-ended. A clear checklist creates completion momentum and makes activation measurable.

Best for

SaaS, healthcare, education, finance, logistics, consulting, agencies, B2B services

Execution Steps

1. Identify required activation actions
2. Reduce the list to essentials
3. Add owner and deadline to each task
4. Explain why each step matters
5. Track completion visibly

Real-world example

An education platform replaces broad onboarding calls with a five-step guided checklist that gets learners active quickly.

Risk Management

1. **Customer** · 3/5 Checklist too long. **Mitigation:** Keep only essential tasks.
2. **Operational** · 3/5 Tasks not owned. **Mitigation:** Assign owner.
3. **Product** · 3/5 Progress not visible. **Mitigation:** Show completion status.
4. **Alignment** · 3/5 Teams add extra tasks. **Mitigation:** Control checklist scope.
5. **Financial** · 3/5 Completion not linked to value. **Mitigation:** Tie steps to first use.

Speed	Effort	Cost	Revenue	Time to cash	Scalability
Fast (0-30 days)	**Low**	**Low**	**Very High**	**Immediate**	**High**

Decision-flow: CFO → Customer Success → Product

281. Assign an activation owner before the customer gets

Give every new customer a named activation owner responsible for guiding first use, removing blockers, and confirming first value.

Why it works

Customers often stall because no one owns their activation. Named ownership prevents post-sale drift and accelerates value realization.

Best for

SaaS, consulting, healthcare, logistics, education, finance, professional services, agencies

Execution Steps

1. Define activation owner role
2. Assign owner. immediately after sale
3. Set first-value target
4. Monitor blockers daily
5. Confirm first value with customer

Real-world example

A professional services firm assigns an activation owner who ensures every new client reaches first output within the first week.

Risk Management

1. **Operational** · 3/5 Owner overloaded. **Mitigation:** Limit account load.
2. **Customer** · 2/5 Customer bypasses owner. **Mitigation:** Introduce role clearly.
3. **Alignment** · 3/5 Sales handoff weak. **Mitigation:** Use handoff checklist.
4. **Financial** · 3/5 Cost rises. **Mitigation:** Prioritize high-value customers.
5. **Operational** · 3/5 Owner lacks authority. **Mitigation:** Give escalation rights.

Speed	Effort	Cost	Revenue	Time to cash	Scalability
Fast (0-30 days)	**Medium**	**Low**	**Very High**	**Immediate**	**High**

Decision-flow: CFO → Customer Success → Operations

282. *Use AI to predict which customers will fail to activate*

Analyze onboarding behavior, inactivity, setup delays, support usage, and engagement signals to identify customers likely to stall before value realization.

Why it works

Most activation failure signals appear early but go unnoticed. Predictive intervention prevents silent drop-off before churn risk grows.

Best for

SaaS, healthcare, education, fintech, logistics, memberships, B2B platforms, professional services

Execution Steps

1. Identify activation failure signals
2. Collect onboarding and usage data
3. Build a risk score or AI model
4. Flag customers likely to stall
5. Trigger intervention playbooks

Real-world example

A SaaS firm flags customers with setup inactivity and support confusion before they fail to activate.

Risk Management

1. **Product** · 4/5 Poor prediction quality. **Mitigation:** Start with simple rules.
2. **Product** · 4/5 Data gaps. **Mitigation:** Track key events.
3. **Customer** · 3/5 Intervention feels intrusive. **Mitigation:** Use helpful tone.
4. **Alignment** · 3/5 No rescue owner. **Mitigation:** Assign playbooks.
5. **Financial** · 3/5 Model cost too high. **Mitigation:** Pilot manually first.

Speed	Effort	Cost	Revenue	Time to cash	Scalability
Medium (1-3 months)	**High**	**Medium**	**Very High**	**Immediate**	**High**

Decision-flow: CFO → Customer Success → IT / Data

283. Create an AI onboarding guide that adapts in real time

Use AI to personalize onboarding steps, explanations, pacing, recommendations, and support based on customer behavior and progress.

Why it works

Different customers activate differently. Adaptive onboarding removes confusion and accelerates first value without requiring large support teams.

Best for

SaaS, education, healthcare, fintech, logistics, memberships, fitness, B2B services

Execution Steps

1. Map common onboarding paths
2. Identify personalization signals
3. Build AI guidance rules
4. Adjust steps based on customer progress
5. Escalate complex blockers to humans

Real-world example

An education platform adapts onboarding based on learner confidence, while a SaaS product changes setup guidance based on user behavior.

Risk Management

1. **Product** · 4/5 AI gives wrong guidance. **Mitigation:** Use controlled recommendations.
2. **Customer** · 3/5 Customer distrusts AI. **Mitigation:** Offer human fallback.
3. **Product** · 3/5 Insufficient signals. **Mitigation:** Start with simple paths.
4. **Legal** · 4/5 Sensitive data use. **Mitigation:** Protect privacy.
5. **Financial** · 3/5 Build cost. **Mitigation:** Pilot narrow use case.

Speed	Effort	Cost	Revenue	Time to cash	Scalability
Medium (1-3 months)	**High**	**Medium**	**Very High**	**Immediate**	**High**

Decision-flow: CFO → Product → IT / Data

284. Use activation heatmaps to find where customers

Track exactly where customers stop, hesitate, abandon setup, delay usage, or fail to complete onboarding steps.

Why it works

Most businesses guess why activation fails. Behavioral heatmaps expose hidden friction points that slow revenue realization.

Best for

SaaS, education, healthcare, fintech, e-commerce services, memberships, B2B tools, digital platforms

Execution Steps

1. Map activation journey
2. Track step completion and drop-off
3. Build heatmap by customer segment
4. Identify highest-friction steps
5. Remove or simplify blockers

Real-world example

A SaaS platform discovers most users disappear during integration setup and redesigns that step.

Risk Management

1. **Product** · 3/5 Tracking incomplete. **Mitigation:** Instrument key steps.
2. **Customer** · 3/5 Behavior misread. **Mitigation:** Conduct buyer interviews to validate demand before launch investment.
3. **Product** · 3/5 Tooling delay. **Mitigation:** Start with simple analytics.
4. **Alignment** · 3/5 Insights not acted on. **Mitigation:** Assign a named owner to every action item before.
5. **Financial** · 3/5 No revenue impact. **Mitigation:** Prioritize high-value drop-offs.

Speed	Effort	Cost	Revenue	Time to cash	Scalability
Fast (0-30 days)	**Medium**	**Low**	**Very High**	**Immediate**	**High**

Decision-flow: CFO → Product → IT / Data

285. Trigger automated rescue flows before activation stalls

Automatically launch reminders, walkthroughs, support offers, video help, or concierge intervention when customers stop progressing.

Why it works

Customers often stall quietly. Automated rescue flows re-engage users before momentum disappears completely.

Best for

SaaS, healthcare, education, fintech, logistics, memberships, subscriptions, B2B platforms

Execution Steps

1. Define stall triggers
2. Create rescue messages and resources
3. Automate reminders. and support offers
4. Escalate high-value customers to humans
5. Test timing. and tone

Real-world example

A SaaS company triggers a guided walkthrough when a customer has not completed setup within 48 hours.

Risk Management

1. **Customer** · 3/5 Messages feel spammy. **Mitigation:** Cap the frequency of outreach or placements to prevent customer fatigue.
2. **Product** · 3/5 Triggers misfire. **Mitigation:** Test logic.
3. **Operational** · 3/5 Human follow-up overloaded. **Mitigation:** Escalate selectively.
4. **Commercial** · 3/5 Rescue content weak. **Mitigation:** Use specific blockers.
5. **Financial** · 3/5 Low rescue rate. **Mitigation:** Refine timing.

Speed	Effort	Cost	Revenue	Time to cash	Scalability
Medium (1-3 months)	**Medium**	**Low**	**Very High**	**Immediate**	**High**

Decision-flow: CFO → Customer Success → IT / Data

286. Create a live activation command center

Build a real-time dashboard showing activation progress, onboarding delays, customer blockers, support tickets, adoption gaps, and time-to-value metrics.

Why it works

Most companies only discover activation problems after churn begins. A live command center allows immediate operational intervention.

Best for

SaaS, healthcare, logistics, fintech, education, manufacturing, B2B services, enterprise platforms

Execution Steps

1. Define activation KPIs
2. Pull onboarding, usage, and support data
3. Build real-time dashboard
4. Assign owner. for stuck accounts
5. Review daily or weekly

Real-world example

A logistics platform uses a live command center to spot customer activation delays before they affect usage.

Risk Management

1. **Product** · 4/5 Dashboard inaccurate. **Mitigation:** Validate sources.
2. **Alignment** · 3/5 No action from insights. **Mitigation:** Assign a named owner to every action item before.
3. **Operational** · 3/5 Too many metrics. **Mitigation:** Focus on critical KPIs.
4. **Product** · 3/5 Data integration cost. **Mitigation:** Launch with the simplest viable version and expand only after validation.
5. **Financial** · 3/5 No ROI. **Mitigation:** Tie metrics to retention.

Speed	Effort	Cost	Revenue	Time to cash	Scalability
Medium (1-3 months)	**Medium**	**Medium**	**Very High**	**Immediate**	**High**

Decision-flow: CFO → Customer Success → Revenue Operations

287. Use AI to generate customer-specific activation plans

Automatically create onboarding plans, timelines, training paths, setup priorities, and stakeholder actions tailored to each customer profile.

Why it works

Generic onboarding slows activation. Personalized AI-generated activation plans reduce confusion and increase implementation speed.

Best for

SaaS, healthcare, consulting, education, logistics, fintech, enterprise software, B2B services

Execution Steps

1. Define customer profile inputs
2. Build plan templates
3. Use AI to generate activation plans
4. Review plans before sharing
5. Track plan completion

Real-world example

A consulting firm generates a tailored 30-day activation plan based on customer size, stakeholders, and goals.

Risk Management

1. **Product** · 4/5 Plan is inaccurate. **Mitigation:** Add a human review checkpoint for all high-value or high-risk outputs.
2. **Customer** · 3/5 Plan feels generic. **Mitigation:** Use customer-specific inputs.
3. **Operational** · 3/5 Too many plan variants. **Mitigation:** Standardize templates.
4. **Legal** · 3/5 Sensitive data concerns. **Mitigation:** Protect inputs.
5. **Financial** · 3/5 Cost too high. **Mitigation:** Pilot for high-value customers.

Speed	Effort	Cost	Revenue	Time to cash	Scalability
Medium (1-3 months)	**High**	**Medium**	**Very High**	**Immediate**	**High**

Decision-flow: CFO → Customer Success → IT / Data

288. Use onboarding data to predict expansion readiness

Analyze activation speed, feature usage, engagement depth, and implementation success to identify customers likely ready for future expansion.

Why it works

Strong activation behavior often predicts future account growth. Early visibility helps businesses prioritize high-potential customers sooner.

Best for

SaaS, healthcare, logistics, education, fintech, memberships, B2B platforms, enterprise software

Execution Steps

1. Identify activation signals linked to expansion
2. Track usage and completion data
3. Score customers for expansion readiness
4. Share signals with customer success
5. Prioritize high-potential accounts

Real-world example

A SaaS firm identifies customers who complete activation quickly and use advanced features as early expansion candidates.

Risk Management

1. **Commercial** · 3/5 Looks like upsell too early. **Mitigation:** Use for readiness only.
2. **Product** · 4/5 Signals unreliable. **Mitigation:** Validate over time.
3. **Customer** · 3/5 Customer feels pushed. **Mitigation:** Focus on value first.
4. **Alignment** · 3/5 Sales acts too soon. **Mitigation:** Define handoff criteria.
5. **Financial** · 3/5 Prediction not monetized. **Mitigation:** Track later expansion.

Speed	Effort	Cost	Revenue	Time to cash	Scalability
Medium (1-3 months)	**Medium**	**Low**	**Very High**	**Immediate**	**High**

Decision-flow: CFO → Customer Success → IT / Data

289. *Reward customers for activating within the first 7 days*

Give customers small operational perks, bonus support, credits, templates, or premium onboarding help when they complete activation milestones quickly.

Why it works

Customers move faster when speed creates visible advantage. Early activation incentives build momentum before procrastination sets in.

Best for

SaaS, education, healthcare, memberships, fintech, logistics, consulting, professional services

Execution Steps

1. Define 7-day activation milestones
2. Choose low-cost rewards
3. Communicate the incentive after purchase
4. Track milestone completion
5. Deliver rewards immediately

Real-world example

A SaaS company gives extra setup templates when customers finish onboarding milestones within seven days.

Risk Management

1. **Financial** · 3/5 Reward cost too high. **Mitigation:** Use low-cost operational perks — admin support.
2. **Customer** · 3/5 Milestone too hard. **Mitigation:** Make achievable.
3. **Operational** · 3/5 Tracking manual. **Mitigation:** Automate milestone tracking.
4. **Commercial** · 2/5 Looks like discounting. **Mitigation:** Avoid price concessions.
5. **Operational** · 3/5 Reward not valued. **Mitigation:** Test incentive options.

Speed	Effort	Cost	Revenue	Time to cash	Scalability
Fast (0-30 days)	**Low**	**Low**	**Very High**	**Immediate**	**High**

Decision-flow: CFO → Customer Success → Product

290. Create an activation progress score customers want to complete

Show customers a visible activation score based on setup completion, usage milestones, stakeholder alignment, and onboarding progress.

Why it works

People naturally respond to visible progress. A measurable activation score gamifies onboarding and increases completion behavior.

Best for

SaaS, healthcare, education, fintech, logistics, memberships, B2B platforms, enterprise software

Execution Steps

1. Define activation score components
2. Make score visible to customers
3. Show how to improve it
4. Tie score to first value milestones
5. Trigger help when score stalls

Real-world example

A SaaS platform shows new customers a 72% activation score and the next action needed to reach full activation.

Risk Management

1. **Customer** · 3/5 Score feels childish. **Mitigation:** Use professional language.
2. **Product** · 4/5 Score inaccurate. **Mitigation:** Use clear inputs.
3. **Product** · 3/5 Score hard to display. **Mitigation:** Launch with the simplest viable version and expand only after validation.
4. **Operational** · 3/5 No follow-up on low score. **Mitigation:** Trigger actions.
5. **Financial** · 3/5 Low impact. **Mitigation:** Tie score to value milestones.

Speed	Effort	Cost	Revenue	Time to cash	Scalability
Medium (1-3 months)	**Medium**	**Low**	**High**	**Immediate**	**High**

Decision-flow: CFO → Product → Customer Success

291. Use activation milestone unlocks to motivate completion

Release helpful tools, templates, shortcuts, integrations, support access, or guided resources as customers complete activation milestones.

Why it works

Customers move faster when progress unlocks something useful. Milestone unlocks turn onboarding from a checklist into a motivating path toward value.

Best for

SaaS, education, fintech, healthcare, memberships, logistics, enterprise software, digital platforms

Execution Steps

1. Identify useful resources customers value
2. Tie each unlock to an activation milestone
3. Make unlocks helpful, not punitive
4. Show the next unlock clearly
5. Track milestone completion

Real-world example

A SaaS company unlocks advanced templates after setup completion, helping customers move faster into practical use.

Risk Management

1. **Customer** · 4/5 Feels like artificial gating. **Mitigation:** Unlock helpful resources only.
2. **Commercial** · 3/5 Looks like upsell. **Mitigation:** Do not tie to paid tiers.
3. **Product** · 3/5 Wrong resources unlocked. **Mitigation:** Match to next activation step.
4. **Operational** · 3/5 Customers cannot clearly distinguish paid support from standard free assistance. Define. **Mitigation:** Explain unlock logic.
5. **Financial** · 3/5 Low usage lift. **Mitigation:** Measure completion behavior.

Speed	Effort	Cost	Revenue	Time to cash	Scalability
Medium (1-3 months)	**Medium**	**Low**	**Very High**	**Immediate**	**High**

Decision-flow: CFO → Product → Customer Success

292. Create activation streak rewards for customer teams

Reward internal customer teams when they complete onboarding tasks consistently over consecutive days or weeks.

Why it works

Activation often fails because customer-side teams lose momentum. Streak-based progress creates accountability and behavioral consistency.

Best for

Enterprise SaaS, education, healthcare, logistics, consulting, fintech, B2B platforms, professional services

Execution Steps

1. Define streak-worthy activation tasks
2. Set streak period
3. Track team progress
4. Notify customers of streak status
5. Reward completion with useful support

Real-world example

An enterprise platform rewards customer teams with bonus support resources after completing onboarding tasks for five straight days.

Risk Management

1. **Customer** · 3/5 Team loses interest. **Mitigation:** Keep streak short.
2. **Operational** · 3/5 Tracking burden. **Mitigation:** Automate simple tracking.
3. **Commercial** · 3/5 Reward not valued. **Mitigation:** Use useful perks.
4. **Alignment** · 3/5 Customer success forgets. **Mitigation:** Add automated reminders at key milestones to prevent drop-off.
5. **Financial** · 2/5 Low impact. **Mitigation:** Use with high-friction onboarding.

Speed	Effort	Cost	Revenue	Time to cash	Scalability
Fast (0-30 days)	**Low**	**Low**	**High**	**Immediate**	**High**

Decision-flow: CFO → Customer Success → Product

293. *Turn activation completion into a customer achievement*

Recognize customers when they complete activation through completion certificates, internal success summaries, executive-ready progress notes, or milestone confirmation.

Why it works

Activation feels more important when it is recognized. Customers are more likely to finish when completion creates visible progress and internal confidence.

Best for

SaaS, healthcare, education, fintech, consulting, memberships, enterprise services, professional services

Execution Steps

1. Define what activation completion means
2. Create a recognition format
3. Ensure every output is immediately useful and actionable for the recipient. for the customer
4. Celebrate completion professionally
5. Confirm next value step

Real-world example

A consulting firm sends an executive-ready activation completion note summarizing progress and next steps after onboarding is complete.

Risk Management

1. **Customer** · 3/5 Recognition feels superficial. **Mitigation:** Ensure every output is immediately useful and actionable for the recipient.
2. **Commercial** · 3/5 Looks like customer marketing. **Mitigation:** Keep it private and activation-focused.
3. **Operational** · 3/5 Completion criteria vague. **Mitigation:** Define all terms, obligations, and conditions in writing before any agreement.
4. **Market** · 2/5 Tone too playful. **Mitigation:** Use professional recognition.
5. **Financial** · 3/5 No measurable effect. **Mitigation:** Track completion lift.

Speed	Effort	Cost	Revenue	Time to cash	Scalability
Fast (0-30 days)	**Low**	**Low**	**High**	**Immediate**	**High**

Decision-flow: CFO → Customer Success → Marketing

294. Create a white-glove activation sprint for the first

Temporarily compress onboarding into an intensive short activation sprint with rapid support, daily checkpoints, instant troubleshooting, and executive visibility.

Why it works

Momentum is highest immediately after purchase. Compressing activation into the first 72 hours dramatically increases usage, confidence, and customer commitment.

Best for

SaaS, healthcare, consulting, logistics, fintech, education, enterprise software, professional services

Execution Steps

1. Define 72-hour activation target
2. Prepare customer inputs before kickoff
3. Schedule daily checkpoints
4. Provide rapid troubleshooting
5. Confirm first value within sprint

Real-world example

An enterprise SaaS company runs a 72-hour activation sprint so new customers reach core usage before momentum fades.

Risk Management

1. **Operational** · 4/5 Support load spikes. **Mitigation:** Limit to key customers.
2. **Customer** · 3/5 Customer not ready. **Mitigation:** Prepare inputs before sprint.
3. **Alignment** · 3/5 Teams unavailable. **Mitigation:** Reserve sprint capacity.
4. **Financial** · 3/5 Cost too high. **Mitigation:** Deploy only in high-confidence accounts before broadening the approach.
5. **Product** · 4/5 Issues block sprint. **Mitigation:** Have escalation path.

Speed	Effort	Cost	Revenue	Time to cash	Scalability
Fast (0-30 days)	**Medium**	**Low**	**Very High**	**Immediate**	**High**

Decision-flow: CFO → Customer Success → Operations

295. Use post-purchase peer benchmarks to speed activation

Show customers benchmark activation progress, completion speed, adoption milestones, or industry averages after purchase so they can compare their progress against peers.

Why it works

Customers move faster when they realize similar customers are already progressing. Peer benchmarks create urgency without discounts or pressure selling.

Best for

SaaS, education, healthcare, memberships, fintech, logistics, enterprise software, B2B platforms

Execution Steps

1. Collect anonymized activation benchmarks
2. Choose relevant peer comparisons
3. Show benchmarks after purchase only
4. Highlight next action to catch up
5. Avoid shaming language

Real-world example

A SaaS company shows new customers that similar teams complete core setup in five days, encouraging faster progress.

Risk Management

1. **Customer** · 3/5 Benchmark feels like pressure. **Mitigation:** Use supportive tone.
2. **Product** · 4/5 Benchmark not credible. **Mitigation:** Use real anonymized data.
3. **Legal** · 4/5 Privacy concerns. **Mitigation:** Aggregate and anonymize.
4. **Commercial** · 3/5 Looks like sales social proof. **Mitigation:** Use only post-purchase.
5. **Financial** · 3/5 No behavior change. **Mitigation:** Tie to next action.

Speed	Effort	Cost	Revenue	Time to cash	Scalability
Medium (1-3 months)	**Medium**	**Low**	**Very High**	**Immediate**	**High**

Decision-flow: CFO → Product → Customer Success

From Ideas to Action

Nineteen ideas. Nineteen ways to accelerate the time between contract signed and revenue actively generating.

The period between signing and first value is where more churn begins than most businesses realise. A customer who does not see results quickly starts to doubt the decision. Speed to value is not a product feature. It is a commercial protection move.

Before continuing, identify the single idea with the clearest commercial case right now. Name who owns it. Set a date for the first step. That is all that is required.

> ***The fastest path to retention is a customer who sees results before they have time to regret buying.***

What Comes Next

4.5 — Pull-Forward Offers addresses businesses where buying intent exists but commitment is delayed. If revenue that is ready to close keeps arriving late in the cycle — the next chapter shows how to move it forward.

4.5 — Pull-Forward Offers

Accelerate revenue through time-based offers designed to shift demand and commitment earlier.

When These Strategies Work Best

Pull-forward offers work best when buying intent already exists but commitment is delayed — where a well-structured time-based incentive would move the decision without creating discount dependency.

- Revenue is consistently back-weighted in the quarter regardless of pipeline quality
- Customers who intend to buy delay without a reason to commit by a specific date
- Early renewal or advance commitment is underutilised despite renewal rates being strong
- Pre-order or forward commitment structures are not currently part of the commercial model
- Quarter-end discounting is the default lever used to pull demand forward

The Benefits

- Revenue that was coming anyway arrives earlier, improving cash and forecast accuracy
- Reduced quarter-end pressure when pipeline is committed rather than still deciding
- Stronger customer relationships when pull-forward offers feel like genuine advantages
- Better capacity planning when future demand is known and committed in advance
- Margin protection when pull-forward mechanisms replace reactive end-of-quarter discounting

The Risks to Manage

- **Discount dependency** — buyers who expect a pull-forward offer every cycle will wait for it. Vary the mechanism, not just the depth.
- **Cannibalisation** — pulling future revenue into this period creates a gap next period. Model the full cycle impact before launching.
- **Urgency fatigue** — customers exposed to too many deadlines stop believing them. Use pull-forward sparingly and credibly.
- **Wrong targeting** — pull-forward offers work on buyers close to deciding, not on prospects still in early stages. Qualify carefully.

296. Sell tomorrow's capacity before customers need it

Offer customers the chance to secure future production slots, service windows, implementation timing, inventory access, or delivery availability before demand peaks.

Why it works

Customers often wait until capacity is already tight. Advance capacity purchase shifts demand earlier and improves planning visibility.

Best for

Manufacturing, logistics, healthcare, consulting, agencies, SaaS, events, construction

Execution Steps

1. Identify future capacity likely to tighten
2. Define what customers can secure in advance
3. Set availability windows and rules
4. Communicate the planning benefit
5. Offer to high-fit customers first

Real-world example

A manufacturer lets customers secure future production slots before seasonal demand spikes, improving both revenue timing and planning.

Risk Management

1. **Operational** · 4/5 Capacity overcommitted. **Mitigation:** Cap advance allocation.
2. **Customer** · 3/5 Feels like forced buying. **Mitigation:** Position as planning option.
3. **Commercial** · 3/5 Demand weak. **Mitigation:** Target known seasonal buyers.
4. **Financial** · 3/5 Cash impact unclear. **Mitigation:** Track shifted revenue.
5. **Alignment** · 4/5 Sales promises too much. **Mitigation:** Use approved capacity rules.

Speed	Effort	Cost	Revenue	Time to cash	Scalability
Fast (0-30 days)	**Low**	**Low**	**Very High**	**Immediate**	**High**

Decision-flow: CFO → Sales → Operations

297. Create decision seasons instead of waiting for random

Train customers to buy during structured commercial windows tied to operational cycles, planning periods, industry timing, or strategic events.

Why it works

Random demand creates forecasting chaos. Decision seasons pull purchases into predictable periods and accelerate revenue timing.

Best for

SaaS, manufacturing, consulting, education, healthcare, logistics, enterprise services, B2B services

Execution Steps

1. Identify natural customer planning windows
2. Create decision-season calendar
3. Build messaging around timing logic
4. Align sales outreach to those windows
5. Add value for earlier decisions

Real-world example

A consulting firm creates quarterly decision seasons tied to board planning cycles, moving late-stage demand earlier.

Risk Management

1. **Customer** · 3/5 Season timing does not fit. **Mitigation:** Align to real cycles.
2. **Commercial** · 3/5 Looks like campaign noise. **Mitigation:** Use strategic timing logic.
3. **Operational** · 3/5 Team not ready. **Mitigation:** Plan capacity. ahead
4. **Financial** · 3/5 Demand bunching creates strain. **Mitigation:** Stage windows carefully.
5. **Alignment** · 3/5 Sales ignores calendar. **Mitigation:** Add pipeline reviews.

Speed	Effort	Cost	Revenue	Time to cash	Scalability
Medium (1-3 months)	**Medium**	**Low**	**Very High**	**Immediate**	**High**

Decision-flow: CFO → PMO / Strategy → Sales

298. Offer priority execution lanes for early commitment

Give earlier buyers faster implementation timing, priority delivery, preferred turnaround, or first-in-line execution when they commit before a defined deadline.

Why it works

Customers move faster when earlier commitment gives them speed advantage. This creates urgency without lowering price.

Best for

Healthcare, SaaS, consulting, logistics, manufacturing, construction, professional services, agencies

Execution Steps

1. Identify execution capacity that can be prioritized
2. Define early-commitment deadline
3. Set clear rules and communicate them before any access. for priority lane access
4. Communicate speed advantage clearly
5. Protect standard customers

Real-world example

A SaaS implementation team gives faster launch scheduling to customers who commit before the monthly implementation cutoff.

Risk Management

1. **Operational** · 4/5 Priority lane disrupts base service. **Mitigation:** Reserve limited slots.
2. **Customer** · 3/5 Feels unfair. **Mitigation:** Keep baseline strong.
3. **Commercial** · 3/5 Deadline feels fake. **Mitigation:** Tie to real schedule.
4. **Financial** · 3/5 Low uplift. **Mitigation:** Track timing shift.
5. **Alignment** · 4/5 Sales overuses lane. **Mitigation:** Require approval. rules

Speed	Effort	Cost	Revenue	Time to cash	Scalability
Fast (0-30 days)	**Low**	**Low**	**Very High**	**Immediate**	**High**

Decision-flow: CFO → Operations → Sales

299. *Turn slow-buying customers into scheduled buyers*

Convert reactive buyers into planned buyers through structured advance purchasing calendars, reorder schedules, renewal planning, or commitment windows.

Why it works

Reactive buying delays revenue unpredictably. Scheduled buying pulls demand forward and stabilizes forecasting.

Best for

Manufacturing, SaaS, healthcare, logistics, education, wholesale, B2B services, subscriptions

Execution Steps

1. Identify repeat or predictable buyers
2. Build purchase calendar with customer
3. Agree advance decision windows
4. Add automated reminders at key milestones to prevent drop-off. and planning checkpoints
5. Capture commitments earlier

Real-world example

A supplier converts reactive monthly reorders into planned quarterly buying windows, improving forecast and earlier revenue visibility.

Risk Management

1. **Customer** · 3/5 Customer resists planning. **Mitigation:** Show operational benefit.
2. **Commercial** · 3/5 Calendar not followed. **Mitigation:** Use reminders.
3. **Operational** · 3/5 Forecast changes. **Mitigation:** Allow controlled updates.
4. **Financial** · 3/5 No earlier commitment. **Mitigation:** Require decision windows.
5. **Alignment** · 3/5 Account owners do not maintain plan. **Mitigation:** Review monthly.

Speed	Effort	Cost	Revenue	Time to cash	Scalability
Medium (1-3 months)	**Medium**	**Low**	**Very High**	**Immediate**	**High**

Decision-flow: CFO → Sales → Customer Success

300. Create a commit now, activate later commercial path

Allow customers to secure pricing, resources, implementation windows, or operational capacity now while delaying actual activation until needed.

Why it works

Customers often delay commitment because usage timing is uncertain. Separating commitment timing from activation timing pulls revenue forward without forcing immediate usage.

Best for

SaaS, healthcare, logistics, manufacturing, consulting, construction, enterprise software, education

Execution Steps

1. Identify customers with future need but timing uncertainty
2. Define what can be committed now
3. Separate commitment from activation date
4. Set activation window. limits
5. Clarify commercial terms

Real-world example

An enterprise software provider lets customers secure implementation capacity now while scheduling activation for a later quarter.

Risk Management

1. **Customer** · 3/5 Customer delays activation too long. **Mitigation:** Set activation window.
2. **Operational** · 4/5 Capacity planning complexity. **Mitigation:** Use clear scheduling rules.
3. **Commercial** · 3/5 Looks like prepay. **Mitigation:** Frame as commitment timing.
4. **Financial** · 4/5 Revenue recognition issue. **Mitigation:** Review accounting treatment.
5. **Legal** · 3/5 Terms ambiguous. **Mitigation:** Use clear contract language.

Speed	Effort	Cost	Revenue	Time to cash	Scalability
Fast (0-30 days)	**Medium**	**Low**	**Very High**	**Immediate**	**High**

Decision-flow: CFO → Sales → Operations

301. Bundle future operational protection into early

Give early buyers a broader protection bundle such as escalation access, continuity planning, risk checks, support readiness, and operational safeguards.

Why it works

Customers commit earlier when they feel protected against future execution risk. This creates confidence without discounting.

Best for

SaaS, healthcare, logistics, consulting, manufacturing, enterprise services, agencies, construction

Execution Steps

1. Identify future risks customers worry about
2. Bundle practical protection elements
3. Tie protection to early commitment
4. Avoid promising guaranteed capacity
5. Communicate risk-reduction value

Real-world example

A logistics provider gives early buyers continuity planning and escalation readiness before a peak season.

Risk Management

1. **Operational** · 4/5 Protection overpromised. **Mitigation:** Define safeguards precisely.
2. **Customer** · 3/5 The value delivered is not clearly communicated. **Mitigation:** Explain risk avoided.
3. **Commercial** · 3/5 Looks like support upsell. **Mitigation:** Tie only to timing.
4. **Financial** · 3/5 Cost too high. **Mitigation:** Use scalable protections.
5. **Alignment** · 3/5 Teams unclear on scope. **Mitigation:** Document bundle.

Speed	Effort	Cost	Revenue	Time to cash	Scalability
Fast (0-30 days)	**Low**	**Low**	**Very High**	**Immediate**	**High**

Decision-flow: CFO → Operations → Customer Success

302. Offer strategic planning access for customers who commit early

Give early buyers access to roadmap sessions, planning workshops, implementation forecasting, or executive strategy discussions before demand peaks.

Why it works

Customers value clarity and preparedness. Strategic access makes earlier commitment feel smarter, not pressured.

Best for

Consulting, SaaS, healthcare, logistics, manufacturing, enterprise services, finance, professional services

Execution Steps

1. Identify planning access customers value
2. Define session format and scope
3. Link access to early commitment
4. Prepare planning materials
5. Deliver planning before peak period

Real-world example

A SaaS firm offers early-commit customers a roadmap planning session before implementation slots tighten.

Risk Management

1. **Operational** · 3/5 Planning sessions consume capacity. **Mitigation:** Limit session length.
2. **Customer** · 3/5 Seen as sales meeting. **Mitigation:** Ensure every output is immediately useful and actionable for the recipient.
3. **Commercial** · 3/5 Urgency signals are insufficient to motivate prompt customer action. Build urgency. **Mitigation:** Tie to planning calendar.
4. **Financial** · 3/5 Low perceived value. **Mitigation:** Use senior insight.
5. **Alignment** · 3/5 Strategy team unavailable. **Mitigation:** Schedule limited slots.

Speed	Effort	Cost	Revenue	Time to cash	Scalability
Medium (1-3 months)	**Medium**	**Low**	**High**	**Immediate**	**High**

Decision-flow: CFO → PMO / Strategy → Customer Success

303. Turn idle periods into bonus-value booking windows

During slower demand periods, add operational value instead of discounts — such as faster turnaround, deeper support, customization help, or extended implementation access.

Why it works

Customers respond to additional value more positively than discounts. Bonus-value windows shift demand into underutilized periods.

Best for

Manufacturing, agencies, SaaS, consulting, healthcare, logistics, education, professional services

Execution Steps

1. Identify idle or underused periods
2. Choose value-adds that use spare capacity
3. Create booking window
4. Communicate bonus value clearly
5. Protect margins by avoiding discounts

Real-world example

An agency offers extra strategy review for clients who book during a slow month instead of discounting fees.

Risk Management

1. **Financial** · 3/5 Bonus value costs too much. **Mitigation:** Use spare capacity only.
2. **Customer** · 3/5 Waits for bonus windows. **Mitigation:** Cap the frequency of outreach or placements to prevent customer fatigue.
3. **Commercial** · 3/5 Looks like discounting. **Mitigation:** Avoid price cuts.
4. **Operational** · 3/5 Idle capacity not available. **Mitigation:** Coordinate calendar.
5. **Alignment** · 3/5 Sales mispositions offer. **Mitigation:** Use clear messaging.

Speed	Effort	Cost	Revenue	Time to cash	Scalability
Fast (0-30 days)	**Low**	**Low**	**Very High**	**Immediate**	**High**

Decision-flow: CFO → Operations → Sales

304. Create future-readiness packages customers secure in advance

Help customers prepare early for future growth, compliance, seasonal demand, hiring, expansion, or operational scaling before urgency hits.

Why it works

Customers often buy too late under pressure. Readiness packaging shifts demand earlier by helping them prepare before the problem becomes urgent.

Best for

Healthcare, SaaS, manufacturing, logistics, consulting, HR services, cybersecurity, finance

Execution Steps

1. Identify future events customers underprepare for
2. Build readiness package around preparation
3. Position around avoiding later urgency
4. Offer before the pressure period
5. Include practical planning assets

Real-world example

A cybersecurity firm sells a future-readiness package before regulatory deadlines create urgent demand.

Risk Management

1. **Customer** · 3/5 Future need feels distant. **Mitigation:** Use clear upcoming triggers.
2. **Commercial** · 3/5 Looks like consulting retainer. **Mitigation:** Keep package defined.
3. **Operational** · 3/5 Scope expands beyond agreed boundaries. **Mitigation:** Limit deliverables.
4. **Financial** · 3/5 Delayed revenue impact. **Mitigation:** Track advance bookings.
5. **Market** · 3/5 Timing changes. **Mitigation:** Update trigger calendar.

Speed	Effort	Cost	Revenue	Time to cash	Scalability
Medium (1-3 months)	**Medium**	**Low**	**Very High**	**Immediate**	**High**

Decision-flow: CFO → PMO / Strategy → Sales

305. Reward early buyers with operational simplicity

Give earlier customers simpler onboarding, faster approvals, pre-configured setups, reduced paperwork, or lighter coordination requirements.

Why it works

Customers delay when future implementation feels operationally painful. Simplicity becomes an incentive to commit earlier.

Best for

SaaS, healthcare, logistics, consulting, finance, education, enterprise software, B2B services

Execution Steps

1. Identify operational pain customers dislike
2. Define simplicity benefits for early buyers
3. Tie benefits to commitment timing
4. Prepare simplified path
5. Communicate reduced effort clearly

Real-world example

A healthcare technology provider offers earlier buyers pre-filled setup documents and simplified onboarding coordination.

Risk Management

1. **Operational** · 3/5 Simplified path strains team. **Mitigation:** Define and enforce eligibility criteria consistently from day one.
2. **Customer** · 3/5 Benefit not compelling. **Mitigation:** Ask what friction matters.
3. **Commercial** · 3/5 Overlaps with onboarding. **Mitigation:** Keep focus on early commitment.
4. **Financial** · 3/5 Low pull-forward effect. **Mitigation:** Track timing shift.
5. **Alignment** · 3/5 Teams deliver inconsistently. **Mitigation:** Document process.

Speed	Effort	Cost	Revenue	Time to cash	Scalability
Fast (0-30 days)	**Medium**	**Low**	**High**	**Immediate**	**High**

Decision-flow: CFO → Operations → Customer Success

306. Offer capacity protection against peak-period

Give early buyers guaranteed protection against peak-period disruption, such as no queue delay, protected delivery timing, reserved support, or continuity assurance.

Why it works

Customers fear being pushed back when demand spikes. Protection-based incentives pull decisions forward because waiting creates operational risk.

Best for

Manufacturing, logistics, healthcare, consulting, SaaS, construction, agencies, enterprise services

Execution Steps

1. Identify peak-period disruption risks
2. Define specific protections early buyers receive
3. Set protection limits
4. Tie eligibility to early commitment
5. Communicate risk of waiting clearly

Real-world example

A logistics provider gives early customers protected delivery timing during peak season rather than simply selling open capacity slots.

Risk Management

1. **Operational** · 4/5 Protection guarantee too broad. **Mitigation:** Define scope, access, and usage limits in writing before launch.
2. **Customer** · 3/5 Misunderstands guarantee. **Mitigation:** Use specific, plain-language contract terms that eliminate ambiguity.
3. **Commercial** · 3/5 Looks like capacity sale. **Mitigation:** Frame as disruption protection.
4. **Financial** · 3/5 Cost of protection rises. **Mitigation:** Cap volume.
5. **Legal** · 4/5 Guarantee exposure. **Mitigation:** Review all external-facing language with legal counsel before publishing.

Speed	Effort	Cost	Revenue	Time to cash	Scalability
Fast (0-30 days)	**Low**	**Low**	**Very High**	**Immediate**	**High**

Decision-flow: CFO → Operations → Sales

307. Create early commitment credits customers can use later

Reward early commitment with future-use operational credits such as support hours, training access, onboarding resources, or service flexibility.

Why it works

Customers commit faster when they feel they gain future optionality instead of simply spending earlier.

Best for

SaaS, consulting, healthcare, logistics, education, professional services, agencies, B2B services

Execution Steps

1. Choose useful future credits
2. Set early-commitment deadline
3. Define credit value and expiry
4. Communicate optionality clearly
5. Deliver credits after commitment

Real-world example

A consulting firm offers early-commit customers future workshop credits that can be used during implementation.

Risk Management

1. **Financial** · 3/5 Credits become expensive. **Mitigation:** Cap credit value.
2. **Customer** · 3/5 Credits not valued. **Mitigation:** Offer choice.
3. **Commercial** · 3/5 Seen as discount. **Mitigation:** Use operational credits only.
4. **Operational** · 3/5 Credit tracking burden. **Mitigation:** Use simple ledger.
5. **Legal** · 2/5 Expiry unclear. **Mitigation:** Define terms.

Speed	Effort	Cost	Revenue	Time to cash	Scalability
Fast (0-30 days)	**Low**	**Low**	**Very High**	**Immediate**	**High**

Decision-flow: CFO → Customer Success → Sales

308. Offer priority innovation access for early buyers

Give customers early access to future features, pilots, beta programs, roadmap previews, or operational improvements when they commit earlier.

Why it works

Customers like feeling strategically ahead. Innovation access creates pull-forward demand without discounting.

Best for

SaaS, healthcare, fintech, logistics, manufacturing, enterprise software, education, professional services

Execution Steps

1. Identify upcoming innovation customers value
2. Define early-access eligibility
3. Link access to early commitment
4. Clarify pilot scope and limitations
5. Manage feedback loop

Real-world example

A SaaS company gives early-commit customers first access to an upcoming workflow automation feature.

Risk Management

1. **Product** · 4/5 Feature delays. **Mitigation:** Avoid overpromising.
2. **Customer** · 3/5 Beta expectations too high. **Mitigation:** Set clear limits.
3. **Commercial** · 3/5 Looks like upsell. **Mitigation:** Tie to timing only.
4. **Operational** · 3/5 Post-launch support demand is higher than planned, straining the delivery team. **Mitigation:** Limit pilot users.
5. **Legal** · 3/5 Beta terms unclear. **Mitigation:** Use pilot agreement.

Speed	Effort	Cost	Revenue	Time to cash	Scalability
Medium (1-3 months)	**Medium**	**Low**	**High**	**Immediate**	**High**

Decision-flow: CFO → Product → Customer Success

309. Reward advance commitment with reduced admin friction

Give early buyers simpler paperwork, fewer coordination steps, pre-filled forms, smoother approvals, or lighter handoffs when they commit ahead of time.

Why it works

Customers delay when buying feels administratively painful. Reducing friction makes earlier commitment feel easier and more attractive.

Best for

Healthcare, SaaS, consulting, logistics, manufacturing, finance, education, B2B services

Execution Steps

1. Identify admin friction in the buying path
2. Define what can be simplified for early buyers
3. Prepare pre-filled or lighter workflows
4. Tie the simplified path to advance commitment
5. Communicate reduced admin burden

Real-world example

A B2B services firm gives early-commit buyers pre-filled forms and simplified handoffs, making it easier to say yes sooner.

Risk Management

1. **Operational** · 3/5 Simplification creates errors. **Mitigation:** Keep control checks.
2. **Customer** · 3/5 Benefit not obvious. **Mitigation:** Quantify the time saved and present it as the.
3. **Commercial** · 2/5 Confused with priority speed. **Mitigation:** Frame as admin reduction.
4. **Legal** · 4/5 Paperwork cannot be reduced. **Mitigation:** Review required documents.
5. **Alignment** · 3/5 Teams revert to old process. **Mitigation:** Use a pre-delivery checklist to catch quality issues before customer contact.

Speed	Effort	Cost	Revenue	Time to cash	Scalability
Fast (0-30 days)	**Medium**	**Low**	**Very High**	**Immediate**	**High**

Decision-flow: CFO → Operations → Customer Success

310. Create executive-only early commitment advantages

Offer senior buyers executive briefings, strategic reviews, implementation visibility, or leadership access when they commit ahead of operational deadlines.

Why it works

Executives respond to strategic visibility and priority treatment more than discounts. Executive advantages accelerate high-value commitments.

Best for

Enterprise SaaS, consulting, healthcare, logistics, manufacturing, finance, infrastructure, professional services

Execution Steps

1. Define executive-level advantage
2. Set early-commitment requirement
3. Limit access to the minimum level required for the commercial purpose. to strategic deals
4. Prepare briefing or review format
5. Deliver with senior credibility

Real-world example

A consulting firm offers early-commit clients a senior leadership strategy review tied to a real planning deadline.

Risk Management

1. **Alignment** · 4/5 Leadership overused. **Mitigation:** Set deal threshold.
2. **Customer** · 3/5 Advantage feels symbolic. **Mitigation:** Make session useful.
3. **Commercial** · 3/5 Sales promises too much. **Mitigation:** Use approved offer.
4. **Operational** · 3/5 Scheduling delays. **Mitigation:** Reserve slots.
5. **Financial** · 3/5 Cost not justified. **Mitigation:** Use for large opportunities.

Speed	Effort	Cost	Revenue	Time to cash	Scalability
Medium (1-3 months)	**Medium**	**Low**	**Very High**	**Immediate**	**High**

Decision-flow: CFO → Cross-functional → Sales

311. Use demand signals to trigger early-buyer advantages

Use live demand, usage, booking, sales, or capacity signals to offer early-buyer advantages when demand is rising but before pressure becomes critical.

Why it works

Customers move faster when urgency is backed by real demand data. Signal-based timing makes early commitment credible.

Best for

SaaS, logistics, healthcare, manufacturing, hospitality, education, consulting, infrastructure

Execution Steps

1. Identify demand signals that predict tightening
2. Set trigger thresholds
3. Define early-buyer advantage
4. Launch offer when signals rise
5. Show the data-backed timing logic

Real-world example

A logistics company uses booking trends to trigger early-buyer advantages before capacity becomes constrained.

Risk Management

1. **Product** · 4/5 Signal is noisy. **Mitigation:** Use simple validated indicators.
2. **Customer** · 3/5 Urgency feels fake. **Mitigation:** Show real signal.
3. **Commercial** · 3/5 Offer too late. **Mitigation:** Set early threshold.
4. **Operational** · 4/5 Capacity forecast wrong. **Mitigation:** Review regularly.
5. **Financial** · 3/5 Weak pull-forward impact. **Mitigation:** Track timing shift.

Speed	Effort	Cost	Revenue	Time to cash	Scalability
Medium (1-3 months)	**Medium**	**Low**	**Very High**	**Immediate**	**High**

Decision-flow: CFO → IT / Data → Sales

312. Create a dynamic early advantage dashboard for committed buyers

Show customers a dashboard with future capacity, timing benefits, forecasted wait times, and the advantages they unlock by committing earlier.

Why it works

Customers delay when the cost of waiting is invisible. A dashboard makes timing consequences clear and pushes earlier commitment.

Best for

Logistics, SaaS, healthcare, manufacturing, education, travel, events, professional services

Execution Steps

1. Identify timing data customers should see
2. Build simple dashboard or customer view
3. Show capacity, wait time, and timing benefits
4. Link early commitment to visible advantages
5. Keep data current

Real-world example

A manufacturer shows customers available production windows and projected wait-time increases if they delay commitment.

Risk Management

1. **Product** · 3/5 Dashboard costly. **Mitigation:** Start with simple view.
2. **Product** · 4/5 Data inaccurate. **Mitigation:** Validate forecasts.
3. **Customer** · 3/5 Dashboard creates pressure. **Mitigation:** Use a transparent.
4. **Commercial** · 3/5 Customers ignore dashboard. **Mitigation:** Add clear next action.
5. **Operational** · 4/5 Availability changes fast. **Mitigation:** Refresh frequently.

Speed	Effort	Cost	Revenue	Time to cash	Scalability
Medium (1-3 months)	**Medium**	**Medium**	**Very High**	**Immediate**	**High**

Decision-flow: CFO → Product → Customer Success

313. Offer predictive buy-before-the-bottleneck incentives

Use forecasts to identify upcoming shortages, delivery delays, staffing limits, seasonal pressure, or implementation bottlenecks, then offer incentives before customers feel the pain.

Why it works

Most customers react too late. Predictive bottleneck incentives turn future operational constraints into earlier demand today.

Best for

Manufacturing, logistics, healthcare, SaaS, consulting, construction, education, infrastructure

Execution Steps

1. Identify recurring bottlenecks
2. Forecast timing and severity
3. Design incentive before bottleneck hits
4. Communicate future risk clearly
5. Offer early action path

Real-world example

A consulting firm forecasts implementation bottlenecks before year-end and offers early buyers extra planning support to commit sooner.

Risk Management

1. **Product** · 4/5 Forecast wrong. **Mitigation:** Use conservative signals.
2. **Customer** · 3/5 Future pain feels distant. **Mitigation:** Show timing clearly.
3. **Commercial** · 3/5 Looks like scare tactic. **Mitigation:** Use factual evidence.
4. **Operational** · 4/5 Bottleneck still occurs. **Mitigation:** Cap total risk commitments to a level the business.
5. **Financial** · 3/5 Incentive cost too high. **Mitigation:** Use low-cost value add.

Speed	Effort	Cost	Revenue	Time to cash	Scalability
Medium (1-3 months)	**Medium**	**Low**	**Very High**	**Immediate**	**High**

Decision-flow: CFO → Operations → IT / Data

From Ideas to Action

Eighteen ideas. Eighteen ways to bring future buying decisions into the current period using structured commercial incentives.

Quarter-end pressure is predictable. The business that waits for it to arrive scrambles. The business that designs around it pulls revenue forward deliberately, on its own terms, with structured incentives rather than last-minute discounts.

Before continuing, identify the single idea with the clearest commercial case right now. Name who owns it. Set a date for the first step. That is all that is required.

> ***Revenue that lands in this quarter instead of next is not new revenue. It is better-timed revenue. That is the difference between a forecast and a result.***

What Comes Next

Part 5 — Expand Revenue is next. The business is now converting and collecting efficiently. Part 5 shows how to scale that model into new channels, segments, geographies, and higher purchase frequency.

PART 5

Expand Revenue

Taking What Works into New Territory

Parts 2 through 4 focused on the commercial potential inside the business as it stands today — creating new revenue, unlocking existing value, and accelerating cash flow. Part 5 moves outward.

Part 5 is about growth. It asks a different question — not how do we get more from what we have, but where else could what we have already works? New channels. New buyer types. New geographies. More frequent purchases from existing customers. More of the right customers coming through the door.

Expansion is the most visible form of growth. It is also the most expensive if attempted without the right foundation. The ideas in this section are built for businesses that have proven something commercially and are ready to take it further.

What This Part Covers

- **New Channels** — selling through new routes to market that the business does not currently use.
- **New Customer Segments** — selling the current offer to a different type of buyer.
- **New Geographies** — taking the current offer into new locations, regions, or countries.
- **Frequency Growth** — increasing how often existing customers buy.
- **Customer Acquisition Growth** — increasing the number of customers acquired from markets the business already serves.

Where to Start

- **Strong offer but limited distribution?** Start with New Channels.
- **Proven offer that solves problems in adjacent segments?** Start with New Customer Segments.
- **Local model ready to replicate in new locations?** Start with New Geographies.
- **Existing customers buying less often than they could?** Start with Frequency Growth.
- **Acquisition volume too low relative to market size?** Start with Customer Acquisition Growth.

5.1 — New Channels

Expand revenue by selling through new routes to market that the business does not currently use.

When These Strategies Work Best

New channel strategies work best when the business has a proven offer but is reaching only a fraction of the available market through its current distribution approach.

- The offer works well but growth is constrained by single-channel dependency
- Potential buyers exist in segments the current sales motion does not reach
- Partners, resellers, or intermediaries already hold the attention of the right customers
- The cost of direct sales is too high to reach smaller or more distributed buyers
- The business depends entirely on inbound or direct sales with no partner-driven revenue

The Benefits

- Revenue growth without proportional increase in direct sales headcount
- Access to buyer relationships that would take years to build independently
- Lower marginal cost of acquisition when partners carry the distribution overhead
- Market coverage that accelerates faster than any direct sales team could achieve
- Resilience from multiple revenue streams that are not all dependent on one channel

The Risks to Manage

- **Channel conflict** — new channels can compete with direct sales. Define usage, access, and delivery boundaries before any commitment, and confirm commercial terms and economics before launch.
- **Brand dilution** — partners represent the business. Set standards. and onboard properly or the brand suffers.
- **Channel dependency** — concentrating too much revenue in one partner creates fragility. Diversify early.
- **Margin compression** — partner economics reduce margin per sale. Model the net return before committing.

314. Turn trusted partners into your second sales force

Create a structured partner channel where complementary businesses recommend, sell, or introduce your offer to customers they already serve.

Why it works

Partners already have customer trust and access. A structured channel lets you expand reach without building all distribution internally.

Best for

SaaS, consulting, healthcare, finance, logistics, education, B2B services, professional services

Execution Steps

1. Identify complementary businesses serving the same buyers
2. Define referral, resale, or intro model
3. Create partner pitch materials
4. Set commercial terms
5. Train initial partners

Real-world example

A SaaS company partners with advisory firms that already serve its target customers and turns them into a structured referral channel.

Risk Management

1. **Commercial** · 3/5 Partner produces weak leads. **Mitigation:** Qualify partner fit.
2. **Market** · 3/5 Partner mispositions offer. **Mitigation:** Provide scripts.
3. **Financial** · 3/5 Commission misaligned. **Mitigation:** Tie payout to quality.
4. **Alignment** · 3/5 Sales channel conflict. **Mitigation:** Set ownership rules.
5. **Operational** · 3/5 Partner support burden. **Mitigation:** Create enablement kit.

Speed	Effort	Cost	Revenue	Time to cash	Scalability
Medium (1-3 months)	**Medium**	**Low**	**Very High**	**Medium**	**High**

Decision-flow: CFO → Partnerships / BD → Sales

315. Sell through businesses that already own the customer

Place your offer inside another company's customer journey at the exact moment their customers need your solution.

Why it works

The best channel is often where demand already appears. Embedded timing reduces acquisition friction and increases conversion.

Best for

Insurance, fintech, healthcare, SaaS, travel, real estate, education, home services

Execution Steps

1. Map when customers naturally need your solution
2. Identify businesses that own that moment
3. Design embedded offer placement
4. Build simple referral or API flow
5. Agree commercial terms

Real-world example

A home service provider embeds its offer inside a real estate closing journey where buyers naturally need support.

Risk Management

1. **Commercial** · 3/5 Moment has weak intent. **Mitigation:** Validate demand timing.
2. **Product** · 4/5 Integration friction. **Mitigation:** Start with manual referral.
3. **Market** · 3/5 Partner experience poor. **Mitigation:** Choose trusted partner.
4. **Financial** · 3/5 Revenue share too high. **Mitigation:** Model full unit economics before setting the launch price.
5. **Customer** · 3/5 Offer feels intrusive. **Mitigation:** Make timing relevant.

Speed	Effort	Cost	Revenue	Time to cash	Scalability
Medium (1-3 months)	**Medium**	**Low**	**Very High**	**Medium**	**High**

Decision-flow: CFO → Partnerships / BD → Product

316. Create a reseller-ready version of your offer

Package your product or service so external resellers can explain, price, sell, and support it with minimal friction.

Why it works

Many offers fail in channels because they are too hard for others to sell. Reseller-ready packaging turns external sellers into scalable distribution.

Best for

SaaS, software, training, consulting, healthcare services, B2B products, equipment, professional services

Execution Steps

1. Identify what makes the offer hard to resell
2. Simplify positioning and pricing
3. Create reseller sales materials
4. Define support boundaries
5. Train initial resellers

Real-world example

A training company creates reseller-ready packages with fixed pricing, clear outcomes, and simple onboarding instructions.

Risk Management

1. **Commercial** · 4/5 Resellers cannot explain offer. **Mitigation:** Simplify messaging.
2. **Market** · 3/5 Poor selling behavior. **Mitigation:** Certify resellers.
3. **Operational** · 3/5 Support expectations unclear. **Mitigation:** Define usage, access, and delivery boundaries before any commitment.
4. **Financial** · 3/5 Margin too thin. **Mitigation:** Set reseller economics.
5. **Legal** · 3/5 Terms inconsistent. **Mitigation:** Use reseller agreement.

Speed	Effort	Cost	Revenue	Time to cash	Scalability
Medium (1-3 months)	**Medium**	**Low**	**Very High**	**Medium**	**High**

Decision-flow: CFO → Sales → Partnerships / BD

317. Use niche communities as distribution channels

Build channel relationships with associations, communities, member groups, industry networks, alumni groups, or professional bodies that already gather your buyers.

Why it works

Communities concentrate trust and attention. Selling through them gives access to buyers without starting from zero awareness.

Best for

Education, SaaS, healthcare, finance, consulting, coaching, professional services, B2B services

Execution Steps

1. Identify communities with concentrated buyer access
2. Define member-relevant offer angle
3. Propose value to the community owner
4. Create co-branded education or offer path
5. Launch to one community first

Real-world example

A finance tool partners with a professional association to reach members through education-led channel access.

Risk Management

1. **Market** · 4/5 Community trust risk. **Mitigation:** Open every buyer conversation with the value delivered, not the price.
2. **Commercial** · 3/5 Audience not buyer-ready. **Mitigation:** Validate fit.
3. **Operational** · 3/5 Community owner slow. **Mitigation:** Use simple proposal.
4. **Financial** · 3/5 Conversion from initial interest to completed purchase is lower than targeted.. **Mitigation:** Test small launch.
5. **Alignment** · 2/5 Marketing treats as campaign only. **Mitigation:** Track as channel.

Speed	Effort	Cost	Revenue	Time to cash	Scalability
Fast (0-30 days)	**Medium**	**Low**	**High**	**Medium**	**High**

Decision-flow: CFO → Marketing → Partnerships / BD

318. Turn service providers into referral engines

Create a formal referral channel with accountants, consultants, agencies, advisors, brokers, installers, trainers, or specialists who already advise your target buyers.

Why it works

Service providers often know the customer's pain before you do. A structured referral channel turns trusted advisors into qualified revenue sources.

Best for

B2B services, SaaS, finance, healthcare, real estate, construction, education, professional services

Execution Steps

1. Identify advisors who see target-buyer pain
2. Define referral trigger criteria
3. Create simple referral process
4. Set compensation or reciprocal value
5. Train providers on good-fit signals

Real-world example

A SaaS firm builds referral relationships with consultants who spot the need during client operations work.

Risk Management

1. **Commercial** · 3/5 Referrals are poor fit. **Mitigation:** Define trigger criteria.
2. **Market** · 3/5 Advisor overpromises. **Mitigation:** Provide approved wording.
3. **Financial** · 3/5 Referral fee too high. **Mitigation:** Pay on qualified outcomes.
4. **Operational** · 3/5 Referral handoff weak. **Mitigation:** Use simple intake form.
5. **Alignment** · 3/5 Sales ignores referrals. **Mitigation:** Set SLA.

Speed	Effort	Cost	Revenue	Time to cash	Scalability
Fast (0-30 days)	**Low**	**Low**	**High**	**Medium**	**High**

Decision-flow: CFO → Partnerships / BD → Sales

319. Build a value-added affiliate channel, not a coupon

Recruit affiliates who educate, compare, guide, diagnose, or explain buyer decisions instead of simply driving discount traffic or generic clicks.

Why it works

Most affiliate programs create low-quality traffic. Value-added affiliates create trust, context, and higher-fit buyers before the sales process even starts.

Best for

SaaS, education, finance, healthcare, wellness, professional services, digital products, B2B tools

Execution Steps

1. Define what value-added affiliate means
2. Exclude coupon-only traffic sources
3. Recruit educators, reviewers, and guides
4. Provide approved positioning
5. Pay for quality outcomes.

Real-world example

A B2B tool recruits niche educators as affiliates instead of coupon sites, improving lead quality and buyer understanding.

Risk Management

1. **Commercial** · 3/5 Affiliates chase volume. **Mitigation:** Pay for quality outcomes.
2. **Market** · 4/5 Low-quality promotion. **Mitigation:** Screen affiliates.
3. **Financial** · 3/5 Commission mispriced. **Mitigation:** Model LTV and margin.
4. **Operational** · 3/5 Program management burden. **Mitigation:** Start small.
5. **Legal** · 3/5 Failure to disclose relationships or terms creates a trust and compliance. **Mitigation:** Require written disclosure of all relationships and commercial arrangements.

Speed	Effort	Cost	Revenue	Time to cash	Scalability
Medium (1-3 months)	**Medium**	**Low**	**Very High**	**Medium**	**High**

Decision-flow: CFO → Marketing → Partnerships / BD

320. Turn expert affiliates into mini-consultants for your buyers

Equip selected affiliates with diagnostic tools, calculators, buyer frameworks, implementation explainers, or evaluation assets so they can guide customer decisions professionally.

Why it works

Expert affiliates convert better when they can actively help buyers make decisions instead of simply referring traffic.

Best for

SaaS, consulting, finance, healthcare, education, B2B services, coaching, professional services

Execution Steps

1. Select affiliates with expertise
2. Build diagnostic tools and calculators
3. Provide approved decision frameworks
4. Train affiliates on use cases
5. Monitor recommendation quality

Real-world example

A finance platform gives expert affiliates calculators and checklists so they can guide buyers before referral.

Risk Management

1. **Market** · 4/5 Affiliate gives wrong advice. **Mitigation:** Train and certify.
2. **Legal** · 4/5 Advice risk. **Mitigation:** Use approved tools.
3. **Operational** · 3/5 Enablement takes effort. **Mitigation:** Prioritize top affiliates.
4. **Commercial** · 3/5 Tools not used. **Mitigation:** Make tools simple.
5. **Financial** · 3/5 Support cost rises. **Mitigation:** Limit to qualified affiliates.

Speed	Effort	Cost	Revenue	Time to cash	Scalability
Medium (1-3 months)	**Medium**	**Low**	**Very High**	**Medium**	**High**

Decision-flow: CFO → Partnerships / BD → Marketing

321. Let affiliates distribute your offer inside their own

Allow affiliates to position your offer as part of a broader workflow, toolkit, operational stack, or customer process they already help manage.

Why it works

Customers buy more easily when the solution fits naturally into a bigger operational context they already understand.

Best for

SaaS, education, healthcare, fitness, finance, creator tools, B2B services, professional services

Execution Steps

1. Identify affiliate-owned workflows
2. Define where your offer fits
3. Create stack positioning guidance
4. Set referral or affiliate links
5. Test with one affiliate workflow

Real-world example

A productivity SaaS is distributed by workflow educators as part of their recommended operating stack.

Risk Management

1. **Commercial** · 3/5 Stack fit weak. **Mitigation:** Validate context.
2. **Market** · 3/5 Affiliate bundles incorrectly. **Mitigation:** Provide guidelines.
3. **Financial** · 3/5 Revenue share unclear. **Mitigation:** Set terms.
4. **Operational** · 3/5 Support questions rise. **Mitigation:** Prepare FAQs.
5. **Customer** · 3/5 Offer feels forced. **Mitigation:** Use natural workflow fit.

Speed	Effort	Cost	Revenue	Time to cash	Scalability
Medium (1-3 months)	**Medium**	**Low**	**High**	**Medium**	**High**

Decision-flow: CFO → Partnerships / BD → Product

322. Reward affiliates for quality, not just clicks

Design affiliate compensation around qualified leads, retained customers, repeat purchase, account value, or activation quality instead of raw traffic.

Why it works

Click-based affiliate programs attract volume games. Quality-based payouts align affiliates with profitable revenue, not vanity traffic.

Best for

SaaS, finance, healthcare, education, B2B services, subscriptions, professional services, digital platforms

Execution Steps

1. Define quality metrics
2. Link payout to qualified outcomes
3. Track activation, retention, or account value
4. Communicate payout rules clearly
5. Remove low-quality affiliates

Real-world example

A SaaS company pays affiliates more for activated customers than for raw sign-ups.

Risk Management

1. **Financial** · 3/5 Payout model too complex. **Mitigation:** Keep tiers simple.
2. **Commercial** · 3/5 Affiliates resist. **Mitigation:** Explain upside.
3. **Product** · 4/5 Attribution gaps. **Mitigation:** Track properly.
4. **Legal** · 3/5 Unclear terms create disputes and undermine trust in the commercial relationship.. **Mitigation:** Publish rules.
5. **Operational** · 3/5 Manual review burden. **Mitigation:** Automate where possible.

Speed	Effort	Cost	Revenue	Time to cash	Scalability
Fast (0-30 days)	**Medium**	**Low**	**Very High**	**Medium**	**High**

Decision-flow: CFO → Marketing → Finance

323. Create a certification layer for affiliates

Require affiliates to complete training, pass a basic certification, and follow approved positioning before they can promote higher-value offers.

Why it works

Certified affiliates protect brand quality and explain the offer better. Better education improves conversion and reduces bad-fit leads.

Best for

SaaS, healthcare, finance, education, B2B tools, professional services, regulated industries

Execution Steps

1. Define affiliate certification requirements
2. Build short training module
3. Test basic understanding
4. Approve higher-value promotion rights
5. Monitor messaging quality

Real-world example

A healthcare technology company certifies affiliates before allowing them to promote regulated enterprise offers.

Risk Management

1. **Commercial** · 3/5 Certification reduces affiliate pool. **Mitigation:** Focus on quality.
2. **Operational** · 3/5 Training burden. **Mitigation:** Keep short.
3. **Market** · 3/5 Uncertified promotion continues. **Mitigation:** Enforce rules.
4. **Legal** · 4/5 Unsubstantiated or overstated claims create legal and reputational exposure. Review before publishing. **Mitigation:** Use approved language.
5. **Financial** · 2/5 Low participation. **Mitigation:** Offer higher payout for certified affiliates.

Speed	Effort	Cost	Revenue	Time to cash	Scalability
Medium (1-3 months)	**Medium**	**Low**	**High**	**Medium**	**High**

Decision-flow: CFO → Partnerships / BD → Customer Success

324. *Use education creators as buyer-acquisition channels*

Partner with educators, analysts, reviewers, trainers, newsletter operators, or niche experts who teach the exact problems your buyers are trying to solve.

Why it works

Educational trust often shapes buying decisions before customers ever speak to sales. Teaching-based channels create warm, informed demand.

Best for

SaaS, finance, healthcare, education, wellness, B2B tools, professional services, digital products

Execution Steps

1. Identify creators teaching buyer problems
2. Evaluate audience fit and trust
3. Build education-led channel offer
4. Provide demos, assets, and tracking links
5. Launch with one creator first

Real-world example

A cybersecurity tool partners with a newsletter educator who teaches security operations problems to the exact buyer audience.

Risk Management

1. **Market** · 3/5 Creator lacks credibility. **Mitigation:** Vet content quality.
2. **Commercial** · 3/5 Audience not ready to buy. **Mitigation:** Choose problem-aware creators.
3. **Financial** · 3/5 Sponsorship creep. **Mitigation:** Use performance terms where possible.
4. **Legal** · 3/5 Failure to disclose relationships or terms creates a trust and compliance. **Mitigation:** Require written disclosure of all relationships and commercial arrangements.
5. **Operational** · 3/5 Creator needs support. **Mitigation:** Provide simple assets.

Speed	Effort	Cost	Revenue	Time to cash	Scalability
Fast (0-30 days)	**Medium**	**Low**	**Very High**	**Medium**	**High**

Decision-flow: CFO → Marketing → Partnerships / BD

325. Turn implementation partners into pre-sale channel

Create a referral or affiliate path for consultants, agencies, integrators, trainers, or specialists who help customers after implementation and already understand buyer needs.

Why it works

Implementation partners see customer pain repeatedly and often influence future purchasing decisions before vendors do.

Best for

SaaS, enterprise software, healthcare tech, education platforms, finance tools, B2B services

Execution Steps

1. Identify implementation partners close to customers
2. Define pre-sale referral triggers
3. Create partner economics
4. Train partners on fit criteria
5. Build handoff process

Real-world example

An enterprise SaaS company turns implementation consultants into referral partners because they see operational needs before the vendor does.

Risk Management

1. **Commercial** · 3/5 Partner focuses only on services. **Mitigation:** Create clear incentive.
2. **Market** · 4/5 Partner quality varies. **Mitigation:** Certify all partners against defined quality criteria before activation.
3. **Customer** · 3/5 Existing channels react negatively to the new route. **Mitigation:** Clarify roles.
4. **Operational** · 3/5 Post-launch support demand is higher than planned, straining the delivery team. **Mitigation:** Provide enablement.
5. **Financial** · 3/5 Revenue share too high. **Mitigation:** Model full unit economics before setting the launch price.

Speed	Effort	Cost	Revenue	Time to cash	Scalability
Medium (1-3 months)	**Medium**	**Low**	**Very High**	**Medium**	**High**

Decision-flow: CFO → Partnerships / BD → Customer Success

326. Turn niche influencers into trusted micro-channels

Partner with smaller, high-trust influencers who speak directly to a specific buyer audience and can explain the offer in practical, relevant terms.

Why it works

Micro-influencers often have stronger trust than large accounts. Their audiences listen because the relationship feels personal and specific.

Best for

SaaS, education, healthcare, finance, wellness, creator tools, retail, professional services

Execution Steps

1. Identify micro-influencers with buyer trust
2. Assess audience relevance
3. Build practical offer angle
4. Set tracked links or codes
5. Launch small test content

Real-world example

A niche healthcare tool partners with specialist creators who speak directly to practitioners rather than broad lifestyle influencers.

Risk Management

1. **Market** · 4/5 Influencer mismatch. **Mitigation:** Vet audience and tone.
2. **Commercial** · 3/5 Engagement does not convert. **Mitigation:** Track revenue.
3. **Financial** · 3/5 Fees too high. **Mitigation:** Use performance components.
4. **Legal** · 3/5 Disclosure issues. **Mitigation:** Require written disclosure of all relationships and commercial arrangements.
5. **Operational** · 3/5 Content approvals slow. **Mitigation:** Use simple approval process.

Speed	Effort	Cost	Revenue	Time to cash	Scalability
Fast (0-30 days)	**Medium**	**Low**	**High**	**Medium**	**High**

Decision-flow: CFO → Marketing → Partnerships / BD

327. Use creators to demonstrate real-world usage as the acquisition channel

Work with creators who actively demonstrate workflows, outcomes, customer experiences, or operational use cases instead of generic product promotion.

Why it works

Customers trust products more when they see them used naturally inside real workflows and environments.

Best for

SaaS, retail, education, healthcare, fitness, finance, creator tools, professional services

Execution Steps

1. Identify creators who can show real usage
2. Define demonstration use case
3. Provide product access or service experience
4. Capture tracked conversion path
5. Launch demonstration content

Real-world example

A SaaS company partners with a workflow creator who shows the tool solving a real operating problem step by step.

Risk Management

1. **Market** · 4/5 Demo is inaccurate. **Mitigation:** Review use case.
2. **Customer** · 3/5 Demo feels staged. **Mitigation:** Use real workflows.
3. **Commercial** · 3/5 No conversion path. **Mitigation:** Add tracked link.
4. **Legal** · 3/5 Unsubstantiated or overstated claims create legal and reputational exposure. Review before publishing. **Mitigation:** Approve claims.
5. **Operational** · 3/5 Creator needs support. **Mitigation:** Provide guided setup.

Speed	Effort	Cost	Revenue	Time to cash	Scalability
Fast (0-30 days)	**Medium**	**Low**	**Very High**	**Medium**	**High**

Decision-flow: CFO → Marketing → Partnerships / BD

328. Build an influencer affiliate program with tracked

Give selected influencers unique links, codes, landing pages, or QR codes so every sale, lead, booking, or sign-up is tracked clearly.

Why it works

Influencer activity becomes measurable when tied to tracked conversion paths. This turns social reach into accountable revenue.

Best for

SaaS, retail, education, healthcare, fitness, finance, consumer products, professional services

Execution Steps

1. Select influencers with buyer fit
2. Create tracked links, codes, or landing pages
3. Define payout rules
4. Launch controlled campaigns
5. Monitor conversion quality

Real-world example

A fitness brand gives each creator a unique landing page and tracks bookings by creator rather than impressions.

Risk Management

1. **Product** · 4/5 Attribution breaks. **Mitigation:** Use unique links.
2. **Financial** · 3/5 Creator ROI unclear. **Mitigation:** Track contribution margin.
3. **Market** · 4/5 Influencer misalignment. **Mitigation:** Vet carefully.
4. **Legal** · 3/5 Disclosure missing. **Mitigation:** Require disclosure.
5. **Commercial** · 3/5 Low-quality leads. **Mitigation:** Optimize by activation.

Speed	Effort	Cost	Revenue	Time to cash	Scalability
Medium (1-3 months)	**Medium**	**Low**	**Very High**	**Medium**	**High**

Decision-flow: CFO → Marketing → Finance

329. Turn audience-building customers into creator-channel

Identify customers who already operate audiences, communities, newsletters, podcasts, or educational platforms and turn them into structured distribution partners.

Why it works

Customers who already use the product and own attention channels create highly trusted distribution pathways.

Best for

SaaS, education, healthcare, memberships, fintech, coaching, professional services, B2B tools

Execution Steps

1. Identify customers with relevant audiences
2. Confirm they are successful users
3. Create partner terms and tracking
4. Provide approved content assets
5. Launch through their audience

Real-world example

An education platform turns a successful customer with a newsletter into a tracked creator-channel partner.

Risk Management

1. **Customer** · 3/5 Customer feels exploited. **Mitigation:** Offer fair economics.
2. **Market** · 3/5 Message too personal or off-brand. **Mitigation:** Provide guidelines.
3. **Commercial** · 2/5 Audience too small. **Mitigation:** Prioritize fit over size.
4. **Legal** · 3/5 Failure to disclose relationships or terms creates a trust and compliance. **Mitigation:** Require clear disclosure.
5. **Alignment** · 2/5 Confused with testimonials. **Mitigation:** Track as channel.

Speed	Effort	Cost	Revenue	Time to cash	Scalability
Medium (1-3 months)	**Medium**	**Low**	**Very High**	**Medium**	**High**

Decision-flow: CFO → Customer Success → Partnerships / BD

330. Turn creator content into reusable multi-channel sales

Secure rights to reuse creator videos, demos, explainers, walkthroughs, or educational content across sales, partnerships, onboarding, and channel enablement.

Why it works

Great creator content compounds in value when reused across multiple distribution paths instead of disappearing after one post.

Best for

SaaS, education, healthcare, fitness, finance, retail, B2B tools, professional services

Execution Steps

1. Identify reusable creator content formats
2. Negotiate usage rights upfront
3. Store content in sales and partner library
4. Adapt assets for multiple channels
5. Train teams to use them

Real-world example

A SaaS firm reuses creator demo videos in partner enablement, sales follow-up, and landing pages after securing rights.

Risk Management

1. **Legal** · 4/5 Usage rights unclear. **Mitigation:** Contract rights explicitly.
2. **Market** · 3/5 Content becomes outdated. **Mitigation:** Review regularly.
3. **Commercial** · 3/5 Assets unused. **Mitigation:** Embed the approach into the standard sales workflow before any rollout.
4. **Financial** · 3/5 Rights cost too much. **Mitigation:** Negotiate practical scope.
5. **Operational** · 2/5 Content hard to organize. **Mitigation:** Build asset library.

Speed	Effort	Cost	Revenue	Time to cash	Scalability
Medium (1-3 months)	**Medium**	**Low**	**High**	**Medium**	**High**

Decision-flow: CFO → Marketing → Sales

331. Turn your customers' vendor ecosystem into a channel

Partner with companies already selling adjacent solutions into your customers so your offer becomes part of the broader operating ecosystem.

Why it works

Vendors already trusted by your buyers can introduce your offer naturally inside existing operational relationships.

Best for

SaaS, logistics, healthcare, finance, construction, manufacturing, B2B services, enterprise software

Execution Steps

1. Map vendors already serving target customers
2. Identify adjacent solution fit
3. Define referral or embedded path
4. Set commercial terms
5. Train vendor teams

Real-world example

A construction technology company partners with materials suppliers already selling into the same contractors.

Risk Management

1. **Commercial** · 3/5 Vendor relationship weak. **Mitigation:** Start with aligned vendors.
2. **Market** · 3/5 Vendor creates confusion. **Mitigation:** Clarify positioning.
3. **Financial** · 3/5 Revenue share too high. **Mitigation:** Model full unit economics before setting the launch price.
4. **Operational** · 3/5 Partner enablement burden. **Mitigation:** Create simple materials.
5. **Alignment** · 3/5 Sales channel conflict. **Mitigation:** Define territory rules.

Speed	Effort	Cost	Revenue	Time to cash	Scalability
Medium (1-3 months)	**Medium**	**Low**	**Very High**	**Medium**	**High**

Decision-flow: CFO → Partnerships / BD → Sales

332. Create a powered-by distribution model

Allow other businesses to embed your capability invisibly inside their own offer while your company powers the backend.

Why it works

Many companies want capabilities without building them. White-labeled infrastructure creates scalable indirect distribution.

Best for

Fintech, SaaS, logistics, healthcare tech, AI tools, payments, analytics, infrastructure software

Execution Steps

1. Identify capabilities others would embed
2. Package backend delivery model
3. Define white-label terms
4. Build partner onboarding process
5. Pilot with one partner

Real-world example

A payments company powers another platform's checkout experience under the partner's brand.

Risk Management

1. **Operational** · 4/5 Partner expectations too high. **Mitigation:** Define service levels.
2. **Product** · 4/5 Integration complexity. **Mitigation:** Start with narrow capability.
3. **Market** · 3/5 Invisible brand value. **Mitigation:** Price for backend value.
4. **Legal** · 4/5 White-label liability. **Mitigation:** Set contractual boundaries.
5. **Financial** · 3/5 Margin compresses if delivery cost is not controlled from the start. **Mitigation:** Model support cost.s

Speed	Effort	Cost	Revenue	Time to cash	Scalability
Medium (1-3 months)	**High**	**Medium**	**Very High**	**Medium**	**High**

Decision-flow: CFO → Product → Partnerships / BD

333. Build channels around customer pain-resolution

Identify specialists already solving painful operational problems for your buyers, then position your offer as part of their problem-resolution workflow.

Why it works

Pain-resolution specialists already have buyer trust at the exact moment urgency exists. That creates highly relevant distribution leverage.

Best for

SaaS, healthcare, enterprise software, logistics, consulting, cybersecurity, HR tech, education

Execution Steps

1. Identify customer pain ecosystems
2. Find specialists solving those pains
3. Map where your offer fits into resolution
4. Build referral or co-solution path
5. Train specialists on fit

Real-world example

An HR tech company partners with workplace consultants who already solve employee retention pain for target customers.

Risk Management

1. **Commercial** · 3/5 Pain specialist sees no fit. **Mitigation:** Choose urgent adjacent pain.
2. **Market** · 3/5 Specialist mispositions offer. **Mitigation:** Provide use cases.
3. **Operational** · 3/5 Handoff unclear. **Mitigation:** Define workflow.
4. **Financial** · 3/5 Low volume. **Mitigation:** Prioritize repeated pain points.
5. **Customer** · 3/5 Solution feels bolted on. **Mitigation:** Integrate naturally.

Speed	Effort	Cost	Revenue	Time to cash	Scalability
Medium (1-3 months)	**Medium**	**Low**	**Very High**	**Medium**	**High**

Decision-flow: CFO → Customer Success → Partnerships / BD

334. Use procurement shortcuts as a distribution advantage

Get approved inside procurement frameworks, preferred-vendor lists, buying cooperatives, or industry purchasing networks that buyers already trust.

Why it works

Many deals die before evaluation because procurement slows everything down. Pre-approved channel access removes buying friction at scale.

Best for

Healthcare, government, enterprise SaaS, manufacturing, education, infrastructure, finance, B2B services

Execution Steps

1. Identify procurement networks buyers use
2. Understand approval requirements
3. Apply for preferred or approved vendor status
4. Build procurement-ready materials
5. Promote availability to buyers

Real-world example

A healthcare supplier joins a trusted purchasing network so hospitals can buy through an approved route faster.

Risk Management

1. **Operational** · 4/5 Approval process slow. **Mitigation:** Prioritize best networks.
2. **Legal** · 4/5 Requirements complex. **Mitigation:** Prepare documentation.
3. **Financial** · 3/5 Fees or margins high. **Mitigation:** Model channel economics.
4. **Commercial** · 3/5 Buyers unaware. **Mitigation:** Promote approved status.
5. **Alignment** · 3/5 Sales does not use route. **Mitigation:** Train sales.

Speed	Effort	Cost	Revenue	Time to cash	Scalability
Medium (1-3 months)	**High**	**Medium**	**Very High**	**Medium**	**High**

Decision-flow: CFO → Operations → Sales

335. Turn your data into a partner-attraction channel

Publish benchmarks, forecasts, scoring systems, operational insights, or intelligence tools that attract ecosystem partners who want access to your market visibility.

Why it works

Useful data creates commercial gravity. Strong insight platforms naturally attract channel relationships, integrations, and distribution partnerships.

Best for

Finance, SaaS, logistics, healthcare, HR tech, cybersecurity, consulting, analytics platforms

Execution Steps

1. Identify valuable data or benchmarks
2. Package insights for ecosystem relevance
3. Publish or share with target partners
4. Invite partner conversations
5. Convert interested partners into channels

Real-world example

A logistics platform publishes shipping benchmarks that attract software and consulting partners seeking distribution collaboration.

Risk Management

1. **Product** · 4/5 Data quality weak. **Mitigation:** Validate methodology.
2. **Legal** · 5/5 Data privacy risk. **Mitigation:** Aggregate and anonymize.
3. **Commercial** · 3/5 Attracts leads not partners. **Mitigation:** Use partner CTA.
4. **Market** · 3/5 Insight lacks authority. **Mitigation:** Use credible methodology.
5. **Financial** · 3/5 No channel conversion. **Mitigation:** Track partner pipeline.

Speed	Effort	Cost	Revenue	Time to cash	Scalability
Medium (1-3 months)	**Medium**	**Low**	**Very High**	**Medium**	**High**

Decision-flow: CFO → IT / Data → Marketing

From Ideas to Action

Twenty-two ideas. Twenty-two ways to reach buyers the business is not currently reaching — through new routes, partners, and platforms.

A new channel does not require a new product or a new customer type. It requires a new route to buyers who already exist. Most businesses are one distribution decision away from a meaningfully larger addressable market.

Before continuing, identify the single idea with the clearest commercial case right now. Name who owns it. Set a date for the first step. That is all that is required.

> ***The right channel does not need to be built from scratch. It needs to be chosen, tested, and owned.***

What Comes Next

5.2 — New Customer Segments addresses businesses whose core offer solves a problem that exists in buyer types, industries, or company sizes the business is not yet serving. If the offer works well and adjacent segments are visible — the next chapter shows how to reach them.

5.2 — New Customer Segments

Expand revenue by selling the current offer to a different type of buyer.

When These Strategies Work Best

New segment strategies work best when the core offer solves a problem that exists in multiple buyer types, industries, or company sizes that the business is not currently serving.

- The core offer solves a problem that clearly exists in adjacent industries or buyer types
- Current customers regularly refer the business to buyers outside its primary segment
- Revenue is concentrated in one segment and expansion would reduce commercial risk
- A new buyer type could be served with minimal change to the core product or delivery
- Competition is lower in adjacent segments than in the primary market

The Benefits

- Revenue growth from existing capabilities without building new products
- Reduced commercial concentration risk across a broader customer base
- New market intelligence that often improves the core offer for existing customers
- Higher average deal values in segments where the problem has greater commercial impact
- Compounding advantage as the business builds multi-segment credibility over time

The Risks to Manage

- **Positioning misfit** — language and proof that works in one segment often fails in another. Adapt before launching.
- **Resource stretch** — serving multiple segments simultaneously dilutes focus. Enter one new segment at a time.
- **Delivery gaps** — new segments often have requirements the current model does not cover. Validate before committing.
- **Brand confusion** — being known for everything quickly means being chosen for nothing. Maintain a clear primary position.

336. Sell the same offer to a different budget owner

Reposition the offer so a different department, executive, or operational owner becomes the buyer without changing the core solution.

Why it works

Many products solve multiple internal problems but are sold to only one budget owner. New budget access expands revenue quickly.

Best for

SaaS, healthcare, logistics, finance, HR tech, cybersecurity, consulting, enterprise services

Execution Steps

1. Map all departments affected by the problem
2. Identify alternative budget owners
3. Reframe the value for each budget owner
4. Build buyer-specific messaging
5. Test with one new department type

Real-world example

A cybersecurity tool sold to IT reframes the same value for finance as loss prevention and audit-risk visibility.

Risk Management

1. **Commercial** · 3/5 New buyer lacks authority. **Mitigation:** Confirm budget ownership.
2. **Commercial** · 3/5 Message too technical. **Mitigation:** Translate value into buyer language.
3. **Alignment** · 3/5 Sales keeps targeting old buyer. **Mitigation:** Create new playbook.
4. **Operational** · 3/5 Different buyer expects different support. **Mitigation:** Set expectations in writing before any engagement or commitment begins.
5. **Financial** · 2/5 Revenue cannibalizes old pipeline. **Mitigation:** Track net new budget.

Speed	Effort	Cost	Revenue	Time to cash	Scalability
Fast (0-30 days)	**Medium**	**Low**	**Very High**	**Medium**	**High**

Decision-flow: CFO → Sales → PMO / Strategy

337. Turn operational tools into executive management tools

Reframe operational products as executive visibility, forecasting, risk, control, or performance-management tools for senior management teams.

Why it works

Executives buy control and confidence, not just operational features. Reframing the same offer opens a higher-level buyer group.

Best for

Analytics, SaaS, logistics, finance, healthcare, cybersecurity, HR tech, enterprise software

Execution Steps

1. Identify executive-level concerns the offer already supports
2. Reframe operational outputs into management outcomes
3. Build executive-oriented messaging and reporting examples
4. Create leadership-level sales material
5. Pilot with management stakeholders

Real-world example

An operations analytics platform reframes workflow reporting as executive performance visibility for leadership teams managing multi-site operations.

Risk Management

1. **Commercial** · 3/5 Positioning confusion. **Mitigation:** Separate operational vs executive messaging.
2. **Customer** · 3/5 Executives ignore tactical features. **Mitigation:** Focus on visibility and control.
3. **Alignment** · 3/5 Sales defaults to old positioning. **Mitigation:** Train on new buyer narrative.
4. **Product** · 4/5 Reporting lacks strategic depth. **Mitigation:** Add executive-ready dashboards.
5. **Operational** · 2/5 Internal product resistance. **Mitigation:** Use existing capabilities first.

Speed	Effort	Cost	Revenue	Time to cash	Scalability
Medium (1-3 months)	**Medium**	**Low**	**Very High**	**Medium**	**High**

Decision-flow: CFO → PMO / Strategy → Marketing

338. *Sell consumer-grade convenience to business buyers*

Position speed, simplicity, ease-of-use, flexibility, or experience quality as the primary reason business buyers should choose the offer.

Why it works

Some business buyers value ease and simplicity more than technical depth. Convenience-led positioning opens a new buyer preference segment.

Best for

SaaS, logistics, finance, healthcare, procurement, education, HR tech, professional services

Execution Steps

1. Identify friction points buyers hate most
2. Simplify messaging. around ease and speed
3. Remove operational jargon from positioning
4. Showcase convenience-driven workflows
5. Target buyers frustrated by complexity

Real-world example

A procurement tool wins mid-market buyers by positioning around consumer-grade simplicity instead of feature depth.

Risk Management

1. **Market** · 3/5 Offer looks less sophisticated. **Mitigation:** Maintain enterprise credibility.
2. **Customer** · 2/5 Existing customers feel ignored. **Mitigation:** Keep technical positioning available.
3. **Product** · 4/5 Simplicity claims unsupported. **Mitigation:** Improve actual onboarding flow.
4. **Market** · 2/5 Competitors copy messaging. **Mitigation:** Tie to operational experience.
5. **Alignment** · 3/5 Teams overcomplicate sales. **Mitigation:** Standardize messaging.

Speed	Effort	Cost	Revenue	Time to cash	Scalability
Fast (0-30 days)	**Low**	**Low**	**High**	**Medium**	**High**

Decision-flow: CFO → Product → Marketing

339. Turn occasional users into recurring operational users

Target teams or workflows that can repeatedly use the same offer as part of regular operations instead of treating it as a one-time purchase.

Why it works

Many offers solve repeat operational pain but are sold as occasional solutions. Recurring-use buyers create more frequent demand.

Best for

SaaS, consulting, logistics, healthcare, education, finance, B2B services, agencies

Execution Steps

1. Identify repeat operational workflows
2. Map recurring pain frequency
3. Reposition the offer around operational continuity
4. Train sales.s on recurring-use cases
5. Target operational departments directly

Real-world example

A consulting firm repositions quarterly operational reviews from an occasional service into a recurring operations-support workflow.

Risk Management

1. **Customer** · 3/5 Customers still perceive one-time usage. **Mitigation:** Show operational cadence.
2. **Operational** · 3/5 Teams resist workflow change. **Mitigation:** Start with pilot users.
3. **Alignment** · 3/5 Sales focuses on one-off projects. **Mitigation:** Add recurring-use KPIs.
4. **Commercial** · 4/5 Operational value unclear. **Mitigation:** Use workflow examples.
5. **Financial** · 2/5 Overlap with subscriptions. **Mitigation:** Keep focus on user behavior.

Speed	Effort	Cost	Revenue	Time to cash	Scalability
Medium (1-3 months)	**Medium**	**Low**	**Very High**	**Medium**	**High**

Decision-flow: CFO → Customer Success → Sales

340. Sell the same outcome to smaller businesses with less

Simplify positioning, onboarding, language, or delivery expectations so smaller companies can buy the same core value more easily.

Why it works

SMBs often avoid enterprise-style complexity. Simplified positioning opens a much larger buyer pool.

Best for

Enterprise software, SaaS, healthcare, finance, logistics, cybersecurity, consulting, education

Execution Steps

1. Identify smaller companies with the same pain
2. Remove enterprise language from messaging
3. Simplify onboarding. expectations
4. Set explicit boundaries on scope and ownership before delivery begins. around scope
5. Pilot with SMB or mid-market buyers

Real-world example

An enterprise compliance tool sells the same core outcome to smaller regulated firms with simpler language and lighter onboarding.

Risk Management

1. **Financial** · 3/5 Segment has lower willingness to pay. **Mitigation:** Model unit economics.
2. **Operational** · 4/5 Support needs are high. **Mitigation:** Set clear scope.
3. **Market** · 3/5 Enterprise positioning diluted. **Mitigation:** Separate segment messaging.
4. **Commercial** · 3/5 Sales chases too small accounts. **Mitigation:** Set minimum fit.
5. **Product** · 3/5 Complexity still too high. **Mitigation:** Simplify process. not product

Speed	Effort	Cost	Revenue	Time to cash	Scalability
Medium (1-3 months)	**Medium**	**Low**	**Very High**	**Medium**	**High**

Decision-flow: CFO → Sales → Operations

341. Target industries with the same hidden operational pain

Identify industries outside your core market that suffer from the same workflow, coordination, compliance, staffing, or efficiency problems.

Why it works

Different industries often share identical operational pain patterns. One proven solution can unlock entirely new sectors.

Best for

SaaS, HR tech, cybersecurity, logistics, healthcare, finance, analytics, professional services

Execution Steps

1. Identify core pain pattern
2. Find other industries with the same pain
3. Validate language and buying process
4. Create industry-specific examples
5. Test with one adjacent sector

Real-world example

A logistics workflow tool originally built for retail expands into healthcare because both sectors face similar coordination problems.

Risk Management

1. **Commercial** · 4/5 Industry pain differs in practice. **Mitigation:** Conduct buyer interviews to validate demand before launch investment.
2. **Commercial** · 3/5 Industry language wrong. **Mitigation:** Localize messaging.
3. **Operational** · 4/5 Compliance requirements differ. **Mitigation:** Review sector requirements.
4. **Financial** · 3/5 Sales cycle longer. **Mitigation:** Pilot before scaling.
5. **Alignment** · 3/5 Team lacks sector credibility. **Mitigation:** Use advisors or partners.

Speed	Effort	Cost	Revenue	Time to cash	Scalability
Medium (1-3 months)	**Medium**	**Low**	**Very High**	**Medium**	**High**

Decision-flow: CFO → PMO / Strategy → Sales

342. Sell the same offer to risk-reduction buyers

Reposition the offer around avoiding loss, downtime, waste, service failure, operational exposure, or business disruption.

Why it works

Some buyers act faster to avoid problems than to chase upside. Risk-reduction framing opens more conservative customer segments.

Best for

Finance, healthcare, cybersecurity, logistics, enterprise software, insurance, consulting, HR tech

Execution Steps

1. Identify operational risks the offer reduces
2. Translate features into avoided losses
3. Build risk-focused case studies
4. Target conservative decision-makers
5. Adjust messaging toward protection

Real-world example

A workflow automation tool shifts positioning from productivity growth to operational risk reduction after costly process failures.

Risk Management

1. **Commercial** · 3/5 Messaging becomes fear-based. **Mitigation:** Use factual positioning.
2. **Customer** · 3/5 Buyers see no urgency. **Mitigation:** Quantify risk exposure.
3. **Legal** · 4/5 Sales overstates protection. **Mitigation:** Use approved claims.
4. **Commercial** · 2/5 Existing growth buyers confused. **Mitigation:** Separate messaging.
5. **Market** · 2/5 Competitors respond similarly. **Mitigation:** Use operational proof.

Speed	Effort	Cost	Revenue	Time to cash	Scalability
Fast (0-30 days)	**Low**	**Low**	**High**	**Medium**	**High**

Decision-flow: CFO → Marketing → Sales

343. Expose existing internal capabilities to external

Offer external customers access to an existing internal capability, workflow, tool, method, or operating advantage with minimal adaptation.

Why it works

Many internal capabilities already solve problems other customers have. Exposing them externally creates new customer segments without building a new product.

Best for

SaaS, analytics, finance, logistics, healthcare, HR tech, consulting, operations platforms

Execution Steps

1. Identify valuable internal operational capabilities
2. Validate external customer demand
3. Expose the capability with minimal adaptation
4. Create customer-safe access and controls
5. Pilot with selected customers

Real-world example

A logistics company exposes its internal route-optimization capability to external fleet customers without rebuilding the core engine.

Risk Management

1. **Product** · 4/5 Capability not customer-ready. **Mitigation:** Pilot carefully.
2. **Operational** · 4/5 Internal systems become overloaded. **Mitigation:** Separate operational environments.
3. **Customer** · 3/5 Customers require heavy customization. **Mitigation:** Define a strict scope boundary and enforce it from. initially
4. **Alignment** · 3/5 Internal teams resist sharing tools. **Mitigation:** Align team and partner incentives with the desired commercial outcome.
5. **Product** · 5/5 Security exposure risk. **Mitigation:** Add proper controls.

Speed	Effort	Cost	Revenue	Time to cash	Scalability
Medium (1-3 months)	**Medium**	**Low**	**Very High**	**Medium**	**High**

Decision-flow: CFO → Product → PMO / Strategy

344. Target companies during moments of organizational

Focus sales efforts on businesses going through hiring, restructuring, scaling, mergers, compliance shifts, leadership change, or rapid growth.

Why it works

Buying urgency increases during operational disruption. Change moments create temporary openness to solutions.

Best for

HR tech, SaaS, consulting, cybersecurity, finance, logistics, healthcare, professional services

Execution Steps

1. Identify change events that create need
2. Build trigger list from public signals
3. Create change-specific messaging
4. Target companies during transition
5. Align offer to immediate pain

Real-world example

An HR platform targets companies after leadership changes or rapid hiring announcements when people processes are under pressure.

Risk Management

1. **Product** · 3/5 Change signals are noisy. **Mitigation:** Use verified triggers.
2. **Commercial** · 3/5 Timing too late. **Mitigation:** Move quickly.
3. **Commercial** · 3/5 Message feels opportunistic. **Mitigation:** Lead with help.
4. **Operational** · 3/5 Needs vary by event. **Mitigation:** Segment trigger types.
5. **Financial** · 3/5 Conversion from initial interest to completed purchase is lower than targeted.. **Mitigation:** Track by trigger source.

Speed	Effort	Cost	Revenue	Time to cash	Scalability
Fast (0-30 days)	**Medium**	**Low**	**Very High**	**Medium**	**High**

Decision-flow: CFO → Sales → Marketing

345. Reposition premium offers for cost-sensitive segments

Change the buying narrative, usage framing, implementation path, or operational scope so cost-sensitive buyers can justify purchasing.

Why it works

Many buyers reject positioning, not value. Reframing the same offer opens lower-budget segments without cutting price.

Best for

SaaS, healthcare, education, consulting, logistics, finance, professional services, enterprise software

Execution Steps

1. Identify cost-sensitive but high-need segments
2. Reframe value around avoided cost or efficiency
3. Clarify practical scope
4. Build proof. of affordability logic
5. Test without discounting

Real-world example

A premium consulting offer is reframed around avoided operational waste for cost-sensitive mid-market buyers.

Risk Management

1. **Financial** · 4/5 Margin compresses if delivery cost is not controlled from the start. **Mitigation:** Do not discount base value.
2. **Market** · 3/5 Premium perception diluted. **Mitigation:** Separate messaging.
3. **Customer** · 3/5 Buyer still lacks budget. **Mitigation:** Qualify ability to pay.
4. **Commercial** · 4/5 Sales discounts anyway. **Mitigation:** Set pricing guardrails.
5. **Commercial** · 3/5 Value case too weak. **Mitigation:** Quantify economic benefit.

Speed	Effort	Cost	Revenue	Time to cash	Scalability
Medium (1-3 months)	**Medium**	**Low**	**High**	**Medium**	**High**

Decision-flow: CFO → Marketing → Sales

346. Sell to departments that inherit the operational pain

Target downstream departments that suffer the consequences of poor processes, delays, errors, or operational inefficiencies created elsewhere.

Why it works

The direct user is not always the economic buyer. Downstream pain owners often have stronger urgency and budget motivation.

Best for

Logistics, HR tech, finance, healthcare, SaaS, operations software, consulting, enterprise tools

Execution Steps

1. Map who suffers from the problem later
2. Identify downstream budget owners
3. Reframe value around consequences avoided
4. Build stakeholder-specific use cases
5. Test outreach to downstream buyers

Real-world example

A data-quality tool sold to operations reframes value for finance because finance suffers from poor reporting accuracy later.

Risk Management

1. **Commercial** · 3/5 Downstream buyer lacks control. **Mitigation:** Map influence path.
2. **Customer** · 3/5 Original user feels bypassed. **Mitigation:** Align stakeholders.
3. **Commercial** · 3/5 Pain chain unclear. **Mitigation:** Show consequence map.
4. **Operational** · 3/5 Different buyer needs different evidence. **Mitigation:** Build proof.
5. **Financial** · 3/5 Longer consensus process. **Mitigation:** Target urgent pain.

Speed	Effort	Cost	Revenue	Time to cash	Scalability
Medium (1-3 months)	**Medium**	**Low**	**Very High**	**Medium**	**High**

Decision-flow: CFO → PMO / Strategy → Sales

347. Turn compliance pressure into a new customer segment

Position the same offer around audit readiness, regulation response, documentation, reporting, or operational governance.

Why it works

Compliance urgency creates budget and faster buying behavior. Regulatory framing opens conservative buyer groups.

Best for

Cybersecurity, finance, healthcare, HR tech, logistics, SaaS, enterprise software, consulting

Execution Steps

1. Identify compliance pressures the offer supports
2. Translate features into compliance outcomes
3. Build audit-ready proof examples
4. Target regulated buyer groups
5. Review claims. for accuracy

Real-world example

A document workflow platform targets regulated healthcare teams by emphasizing audit readiness and operational governance.

Risk Management

1. **Legal** · 5/5 Claims overstate compliance value. **Mitigation:** Review messaging.
2. **Customer** · 4/5 Buyer expects legal advice. **Mitigation:** Clarify scope.
3. **Commercial** · 3/5 Regulatory language weak. **Mitigation:** Use expert review.
4. **Operational** · 3/5 Documentation support needed. **Mitigation:** Prepare evidence.
5. **Financial** · 3/5 Sales cycle longer. **Mitigation:** Target high-urgency rules.

Speed	Effort	Cost	Revenue	Time to cash	Scalability
Fast (0-30 days)	**Low**	**Low**	**Very High**	**Medium**	**High**

Decision-flow: CFO → Marketing → Sales

348. Sell operational visibility to finance teams

Reframe operational data, workflows, or reporting capabilities as tools for forecasting, cost control, margin protection, or financial visibility.

Why it works

Finance teams increasingly influence operational decisions. Visibility-driven positioning unlocks new executive buyers.

Best for

Logistics, SaaS, manufacturing, healthcare, HR tech, analytics, enterprise software, operations platforms

Execution Steps

1. Identify financial decisions the offer informs
2. Translate operational data into finance outcomes
3. Build CFO-friendly examples
4. Target finance stakeholders
5. Equip sales with financial language

Real-world example

A logistics platform reframes delivery visibility as margin and working-capital visibility for finance teams.

Risk Management

1. **Commercial** · 3/5 Too operational for finance. **Mitigation:** Translate into financial impact.
2. **Customer** · 3/5 Finance lacks ownership. **Mitigation:** Map decision influence.
3. **Financial** · 4/5 ROI assumptions weak. **Mitigation:** Use conservative model.
4. **Alignment** · 4/5 Sales cannot speak CFO language. **Mitigation:** Train sales.
5. **Product** · 3/5 Metrics not finance-ready. **Mitigation:** Clean definitions.

Speed	Effort	Cost	Revenue	Time to cash	Scalability
Fast (0-30 days)	**Medium**	**Low**	**Very High**	**Medium**	**High**

Decision-flow: CFO → Finance → Sales

349. Use education to reach future operational buyers

Use workshops, guides, learning sessions, certifications, or practical education to attract buyers who are not yet ready to purchase but will need the offer later.

Why it works

Education builds trust before buying urgency appears. It gives access to future buyer segments earlier than direct selling would.

Best for

SaaS, healthcare, finance, cybersecurity, logistics, consulting, HR tech, professional services

Execution Steps

1. Identify future buyer pain themes
2. Build practical education around those pains
3. Offer learning without hard selling
4. Capture audience relationships early
5. Nurture buyers over time

Real-world example

A cybersecurity company runs operational risk workshops for IT managers before they formally enter procurement cycles.

Risk Management

1. **Commercial** · 3/5 Education attracts non-buyers. **Mitigation:** Target practical pains.
2. **Market** · 3/5 Content lacks authority. **Mitigation:** Use real expertise.
3. **Commercial** · 4/5 No conversion path. **Mitigation:** Add nurture process.
4. **Alignment** · 3/5 Teams push sales too early. **Mitigation:** Separate education from pitching.
5. **Financial** · 2/5 Program becomes expensive. **Mitigation:** Reuse scalable content.

Speed	Effort	Cost	Revenue	Time to cash	Scalability
Medium (1-3 months)	**Medium**	**Low**	**High**	**Medium**	**High**

Decision-flow: CFO → Marketing → Customer Success

350. *Sell to companies trying to replace manual work*

Position the offer around reducing spreadsheets, coordination burden, repetitive tasks, approvals, or operational dependency on people.

Why it works

Manual operations create scaling pain. Automation-oriented positioning attracts efficiency-focused buyer segments.

Best for

SaaS, logistics, HR tech, finance, healthcare, consulting, enterprise software, operations platforms

Execution Steps

1. Identify manual workflows the offer replaces
2. Build messaging around workload reduction
3. Target teams overwhelmed by manual work
4. Show before-and-after workflow examples
5. Test with operations-heavy buyers

Real-world example

A workflow tool targets spreadsheet-heavy operations teams by showing how manual coordination work is reduced.

Risk Management

1. **Customer** · 3/5 Buyer fears job replacement. **Mitigation:** Frame as burden reduction.
2. **Commercial** · 3/5 Automation claim too broad. **Mitigation:** Use specific workflows.
3. **Operational** · 3/5 Implementation effort hidden. **Mitigation:** Explain transition.
4. **Product** · 3/5 Feature gaps exposed. **Mitigation:** Target fit carefully.
5. **Financial** · 3/5 Value hard to quantify. **Mitigation:** Estimate time saved.

Speed	Effort	Cost	Revenue	Time to cash	Scalability
Fast (0-30 days)	**Low**	**Low**	**Very High**	**Medium**	**High**

Decision-flow: CFO → Sales → Product

351. Use benchmark comparisons to attract underperforming

Show industries, departments, or company types how they compare operationally against peers to trigger buying urgency.

Why it works

Buyers act faster when they see measurable underperformance relative to competitors or peers.

Best for

Analytics, SaaS, finance, healthcare, logistics, HR tech, cybersecurity, consulting

Execution Steps

1. Identify measurable performance gaps
2. Build peer benchmark views
3. Target underperforming segments
4. Show gap without shaming
5. Connect offer to improvement path

Real-world example

An HR analytics tool shows mid-market firms how their employee churn compares with peers and uses that gap to open conversations.

Risk Management

1. **Product** · 4/5 Benchmark data weak. **Mitigation:** Validate methodology.
2. **Customer** · 3/5 Comparison feels negative. **Mitigation:** Use constructive framing.
3. **Legal** · 4/5 Data privacy risk. **Mitigation:** Aggregate data.
4. **Commercial** · 3/5 Benchmarks too generic. **Mitigation:** Segment carefully.
5. **Financial** · 3/5 Conversion from initial interest to completed purchase is lower than targeted.. **Mitigation:** Ensure every output ends with a single.

Speed	Effort	Cost	Revenue	Time to cash	Scalability
Medium (1-3 months)	**Medium**	**Low**	**Very High**	**Medium**	**High**

Decision-flow: CFO → IT / Data → Marketing

352. Sell proven workflows to less mature customer segments

Reframe successful workflows, playbooks, or operating patterns from advanced customers so less mature buyers can adopt the same underlying offer with confidence.

Why it works

Less mature buyers want proven paths without enterprise complexity. Workflow framing makes the same offer feel safer and easier to adopt.

Best for

SaaS, consulting, logistics, healthcare, finance, HR tech, education, operations software

Execution Steps

1. Identify successful enterprise workflows
2. Simplify them for less mature buyers
3. Build practical adoption playbooks
4. Remove unnecessary complexity
5. Position as proven operational path

Real-world example

An operations platform adapts enterprise-grade operating workflows into simplified templates for growing mid-market companies.

Risk Management

1. **Product** · 3/5 Workflow oversimplified. **Mitigation:** Preserve core outcomes.
2. **Customer** · 3/5 Customers still feel overwhelmed. **Mitigation:** Simplify onboarding.
3. **Market** · 2/5 Enterprise clients fear dilution. **Mitigation:** Keep advanced paths separate.
4. **Product** · 4/5 Teams accidentally build new products. **Mitigation:** Reuse existing capability.
5. **Commercial** · 3/5 Adoption remains low. **Mitigation:** Use guided rollout.

Speed	Effort	Cost	Revenue	Time to cash	Scalability
Medium (1-3 months)	**Medium**	**Low**	**Very High**	**Medium**	**High**

Decision-flow: CFO → Product → Customer Success

353. Sell to companies before they officially become your ideal customer

Target emerging companies early, before they reach the maturity level where competitors normally begin selling to them.

Why it works

Early positioning builds long-term customer relationships before the market becomes crowded and expensive.

Best for

SaaS, finance, logistics, healthcare, HR tech, cybersecurity, analytics, professional services

Execution Steps

1. Define pre-target maturity signals
2. Identify emerging companies before competitors
3. Create early-fit messaging
4. Offer a right-sized adoption path
5. Build relationship before full budget arrives

Real-world example

A cybersecurity provider targets fast-growing startups before they become enterprise security buyers.

Risk Management

1. **Financial** · 4/5 Early-stage buyers lack budget. **Mitigation:** Qualify resources.
2. **Commercial** · 3/5 Long payback. **Mitigation:** Track lifetime potential.
3. **Operational** · 3/5 Support needs high. **Mitigation:** Use right-sized scope.
4. **Customer** · 3/5 Buyer not ready. **Mitigation:** Use education-led approach.
5. **Alignment** · 3/5 Sales wants mature accounts only. **Mitigation:** Create strategic target list.

Speed	Effort	Cost	Revenue	Time to cash	Scalability
Medium (1-3 months)	**Medium**	**Low**	**High**	**Medium**	**High**

Decision-flow: CFO → Sales → PMO / Strategy

354. Sell operational visibility to boards and governance

Reframe reporting, analytics, or workflow visibility as board oversight, governance confidence, audit readiness, or executive accountability support.

Why it works

Boards and governance stakeholders buy visibility, assurance, and control. This opens a distinct buyer group above operational management.

Best for

Analytics, SaaS, finance, logistics, healthcare, cybersecurity, HR tech, enterprise software

Execution Steps

1. Identify governance-level reporting needs
2. Reframe operational visibility into oversight language
3. Build governance-oriented reporting examples
4. Target boards, audit committees, and governance leaders
5. Pilot governance-led sales conversations

Real-world example

A compliance analytics platform repositions operational reporting as board-level governance assurance for regulated enterprises.

Risk Management

1. **Product** · 4/5 Reporting lacks governance depth. **Mitigation:** Add oversight metrics.
2. **Alignment** · 4/5 Sales teams cannot sell to boards. **Mitigation:** Train executive-selling approach.
3. **Commercial** · 3/5 Buyers perceive overlap with audit tools. **Mitigation:** Clarify governance value.
4. **Legal** · 4/5 Governance claims overpromised. **Mitigation:** Use real evidence.
5. **Financial** · 3/5 Long enterprise sales cycles. **Mitigation:** Target high-pain sectors first.

Speed	Effort	Cost	Revenue	Time to cash	Scalability
Medium (1-3 months)	**Medium**	**Low**	**Very High**	**Medium**	**High**

Decision-flow: CFO → PMO / Strategy → Marketing

355. Sell the same offer to buyers trying to reduce vendor

Position the offer as a consolidation tool that replaces fragmented vendors, disconnected systems, or overlapping operational tools.

Why it works

Many companies want fewer vendors, not more features. Consolidation positioning unlocks efficiency-driven buyer segments.

Best for

SaaS, enterprise software, logistics, healthcare, finance, HR tech, cybersecurity, operations platforms

Execution Steps

1. Identify customers with vendor sprawl pain
2. Map overlapping tools or vendors
3. Position the offer as consolidation path
4. Build economic case for fewer vendors
5. Target efficiency-focused buyers

Real-world example

An enterprise software platform positions itself to operations leaders as a way to replace three disconnected tools.

Risk Management

1. **Customer** · 4/5 Migration feels risky. **Mitigation:** Show transition plan.
2. **Commercial** · 3/5 Incumbent vendors resist. **Mitigation:** Target pain owners.
3. **Product** · 4/5 Offer cannot replace enough tools. **Mitigation:** Be specific on scope.
4. **Financial** · 3/5 Savings case weak. **Mitigation:** Model total cost.
5. **Operational** · 3/5 Implementation complexity. **Mitigation:** Provide phased path.

Speed	Effort	Cost	Revenue	Time to cash	Scalability
Medium (1-3 months)	**Medium**	**Low**	**Very High**	**Medium**	**High**

Decision-flow: CFO → Sales → Product

From Ideas to Action

Twenty ideas. Twenty ways to take a proven offer into adjacent customer profiles already predisposed to buy it.

Adjacent segments share the same underlying problem. The offer does not need to be reinvented — it needs to be repositioned. The buyer profile changes. The value proposition shifts. The product stays the same. This is the lowest-cost form of expansion a business can execute.

Before continuing, identify the single idea with the clearest commercial case right now. Name who owns it. Set a date for the first step. That is all that is required.

> ***A proven offer sold to a new segment is not a new business. It is an existing business with a larger market.***

What Comes Next

5.3 — New Geographies addresses businesses whose commercial model is proven and ready to be taken into new locations, regions, or countries. If the offer works locally and the conditions for replication exist elsewhere — the next chapter is where the expansion begins.

5.3 — New Geographies

Expand revenue by taking the current offer into new locations, regions, or countries.

When These Strategies Work Best

New geography strategies work best when the commercial model is proven in the home market and the conditions that made it work are replicable in another location.

- The core offer has strong unit economics and a repeatable delivery model
- Inbound enquiries are already arriving from outside the current geographic footprint
- The problem the business solves is not specific to a single location or culture
- Local partners, distributors, or talent exist in the target market
- Competitors are already proving demand in the target geography

The Benefits

- Revenue growth that does not depend on increasing market share in the home market
- Commercial risk spread across multiple geographies and economic conditions
- Brand building in markets where first-mover advantage is still available
- Economies of scale in product development and delivery as the geographic base widens
- New customer and partner relationships that create compounding commercial value

The Risks to Manage

- **Market misread** — what works locally may not translate. Validate demand before committing capital.
- **Execution overstretch** — geographic expansion without sufficient management attention fails consistently. Resource properly.
- **Regulatory exposure** — new markets carry legal, compliance, and tax obligations. Assess fully before entering.
- **Cultural misalignment** — buyer behaviour, trust, and decision-making vary significantly. Local knowledge is not optional.

356. *Enter each new market through one narrow beachhead*

Start inside a chosen geography with one narrow buyer use case, customer type, city cluster, or problem area before expanding wider.

Why it works

New markets become risky when companies enter too broadly. A narrow beachhead creates proof, learning, and lower entry cost.

Best for

SaaS, consulting, healthcare, logistics, education, fintech, B2B services, professional services

Execution Steps

1. Select the target geography
2. Identify the narrowest high-potential buyer group
3. Define the specific use case or local problem
4. Build a focused entry message
5. Win proof inside the beachhead

Real-world example

A SaaS firm enters a new country through one city cluster and one use case before pursuing the full national market.

Risk Management

1. **Commercial** · 3/5 Beachhead too narrow. **Mitigation:** Choose segment with expansion path.
2. **Market** · 4/5 Wrong entry niche. **Mitigation:** Validate with local interviews.
3. **Financial** · 3/5 Early revenue small. **Mitigation:** Treat as proof stage.
4. **Alignment** · 3/5 Team expands too fast. **Mitigation:** Set stage gates.
5. **Operational** · 3/5 Delivery learning incomplete. **Mitigation:** Capture lessons before scaling.

Speed	Effort	Cost	Revenue	Time to cash	Scalability
Medium (1-3 months)	**Medium**	**Low**	**Very High**	**Medium**	**High**

Decision-flow: CFO → PMO / Strategy → Sales

357. Use existing customers as bridges into new geographies

Identify current customers with operations, suppliers, teams, branches, or partners in other markets, then use them as warm entry points.

Why it works

Trust travels faster through existing relationships. Customer bridges reduce cold-market entry risk and create credible early references.

Best for

B2B services, SaaS, logistics, consulting, manufacturing, healthcare, finance, enterprise software

Execution Steps

1. Map current customers with cross-border links
2. Identify branch, supplier, or partner entry points
3. Request warm introductions where appropriate
4. Adapt the case for the new geography
5. Pilot with the connected buyer

Real-world example

A consulting firm expands into a new region by following an existing client's regional subsidiary and using the relationship as entry proof.

Risk Management

1. **Customer** · 3/5 Customer does not want to introduce. **Mitigation:** Ask respectfully.
2. **Commercial** · 3/5 Bridge buyer lacks budget. **Mitigation:** Qualify before investing.
3. **Market** · 3/5 Local needs differ. **Mitigation:** Validate use case.
4. **Market** · 3/5 Relationship strained. **Mitigation:** Keep value-first.
5. **Financial** · 3/5 Expansion depends on one client. **Mitigation:** Build broader pipeline.

Speed	Effort	Cost	Revenue	Time to cash	Scalability
Fast (0-30 days)	**Low**	**Low**	**Very High**	**Medium**	**High**

Decision-flow: CFO → Customer Success → Sales

358. Test buyer demand before building local presence

Run remote sales tests, paid pilots, webinars, landing pages, partner introductions, or small campaigns before committing local teams or infrastructure.

Why it works

Geographic expansion fails when companies invest before validating demand. Low-cost customer testing protects capital and reveals real market pull.

Best for

SaaS, education, consulting, fintech, professional services, digital products, B2B services

Execution Steps

1. Choose the geography to test
2. Create one clear offer test
3. Run remote sales or marketing experiments
4. Track qualified buyer response
5. Compare demand with entry cost

Real-world example

An education company tests demand in a new market through webinars and paid pilots before opening any local office.

Risk Management

1. **Product** · 3/5 Test signals misleading. **Mitigation:** Use qualified buyer actions.
2. **Commercial** · 3/5 Interest does not convert. **Mitigation:** Test paid intent.
3. **Commercial** · 3/5 Campaign too broad. **Mitigation:** Target tightly.
4. **Financial** · 4/5 Overinvest after weak signal. **Mitigation:** Set go/no-go thresholds.
5. **Market** · 3/5 Local objections missed. **Mitigation:** Pair with local feedback.

Speed	Effort	Cost	Revenue	Time to cash	Scalability
Fast (0-30 days)	**Low**	**Low**	**Very High**	**Medium**	**High**

Decision-flow: CFO → Marketing → PMO / Strategy

359. Enter through local trust partners before hiring

Partner with local advisors, associations, distributors, agencies, consultants, operators, or ecosystem players before building a direct local presence.

Why it works

Local trust is expensive to build from scratch. Trust partners shorten credibility gaps and reduce early market-entry mistakes.

Best for

Consulting, SaaS, healthcare, finance, logistics, education, B2B services, manufacturing

Execution Steps

1. Identify trusted local ecosystem players
2. Validate their buyer access and credibility
3. Define entry role and expectations
4. Build co-introduction or referral process
5. Launch with limited market scope

Real-world example

A healthcare technology company enters a new market through a trusted local healthcare association before hiring a local sales team.

Risk Management

1. **Market** · 4/5 Partner trust is overstated. **Mitigation:** Reference-check partner.
2. **Commercial** · 3/5 Partner lacks real access. **Mitigation:** Validate introductions.
3. **Financial** · 3/5 Partner economics unclear. **Mitigation:** Set terms. upfront
4. **Operational** · 3/5 Partner creates false expectations. **Mitigation:** Provide approved messaging.
5. **Alignment** · 2/5 Team bypasses partner. **Mitigation:** Define roles.

Speed	Effort	Cost	Revenue	Time to cash	Scalability
Medium (1-3 months)	**Medium**	**Low**	**Very High**	**Medium**	**High**

Decision-flow: CFO → Partnerships / BD → PMO / Strategy

360. Build local proof before scaling the market

Secure one visible customer, pilot, case study, local testimonial, partner win, or reference before expanding sales activity in the geography.

Why it works

Buyers trust local proof more than distant success stories. Local evidence reduces skepticism and improves conversion.

Best for

SaaS, healthcare, logistics, consulting, education, finance, construction, B2B services

Execution Steps

1. Identify the fastest path to local proof
2. Choose a credible first customer or partner
3. Deliver a small visible win
4. Convert the win into local proof
5. Use proof in targeted outreach

Real-world example

A logistics platform wins one respected local customer and uses that reference to build confidence with similar buyers in the market.

Risk Management

1. **Customer** · 3/5 First proof not credible. **Mitigation:** Choose visible customer.
2. **Commercial** · 3/5 Pilot does not convert. **Mitigation:** Set success criteria.
3. **Commercial** · 2/5 Proof too generic. **Mitigation:** Make it local.
4. **Operational** · 4/5 Pilot delivery weak. **Mitigation:** Prioritize quality.
5. **Financial** · 3/5 Discounted pilot becomes precedent. **Mitigation:** Protect commercial terms.

Speed	Effort	Cost	Revenue	Time to cash	Scalability
Medium (1-3 months)	**Medium**	**Low**	**Very High**	**Medium**	**High**

Decision-flow: CFO → Sales → Marketing

361. Use diaspora networks as geographic entry routes

Target diaspora founders, executives, investors, business councils, chambers, or community networks connected to the new market.

Why it works

Diaspora networks often hold cross-border trust, cultural knowledge, and warm commercial bridges into new locations.

Best for

Professional services, consulting, education, fintech, trade services, investment services, B2B services

Execution Steps

1. Identify diaspora networks linked to the target geography
2. Map commercially relevant members
3. Build a cross-border value message
4. Request introductions or small events
5. Convert warm contacts into pilots

Real-world example

A professional services firm enters a new country by working through diaspora business councils and founders connected to that market.

Risk Management

1. **Commercial** · 3/5 Network is social not commercial. **Mitigation:** Target business members.
2. **Market** · 3/5 Approach feels transactional. **Mitigation:** Open every buyer conversation with the value delivered, not the price.
3. **Operational** · 3/5 Introductions lack fit. **Mitigation:** Qualify quickly.
4. **Financial** · 2/5 Slow conversion. **Mitigation:** Use low-cost outreach.
5. **Market** · 3/5 Cultural signals misunderstood. **Mitigation:** Use local advisors.

Speed	Effort	Cost	Revenue	Time to cash	Scalability
Fast (0-30 days)	**Low**	**Low**	**High**	**Medium**	**High**

Decision-flow: CFO → Partnerships / BD → Sales

362. Localize the buying story, not the whole product

Adapt messaging, proof points, pricing context, objections, examples, and buyer language for the new geography without rebuilding the core offer.

Why it works

Most early geographic friction is narrative, not product. Localized positioning improves adoption while keeping entry cost low.

Best for

SaaS, consulting, healthcare, education, finance, logistics, B2B services, professional services

Execution Steps

1. Identify local buyer language and objections
2. Adapt proof points and examples
3. Translate value into local context
4. Keep the core offer unchanged
5. Test localized messaging

Real-world example

A fintech company keeps the same offer but changes examples, objections, and proof points for a new regional buyer audience.

Risk Management

1. **Commercial** · 3/5 Localization is superficial. **Mitigation:** Use local interviews.
2. **Market** · 2/5 Message drifts from core value. **Mitigation:** Keep core promise intact.
3. **Commercial** · 3/5 Wrong local objections. **Mitigation:** Test with buyers.
4. **Legal** · 3/5 Pricing context misleading. **Mitigation:** Review local claims.
5. **Alignment** · 3/5 Team rebuilds product unnecessarily. **Mitigation:** Set scope limits.

Speed	Effort	Cost	Revenue	Time to cash	Scalability
Fast (0-30 days)	**Low**	**Low**	**High**	**Medium**	**High**

Decision-flow: CFO → Marketing → Sales

363. Choose geographies where the problem is already

Prioritize markets where buyers already recognize the pain, category, regulation, workflow, or business need your offer solves.

Why it works

Problem-aware markets convert faster because less spending is needed to educate buyers from zero.

Best for

SaaS, cybersecurity, healthcare, logistics, fintech, education, compliance services, B2B services

Execution Steps

1. List potential geographies
2. Score problem awareness in each market
3. Check buyer education needs
4. Prioritize markets with existing demand language
5. Launch first into high-awareness markets

Real-world example

A cybersecurity company enters markets where regulatory pressure already makes buyers aware of the problem.

Risk Management

1. **Market** · 4/5 Problem awareness overstated. **Mitigation:** Validate with local searches and interviews.
2. **Commercial** · 3/5 Competition already strong. **Mitigation:** Differentiate clearly.
3. **Financial** · 3/5 High-awareness market costly. **Mitigation:** Model CAC.
4. **Commercial** · 3/5 Category language differs. **Mitigation:** Localize narrative.
5. **Alignment** · 3/5 Team chases market size only. **Mitigation:** Use scorecard.

Speed	Effort	Cost	Revenue	Time to cash	Scalability
Medium (1-3 months)	**Medium**	**Low**	**Very High**	**Medium**	**High**

Decision-flow: CFO → PMO / Strategy → Marketing

364. Create a remote-first market-entry motion

Sell, onboard, support, and service new geographic customers remotely before establishing offices, local hires, or physical operations.

Why it works

Remote-first entry lowers fixed cost and lets the company prove demand before making permanent market commitments.

Best for

SaaS, education, consulting, fintech, professional services, digital products, B2B platforms

Execution Steps

1. Identify offers deliverable remotely
2. Build remote sales and onboarding flow
3. Set support hours and service boundaries
4. Launch into one geography remotely
5. Track customer success and revenue

Real-world example

A consulting firm sells and delivers initial projects remotely in a new market before considering local hiring.

Risk Management

1. **Customer** · 3/5 Buyers expect local presence. **Mitigation:** Clarify remote delivery value.
2. **Operational** · 3/5 Time-zone support gaps. **Mitigation:** Define coverage.
3. **Commercial** · 3/5 Trust is lower remotely. **Mitigation:** Use proof and references.
4. **Financial** · 3/5 Remote delivery hides true costs. **Mitigation:** Track service effort.
5. **Market** · 4/5 Local requirements block remote delivery. **Mitigation:** Check constraints.

Speed	Effort	Cost	Revenue	Time to cash	Scalability
Fast (0-30 days)	**Medium**	**Low**	**Very High**	**Medium**	**High**

Decision-flow: CFO → Sales → Operations

365. Use regional anchor clients to unlock nearby markets

Win one respected customer, institution, distributor, or enterprise in a region, then use that anchor to expand into nearby markets.

Why it works

Regional credibility compounds. One anchor win can create proof, referrals, and confidence across neighboring geographies.

Best for

B2B services, SaaS, logistics, healthcare, finance, consulting, manufacturing, enterprise software

Execution Steps

1. Identify anchor prospects with regional credibility
2. Prioritize one high-trust win
3. Deliver a strong result
4. Convert the result into regional proof
5. Use anchor reference for nearby markets

Real-world example

A manufacturing supplier wins one respected regional enterprise and uses that proof to enter neighboring markets.

Risk Management

1. **Commercial** · 3/5 Anchor takes too long to close. **Mitigation:** Choose realistic target.
2. **Customer** · 3/5 Anchor refuses reference. **Mitigation:** Agree proof rights early.
3. **Operational** · 4/5 Service quality weak. **Mitigation:** Prioritize delivery.
4. **Financial** · 3/5 Overinvestment in one account. **Mitigation:** Set limits.
5. **Market** · 3/5 Nearby markets differ. **Mitigation:** Validate before replication.

Speed	Effort	Cost	Revenue	Time to cash	Scalability
Medium (1-3 months)	**Medium**	**Low**	**Very High**	**Medium**	**High**

Decision-flow: CFO → Sales → Partnerships / BD

366. *Give local partners a ready-to-sell market-entry*

Create partner-ready packages that local partners can sell, explain, support, or introduce in their geography with clear roles, materials, and economics.

Why it works

Local partners move faster when the offer is easy to sell. Partner-ready packaging reduces friction and accelerates geographic reach.

Best for

SaaS, education, consulting, logistics, healthcare, finance, B2B services, professional services

Execution Steps

1. Identify what local partners need to sell
2. Build sales materials and role clarity
3. Define partner economics
4. Create support and escalation rules
5. Train partners in the geography

Real-world example

A SaaS company creates a local partner kit with offer positioning, pricing rules, demos, FAQs, and referral economics.

Risk Management

1. **Commercial** · 3/5 Partner package too complex. **Mitigation:** Simplify materials.
2. **Market** · 4/5 Partner misrepresents offer. **Mitigation:** Use approved messaging.
3. **Financial** · 3/5 Economics unattractive. **Mitigation:** Model partner margin.
4. **Operational** · 3/5 Support roles unclear. **Mitigation:** Define responsibilities.
5. **Alignment** · 3/5 Sales competes with partners. **Mitigation:** Set channel rules.

Speed	Effort	Cost	Revenue	Time to cash	Scalability
Medium (1-3 months)	**Medium**	**Low**	**Very High**	**Medium**	**High**

Decision-flow: CFO → Partnerships / BD → Sales

367. Use regulatory-light entry before heavy market

Start with offers, customer types, or delivery models that require the least licensing, compliance burden, staffing, or local infrastructure.

Why it works

Regulatory complexity can delay expansion. Starting with lighter entry paths creates revenue while deeper market readiness is built.

Best for

Healthcare, finance, fintech, education, logistics, consulting, SaaS, professional services

Execution Steps

1. Map regulatory complexity by offer and customer type
2. Identify the lightest legal entry path
3. Confirm allowed delivery model
4. Start with lower-complexity customers
5. Build deeper compliance readiness in parallel

Real-world example

A fintech education provider enters with advisory and training services first while evaluating heavier licensing requirements.

Risk Management

1. **Legal** · 5/5 Regulatory interpretation wrong. **Mitigation:** Get local legal review.
2. **Commercial** · 3/5 Light entry limits revenue. **Mitigation:** Use as first stage.
3. **Market** · 2/5 Offer seems incomplete. **Mitigation:** Explain phased entry.
4. **Operational** · 4/5 Compliance work delayed. **Mitigation:** Create parallel roadmap.
5. **Financial** · 3/5 Market not worth deeper entry. **Mitigation:** Use go/no-go criteria.

Speed	Effort	Cost	Revenue	Time to cash	Scalability
Medium (1-3 months)	**Medium**	**Low**	**High**	**Medium**	**High**

Decision-flow: CFO → Legal → PMO / Strategy

368. Sequence markets by ease of revenue, not market size

Prioritize new geographies based on buyer readiness, trust access, regulation, payment ability, competition, and speed-to-revenue instead of TAM alone.

Why it works

Large markets can be slow and expensive. Easier revenue markets often create faster cash, proof, and learning.

Best for

SaaS, consulting, logistics, healthcare, education, fintech, B2B services, manufacturing

Execution Steps

1. List candidate geographies
2. Score ease of revenue factors
3. Compare against market size
4. Prioritize fast-proof markets
5. Launch staged entry

Real-world example

A B2B services company delays a huge but slow market and enters a smaller market with faster buyer readiness and partner access.

Risk Management

1. **Alignment** · 3/5 Team chases prestige markets. **Mitigation:** Use scoring discipline.
2. **Financial** · 2/5 Small market caps upside. **Mitigation:** Use for proof and cash.
3. **Commercial** · 3/5 Ease score wrong. **Mitigation:** Validate with tests.
4. **Alignment** · 3/5 Leadership disagrees. **Mitigation:** Show decision criteria.
5. **Market** · 3/5 Competition surprises. **Mitigation:** Review local dynamics.

Speed	Effort	Cost	Revenue	Time to cash	Scalability
Medium (1-3 months)	**Medium**	**Low**	**Very High**	**Medium**	**High**

Decision-flow: CFO → PMO / Strategy → Finance

369. Turn export demand signals into market-entry priorities

Use inbound leads, website traffic, search queries, partner requests, demo bookings, or support inquiries from new regions to prioritize expansion.

Why it works

Existing demand signals reduce guesswork. The best next market is often already raising its hand.

Best for

SaaS, education, e-commerce, consulting, fintech, digital products, B2B services, professional services

Execution Steps

1. Track demand signals by geography
2. Separate curiosity from buying intent
3. Score regions by qualified demand
4. Run focused follow-up tests
5. Prioritize regions with repeated signals

Real-world example

A SaaS company notices repeated demo requests from one country and uses that demand signal to prioritize local expansion testing.

Risk Management

1. **Product** · 3/5 Traffic is not buyer intent. **Mitigation:** Use qualified signals.
2. **Commercial** · 3/5 Signals are too scattered. **Mitigation:** Look for repeated patterns.
3. **Commercial** · 3/5 Attribution unclear. **Mitigation:** Tag geography data.
4. **Financial** · 3/5 Overreacting to small samples. **Mitigation:** Define a minimum performance threshold before committing to scale.s.
5. **Operational** · 3/5 Support cannot serve region. **Mitigation:** Check delivery fit.

Speed	Effort	Cost	Revenue	Time to cash	Scalability
Fast (0-30 days)	**Low**	**Low**	**Very High**	**Medium**	**High**

Decision-flow: CFO → IT / Data → Sales

370. Create a repeatable market-entry playbook

Document the exact process for testing, validating, localizing, partnering, selling, servicing, and scaling each new geography.

Why it works

Geographic expansion becomes more profitable when learning compounds. A repeatable playbook turns one market entry into a scalable growth system.

Best for

SaaS, consulting, education, healthcare, logistics, fintech, B2B services, professional services

Execution Steps

1. Document current market-entry steps
2. Define validation and go/no-go criteria
3. Create templates for localization and partners
4. Add operating and sales handoffs
5. Use the playbook in the next geography

Real-world example

A professional services firm turns its first successful regional entry into a repeatable checklist for future markets.

Risk Management

1. **Operational** · 3/5 Playbook too generic. **Mitigation:** Base on real entries.
2. **Alignment** · 3/5 Teams do not follow it. **Mitigation:** Use stage gates.
3. **Commercial** · 3/5 Markets differ too much. **Mitigation:** Allow local adaptations.
4. **Financial** · 3/5 Learning not captured. **Mitigation:** Review after each market.
5. **Alignment** · 2/5 Over-standardization. **Mitigation:** Keep flexible modules.

Speed	Effort	Cost	Revenue	Time to cash	Scalability
Medium (1-3 months)	**Medium**	**Low**	**Very High**	**Medium**	**High**

Decision-flow: CFO → PMO / Strategy → Operations

371. Use local freelancers as micro-market scouts

Hire low-cost local freelancers, researchers, or commercial scouts to collect buyer objections, identify local players, map competitors, and validate market context.

Why it works

Local learning is expensive when done through full market-entry projects. Micro-scouting gives fast local intelligence at low cost and low risk.

Best for

SaaS, consulting, education, logistics, healthcare, fintech, B2B services, professional services

Execution Steps

1. Define what local intelligence is needed
2. Hire local freelancers or scouts
3. Give structured research questions
4. Validate findings with multiple sources
5. Use insights to shape entry tests

Real-world example

A consulting firm hires local commercial scouts to map buyer objections and competitor presence before committing to a new market.

Risk Management

1. **Product** · 4/5 Scout research is low quality. **Mitigation:** Use structured briefs.
2. **Commercial** · 3/5 Insights not tied to action. **Mitigation:** Link to entry decisions.
3. **Legal** · 3/5 Improper data collection. **Mitigation:** Set ethical rules.
4. **Financial** · 3/5 False confidence. **Mitigation:** Cross-check findings.
5. **Alignment** · 2/5 Team ignores local insight. **Mitigation:** Review with decision-makers.

Speed	Effort	Cost	Revenue	Time to cash	Scalability
Fast (0-30 days)	**Low**	**Low**	**High**	**Medium**	**High**

Decision-flow: CFO → PMO / Strategy → Partnerships / BD

372. Lead with one urgent local pain

Use interviews, surveys, support questions, or local partner feedback to identify one urgent geography-specific pain and lead market entry with that angle.

Why it works

New-market entry fails when companies push generic offers. One sharp local pain creates relevance faster without rebuilding the product.

Best for

SaaS, consulting, healthcare, logistics, education, finance, HR tech, professional services

Execution Steps

1. Collect local buyer and partner feedback
2. Identify one urgent local pain
3. Connect the existing offer to that pain
4. Build entry messaging around it
5. Test with local prospects

Real-world example

A logistics platform leads with local customs-delay pain in one market while keeping the same core solution.

Risk Management

1. **Commercial** · 3/5 Pain chosen is too narrow. **Mitigation:** Validate urgency.
2. **Commercial** · 4/5 Pain does not map to offer. **Mitigation:** Check fit honestly.
3. **Customer** · 3/5 Local language misses nuance. **Mitigation:** Use local feedback.
4. **Operational** · 3/5 Delivery cannot support promise. **Mitigation:** Align capabilities.
5. **Financial** · 2/5 Limited scalability. **Mitigation:** Use as entry wedge.

Speed	Effort	Cost	Revenue	Time to cash	Scalability
Fast (0-30 days)	**Low**	**Low**	**High**	**Medium**	**High**

Decision-flow: CFO → Marketing → PMO / Strategy

373. Use shared local infrastructure instead of building

Leverage coworking spaces, partner offices, fractional country managers, outsourced support, local agencies, or shared logistics providers before investing in owned infrastructure.

Why it works

Owned infrastructure increases expansion risk. Shared infrastructure gives local presence and capability without heavy fixed cost.

Best for

Consulting, education, logistics, healthcare, professional services, SaaS, B2B services, trade services

Execution Steps

1. Identify what local presence is actually needed
2. Find shared infrastructure options
3. Define service levels. and responsibilities
4. Pilot with minimal fixed cost
5. Monitor customer experience

Real-world example

A professional services firm uses a partner office and fractional country lead before opening a full local office.

Risk Management

1. **Operational** · 4/5 Shared infrastructure quality varies. **Mitigation:** Vet providers.
2. **Market** · 3/5 Local presence feels weak. **Mitigation:** Use credible partners.
3. **Customer** · 3/5 Service experience inconsistent. **Mitigation:** Set standards.
4. **Financial** · 3/5 Hidden costs emerge. **Mitigation:** Review total cost.
5. **Legal** · 4/5 Local obligations unclear. **Mitigation:** Check requirements.

Speed	Effort	Cost	Revenue	Time to cash	Scalability
Medium (1-3 months)	**Medium**	**Low**	**Very High**	**Medium**	**High**

Decision-flow: CFO → Operations → PMO / Strategy

From Ideas to Action

Eighteen ideas. Eighteen ways to extend a commercial model that works in one geography into new markets.

Geographic expansion fails when businesses underestimate local friction and overestimate how directly a model transfers. Every idea here is designed to reduce that friction — to find the shortest path from a working model to a new market without rebuilding what already works.

Before continuing, identify the single idea with the clearest commercial case right now. Name who owns it. Set a date for the first step. That is all that is required.

> ***The business that works in one market is not automatically ready for another. But it is far closer than starting from zero.***

What Comes Next

5.4 — Frequency Growth addresses businesses where existing customers buy less often than their need or satisfaction level would support. If purchase frequency is below what the relationship warrants — the next chapter closes the gap.

5.4 — Frequency Growth

Expand revenue by increasing how often existing customers buy.

When These Strategies Work Best

Frequency growth strategies work best when the business already has satisfied customers who buy less often than the value they receive or the need they have would logically support.

- Customers buy once or infrequently despite having an ongoing or repeating need
- Repurchase rates are below what customer satisfaction scores would predict
- There is no systematic trigger, prompt, or incentive to encourage repeat purchasing
- Time between purchases is longer than the natural consumption or usage cycle
- Competitor retention data suggests customers are buying the same need elsewhere

The Benefits

- Revenue growth from customers already acquired without additional acquisition cost
- Higher customer lifetime value that makes the original acquisition cost more efficient
- Stronger customer relationships that make competitive displacement harder over time
- More predictable revenue when purchase cycles become regular rather than random
- Better data on customer behaviour that improves product and service development

The Risks to Manage

- **Pressure without value** — prompting more purchases without a genuine customer reason creates resentment, not revenue.
- **Wrong trigger timing** — contacting customers before they are ready accelerates opt-outs. Align timing to actual usage cycles.
- **Channel fatigue** — over-communicating to drive frequency reduces the impact of all future communication.
- **Margin trade-offs** — incentives to increase frequency must generate net positive economics. Model before launching.

374. Use predictive reorder timing by customer pattern

Use purchase history, usage patterns, seasonality, and customer segments to predict when groups of customers are likely ready to reorder.

Why it works

Most businesses wait for customers to return naturally. Pattern-based prediction prompts repeat buying before customers forget or switch.

Best for

E-commerce, SaaS, healthcare, logistics, food, industrial supply, subscription products, B2B services

Execution Steps

1. Collect reorder and usage history
2. Group customers by buying pattern
3. Identify likely reorder timing
4. Build automated reorder prompts
5. Test timing. by customer group

Real-world example

An industrial supplier predicts when similar customer groups usually run low on consumables and sends reorder prompts before stockouts happen.

Risk Management

1. **Product** · 4/5 Weak data quality. **Mitigation:** Clean purchase history first.
2. **Commercial** · 3/5 Offer arrives at the wrong point in the journey. **Mitigation:** Test in one controlled segment before expanding to the broader market.
3. **Customer** · 3/5 Customer fatigue. **Mitigation:** Limit prompt frequency.
4. **Operational** · 3/5 Inventory mismatch. **Mitigation:** Align with stock planning.
5. **Financial** · 3/5 Adoption is slower than expected. **Mitigation:** Track conversion by group.

Speed	Effort	Cost	Revenue	Time to cash	Scalability
Medium (1-3 months)	**Medium**	**Medium**	**Very High**	**Medium**	**High**

Decision-flow: CFO → IT / Data → Marketing

375. Create automatic replenishment flows

Allow customers to automatically refill, reorder, restock, renew, or replenish based on time, usage, or thresholds.

Why it works

Automation removes the effort of remembering to reorder, increasing purchase frequency naturally.

Best for

Healthcare, food, SaaS, industrial supply, e-commerce, office supply, beauty, logistics

Execution Steps

1. Identify repeat-purchase items
2. Define replenishment rules
3. Add customer control settings
4. Automate reorder execution
5. Pilot with frequent buyers

Real-world example

A clinic supplier lets clinics auto-reorder medical consumables based on expected usage cycles.

Risk Management

1. **Customer** · 3/5 Wrong reorder timing. **Mitigation:** Allow edits and pauses.
2. **Customer** · 3/5 Customer distrust. **Mitigation:** Show clear controls.
3. **Operational** · 4/5 Stock shortages. **Mitigation:** Align inventory forecasts.
4. **Financial** · 3/5 Payment failures. **Mitigation:** Add payment safeguards.
5. **Customer** · 2/5 Over-ordering. **Mitigation:** Add usage checks.

Speed	Effort	Cost	Revenue	Time to cash	Scalability
Medium (1-3 months)	**Medium**	**Medium**	**Very High**	**Medium**	**High**

Decision-flow: CFO → Product → Operations

376. Use consumption acceleration bundles

Bundle products, services, features, or usage behaviors in ways that increase how quickly customers consume and need to repurchase.

Why it works

Faster consumption shortens reorder cycles and increases annual revenue per customer.

Best for

Food, beauty, SaaS, supplements, office products, industrial consumables, healthcare, e-commerce

Execution Steps

1. Identify products with repeat usage
2. Find natural companion use cases
3. Bundle around higher consumption cadence
4. Position around better outcomes or convenience
5. Test reorder-cycle reduction

Real-world example

A supplement brand bundles morning and evening routines to increase monthly usage frequency.

Risk Management

1. **Customer** · 4/5 Overconsumption risk. **Mitigation:** Keep usage responsible.
2. **Financial** · 3/5 Margin dilution. **Mitigation:** Protect bundle economics.
3. **Commercial** · 2/5 Bundle confusion. **Mitigation:** Keep use case simple.
4. **Operational** · 3/5 Inventory pressure. **Mitigation:** Forecast demand.
5. **Financial** · 3/5 The new offer cannibalizes existing higher-margin revenue if segmentation is not. **Mitigation:** Track customer behavior.

Speed	Effort	Cost	Revenue	Time to cash	Scalability
Fast (0-30 days)	**Low**	**Low**	**Very High**	**Medium**	**High**

Decision-flow: CFO → Product → Marketing

377. Reward shorter reorder cycles

Create incentives, credits, perks, or exclusive access for customers who reorder earlier than their usual cycle.

Why it works

Most loyalty systems reward spend. This rewards buying sooner, directly increasing frequency.

Best for

Retail, SaaS, healthcare, food, e-commerce, industrial supply, B2B services, logistics

Execution Steps

1. Define normal reorder cycle
2. Set shorter-cycle target
3. Create low-cost incentive
4. Communicate timing benefit
5. Track earlier reorder behavior

Real-world example

A B2B supplier gives priority handling to customers who reorder before their usual restock window.

Risk Management

1. **Commercial** · 3/5 Incentive too weak. **Mitigation:** Test stronger benefits.
2. **Financial** · 3/5 Incentive too costly. **Mitigation:** Cap reward value.
3. **Customer** · 3/5 Customer gaming. **Mitigation:** Set eligibility.
4. **Commercial** · 2/5 Low awareness. **Mitigation:** Show reorder target clearly.
5. **Financial** · 3/5 Margin compresses if delivery cost is not controlled from the start. **Mitigation:** Measure net profit.

Speed	Effort	Cost	Revenue	Time to cash	Scalability
Fast (0-30 days)	**Low**	**Low**	**High**	**Medium**	**High**

Decision-flow: CFO → Marketing → Customer Success

378. Use AI to detect customers drifting toward inactivity

Use engagement, usage, transaction, login, or behavior signals to predict declining buying frequency before full churn occurs.

Why it works

Revenue loss often starts with slower buying cadence. Early intervention preserves revenue velocity.

Best for

SaaS, e-commerce, fintech, healthcare, logistics, education, subscriptions, B2B platforms

Execution Steps

1. Define normal customer activity
2. Identify early frequency-decline signals
3. Build AI or rule-based risk scoring
4. Trigger intervention workflows
5. Test recovery actions

Real-world example

A SaaS company detects lower weekly usage and triggers a customer success intervention before renewals are at risk.

Risk Management

1. **Product** · 4/5 False alerts. **Mitigation:** Improve signal quality.
2. **Product** · 3/5 Late detection. **Mitigation:** Shorten monitoring cycles.
3. **Customer** · 3/5 Outreach fatigue. **Mitigation:** Personalize intervention.
4. **Alignment** · 3/5 Team ignores alerts. **Mitigation:** Automate escalation.
5. **Commercial** · 3/5 Weak recovery offer. **Mitigation:** Test playbooks.

Speed	Effort	Cost	Revenue	Time to cash	Scalability
Medium (1-3 months)	**Medium**	**Medium**	**Very High**	**Medium**	**High**

Decision-flow: CFO → IT / Data → Customer Success

379. Turn customer milestones into buying triggers

Use birthdays, anniversaries, onboarding milestones, renewal periods, operational cycles, or business events as repeat-purchase triggers.

Why it works

Event-based prompts increase frequency without aggressive selling because the timing feels relevant and natural.

Best for

Retail, SaaS, healthcare, finance, education, hospitality, beauty, B2B services

Execution Steps

1. Map meaningful customer milestones
2. Choose milestones linked to repeat need
3. Build relevant buying prompts
4. Add CRM triggers
5. Test by milestone type

Real-world example

A professional services firm uses annual planning anniversaries to trigger repeat advisory reviews.

Risk Management

1. **Commercial** · 3/5 Milestone feels generic. **Mitigation:** Use meaningful triggers.
2. **Customer** · 3/5 Message feels opportunistic. **Mitigation:** Open every buyer conversation with the value delivered, not the price.
3. **Product** · 3/5 Milestone data incomplete. **Mitigation:** Clean CRM fields.
4. **Commercial** · 3/5 Conversion from initial interest to completed purchase is lower than targeted.. **Mitigation:** Test different triggers.
5. **Market** · 2/5 Too many messages. **Mitigation:** Cap the frequency of outreach or placements to prevent customer fatigue.

Speed	Effort	Cost	Revenue	Time to cash	Scalability
Fast (0-30 days)	**Low**	**Low**	**High**	**Medium**	**High**

Decision-flow: CFO → Marketing → IT / Data

380. Build habit loops into product usage

Design product workflows, reminders, dashboards, streaks, or routines that make repeat usage habitual.

Why it works

Habitual usage increases the likelihood of repeat buying and reduces competitor disruption.

Best for

SaaS, fitness, education, healthcare, productivity tools, fintech, consumer apps, subscriptions

Execution Steps

1. Identify the desired repeat usage behavior
2. Add cue, action, reward, and progress loop
3. Make the loop visible to customers
4. Test frequency of engagement
5. Connect usage to repeat purchase moments

Real-world example

A learning platform builds weekly progress routines that increase course usage and repeat purchases.

Risk Management

1. **Customer** · 3/5 Habit loop feels forced. **Mitigation:** Ensure every output is immediately useful and actionable for the recipient.
2. **Product** · 3/5 Loop does not connect to purchase. **Mitigation:** Tie to value moments.
3. **Operational** · 2/5 Support burden rises. **Mitigation:** Automate nudges.
4. **Product** · 3/5 Usage metrics unclear. **Mitigation:** Track behavior events.
5. **Commercial** · 3/5 Engagement grows without revenue. **Mitigation:** Link to purchase cadence.

Speed	Effort	Cost	Revenue	Time to cash	Scalability
Medium (1-3 months)	**Medium**	**Low**	**Very High**	**Medium**	**High**

Decision-flow: CFO → Product → Customer Success

381. Use smart reminders tied to actual usage patterns

Trigger reminders based on real customer behavior, consumption, engagement, or usage timing instead of generic calendar dates.

Why it works

Usage-aware reminders feel more relevant and convert better than fixed-date campaigns.

Best for

Healthcare, SaaS, retail, industrial supply, food, subscriptions, e-commerce, logistics

Execution Steps

1. Identify usage behaviors linked to repeat need
2. Define reminder rules
3. Personalize reminder timing
4. Test message relevance
5. Track reorder response rates

Real-world example

A beauty brand sends replenishment reminders based on expected usage behavior instead of a fixed monthly calendar.

Risk Management

1. **Product** · 3/5 Behavior signals inaccurate. **Mitigation:** Validate patterns.
2. **Customer** · 3/5 Reminder fatigue. **Mitigation:** Cap frequency.
3. **Commercial** · 2/5 Message too generic. **Mitigation:** Personalize content.
4. **Commercial** · 3/5 Conversion from initial interest to completed purchase is lower than targeted.. **Mitigation:** Run an A/B test on a small cohort before deploying broadly.
5. **Legal** · 3/5 Consent issues. **Mitigation:** Respect opt-in rules.

Speed	Effort	Cost	Revenue	Time to cash	Scalability
Fast (0-30 days)	**Medium**	**Low**	**High**	**Medium**	**High**

Decision-flow: CFO → IT / Data → Marketing

382. Gamify repeat purchasing behavior

Use streaks, badges, unlocks, progress tracking, or rewards tied to repeat purchase actions.

Why it works

Gamification creates emotional momentum around buying more consistently.

Best for

Retail, SaaS, fitness, education, gaming, subscriptions, e-commerce, hospitality

Execution Steps

1. Define purchase actions to gamify
2. Create simple progress mechanics
3. Add rewards or unlocks
4. Make progress visible
5. Test customer response

Real-world example

A fitness app gives customers streak rewards for consistent monthly program renewals.

Risk Management

1. **Customer** · 3/5 Gamification feels childish. **Mitigation:** Keep tone professional.
2. **Financial** · 3/5 Rewards too costly. **Mitigation:** Use low-cost operational perks — admin support.
3. **Product** · 3/5 Progress tracking complex. **Mitigation:** Launch with the simplest viable version and expand only after validation.
4. **Commercial** · 3/5 Customers game actions. **Mitigation:** Set clear rules and communicate them before any access.
5. **Market** · 2/5 Mechanics distract from value. **Mitigation:** Anchor to outcomes.

Speed	Effort	Cost	Revenue	Time to cash	Scalability
Medium (1-3 months)	**Medium**	**Low**	**High**	**Medium**	**High**

Decision-flow: CFO → Product → Marketing

383. Use AI to identify the ideal reorder window per customer

Use machine learning to estimate the best reorder timing for each individual customer.

Why it works

Customers buy at different cadences. Personalized timing improves repeat conversion.

Best for

E-commerce, healthcare, SaaS, industrial supply, food, logistics, subscriptions, B2B services

Execution Steps

1. Collect customer-level purchase data
2. Identify personal cadence patterns
3. Build individual reorder timing model
4. Trigger personalized prompts
5. Compare against generic timing

Real-world example

An e-commerce brand predicts reorder timing for each customer based on individual buying history and usage signals.

Risk Management

1. **Product** · 4/5 Insufficient customer data. **Mitigation:** Start with high-repeat customers.
2. **Product** · 4/5 Model complexity. **Mitigation:** Begin rule-based.
3. **Customer** · 3/5 Timing feels intrusive. **Mitigation:** Use helpful framing.
4. **Financial** · 3/5 High implementation cost. **Mitigation:** Run a controlled pilot with three to five accounts.
5. **Commercial** · 3/5 Small uplift. **Mitigation:** Measure by cohort.

Speed	Effort	Cost	Revenue	Time to cash	Scalability
Medium (1-3 months)	**High**	**Medium**	**Very High**	**Medium**	**High**

Decision-flow: CFO → IT / Data → Product

384. Turn support interactions into repurchase opportunities

Use support tickets, service interactions, maintenance cycles, or customer questions as structured repeat-purchase triggers.

Why it works

Customers already engaged with support are easier to guide toward the next purchase.

Best for

SaaS, healthcare, industrial services, logistics, telecom, B2B services, retail, subscriptions

Execution Steps

1. Map support interactions linked to repeat need
2. Create helpful repurchase prompts
3. Train support on timing and tone
4. Add CRM trigger after relevant tickets
5. Test conversion from support moments

Real-world example

An equipment service company prompts replacement consumable purchases after maintenance support interactions.

Risk Management

1. **Customer** · 3/5 Feels like hard sell. **Mitigation:** Lead with problem resolution.
2. **Operational** · 3/5 Support team resists selling. **Mitigation:** Keep prompts helpful.
3. **Commercial** · 3/5 Wrong timing. **Mitigation:** Use issue-specific triggers.
4. **Market** · 3/5 Customer trust damaged if delivery falls short. **Mitigation:** Separate help from pressure.
5. **Financial** · 2/5 Conversion from initial interest to completed purchase is lower than targeted.. **Mitigation:** Track by interaction type.

Speed	Effort	Cost	Revenue	Time to cash	Scalability
Fast (0-30 days)	**Low**	**Low**	**High**	**Medium**	**High**

Decision-flow: CFO → Customer Success → Customer Success

385. Create always-on micro-purchases

Introduce small repeatable purchases, add-ons, refills, credits, boosts, or usage increments customers can buy frequently.

Why it works

Small purchases lower friction and create more frequent revenue moments.

Best for

Gaming, SaaS, fintech, education, retail, subscriptions, digital products, hospitality

Execution Steps

1. Identify small repeatable value units
2. Price them simply
3. Make purchase friction low
4. Add clear usage moments
5. Track repeat micro-purchase behavior

Real-world example

A design software platform sells small credit packs for occasional premium processing needs.

Risk Management

1. **Customer** · 4/5 Feels nickel-and-dimed. **Mitigation:** Ensure clear value.
2. **Financial** · 3/5 Unit economics weak. **Mitigation:** Model transaction cost.
3. **Product** · 3/5 Micro-offers clutter experience. **Mitigation:** Keep version one as simple as possible and add.
4. **Market** · 3/5 Perceived as low value. **Mitigation:** Maintain premium framing.
5. **Legal** · 2/5 Payment complexity. **Mitigation:** Use clean billing rules.

Speed	Effort	Cost	Revenue	Time to cash	Scalability
Medium (1-3 months)	**Medium**	**Low**	**High**	**Medium**	**High**

Decision-flow: CFO → Product → Finance

386. Use predictive inventory alerts for customers

Alert customers when stock, supplies, credits, usage quotas, or operational thresholds are likely running low.

Why it works

Customers reorder faster when they are warned before operational interruption.

Best for

Industrial supply, healthcare, SaaS, logistics, retail, office supply, food, B2B services

Execution Steps

1. Define thresholds that signal low stock or usage
2. Track consumption or quota indicators
3. Create customer alerts
4. Link alerts to simple reorder action
5. Test alert timing

Real-world example

A SaaS company alerts customers when credits or usage quotas are likely to run out before month-end.

Risk Management

1. **Product** · 3/5 Thresholds inaccurate. **Mitigation:** Tune with usage data.
2. **Customer** · 3/5 Alerts ignored. **Mitigation:** Make next action simple.
3. **Operational** · 4/5 Inventory unavailable. **Mitigation:** Sync with stock.
4. **Commercial** · 3/5 Too many alerts. **Mitigation:** Prioritize critical thresholds.
5. **Financial** · 3/5 Low response. **Mitigation:** Test timing.

Speed	Effort	Cost	Revenue	Time to cash	Scalability
Medium (1-3 months)	**Medium**	**Low**	**High**	**Medium**	**High**

Decision-flow: CFO → IT / Data → Operations

387. Reward consistent buying behavior over time

Offer benefits to customers who maintain stable repeat purchase behavior across weeks, months, or cycles.

Why it works

Consistency creates more predictable revenue than irregular large purchases.

Best for

Retail, SaaS, healthcare, logistics, industrial supply, subscriptions, hospitality, e-commerce

Execution Steps

1. Define consistent buying behavior
2. Create stable-cadence benefits
3. Track customers by consistency
4. Communicate progress toward benefits
5. Reward stable behavior

Real-world example

A logistics provider gives preferred scheduling to customers who maintain consistent monthly shipping volumes.

Risk Management

1. **Financial** · 3/5 Rewards exceed value. **Mitigation:** Tie to profitability.
2. **Customer** · 3/5 Rules unclear. **Mitigation:** Show simple criteria.
3. **Commercial** · 2/5 Large irregular buyers feel excluded. **Mitigation:** Keep separate benefits.
4. **Operational** · 2/5 Tracking burden. **Mitigation:** Automate scoring.
5. **Customer** · 3/5 Behavior does not change. **Mitigation:** Test reward appeal.

Speed	Effort	Cost	Revenue	Time to cash	Scalability
Fast (0-30 days)	**Low**	**Low**	**High**	**Medium**	**High**

Decision-flow: CFO → Marketing → Finance

388. Use operational deadlines to trigger repeat purchases

Tie purchasing prompts to payroll cycles, compliance deadlines, maintenance schedules, reporting periods, or operational calendars.

Why it works

Operational deadlines create natural urgency and repeat buying momentum.

Best for

Finance, SaaS, healthcare, logistics, HR tech, compliance services, industrial services, B2B software

Execution Steps

1. Identify recurring operational deadlines
2. Link deadlines to purchase need
3. Build calendar-based triggers
4. Send relevant prompts before deadline
5. Offer easy repeat purchase path

Real-world example

A compliance service provider prompts repeat reporting support before recurring regulatory deadlines.

Risk Management

1. **Commercial** · 3/5 Deadline not relevant. **Mitigation:** Map real cycles.
2. **Customer** · 3/5 Prompt arrives too late. **Mitigation:** Send earlier.
3. **Commercial** · 3/5 Message feels artificial. **Mitigation:** Use actual operating needs.
4. **Product** · 3/5 Calendar data incomplete. **Mitigation:** Build deadline library.
5. **Financial** · 2/5 Revenue bunching. **Mitigation:** Forecast cycle timing.

Speed	Effort	Cost	Revenue	Time to cash	Scalability
Fast (0-30 days)	**Low**	**Low**	**High**	**Medium**	**High**

Decision-flow: CFO → IT / Data → Sales

389. Create a frequency scorecard customers can see

Show customers a visible buying consistency score tied to perks, reliability status, priority, or preferred-customer benefits.

Why it works

Visible status systems influence repeat behavior and create self-reinforcing purchase habits.

Best for

B2B services, logistics, SaaS, industrial supply, healthcare, retail, fintech, subscriptions

Execution Steps

1. Define frequency score inputs
2. Make score visible to customers
3. Link score to practical benefits
4. Show how to improve score
5. Trigger customer success follow-up

Real-world example

A B2B supplier shows customers a reliability score based on consistent ordering and rewards high scores with priority fulfillment.

Risk Management

1. **Customer** · 4/5 Score feels punitive. **Mitigation:** Use positive framing.
2. **Product** · 4/5 Score inaccurate. **Mitigation:** Use simple inputs.
3. **Financial** · 3/5 Benefits too costly. **Mitigation:** Tie benefits to margin.
4. **Market** · 3/5 Customers dislike ranking. **Mitigation:** Keep private.
5. **Commercial** · 3/5 No behavior change. **Mitigation:** Test benefit strength.

Speed	Effort	Cost	Revenue	Time to cash	Scalability
Medium (1-3 months)	**Medium**	**Low**	**High**	**Medium**	**High**

Decision-flow: CFO → Product → Customer Success

390. Use embedded workflows that naturally trigger reorders

Integrate the offer directly into operational workflows so usage naturally creates repeat-purchase moments.

Why it works

Workflow dependency creates frequency without constant marketing pressure.

Best for

SaaS, healthcare, logistics, finance, HR tech, industrial supply, operations platforms, B2B services

Execution Steps

1. Identify workflows that create repeat need
2. Embed reorder prompts into the workflow
3. Make repeat purchase part of normal operations
4. Reduce handoff friction
5. Test with frequent users

Real-world example

An industrial supply platform embeds reorder prompts directly into a maintenance workflow used by operations teams.

Risk Management

1. **Product** · 4/5 Workflow integration too complex. **Mitigation:** Start with lightweight prompt.
2. **Customer** · 3/5 Workflow disruption. **Mitigation:** Make it optional.
3. **Commercial** · 3/5 Prompt ignored. **Mitigation:** Tie to real task.
4. **Operational** · 3/5 Fulfillment delays. **Mitigation:** Coordinate operations.
5. **Financial** · 3/5 Development cost. **Mitigation:** Pilot narrow workflow.

Speed	Effort	Cost	Revenue	Time to cash	Scalability
Medium (1-3 months)	**Medium**	**Medium**	**Very High**	**Medium**	**High**

Decision-flow: CFO → Product → Operations

391. Use AI to recommend the next best repeat purchase

Analyze usage, behavior, timing, and operational patterns to predict the most likely next repeat purchase.

Why it works

Predictive recommendations increase repeat buying precision and reduce buying friction.

Best for

Retail, SaaS, healthcare, fintech, e-commerce, logistics, subscriptions, B2B platforms

Execution Steps

1. Identify repeat purchase categories
2. Collect usage and transaction data
3. Build next-best-purchase rules or model
4. Present recommendation at the right moment
5. Test recommendation acceptance

Real-world example

A B2B platform recommends the next likely repeat service based on prior usage and operating patterns.

Risk Management

1. **Product** · 4/5 Recommendation irrelevant. **Mitigation:** Use better signals.
2. **Customer** · 3/5 Feels like cross-sell. **Mitigation:** Limit to repeat needs.
3. **Product** · 3/5 Poor placement. **Mitigation:** Show at decision moment.
4. **Financial** · 3/5 Low margin items recommended. **Mitigation:** Include margin rules.
5. **Commercial** · 2/5 Sales misuses recommendations. **Mitigation:** Set clear boundaries.

Speed	Effort	Cost	Revenue	Time to cash	Scalability
Medium (1-3 months)	**Medium**	**Medium**	**Very High**	**Medium**	**High**

Decision-flow: CFO → IT / Data → Product

392. Create revenue rituals customers repeat automatically

Design scheduled reviews, check-ins, reports, replenishment moments, monthly routines, or value rituals tied to recurring purchases.

Why it works

Ritualized behavior becomes predictable, increasing long-term buying frequency.

Best for

Consulting, SaaS, finance, healthcare, education, fitness, B2B services, subscriptions

Execution Steps

1. Identify a useful recurring customer ritual
2. Link the ritual to repeat purchase value
3. Schedule it into customer routines
4. Add automated reminders at key milestones to prevent drop-off. and value outputs
5. Train teams to run it consistently

Real-world example

A consulting firm creates a monthly operating review ritual that naturally leads to recurring advisory work.

Risk Management

1. **Customer** · 3/5 Ritual feels like meeting overload. **Mitigation:** Make it valuable.
2. **Operational** · 3/5 Team consistency weak. **Mitigation:** Use templates.
3. **Commercial** · 3/5 Ritual does not lead to purchase. **Mitigation:** Tie to action.
4. **Financial** · 3/5 Too much delivery time. **Mitigation:** Keep lightweight.
5. **Operational** · 2/5 Ownership unclear. **Mitigation:** Assign owner.

Speed	Effort	Cost	Revenue	Time to cash	Scalability
Medium (1-3 months)	**Medium**	**Low**	**High**	**Medium**	**High**

Decision-flow: CFO → Customer Success → Operations

393. Increase frequency by reducing reorder effort to near

Remove approvals, checkout friction, repeated forms, manual confirmations, or operational complexity from the reorder process.

Why it works

Customers delay purchases when reordering feels annoying. Simpler reordering increases cadence.

Best for

E-commerce, SaaS, industrial supply, healthcare, logistics, subscriptions, B2B services, retail

Execution Steps

1. Map every reorder step
2. Identify friction and delay points
3. Remove repeated forms or approvals where possible
4. Add one-click or prefilled reorder paths
5. Test with repeat customers

Real-world example

A B2B supply company uses saved orders and prefilled approvals to make repeat purchasing almost instant.

Risk Management

1. **Operational** · 4/5 Controls removed too far. **Mitigation:** Keep necessary approvals.
2. **Customer** · 3/5 Mistaken orders increase. **Mitigation:** Add confirmation controls.
3. **Product** · 3/5 System changes needed. **Mitigation:** Start with saved orders.
4. **Financial** · 3/5 Adoption is slower than expected. **Mitigation:** Promote to frequent buyers.
5. **Legal** · 4/5 Approval rules violated. **Mitigation:** Review requirements.

Speed	Effort	Cost	Revenue	Time to cash	Scalability
Fast (0-30 days)	**Medium**	**Low**	**Very High**	**Medium**	**High**

Decision-flow: CFO → Operations → Product

From Ideas to Action

Twenty ideas. Twenty ways to increase how often existing customers buy — without expanding the customer base.

Frequency is the most overlooked revenue lever in most businesses. Acquiring a new customer costs many times more than selling again to one who already trusts the business. These ideas exist entirely in that gap — between the last sale and the next one that should have happened already.

Before continuing, identify the single idea with the clearest commercial case right now. Name who owns it. Set a date for the first step. That is all that is required.

> ***The customer who bought last month is the most likely person to buy this month. Most businesses have not asked.***

What Comes Next

5.5 — Customer Acquisition Growth addresses businesses with a proven offer and conversion model where the primary growth constraint is the volume of qualified prospects entering the funnel. If the commercial engine works but not enough people are seeing it — the next chapter increases the flow.

5.5 — Customer Acquisition Growth

Expand revenue by increasing the number of customers acquired from the markets and channels the business already serves.

When These Strategies Work Best

Customer acquisition growth strategies work best when the business has a proven commercial model and the primary constraint on growth is the volume of new customers entering the funnel rather than conversion rates or market fit.

- The offer converts well but too few qualified prospects see it
- Acquisition is largely passive or inbound with no systematic outbound motion
- The cost of customer acquisition is high relative to what more disciplined targeting could achieve
- The business is significantly below its addressable market share in current channels
- Word of mouth and referrals are happening organically but are not being systematically amplified

The Benefits

- Direct revenue growth from a larger customer base in the existing commercial model
- Economies of scale in delivery as fixed costs are spread across more customers
- Stronger competitive position as market share increases in current segments
- Better data on what converts that continuously improves acquisition efficiency
- A growth foundation that supports future expansion into new channels and segments

The Risks to Manage

- **Growth before readiness** — acquiring customers faster than delivery can absorb them destroys the commercial relationships being built.
- **Wrong customer acquisition** — volume without qualification increases churn, reduces margins, and wastes delivery capacity.
- **Channel concentration** — dependence on one acquisition source creates fragility. Diversify acquisition channels over time.
- **Cost escalation** — acquisition cost grows faster than customer value when targeting is not disciplined. Monitor unit economics continuously.

394. Turn existing customers into acquisition ambassadors

Build automated referral, introduction, review, testimonial, and advocacy prompts that continuously encourage happy customers to bring in new buyers.

Why it works

Customer trust converts faster than cold acquisition. Automating the ask creates a repeatable referral engine without relying on manual follow-up.

Best for

SaaS, services, education, healthcare, fitness, retail, fintech, B2B platforms

Execution Steps

1. Identify happy customer moments
2. Build referral and review prompts
3. Automate timing after success moments
4. Provide easy sharing links
5. Track referred prospects

Real-world example

A SaaS company triggers referral prompts after customers complete a successful milestone or publish a positive support rating.

Risk Management

1. **Customer** · 3/5 Customers ignore prompts. **Mitigation:** Trigger after success moments.
2. **Commercial** · 3/5 Poor-fit referrals. **Mitigation:** Define ideal referral profile.
3. **Customer** · 3/5 Over-messaging. **Mitigation:** Cap the frequency of outreach or placements to prevent customer fatigue.
4. **Product** · 3/5 Weak tracking. **Mitigation:** Use referral links.
5. **Financial** · 2/5 Incentive cost. **Mitigation:** Reward only qualified outcomes.

Speed	Effort	Cost	Revenue	Time to cash	Scalability
Fast (0-30 days)	**Medium**	**Low**	**Very High**	**Medium**	**High**

Decision-flow: CFO → Customer Success → Marketing

395. Use AI to identify the highest-converting customer

Use behavioral, transactional, demographic, firmographic, and engagement data to identify which prospect profiles are most likely to become customers.

Why it works

Acquisition waste often comes from targeting weak-fit prospects. Better-fit targeting improves conversion and reduces CAC.

Best for

SaaS, fintech, healthcare, education, B2B services, e-commerce, subscriptions, marketplaces

Execution Steps

1. Collect customer and prospect data
2. Identify traits of converted customers
3. Build AI or rules-based profile scoring
4. Prioritize acquisition spend by fit
5. Test campaigns against high-fit profiles

Real-world example

A B2B SaaS company discovers that mid-sized logistics firms convert twice as well as broad enterprise targets and shifts acquisition focus.

Risk Management

1. **Product** · 4/5 Bad data quality. **Mitigation:** Clean data first.
2. **Product** · 3/5 Bias in model. **Mitigation:** Review assumptions.
3. **Commercial** · 3/5 Over-narrow targeting. **Mitigation:** Keep test segments open.
4. **Alignment** · 3/5 Sales misalignment. **Mitigation:** Share profile logic.
5. **Financial** · 3/5 Weak uplift. **Mitigation:** Compare against control campaigns.

Speed	Effort	Cost	Revenue	Time to cash	Scalability
Medium (1-3 months)	**Medium**	**Medium**	**Very High**	**Medium**	**High**

Decision-flow: CFO → IT / Data → Marketing

396. Create instant trust packages for first-time buyers

Bundle proof, testimonials, certifications, case studies, reviews, risk answers, and onboarding clarity into one acquisition asset for new buyers.

Why it works

First-time buyers hesitate when trust is incomplete. A proof package removes doubt and improves conversion.

Best for

SaaS, consulting, healthcare, finance, education, professional services, B2B services, consumer products

Execution Steps

1. List common first-buyer doubts
2. Collect proof assets
3. Build one trust package
4. Add it to landing pages and sales flows
5. Test conversion impact

Real-world example

A healthcare service gives first-time buyers a trust pack with certifications, reviews, case examples, and onboarding clarity.

Risk Management

1. **Commercial** · 3/5 Proof feels generic. **Mitigation:** Match proof to buyer concerns.
2. **Market** · 3/5 Outdated evidence. **Mitigation:** Refresh quarterly.
3. **Legal** · 4/5 Overclaiming. **Mitigation:** Verify claims.
4. **Commercial** · 2/5 Low visibility. **Mitigation:** Place before decision point.
5. **Market** · 2/5 Weak design. **Mitigation:** Make it easy. to scan

Speed	Effort	Cost	Revenue	Time to cash	Scalability
Fast (0-30 days)	**Low**	**Low**	**High**	**Medium**	**High**

Decision-flow: CFO → Marketing → Sales

397. Use acquisition partnerships instead of buying more ads

Partner with complementary businesses that already serve your target customers and collaborate through warm introductions, shared campaigns, or co-marketing.

Why it works

Partner trust can reduce CAC and increase conversion without relying only on paid advertising.

Best for

SaaS, consulting, education, healthcare, fintech, B2B services, professional services, consumer brands

Execution Steps

1. Identify complementary partners
2. Define shared target customer
3. Create acquisition collaboration model
4. Build co-branded offer or campaign
5. Track partner-sourced customers

Real-world example

A payroll platform partners with HR consultants to reach the same buyer through trusted advisory relationships.

Risk Management

1. **Commercial** · 3/5 Partner produces weak leads. **Mitigation:** Qualify partner fit.
2. **Market** · 3/5 Partner profile does not align with brand standards. **Mitigation:** Vet partner reputation.
3. **Operational** · 3/5 Unclear ownership. **Mitigation:** Define lead handoff.
4. **Alignment** · 3/5 Low effort from partner. **Mitigation:** Create mutual benefit.
5. **Financial** · 3/5 CAC unclear. **Mitigation:** Track acquisition cost.

Speed	Effort	Cost	Revenue	Time to cash	Scalability
Medium (1-3 months)	**Medium**	**Low**	**Very High**	**Medium**	**High**

Decision-flow: CFO → Partnerships / BD → Marketing

398. *Build micro-commitment entry offers*

Create small, low-risk first purchases, trials, diagnostics, audits, assessments, or starter offers that make it easier for prospects to become customers.

Why it works

People commit faster to small, low-risk decisions than large, high-friction purchases.

Best for

Consulting, SaaS, healthcare, education, finance, agencies, professional services, B2B services

Execution Steps

1. Identify the smallest valuable first step
2. Package it clearly
3. Price or position it as low risk
4. Create conversion path to core offer
5. Test with cold prospects

Real-world example

A consulting firm offers a low-cost diagnostic that gives prospects a useful first result before a larger engagement.

Risk Management

1. **Commercial** · 3/5 Entry offer too small. **Mitigation:** Ensure real value.
2. **Commercial** · 3/5 Poor conversion to core offer. **Mitigation:** Build follow-up path.
3. **Financial** · 3/5 Margin compresses if delivery cost is not controlled from the start. **Mitigation:** Limit delivery scope.
4. **Customer** · 3/5 Attracts low-fit buyers. **Mitigation:** Qualify upfront.
5. **Commercial** · 2/5 Confuses main offer. **Mitigation:** Position as first step.

Speed	Effort	Cost	Revenue	Time to cash	Scalability
Fast (0-30 days)	**Low**	**Low**	**High**	**Medium**	**High**

Decision-flow: CFO → Sales → Product

399. Use AI-powered lead prioritization before sales

Automatically rank existing inbound leads by conversion likelihood, urgency, timing, fit, and expected value before sales engagement begins.

Why it works

Sales teams waste time on weak-fit leads. Prioritization increases acquisition efficiency and improves speed to first customer conversion.

Best for

SaaS, fintech, healthcare, B2B services, education, marketplaces, subscriptions, enterprise software

Execution Steps

1. Define lead-quality signals
2. Connect CRM and engagement data
3. Build lead-priority model
4. Route high-priority leads first
5. Track conversion by lead rank

Real-world example

A SaaS company ranks demo requests by fit and urgency so sales prioritizes leads most likely to become customers.

Risk Management

1. **Product** · 4/5 Model ranks leads poorly. **Mitigation:** Validate with outcomes.
2. **Alignment** · 3/5 Sales ignores scores. **Mitigation:** Train and monitor usage.
3. **Commercial** · 4/5 High-value leads missed. **Mitigation:** Keep manual override.
4. **Product** · 3/5 CRM data incomplete. **Mitigation:** Clean fields.
5. **Financial** · 3/5 No CAC impact. **Mitigation:** Track cost per acquired customer.

Speed	Effort	Cost	Revenue	Time to cash	Scalability
Medium (1-3 months)	**Medium**	**Medium**	**Very High**	**Medium**	**High**

Decision-flow: CFO → IT / Data → Sales

400. Turn social proof into a real-time acquisition engine

Show live purchases, customer activity, usage growth, waitlists, adoption metrics, or business momentum directly in the buying journey.

Why it works

People trust momentum and visible adoption. Real-time proof reduces hesitation and increases first-time conversion.

Best for

SaaS, e-commerce, education, events, healthcare, consumer products, marketplaces, hospitality

Execution Steps

1. Identify truthful momentum signals
2. Choose where buyers need proof
3. Add live or recent activity proof
4. Avoid fake scarcity or inflated claims
5. Test conversion lift

Real-world example

An online course provider shows recent sign-ups and completion activity during the buying journey.

Risk Management

1. **Legal** · 4/5 Proof claims inflated. **Mitigation:** Use real data.
2. **Customer** · 3/5 Feels manipulative. **Mitigation:** Keep tone factual.
3. **Product** · 3/5 Live data unreliable. **Mitigation:** Use recent activity fallback.
4. **Market** · 3/5 Low activity hurts trust. **Mitigation:** Show only meaningful signals.
5. **Financial** · 2/5 Weak conversion lift. **Mitigation:** Run an A/B test on a small cohort before deploying broadly.

Speed	Effort	Cost	Revenue	Time to cash	Scalability
Fast (0-30 days)	**Medium**	**Low**	**High**	**Medium**	**High**

Decision-flow: CFO → Marketing → Product

401. Use community-led acquisition systems

Build communities, groups, ecosystems, masterminds, events, or shared spaces where prospects naturally discover, trust, and eventually buy from the business.

Why it works

Communities compound trust and lower acquisition cost over time by making prospects familiar before they enter a buying process.

Best for

SaaS, education, coaching, fitness, fintech, professional services, B2B tools, consumer brands

Execution Steps

1. Define the community's shared problem
2. Create valuable recurring community activity
3. Invite target prospects
4. Build trust before selling
5. Add soft conversion paths

Real-world example

A B2B software company hosts an operator community where prospects learn from peers and later convert into customers.

Risk Management

1. **Commercial** · 3/5 Community becomes non-commercial. **Mitigation:** Add conversion paths.
2. **Operational** · 3/5 Moderation burden. **Mitigation:** Set community rules.
3. **Market** · 3/5 Low-quality engagement. **Mitigation:** Curate participants.
4. **Financial** · 3/5 Slow payback. **Mitigation:** Track pipeline influence.
5. **Commercial** · 3/5 Too much selling. **Mitigation:** Open every buyer conversation with the value delivered, not the price.

Speed	Effort	Cost	Revenue	Time to cash	Scalability
Medium (1-3 months)	**Medium**	**Low**	**Very High**	**Medium**	**High**

Decision-flow: CFO → Marketing → Marketing

402. Create acquisition incentives tied to outcomes

Reward customers, partners, or advocates only when real acquisition outcomes occur, such as signed customers, completed purchases, or qualified new accounts.

Why it works

Outcome-based incentives align acquisition spending with actual customer growth instead of activity or exposure.

Best for

SaaS, retail, education, healthcare, fintech, B2B services, subscriptions, marketplaces

Execution Steps

1. Define qualified acquisition outcome
2. Set payout or reward logic
3. Communicate rules clearly
4. Track source attribution
5. Pay only on verified outcomes

Real-world example

A subscription company pays partners only when referred prospects become active paying customers.

Risk Management

1. **Product** · 4/5 Attribution disputes. **Mitigation:** Use tracked links and rules.
2. **Financial** · 3/5 Payout too generous. **Mitigation:** Model margin.
3. **Commercial** · 2/5 Participants lose motivation. **Mitigation:** Make payout attractive.
4. **Legal** · 3/5 Unclear terms create disputes and undermine trust in the commercial relationship.. **Mitigation:** Document all rules and exceptions before the first live engagement.
5. **Customer** · 3/5 Low-quality customers. **Mitigation:** Pay on qualified outcomes.

Speed	Effort	Cost	Revenue	Time to cash	Scalability
Fast (0-30 days)	**Low**	**Low**	**High**	**Medium**	**High**

Decision-flow: CFO → Finance → Marketing

403. Use AI chat acquisition assistants that qualify

Deploy AI assistants that engage, qualify, educate, answer objections, and route prospects immediately when they show buying intent.

Why it works

Fast response improves acquisition conversion. AI qualification captures interest before prospects leave or cool down.

Best for

SaaS, education, healthcare, fintech, professional services, e-commerce, B2B services, agencies

Execution Steps

1. Identify high-intent visitor moments
2. Build qualification questions
3. Train AI on approved answers
4. Route qualified leads. instantly
5. Monitor conversation quality

Real-world example

A consulting firm uses an AI assistant to qualify website visitors and route serious prospects to the right advisor immediately.

Risk Management

1. **Customer** · 4/5 AI gives poor answers. **Mitigation:** Use approved knowledge base.
2. **Market** · 3/5 AI tone feels wrong. **Mitigation:** Tune brand voice.
3. **Legal** · 4/5 Unsubstantiated or overstated claims create legal and reputational exposure. Review before publishing. **Mitigation:** Restrict sensitive answers.
4. **Operational** · 3/5 Sales follow-up slow. **Mitigation:** Set SLA.
5. **Product** · 3/5 Poor tracking. **Mitigation:** Tag AI-qualified leads.

Speed	Effort	Cost	Revenue	Time to cash	Scalability
Medium (1-3 months)	**Medium**	**Medium**	**Very High**	**Medium**	**High**

Decision-flow: CFO → Product → Sales

404. Create buyer confidence guarantees for new customers

Reduce acquisition fear with guarantees, reversibility, pilot options, easy exits, low-risk commitments, or outcome assurances.

Why it works

Many prospects want the outcome but fear making the wrong decision. Confidence mechanisms reduce hesitation.

Best for

SaaS, consulting, healthcare, education, consumer products, B2B services, professional services, subscriptions

Execution Steps

1. Identify top first-buyer fears
2. Choose a guarantee or reversibility mechanism
3. Set eligibility. and limits
4. Add to acquisition journey
5. Train sales. on proper use

Real-world example

A professional services firm offers a paid pilot with clear exit terms to reduce new-customer hesitation.

Risk Management

1. **Financial** · 4/5 Guarantee claims too high. **Mitigation:** Set explicit boundaries on scope and ownership before delivery begins.
2. **Customer** · 3/5 Customers exploit policy. **Mitigation:** Define eligibility.
3. **Legal** · 4/5 Guarantee wording risky. **Mitigation:** Review all external-facing language with legal counsel before publishing.
4. **Commercial** · 3/5 Sales overuses guarantee. **Mitigation:** Use only where needed.
5. **Market** · 2/5 Guarantee implies weakness. **Mitigation:** Position as confidence.

Speed	Effort	Cost	Revenue	Time to cash	Scalability
Fast (0-30 days)	**Low**	**Low**	**High**	**Medium**	**High**

Decision-flow: CFO → Sales → Finance

405. Use competitor frustration as an acquisition trigger

Target prospects immediately after competitor outages, delays, complaints, pricing changes, support failures, or public dissatisfaction.

Why it works

Switching intent rises when frustration is highest. Timely outreach captures buyers already open to change.

Best for

SaaS, telecom, logistics, fintech, healthcare, B2B services, marketplaces, consumer services

Execution Steps

1. Monitor competitor frustration signals
2. Define ethical outreach triggers
3. Prepare helpful switching messages
4. Offer low-friction comparison or migration path
5. Route interested prospects quickly

Real-world example

A SaaS company runs helpful migration outreach after a competitor's public outage creates customer frustration.

Risk Management

1. **Market** · 4/5 Looks opportunistic. **Mitigation:** Use respectful tone.
2. **Legal** · 4/5 Unsubstantiated or overstated claims create legal and reputational exposure. Review before publishing. **Mitigation:** Avoid false comparisons.
3. **Commercial** · 3/5 Wrong prospects targeted. **Mitigation:** Use clear intent signals.
4. **Operational** · 3/5 Migration support burden. **Mitigation:** Prepare resources.
5. **Market** · 2/5 Competitor responds aggressively. **Mitigation:** Stay factual.

Speed	Effort	Cost	Revenue	Time to cash	Scalability
Fast (0-30 days)	**Medium**	**Low**	**High**	**Medium**	**High**

Decision-flow: CFO → Marketing → Sales

406. Build acquisition loops into the product itself

Design the product so usage naturally exposes, invites, or introduces new potential customers automatically.

Why it works

Product-driven acquisition compounds without proportional acquisition spending because usage creates organic discovery.

Best for

SaaS, collaboration tools, fintech, education, marketplaces, productivity tools, consumer apps, B2B platforms

Execution Steps

1. Identify where product usage touches non-customers
2. Add natural invite or exposure moments
3. Make sharing useful, not forced
4. Track invited or exposed prospects
5. Reduce friction to signup

Real-world example

A collaboration tool grows when users invite external stakeholders into shared workspaces during normal use.

Risk Management

1. **Product** · 4/5 Loop feels forced. **Mitigation:** Ensure every output is immediately useful and actionable for the recipient.
2. **Customer** · 3/5 Users resist inviting others. **Mitigation:** Add clear value.
3. **Product** · 3/5 Tracking complex. **Mitigation:** Start with simple invites.
4. **Market** · 4/5 Spam risk **Mitigation:** Control frequency.
5. **Financial** · 3/5 Loop does not convert. **Mitigation:** Measure activation.

Speed	Effort	Cost	Revenue	Time to cash	Scalability
Medium (1-3 months)	**High**	**Medium**	**Very High**	**Medium**	**High**

Decision-flow: CFO → Product → Sales

407. Use founder or executive visibility as an acquisition

Leverage founders, executives, specialists, or operators as trusted visible voices that attract customers directly through authority and insight.

Why it works

People trust people faster than brands, especially in high-trust purchases where credibility reduces acquisition friction.

Best for

B2B services, consulting, SaaS, healthcare, fintech, education, professional services, agencies

Execution Steps

1. Identify credible internal voices
2. Define authority topics linked to buyer pain
3. Publish practical insight consistently
4. Route engaged prospects into acquisition paths
5. Track inbound from executive visibility

Real-world example

A consulting founder publishes sharp operational insights that generate inbound conversations from target executives.

Risk Management

1. **Alignment** · 3/5 Leader lacks consistency. **Mitigation:** Use content system.
2. **Market** · 2/5 Message becomes too personal. **Mitigation:** Tie to business value.
3. **Commercial** · 3/5 Audience does not convert. **Mitigation:** Add clear CTA.
4. **Operational** · 3/5 Content takes time. **Mitigation:** Batch production.
5. **Market** · 2/5 Public criticism. **Mitigation:** Stay thoughtful.

Speed	Effort	Cost	Revenue	Time to cash	Scalability
Medium (1-3 months)	**Medium**	**Low**	**High**	**Medium**	**High**

Decision-flow: CFO → Cross-functional → Marketing

408. Create instant proposal generation systems

Allow first-time prospects to receive instant pricing, proposals, estimates, simulations, or recommendations without waiting for sales teams.

Why it works

Acquisition slows when prospects wait too long for clarity. Instant answers help prospects become customers faster.

Best for

SaaS, consulting, services, healthcare, logistics, finance, agencies, home services

Execution Steps

1. Identify common proposal inputs
2. Build pricing or estimate logic
3. Create instant proposal flow
4. Add guardrails for complex cases
5. Route qualified prospects to sales

Real-world example

A services company lets prospects generate a guided estimate instantly before speaking to a consultant.

Risk Management

1. **Financial** · 4/5 Estimates inaccurate. **Mitigation:** Use pricing guardrails.
2. **Commercial** · 3/5 Complex deals oversimplified. **Mitigation:** Escalate exceptions.
3. **Customer** · 3/5 Prospect misunderstands scope. **Mitigation:** Add assumptions.
4. **Legal** · 3/5 Proposal terms incomplete. **Mitigation:** Review all external-facing language with legal counsel before publishing.
5. **Commercial** · 2/5 Sales bypassed improperly. **Mitigation:** Route qualified leads.

Speed	Effort	Cost	Revenue	Time to cash	Scalability
Medium (1-3 months)	**Medium**	**Medium**	**High**	**Medium**	**High**

Decision-flow: CFO → Product → Sales

409. Use customer success stories matched by buyer type

Show prospects success stories specifically matched to their industry, size, geography, role, maturity level, or pain point.

Why it works

People convert faster when they see someone like them succeeding with the offer.

Best for

SaaS, consulting, healthcare, finance, education, logistics, B2B services, professional services

Execution Steps

1. Segment prospects by buyer type
2. Map relevant proof to each type
3. Build matched story library
4. Add proof to landing pages and sales flows
5. Test conversion by proof match

Real-world example

A B2B platform shows healthcare prospects healthcare case studies and logistics prospects logistics proof.

Risk Management

1. **Commercial** · 3/5 Not enough proof assets. **Mitigation:** Start with closest match.
2. **Customer** · 3/5 Proof feels irrelevant. **Mitigation:** Segment carefully.
3. **Legal** · 4/5 Customer permissions missing. **Mitigation:** Get approval.
4. **Commercial** · 3/5 Team uses generic proof. **Mitigation:** Create easy library.
5. **Commercial** · 2/5 Weak conversion lift. **Mitigation:** Run an A/B test on a small cohort before deploying broadly.

Speed	Effort	Cost	Revenue	Time to cash	Scalability
Fast (0-30 days)	**Low**	**Low**	**High**	**Medium**	**High**

Decision-flow: CFO → Marketing → Sales

410. Create acquisition urgency through capacity visibility

Show real operational limits such as onboarding slots, implementation capacity, inventory windows, scheduling availability, or service bandwidth.

Why it works

Real scarcity increases decision speed when it reflects operational truth and helps prospects understand timing consequences.

Best for

SaaS, healthcare, logistics, consulting, education, hospitality, services, consumer products

Execution Steps

1. Identify real capacity limits
2. Decide what prospects should see
3. Show availability truthfully
4. Link capacity to decision timing
5. Monitor conversion impact

Real-world example

A consulting firm shows limited onboarding slots for the month to help prospects understand real delivery capacity.

Risk Management

1. **Market** · 4/5 Looks like fake scarcity. **Mitigation:** Use only real limits.
2. **Operational** · 3/5 Capacity data outdated. **Mitigation:** Update data, pricing, and claims on a defined regular schedule.
3. **Commercial** · 3/5 Prospects feel pressured. **Mitigation:** Use a transparent.
4. **Legal** · 4/5 Misleading claims. **Mitigation:** Review all external-facing language with legal counsel before publishing.
5. **Financial** · 3/5 Demand exceeds capacity. **Mitigation:** Control intake volume to protect delivery quality during peak periods.

Speed	Effort	Cost	Revenue	Time to cash	Scalability
Fast (0-30 days)	**Low**	**Low**	**High**	**Medium**	**High**

Decision-flow: CFO → Operations → Marketing

411. Use acquisition automation sequences across channels

Automate coordinated acquisition flows across email, SMS, social, ads, CRM, chat, and outbound touchpoints.

Why it works

Coordinated follow-up increases conversion while lowering manual acquisition effort.

Best for

SaaS, e-commerce, healthcare, education, fintech, B2B services, agencies, subscriptions

Execution Steps

1. Map acquisition touchpoints
2. Define channel sequence logic
3. Build coordinated automations
4. Personalize by prospect behavior
5. Monitor conversion by sequence

Real-world example

An education company coordinates email, SMS, and chat follow-up after webinar attendance to convert prospects into customers.

Risk Management

1. **Customer** · 4/5 Sequence feels spammy. **Mitigation:** Cap the frequency of outreach or placements to prevent customer fatigue.
2. **Product** · 3/5 Systems not connected. **Mitigation:** Start with core channels.
3. **Product** · 3/5 Attribution messy. **Mitigation:** Tag source and sequence.
4. **Commercial** · 3/5 Message repetition. **Mitigation:** Vary content.
5. **Financial** · 2/5 Tool cost grows. **Mitigation:** Track ROI.

Speed	Effort	Cost	Revenue	Time to cash	Scalability
Medium (1-3 months)	**Medium**	**Medium**	**Very High**	**Medium**	**High**

Decision-flow: CFO → Marketing → Revenue Operations

412. Turn educational content into acquisition diagnostics

Convert educational material into assessments, calculators, benchmarks, audits, or interactive tools that capture and qualify prospects.

Why it works

Interactive education reveals buyer intent and converts better than passive content because prospects diagnose their own need.

Best for

SaaS, consulting, fintech, healthcare, education, cybersecurity, HR tech, professional services

Execution Steps

1. Identify an educational topic with buyer pain
2. Convert it into diagnostic tool
3. Capture useful prospect inputs
4. Return immediate value
5. Route qualified prospects

Real-world example

A cybersecurity firm turns a guide into a risk-readiness calculator that captures qualified prospects.

Risk Management

1. **Commercial** · 3/5 Diagnostic too shallow. **Mitigation:** Make output useful.
2. **Product** · 3/5 Inputs not qualifying. **Mitigation:** Ask better questions.
3. **Customer** · 3/5 Tool feels like lead trap. **Mitigation:** Give real value.
4. **Product** · 2/5 Build takes too long. **Mitigation:** Launch with the simplest viable version and expand only after validation.
5. **Commercial** · 3/5 Low follow-up conversion. **Mitigation:** Create nurture path.

Speed	Effort	Cost	Revenue	Time to cash	Scalability
Medium (1-3 months)	**Medium**	**Low**	**Very High**	**Medium**	**High**

Decision-flow: CFO → Marketing → Product

413. Use speed-to-value acquisition positioning

Position the offer around how quickly prospects can see value, results, relief, savings, or operational improvement.

Why it works

Buyers often choose the fastest path to value when solutions appear similar.

Best for

SaaS, consulting, healthcare, logistics, education, fintech, professional services, B2B tools

Execution Steps

1. Define the fastest real value moment
2. Translate it into acquisition messaging
3. Build proof. around time-to-value
4. Add to landing pages and sales scripts
5. Test against current positioning

Real-world example

A SaaS company leads acquisition messaging with customers seeing their first dashboard in 24 hours.

Risk Management

1. **Commercial** · 3/5 Speed claim weak. **Mitigation:** Use real evidence.
2. **Operational** · 4/5 Delivery cannot match promise. **Mitigation:** Align operations.
3. **Customer** · 2/5 Fast value seen as shallow. **Mitigation:** Show meaningful outcome.
4. **Legal** · 4/5 Overpromising. **Mitigation:** Review claims.
5. **Commercial** · 2/5 Positioning too narrow. **Mitigation:** Use in right segments.

Speed	Effort	Cost	Revenue	Time to cash	Scalability
Fast (0-30 days)	**Low**	**Low**	**High**	**Medium**	**High**

Decision-flow: CFO → Marketing → Sales

414. Turn customers into mini franchises without calling

Give selected customers tools, branding, templates, incentives, and support to resell, host, demonstrate, recommend, or locally distribute the offer inside their own networks.

Why it works

Selected customers already hold trust and relationships. Structured micro-distribution creates decentralized acquisition without opening new branches.

Best for

Education, SaaS, consulting, fitness, food, beauty, coaching, professional services

Execution Steps

1. Identify highly engaged customers
2. Create lightweight reseller or host toolkit
3. Build revenue-sharing structure
4. Provide templates and onboarding
5. Launch in controlled pilot markets

Real-world example

A wellness company enables power users to host local product circles and earn referral revenue without formal franchise complexity.

Risk Management

1. **Market** · 4/5 Brand inconsistency. **Mitigation:** Use approved materials.
2. **Customer** · 3/5 Poor representation. **Mitigation:** Vet participants.
3. **Legal** · 4/5 Franchise structure triggers. **Mitigation:** Get legal review.
4. **Financial** · 3/5 Unit economics are weaker than projected once real delivery costs are measured. **Mitigation:** Model payouts carefully.
5. **Commercial** · 3/5 Low participation. **Mitigation:** Reward early success visibly.

Speed	Effort	Cost	Revenue	Time to cash	Scalability
Medium (1-3 months)	**Medium**	**Low**	**Very High**	**Medium**	**High**

Decision-flow: CFO → Partnerships / BD → Marketing

415. Use acquisition swarms instead of campaigns

Trigger coordinated small acquisition actions simultaneously across employees, customers, partners, founders, communities, and advocates over short time windows.

Why it works

Large synchronized visibility creates disproportionate attention and trust momentum compared to isolated campaigns.

Best for

SaaS, consumer brands, education, fintech, communities, media, B2B services, launches

Execution Steps

1. Define swarm objective and timing
2. Recruit internal and external advocates
3. Prepare coordinated messaging assets
4. Launch synchronized posting and outreach
5. Amplify highest-performing responses

Real-world example

A SaaS company coordinates customers, founders, employees, and partners to all share proof and use cases during one launch week.

Risk Management

1. **Market** · 3/5 Messaging inconsistency. **Mitigation:** Use approved assets.
2. **Commercial** · 3/5 Weak participation. **Mitigation:** Incentivize involvement.
3. **Market** · 4/5 Looks artificial. **Mitigation:** Keep authentic voices.
4. **Commercial** · 3/5 Short-lived momentum. **Mitigation:** Build a conversion funnel that moves interested parties to.
5. **Market** · 3/5 Reputation risk. **Mitigation:** Monitor responses quickly.

Speed	Effort	Cost	Revenue	Time to cash	Scalability
Fast (0-30 days)	**Medium**	**Low**	**Very High**	**Medium**	**High**

Decision-flow: CFO → Marketing → Marketing

416. Create acquisition gravity through public scoreboards

Build public rankings, indexes, leaderboards, benchmarks, maps, or industry scoreboards that prospects want to appear on or improve within.

Why it works

People and companies are drawn toward visibility, recognition, and competitive positioning. Public scoreboards create inbound acquisition gravity.

Best for

B2B services, SaaS, fintech, HR tech, education, consulting, marketplaces, media

Execution Steps

1. Define the benchmark or ranking system
2. Build measurable scoring logic
3. Publish public visibility platform
4. Invite participation and comparisons
5. Link participation to acquisition funnels

Real-world example

A cybersecurity platform creates a public security readiness index companies want to improve and share publicly.

Risk Management

1. **Product** · 4/5 Scoring credibility challenged. **Mitigation:** Use transparent methodology.
2. **Legal** · 4/5 Legal concerns. **Mitigation:** Avoid defamatory comparisons.
3. **Commercial** · 3/5 Low engagement. **Mitigation:** Tie to visibility benefits.
4. **Operational** · 3/5 High maintenance burden. **Mitigation:** Automate updates.
5. **Customer** · 3/5 Manipulation attempts. **Mitigation:** Add verification rules.

Speed	Effort	Cost	Revenue	Time to cash	Scalability
Medium (1-3 months)	**High**	**Medium**	**Very High**	**Medium**	**High**

Decision-flow: CFO → Product → Marketing

417. Build acquisition moments into real-world behavior

Design the product, packaging, experience, workflow, or customer interaction so people naturally showcase or discuss it publicly during normal use.

Why it works

The strongest acquisition often happens when customers market the product unintentionally through visible behavior.

Best for

Consumer products, hospitality, fitness, fintech, SaaS, retail, food, creator tools

Execution Steps

1. Identify moments customers naturally share
2. Design visible or discussable experiences
3. Reduce friction to social sharing
4. Add identity, status, or value triggers
5. Encourage repeat visibility moments

Real-world example

A fintech app creates visually shareable savings milestones customers post publicly without being asked.

Risk Management

1. **Customer** · 3/5 Sharing feels forced. **Mitigation:** Keep it organic.
2. **Commercial** · 3/5 Low visibility impact. **Mitigation:** Focus on emotional moments.
3. **Market** · 2/5 Partner profile does not align with brand standards. **Mitigation:** Align with audience identity.
4. **Market** · 2/5 Copycat competitors. **Mitigation:** Move quickly.
5. **Product** · 3/5 Weak attribution. **Mitigation:** Use referral tracking.

Speed	Effort	Cost	Revenue	Time to cash	Scalability
Medium (1-3 months)	**Medium**	**Medium**	**Very High**	**Medium**	**High**

Decision-flow: CFO → Product → Marketing

418. *Use AI-generated personalized acquisition experiences*

Generate personalized landing pages, videos, proposals, demos, onboarding previews, or value simulations dynamically for each prospect automatically.

Why it works

People convert faster when the acquisition experience feels designed specifically for them rather than for the mass market.

Best for

SaaS, consulting, fintech, healthcare, education, B2B services, enterprise sales, agencies

Execution Steps

1. Identify high-value personalization opportunities
2. Build AI-driven personalization templates
3. Connect CRM and prospect data
4. Generate tailored acquisition assets automatically
5. Test conversion uplift by segment

Real-world example

An enterprise software company auto-generates personalized ROI demos for each prospect using their industry and operational data.

Risk Management

1. **Customer** · 4/5 Personalization feels invasive. **Mitigation:** Use transparent inputs.
2. **Product** · 4/5 AI quality inconsistency. **Mitigation:** Human-review high-value outputs.
3. **Product** · 3/5 Technical complexity. **Mitigation:** Start with one tightly defined use case and expand.
4. **Product** · 4/5 Data quality problems. **Mitigation:** Clean CRM sources.
5. **Commercial** · 3/5 Over-automation risk. **Mitigation:** Keep human escalation path.

Speed	Effort	Cost	Revenue	Time to cash	Scalability
Medium (1-3 months)	**High**	**Medium**	**Very High**	**Medium**	**High**

Decision-flow: CFO → IT / Data → Product

From Ideas to Action

Twenty-five ideas. Twenty-five ways to accelerate the rate at which qualified new customers enter the business.

Acquisition is expensive when it is unstructured. Every idea here creates a more systematic, repeatable path from prospect to customer — reducing cost, improving quality, and building a commercial engine that does not depend entirely on individual effort or unpredictable timing.

Before continuing, identify the single idea with the clearest commercial case right now. Name who owns it. Set a date for the first step. That is all that is required.

> ***Acquisition that relies on relationships and effort alone does not scale. Build the system first.***

What Comes Next

Part 6 — Protect Revenue is the final step. The business has built and expanded revenue. Part 6 ensures it keeps what it wins — by preventing churn, protecting renewals, controlling discounts, and defending margin.

PART 6
Protect Revenue

The Revenue Already Won That Is Still at Risk

Parts 2 through 5 were about growth — creating, unlocking, accelerating, and expanding revenue. Part 6 is about something equally important and consistently underinvested in.

Part 6 is about protection. It asks a different question — not how do we grow, but how do we keep what we have already built? Revenue won is not revenue kept. Customers leave. Discounts erode margins. Deals that should close at full value get chipped away. Delivery failures undo commercial relationships that took years to build.

The ideas in this section protect the revenue that already exists. In most businesses, plugging the leaks is faster and cheaper than adding new growth.

What This Part Covers

- **Churn Prevention** — reducing customer loss before formal renewal or repeat-purchase failure occurs.
- **Renewal Protection** — defending renewals before they are lost at formal contract renewal moments.
- **Discount Control** — reducing unnecessary discounting and preventing price leakage in live selling.
- **Deal & Margin Protection** — defending deal economics, scope discipline, and margin integrity.
- **Delivery Reliability** — preventing operational failures that cause churn, refunds, and lost renewals.

Where to Start

- **Customers leaving before renewal?** Start with Churn Prevention.
- **Renewals being lost at contract time?** Start with Renewal Protection.
- **Discounts being given away without discipline?** Start with Discount Control.
- **Deal margins eroding from scope and structure issues?** Start with Deal & Margin Protection.
- **Delivery failures costing commercial relationships?** Start with Delivery Reliability.

6.1 — Churn Prevention

Protect revenue by reducing customer loss before formal renewal or repeat-purchase failure occurs.

When These Strategies Work Best

Churn prevention strategies work best when customers are leaving or disengaging in ways that could have been caught and addressed earlier with the right signals and interventions.

- Customers are leaving and the business learns about it only after cancellation
- Usage, engagement, or activity data shows declining signals that are not being acted on
- Customer success is treated as a service function rather than a commercial one
- Churn is measured but not owned by a specific team with specific revenue accountability
- Satisfaction is high at point of purchase but the experience degrades between transactions

The Benefits

- Revenue protection that is significantly cheaper than replacing lost customers with new ones
- Higher lifetime value from customers retained through proactive engagement
- Better commercial intelligence about why customers leave that improves the whole business
- Stronger referral and reference rates from customers who feel genuinely looked after
- More predictable revenue forecasting when churn is measured and systematically managed

The Risks to Manage

- **Reactive not proactive** — intervening only when customers announce they are leaving is too late. Build early warning systems.
- **Wrong intervention** — the same save offer sent to all at-risk customers underperforms. Diagnose before responding.
- **Measurement gaps** — churn that is not measured cannot be managed. Define and track the metric before building interventions.
- **Saving unprofitable customers** — not every churning customer is worth saving. Qualify before investing. in retention effort.

419. Use AI to detect churn risk before customers complain

Use engagement, usage, support, operational, and behavioral signals to identify customers likely to leave before visible warning signs appear.

Why it works

Most churn signals appear long before cancellation. AI prediction helps intervene before revenue loss compounds.

Best for

SaaS, fintech, telecom, healthcare, logistics, education, subscriptions, B2B platforms

Execution Steps

1. Collect usage, support, billing, and engagement data
2. Define churn outcomes and warning signs
3. Build AI or rules-based prediction model
4. Score customers by churn risk
5. Trigger retention workflows

Real-world example

A subscription platform predicts cancellation risk from lower usage, support issues, and billing friction before customers submit cancellation requests.

Risk Management

1. **Product** · 4/5 Prediction accuracy is weak. **Mitigation:** Validate against churn history.
2. **Customer** · 3/5 Outreach feels intrusive. **Mitigation:** Use helpful intervention tone.
3. **Operational** · 3/5 Teams ignore alerts. **Mitigation:** Assign a named owner to every action item before.
4. **Financial** · 3/5 Model cost too high. **Mitigation:** Pilot on high-value accounts.
5. **Product** · 4/5 Data quality gaps. **Mitigation:** Clean source data first.

Speed	Effort	Cost	Revenue	Time to cash	Scalability
Medium (1-3 months)	**Medium**	**Medium**	**Very High**	**Medium**	**High**

Decision-flow: CFO → IT / Data → Customer Success

420. Create customer health score systems tied to action

Build measurable customer health scoring tied directly to intervention workflows, escalation rules, and retention actions.

Why it works

Health scoring creates simple visibility before customers disengage fully and helps teams act consistently.

Best for

SaaS, healthcare, B2B services, education, logistics, fintech, subscriptions, professional services

Execution Steps

1. Define health score inputs
2. Weight usage, relationship, support, and value signals
3. Create clear risk bands
4. Link each band to actions
5. Review scores weekly

Real-world example

A SaaS company creates red, amber, and green health scores with specific customer success actions for each band.

Risk Management

1. **Product** · 3/5 Score is too simplistic. **Mitigation:** Review score logic regularly.
2. **Alignment** · 4/5 No one acts on scores. **Mitigation:** Attach owners and SLAs.
3. **Customer** · 3/5 Customers are mislabeled. **Mitigation:** Add a human review checkpoint for all high-value or high-risk outputs.
4. **Operational** · 3/5 Too many accounts flagged. **Mitigation:** Prioritize value. at risk
5. **Financial** · 3/5 Impact unclear. **Mitigation:** Track retained revenue.

Speed	Effort	Cost	Revenue	Time to cash	Scalability
Medium (1-3 months)	**Medium**	**Low**	**High**	**Medium**	**High**

Decision-flow: CFO → Customer Success → Revenue Operations

421. Turn onboarding completion into a retention milestone

Design onboarding so customers reach a clear success milestone that proves value and strengthens long-term retention.

Why it works

Customers who experience value early are less likely to churn later, even if the intervention is designed for retention rather than activation speed.

Best for

SaaS, healthcare, education, fintech, logistics, consulting, B2B services, subscriptions

Execution Steps

1. Define the retention-critical success milestone
2. Map onboarding steps to that milestone
3. Remove blockers to completion
4. Celebrate milestone achievement
5. Monitor future retention by completion status

Real-world example

A B2B platform tracks whether customers complete the first business-critical workflow because completion strongly predicts retention.

Risk Management

1. **Operational** · 3/5 Milestone is not meaningful. **Mitigation:** Tie to customer value.
2. **Operational** · 3/5 Onboarding steps too heavy. **Mitigation:** Simplify process.
3. **Product** · 3/5 Completion not tracked. **Mitigation:** Add milestone field.
4. **Customer** · 4/5 Customer misses milestone. **Mitigation:** Escalate risk signals early — do not wait for.
5. **Financial** · 2/5 Retention link weak **Mitigation:** Analyze cohort data.

Speed	Effort	Cost	Revenue	Time to cash	Scalability
Fast (0-30 days)	**Medium**	**Low**	**High**	**Medium**	**High**

Decision-flow: CFO → Customer Success → Operations

422. Use retention incentives before renewal risk appears

Offer proactive benefits, loyalty perks, service upgrades, helpful credits, or value-adds before customers begin considering leaving.

Why it works

Retention becomes harder once customers mentally disengage. Early reinforcement protects loyalty before risk grows.

Best for

SaaS, retail, healthcare, education, subscriptions, logistics, B2B services, professional services

Execution Steps

1. Identify customers worth proactively reinforcing
2. Define low-cost retention benefits
3. Trigger benefits before risk moments
4. Communicate the value clearly
5. Track retention by incentive cohort

Real-world example

A subscription business gives loyal customers an unexpected service upgrade before annual decision fatigue appears.

Risk Management

1. **Financial** · 3/5 Benefits become too costly. **Mitigation:** Cap reward value.
2. **Customer** · 3/5 Customers expect constant perks. **Mitigation:** Use selective timing.
3. **Commercial** · 3/5 Wrong customers rewarded. **Mitigation:** Prioritize value. at risk
4. **Commercial** · 2/5 Benefit feels generic. **Mitigation:** Personalize where possible.
5. **Alignment** · 3/5 Sales uses as discount. **Mitigation:** Set clear rules and communicate them before any access.

Speed	Effort	Cost	Revenue	Time to cash	Scalability
Fast (0-30 days)	**Low**	**Low**	**High**	**Medium**	**High**

Decision-flow: CFO → Marketing → Customer Success

423. Create operational dependency around the product or service

Embed the business deeply into customer workflows, reporting, processes, or operating routines so the customer relies on it to run work effectively.

Why it works

The more operationally integrated the business becomes, the harder it is for customers to leave without disruption.

Best for

SaaS, logistics, healthcare, fintech, HR tech, education, operations platforms, B2B services

Execution Steps

1. Identify customer workflows where the offer adds daily value
2. Embed outputs into routine operations
3. Connect reporting or process handoffs
4. Train users around the integrated workflow
5. Monitor dependency and satisfaction

Real-world example

A logistics platform becomes part of daily dispatch planning and reporting, making replacement operationally difficult.

Risk Management

1. **Customer** · 4/5 Dependency feels like lock-in. **Mitigation:** Keep value transparent.
2. **Product** · 3/5 Integration complexity rises. **Mitigation:** Start with core workflows.
3. **Operational** · 3/5 Support burden increases. **Mitigation:** Document process.es
4. **Commercial** · 3/5 Customer adoption is shallow. **Mitigation:** Train active users.
5. **Legal** · 4/5 Data integration risk. **Mitigation:** Use sccure controls.

Speed	Effort	Cost	Revenue	Time to cash	Scalability
Medium (1-3 months)	**Medium**	**Medium**	**Very High**	**Medium**	**High**

Decision-flow: CFO → Product → Customer Success

424. Use AI to identify declining engagement patterns

Monitor narrow engagement signals such as logins, feature use, response rates, transactions, or interaction patterns that indicate weakening commitment.

Why it works

Declining engagement often predicts churn earlier than financial metrics and can be detected before formal dissatisfaction appears.

Best for

SaaS, e-commerce, fintech, education, healthcare, subscriptions, marketplaces, B2B platforms

Execution Steps

1. Define engagement behaviors that matter
2. Track baseline customer engagement
3. Detect declines from normal patterns
4. Trigger light-touch interventions
5. Measure usage recovery

Real-world example

An education platform flags learners whose activity drops sharply and triggers a support check-in before cancellation risk rises.

Risk Management

1. **Product** · 3/5 Engagement signals are noisy. **Mitigation:** Use behavior baselines.
2. **Customer** · 2/5 Outreach feels unnecessary. **Mitigation:** Use light-touch messaging.
3. **Operational** · 3/5 Too many alerts. **Mitigation:** Define a minimum performance threshold before committing to scale.s.
4. **Commercial** · 3/5 Engagement does not equal retention. **Mitigation:** Validate link.
5. **Alignment** · 3/5 No action taken. **Mitigation:** Assign a named owner to every action item before.hip

Speed	Effort	Cost	Revenue	Time to cash	Scalability
Medium (1-3 months)	**Medium**	**Low**	**High**	**Medium**	**High**

Decision-flow: CFO → IT / Data → Customer Success

425. Build retention rituals into customer relationships

Create recurring reviews, check-ins, insights, planning sessions, or strategic touchpoints customers expect as part of the relationship.

Why it works

Consistent relationship cadence strengthens attachment and prevents silent disengagement.

Best for

SaaS, consulting, healthcare, finance, education, logistics, B2B services, professional services

Execution Steps

1. Identify the most valuable recurring touchpoint
2. Set customer cadence by segment
3. Create repeatable agenda or report
4. Assign relationship owner
5. Track attendance and customer sentiment

Real-world example

A consulting firm runs quarterly value reviews that keep customer priorities aligned and reduce silent churn.

Risk Management

1. **Customer** · 3/5 Ritual feels like busywork. **Mitigation:** Make each touchpoint useful.
2. **Operational** · 3/5 Team consistency weak. **Mitigation:** Use templates.
3. **Financial** · 3/5 Time cost too high. **Mitigation:** Segment by customer value.
4. **Commercial** · 3/5 No retention lift. **Mitigation:** Track outcomes.
5. **Alignment** · 2/5 Owner unclear. **Mitigation:** Assign account owner.

Speed	Effort	Cost	Revenue	Time to cash	Scalability
Medium (1-3 months)	**Medium**	**Low**	**High**	**Medium**	**High**

Decision-flow: CFO → Customer Success → Sales

426. Use surprise value-add moments to strengthen loyalty

Deliver unexpected value, insights, upgrades, recognition, or helpful actions at strategic moments during the customer lifecycle.

Why it works

Unexpected positive experiences increase emotional loyalty and reduce switching intent without relying only on discounts.

Best for

SaaS, retail, hospitality, healthcare, education, subscriptions, B2B services, professional services

Execution Steps

1. Identify lifecycle moments where surprise matters
2. Choose low-cost value-adds
3. Trigger surprises selectively
4. Make the value feel personal
5. Track response and retention impact

Real-world example

A SaaS business sends unexpected custom insight reports to customers reaching their six-month mark.

Risk Management

1. **Financial** · 3/5 Value-adds become expensive. **Mitigation:** Use low-cost high-value actions.
2. **Customer** · 2/5 Surprise feels random. **Mitigation:** Tie to lifecycle moment.
3. **Operational** · 3/5 Execution inconsistent. **Mitigation:** Use usage data to trigger the expansion offer automatically.s
4. **Commercial** · 2/5 Looks like promotion. **Mitigation:** Make it genuinely useful.
5. **Commercial** · 3/5 Retention impact unclear. **Mitigation:** Measure cohort retention.

Speed	Effort	Cost	Revenue	Time to cash	Scalability
Fast (0-30 days)	**Low**	**Low**	**High**	**Medium**	**High**

Decision-flow: CFO → Customer Success → Marketing

427. Create customer rescue workflows for at-risk accounts

Build human-led intervention systems for customers showing signs of disengagement, frustration, inactivity, or reduced usage.

Why it works

Most businesses respond inconsistently to churn risk. Structured rescue systems improve retention outcomes for at-risk accounts.

Best for

SaaS, B2B services, healthcare, education, logistics, fintech, subscriptions, professional services

Execution Steps

1. Define at-risk account triggers
2. Create rescue workflow steps
3. Assign escalation owner.
4. Prepare save conversation scripts
5. Offer practical recovery path

Real-world example

A SaaS company creates a red-account playbook with executive escalation, customer success review, and recovery plan.

Risk Management

1. **Customer** · 4/5 Intervention arrives too late. **Mitigation:** Trigger earlier.
2. **Alignment** · 4/5 No owner. **Mitigation:** Assign accountable lead.
3. **Commercial** · 3/5 Save offer too costly. **Mitigation:** Use value-first fixes.
4. **Operational** · 4/5 Root cause unresolved. **Mitigation:** Fix systemic issue.
5. **Product** · 3/5 Risk flags weak. **Mitigation:** Improve trigger rules.

Speed	Effort	Cost	Revenue	Time to cash	Scalability
Fast (0-30 days)	**Medium**	**Low**	**Very High**	**Medium**	**High**

Decision-flow: CFO → Customer Success → Sales

428. Use customer success benchmarking to reinforce value

Show customers measurable progress, ROI, savings, usage improvement, operational gains, or success metrics over time.

Why it works

Customers stay longer when value remains visible, measurable, and connected to outcomes they care about.

Best for

SaaS, consulting, healthcare, finance, logistics, education, HR tech, professional services

Execution Steps

1. Define customer value metrics
2. Establish baseline performance
3. Track improvement over time
4. Package progress into simple reports
5. Review results with customers

Real-world example

A logistics platform shows customers monthly reductions in delay rates and cost leakage from using the service.

Risk Management

1. **Product** · 4/5 Value metrics weak. **Mitigation:** Use credible measures.
2. **Customer** · 3/5 Customer does not care about metric. **Mitigation:** Tie to their goals.
3. **Operational** · 3/5 Reporting takes too long. **Mitigation:** Automate reports.
4. **Commercial** · 4/5 Value not improving. **Mitigation:** Trigger action plan.
5. **Legal** · 4/5 ROI claims overstated. **Mitigation:** Use conservative assumptions.

Speed	Effort	Cost	Revenue	Time to cash	Scalability
Medium (1-3 months)	**Medium**	**Low**	**High**	**Medium**	**High**

Decision-flow: CFO → Customer Success → IT / Data

429. Reduce silent churn through automated engagement

Automatically re-engage customers when usage, activity, purchasing, or communication suddenly declines before they formally leave.

Why it works

Many customers leave gradually without signaling dissatisfaction. Automated recovery catches disengagement early at scale.

Best for

SaaS, e-commerce, education, healthcare, subscriptions, fintech, marketplaces, B2B platforms

Execution Steps

1. Define silent disengagement signals
2. Create automated recovery messages
3. Personalize by customer behavior
4. Offer helpful next steps
5. Escalate high-value accounts to humans

Real-world example

A subscription platform automatically sends helpful usage prompts when customer activity drops for two consecutive weeks.

Risk Management

1. **Customer** · 3/5 Automation feels generic. **Mitigation:** Personalize content.
2. **Commercial** · 3/5 Too many recovery messages. **Mitigation:** Throttle frequency.
3. **Product** · 3/5 False triggers. **Mitigation:** Tune signal thresholds regularly using real performance data.
4. **Commercial** · 3/5 High-value accounts need human touch. **Mitigation:** Escalate VIPs.
5. **Financial** · 3/5 Low recovery impact. **Mitigation:** Test sequences.

Speed	Effort	Cost	Revenue	Time to cash	Scalability
Fast (0-30 days)	**Medium**	**Low**	**High**	**Medium**	**High**

Decision-flow: CFO → Marketing → Customer Success

430. Use retention-focused account segmentation

Segment customers by retention risk, profitability, engagement level, strategic value, or churn likelihood and apply different retention strategies.

Why it works

Different customers churn for different reasons. Segmentation improves retention precision and resource allocation.

Best for

SaaS, healthcare, education, logistics, fintech, B2B services, subscriptions, professional services

Execution Steps

1. Define retention-relevant segments
2. Score customers by value and risk
3. Assign retention play by segment
4. Allocate team effort accordingly
5. Track retention by segment

Real-world example

A B2B services firm gives high-value at-risk customers human retention support and low-value accounts automated check-ins.

Risk Management

1. **Product** · 3/5 Segments too broad. **Mitigation:** Use behavioral and value data.
2. **Customer** · 3/5 Some customers underserved. **Mitigation:** Set minimum service standard.
3. **Financial** · 3/5 Resources misallocated. **Mitigation:** Track ROI. by segment
4. **Alignment** · 2/5 Teams resist segmentation. **Mitigation:** Explain logic.
5. **Commercial** · 3/5 Risk changes quickly. **Mitigation:** Refresh all content, data, and offer elements on a defined schedule.

Speed	Effort	Cost	Revenue	Time to cash	Scalability
Medium (1-3 months)	**Medium**	**Low**	**High**	**Medium**	**High**

Decision-flow: CFO → Customer Success → Finance

431. Create switching-friction advantages ethically

Increase the educational, documentation, integration, process-depth, relationship, or workflow effort required for customers to switch while still delivering strong value.

Why it works

Ethical switching friction reduces impulsive churn because customers recognize real effort and value embedded in the relationship.

Best for

SaaS, consulting, logistics, healthcare, finance, HR tech, education, B2B services

Execution Steps

1. Identify value-based switching friction opportunities
2. Deepen useful integrations or documentation
3. Train users on unique workflows
4. Build relationship depth across teams
5. Avoid abusive lock-in tactics

Real-world example

A software platform becomes sticky by training customer teams, integrating workflows, and documenting processes around the platform.

Risk Management

1. **Customer** · 4/5 Feels like lock-in abuse. **Mitigation:** Anchor friction in real value.
2. **Market** · 3/5 Reputation risk. **Mitigation:** Keep exits fair.
3. **Operational** · 3/5 Too much customization. **Mitigation:** Use repeatable depth.
4. **Legal** · 3/5 Contractual concerns. **Mitigation:** Avoid restrictive terms.
5. **Financial** · 3/5 High service cost. **Mitigation:** Prioritize valuable accounts.

Speed	Effort	Cost	Revenue	Time to cash	Scalability
Medium (1-3 months)	**Medium**	**Low**	**Very High**	**Medium**	**High**

Decision-flow: CFO → Product → Customer Success

432. Use executive relationship mapping for retention

Map and strengthen relationships across multiple decision-makers, influencers, operators, and stakeholders inside customer organizations.

Why it works

Revenue risk increases when relationships depend on one contact only. Multi-stakeholder relationships protect accounts from personnel changes.

Best for

Enterprise SaaS, consulting, healthcare, logistics, finance, B2B services, professional services, education

Execution Steps

1. Map key customer stakeholders
2. Identify relationship gaps
3. Build contact plan by role
4. Create executive touchpoints
5. Document relationship strength

Real-world example

A consulting firm reduces churn risk by building relationships with finance, operations, and executive sponsors rather than one buyer only.

Risk Management

1. **Commercial** · 3/5 Access to stakeholders is limited. **Mitigation:** Ask sponsor for introductions.
2. **Customer** · 2/5 Stakeholders feel overmanaged. **Mitigation:** Add value in each touch.
3. **Alignment** · 3/5 Relationship data not updated. **Mitigation:** Use CRM discipline.
4. **Commercial** · 3/5 Account owner resists sharing. **Mitigation:** Align team and partner incentives with the desired commercial outcome.
5. **Financial** · 2/5 Time cost high. **Mitigation:** Focus on strategic accounts.

Speed	Effort	Cost	Revenue	Time to cash	Scalability
Medium (1-3 months)	**Medium**	**Low**	**High**	**Medium**	**High**

Decision-flow: CFO → Sales → Customer Success

433. Turn customer feedback into visible retention action

Collect feedback systematically and visibly show customers how their feedback improved products, services, processes, or relationship quality.

Why it works

Customers stay longer when they feel heard and see real responsiveness from the business.

Best for

SaaS, healthcare, education, logistics, retail, B2B services, subscriptions, professional services

Execution Steps

1. Collect structured customer feedback
2. Prioritize feedback linked to churn risk
3. Act on selected improvements
4. Communicate what changed
5. Thank customers for input

Real-world example

A SaaS company sends customers a "you said, we changed" update after implementing high-priority feedback.

Risk Management

1. **Customer** · 4/5 Feedback ignored. **Mitigation:** Close the loop visibly.
2. **Product** · 3/5 Too many requests. **Mitigation:** Prioritize by impact.
3. **Market** · 4/5 Overpromising changes. **Mitigation:** Communicate the basis for all decisions and relationships clearly upfront.
4. **Operational** · 3/5 Slow response. **Mitigation:** Set timelines.
5. **Financial** · 2/5 Low retention impact. **Mitigation:** Track participant cohorts.

Speed	Effort	Cost	Revenue	Time to cash	Scalability
Medium (1-3 months)	**Medium**	**Low**	**High**	**Medium**	**High**

Decision-flow: CFO → Customer Success → Product

434. Build a digital twin of customer churn behavior

Create AI-driven customer behavioral twins that simulate future churn risk, engagement decline, buying changes, and switching probability before customers act.

Why it works

Most retention systems react to historical behavior. Digital twins predict future customer states and enable proactive intervention.

Best for

SaaS, fintech, telecom, healthcare, logistics, enterprise software, subscriptions, marketplaces

Execution Steps

1. Aggregate customer behavioral data
2. Build predictive churn-behavior models
3. Simulate future customer states
4. Detect high-risk future scenarios
5. Trigger intervention workflows automatically

Real-world example

A telecom provider predicts which customers are likely to reduce usage months before formal cancellation signals appear.

Risk Management

1. **Product** · 4/5 Poor prediction accuracy. **Mitigation:** Retrain continuously.
2. **Product** · 4/5 Weak data quality. **Mitigation:** Clean source systems.
3. **Product** · 3/5 Over-complexity. **Mitigation:** Start with high-value accounts.
4. **Alignment** · 3/5 Teams ignore outputs. **Mitigation:** Tie alerts to workflows.
5. **Financial** · 3/5 High implementation cost. **Mitigation:** Pilot before scaling.

Speed	Effort	Cost	Revenue	Time to cash	Scalability
Slow (3+ months)	**High**	**High**	**Very High**	**Medium**	**High**

Decision-flow: CFO → IT / Data → Customer Success

435. Use hidden network analysis to identify churn contagion

Analyze customer relationship patterns to detect when churn risk spreads across connected users, teams, departments, or customer groups.

Why it works

Churn can spread socially or operationally. One unhappy stakeholder can influence many others silently.

Best for

Enterprise SaaS, telecom, fintech, education, healthcare, collaboration tools, marketplaces, B2B platforms

Execution Steps

1. Map customer interaction networks
2. Identify influence relationships
3. Detect concentrated dissatisfaction patterns
4. Build churn contagion alerts
5. Intervene at influential nodes

Real-world example

An enterprise software company detects that dissatisfaction from one department head spreads reduced platform adoption across multiple teams.

Risk Management

1. **Product** · 4/5 False relationship assumptions. **Mitigation:** Validate network logic.
2. **Legal** · 4/5 Privacy concerns. **Mitigation:** Respect governance rules.
3. **Product** · 3/5 Complex implementation. **Mitigation:** Start with enterprise accounts.
4. **Operational** · 3/5 Weak intervention strategy. **Mitigation:** Prioritize key influencers.
5. **Product** · 3/5 Data fragmentation. **Mitigation:** Unify customer systems.

Speed	Effort	Cost	Revenue	Time to cash	Scalability
Medium (1-3 months)	**High**	**Medium**	**Very High**	**Medium**	**High**

Decision-flow: CFO → IT / Data → Customer Success

436. Create real-time retention command centers

Build live retention dashboards that monitor churn risk, engagement decline, usage anomalies, support friction, payment issues, and operational risk continuously.

Why it works

Most retention reporting is delayed. Real-time visibility enables faster intervention before customers disengage fully.

Best for

SaaS, fintech, telecom, healthcare, logistics, subscriptions, enterprise platforms, marketplaces

Execution Steps

1. Identify real-time retention signals
2. Integrate customer systems and feeds
3. Build live retention dashboards
4. Configure alert thresholds
5. Route alerts to responsible teams

Real-world example

A subscription platform monitors payment failures, login decline, support escalation, and usage drops in one retention control center.

Risk Management

1. **Operational** · 4/5 Alert overload. **Mitigation:** Prioritize high-risk signals.
2. **Alignment** · 3/5 Teams ignore dashboards. **Mitigation:** Tie alerts to ownership.
3. **Product** · 3/5 Data latency problems. **Mitigation:** Invest in integration quality early to prevent downstream system failures.
4. **Product** · 3/5 Operational complexity increases faster than the team is resourced to manage.. **Mitigation:** Start with core metrics.
5. **Financial** · 2/5 High maintenance burden. **Mitigation:** Automate reporting to reduce manual effort and improve data reliability.

Speed	Effort	Cost	Revenue	Time to cash	Scalability
Medium (1-3 months)	**High**	**Medium**	**Very High**	**Medium**	**High**

Decision-flow: CFO → Revenue Operations → Customer Success

From Ideas to Action

Eighteen ideas. Eighteen ways to stop customers from leaving before the warning signs become a cancellation.

Churn is rarely sudden. It builds quietly — through declining usage, unanswered questions, unacknowledged frustration, and a slow accumulation of reasons to leave. By the time a customer announces they are going, the decision was made weeks earlier. These ideas exist to catch it before that point.

Before continuing, identify the single idea with the clearest commercial case right now. Name who owns it. Set a date for the first step. That is all that is required.

> ***The cheapest customer to keep is the one who has not yet decided to leave. Most businesses wait too long.***

What Comes Next

6.2 — Renewal Protection addresses businesses with recurring contract revenue where renewals are being lost at formal decision points that could have been influenced earlier. If renewals are treated as events rather than outcomes — the next chapter changes that.

6.2 — Renewal Protection

Protect revenue tied to formal renewal cycles by defending renewals before they are lost.

When These Strategies Work Best

Renewal protection strategies work best when recurring contract revenue exists and renewals are being lost at formal decision points that could have been influenced earlier in the cycle.

- Renewals are treated as administrative events rather than commercial ones
- The first renewal conversation happens within 90 days of the renewal date
- No systematic process tracks renewal risk across the customer base
- Customers who renew do so passively rather than because they chose to stay
- Renewal rates are below what product quality and customer satisfaction would suggest they should be

The Benefits

- Direct revenue protection from the most predictable income stream in the business
- Higher customer lifetime value when renewals compound over multiple cycles
- Reduced acquisition pressure when retention rates make replacement less necessary
- Expansion revenue opportunities that emerge naturally from strong renewal relationships
- Commercial stability and better forecasting when renewal rates become predictable

The Risks to Manage

- **Starting too late** — renewal conversations that begin within 90 days of the date are already reactive. Start earlier.
- **Treating renewal as an event** — renewal is won or lost in the months before the date. The outcome is determined by what happens daily.
- **Over-relying on relationships** — personal relationships do not survive restructuring. Multi-thread commercial contacts deliberately.
- **Discounting to retain** — price reductions that save renewals train customers to negotiate every cycle. Use value, not discount.

437. *Use AI to predict renewal probability months in advance*

Analyze usage, stakeholder engagement, support trends, ROI realization, sentiment, and operational dependency to forecast renewal likelihood early.

Why it works

Most renewal risk becomes visible too late. Early probability forecasting creates time for intervention before competitors gain influence.

Best for

SaaS, enterprise software, telecom, fintech, healthcare, subscriptions, B2B services, logistics

Execution Steps

1. Collect renewal history and account signals
2. Define renewal probability drivers
3. Build AI or rules-based prediction model
4. Score accounts months before renewal
5. Trigger renewal protection actions

Real-world example

A SaaS company predicts renewal probability six months ahead using usage, stakeholder engagement, and support trends.

Risk Management

1. **Product** · 4/5 Probability model inaccurate. **Mitigation:** Validate against renewal history.
2. **Alignment** · 3/5 Teams ignore predictions. **Mitigation:** Tie scores to playbooks.
3. **Customer** · 2/5 Intervention feels premature. **Mitigation:** Use value-led outreach.
4. **Financial** · 3/5 Model cost too high. **Mitigation:** Pilot on strategic accounts.
5. **Commercial** · 3/5 Competitor signals missing. **Mitigation:** Add account intelligence.

Speed	Effort	Cost	Revenue	Time to cash	Scalability
Medium (1-3 months)	**Medium**	**Medium**	**Very High**	**Medium**	**High**

Decision-flow: CFO → IT / Data → Customer Success

438. Create renewal proof packs before negotiation begins

Automatically generate customer-specific ROI, savings, adoption metrics, usage progress, operational improvements, and business outcomes before renewal discussions start.

Why it works

Customers renew more confidently when their own measurable value is organized and visible before negotiation begins.

Best for

SaaS, consulting, healthcare, logistics, education, fintech, B2B services, professional services

Execution Steps

1. Identify renewal value metrics
2. Pull customer-specific outcomes
3. Package ROI and progress clearly
4. Share before renewal conversation
5. Use proof in renewal negotiation

Real-world example

A logistics platform sends a renewal proof pack showing each customer's delay reduction, cost savings, and usage adoption.

Risk Management

1. **Product** · 4/5 Value data incomplete. **Mitigation:** Improve tracking.
2. **Customer** · 3/5 Proof not tied to customer goals. **Mitigation:** Use customer-specific outcomes.
3. **Legal** · 4/5 ROI claims overstated. **Mitigation:** Use conservative assumptions.
4. **Operational** · 3/5 Pack takes too long. **Mitigation:** Automate template.
5. **Commercial** · 3/5 Proof shared too late. **Mitigation:** Send before negotiation.

Speed	Effort	Cost	Revenue	Time to cash	Scalability
Fast (0-30 days)	**Medium**	**Low**	**Very High**	**Medium**	**High**

Decision-flow: CFO → Customer Success → IT / Data

439. Build multi-threaded renewal relationships across the account

Expand relationships beyond one buyer into finance, operations, executives, users, procurement, and influencers before renewal periods begin.

Why it works

Single-threaded accounts are fragile. Multi-stakeholder relationships reduce renewal dependency risk.

Best for

Enterprise SaaS, consulting, healthcare, logistics, finance, B2B services, education, professional services

Execution Steps

1. Map existing customer relationships
2. Identify missing stakeholder groups
3. Build role-specific relationship plan
4. Create value touchpoints by stakeholder
5. Track relationship depth before renewal

Real-world example

A consulting firm strengthens relationships with finance, operations, and executive sponsors before a major annual renewal.

Risk Management

1. **Commercial** · 3/5 Stakeholder access limited. **Mitigation:** Ask sponsor for introductions.
2. **Customer** · 2/5 Too many touchpoints. **Mitigation:** Add clear value.
3. **Alignment** · 3/5 CRM not updated. **Mitigation:** Track relationship map.
4. **Commercial** · 3/5 Account owner resists sharing. **Mitigation:** Align team and partner incentives with the desired commercial outcome.
5. **Financial** · 2/5 Time cost high. **Mitigation:** Prioritize high-value renewals.

Speed	Effort	Cost	Revenue	Time to cash	Scalability
Medium (1-3 months)	**Medium**	**Low**	**Very High**	**Medium**	**High**

Decision-flow: CFO → Sales → Customer Success

440. Use renewal incentives tied to commitment length

Offer strategic incentives, value-adds, support upgrades, or pricing advantages tied to longer renewal commitments.

Why it works

Longer commitments improve revenue predictability and reduce repeated renewal risk.

Best for

SaaS, subscriptions, healthcare, logistics, education, consulting, B2B services, professional services

Execution Steps

1. Define renewal term options
2. Identify value-adds for longer commitments
3. Model margin. and cash impact
4. Prepare renewal incentive rules
5. Offer selectively to eligible accounts

Real-world example

A SaaS company offers dedicated support and price protection for customers committing to longer renewal terms.

Risk Management

1. **Financial** · 4/5 Incentive erodes margin. **Mitigation:** Model full unit economics before setting the launch price.
2. **Customer** · 3/5 Customer expects discount. **Mitigation:** Use value-adds over price cuts.
3. **Commercial** · 3/5 Wrong accounts receive offer. **Mitigation:** Set eligibility.
4. **Legal** · 3/5 Contract terms unclear. **Mitigation:** Review all external-facing language with legal counsel before publishing.
5. **Alignment** · 4/5 Sales over-discounts. **Mitigation:** Require written manager approval for any deviation from standard terms.

Speed	Effort	Cost	Revenue	Time to cash	Scalability
Fast (0-30 days)	**Low**	**Low**	**High**	**Medium**	**High**

Decision-flow: CFO → Finance → Sales

441. Create AI-driven renewal objection prediction

Use historical negotiations, support history, usage behavior, stakeholder signals, and commercial data to predict likely renewal objections before meetings occur.

Why it works

Prepared responses improve renewal defense and reduce reactive negotiation pressure.

Best for

SaaS, enterprise software, consulting, healthcare, logistics, subscriptions, B2B services

Execution Steps

1. Collect past renewal objections
2. Map objections to account signals
3. Build objection prediction logic
4. Prepare response materials by objection
5. Train account owners before meetings

Real-world example

A software company predicts that a customer will challenge adoption levels and prepares usage proof before the renewal meeting.

Risk Management

1. **Product** · 3/5 Predicted objections wrong. **Mitigation:** Validate with sales feedback.
2. **Commercial** · 3/5 Team underprepares. **Mitigation:** Embed into renewal prep.
3. **Customer** · 2/5 Response feels scripted. **Mitigation:** Use authentic conversation.
4. **Commercial** · 4/5 Objection root cause unresolved. **Mitigation:** Fix issue, not just message.
5. **Financial** · 2/5 Tool overbuilt. **Mitigation:** Start with top objections.

Speed	Effort	Cost	Revenue	Time to cash	Scalability
Medium (1-3 months)	**Medium**	**Medium**	**High**	**Medium**	**High**

Decision-flow: CFO → IT / Data → Sales

442. Use executive-to-executive renewal engagement

Involve senior leadership in strategic renewal conversations for high-value, high-risk, or strategically important accounts.

Why it works

Executive alignment reinforces trust, strategic importance, and long-term partnership value during renewal decisions.

Best for

Enterprise SaaS, consulting, healthcare, finance, logistics, infrastructure, B2B services, professional services

Execution Steps

1. Identify renewals needing executive engagement
2. Match executive sponsor to customer stakeholder
3. Prepare strategic discussion points
4. Schedule touchpoint before negotiation peak
5. Reinforce partnership value

Real-world example

A CEO joins a strategic renewal meeting to reinforce commitment and alignment with the customer's executive sponsor.

Risk Management

1. **Alignment** · 3/5 Executive time overused. **Mitigation:** Reserve for strategic renewals.
2. **Customer** · 3/5 Engagement feels performative. **Mitigation:** Prepare real value.
3. **Commercial** · 4/5 Executive not briefed. **Mitigation:** Create briefing pack.
4. **Commercial** · 3/5 Price issue remains unresolved. **Mitigation:** Coordinate commercial position.
5. **Alignment** · 2/5 Ownership confusion. **Mitigation:** Define account lead.

Speed	Effort	Cost	Revenue	Time to cash	Scalability
Medium (1-3 months)	**Medium**	**Low**	**Very High**	**Medium**	**High**

Decision-flow: CFO → Cross-functional → Customer Success

443. Create renewal urgency through future roadmap

Show customers upcoming features, capabilities, integrations, innovations, or strategic improvements tied to continued partnership.

Why it works

Customers are more likely to renew when future value appears stronger than switching alternatives.

Best for

SaaS, technology, healthcare, fintech, education, logistics, platforms, B2B services

Execution Steps

1. Identify roadmap items relevant to renewal accounts
2. Connect future value to customer priorities
3. Prepare roadmap preview responsibly
4. Share before renewal decision
5. Capture customer questions

Real-world example

A software company shows a renewing customer upcoming integrations directly tied to their operational priorities.

Risk Management

1. **Product** · 4/5 Roadmap slips. **Mitigation:** Avoid overpromising.
2. **Legal** · 3/5 Future claims unclear. **Mitigation:** Use careful language.
3. **Customer** · 3/5 Roadmap not relevant. **Mitigation:** Personalize by account.
4. **Commercial** · 2/5 Seen as upsell. **Mitigation:** Tie to current partnership.
5. **Alignment** · 3/5 Product and sales misaligned. **Mitigation:** Approve roadmap messaging.

Speed	Effort	Cost	Revenue	Time to cash	Scalability
Medium (1-3 months)	**Medium**	**Low**	**High**	**Medium**	**High**

Decision-flow: CFO → Product → Customer Success

444. Build renewal defense competitive intelligence systems

Monitor competitor activity, pricing shifts, positioning, hiring, messaging, customer movement, and market claims to defend renewals proactively.

Why it works

Competitors often target accounts before renewal periods. Early competitive visibility strengthens renewal defense strategy.

Best for

SaaS, telecom, fintech, logistics, healthcare, enterprise software, B2B services, subscriptions

Execution Steps

1. Identify competitors targeting renewals
2. Track pricing, messaging, and account signals
3. Build competitive renewal briefs
4. Prepare renewal defense responses
5. Train account teams before renewal windows

Real-world example

A telecom provider monitors competitor promotions before contract renewal windows and prepares account-specific defenses.

Risk Management

1. **Market** · 3/5 Competitive data inaccurate. **Mitigation:** Verify sources.
2. **Commercial** · 2/5 Team over-focuses on competitor. **Mitigation:** Open every buyer conversation with the value delivered, not the price.
3. **Legal** · 4/5 Unsubstantiated or overstated claims create legal and reputational exposure. Review before publishing. **Mitigation:** Avoid false comparisons.
4. **Commercial** · 3/5 Defense too reactive. **Mitigation:** Start early.
5. **Alignment** · 3/5 Insights not used. **Mitigation:** Embed in renewal planning.

Speed	Effort	Cost	Revenue	Time to cash	Scalability
Medium (1-3 months)	**Medium**	**Low**	**High**	**Medium**	**High**

Decision-flow: CFO → PMO / Strategy → Sales

445. *Use AI-generated renewal playbooks per account*

Automatically generate account-specific renewal strategies based on customer behavior, history, stakeholders, risk signals, objections, and commercial dynamics.

Why it works

Standard renewal scripts miss account complexity. Personalized playbooks improve renewal defense precision.

Best for

SaaS, enterprise software, consulting, healthcare, logistics, subscriptions, B2B services

Execution Steps

1. Collect account renewal data
2. Define playbook components
3. Generate account-specific strategy drafts
4. Review with account owner
5. Execute renewal actions

Real-world example

A SaaS firm generates account renewal plans covering risks, stakeholders, value proof, and likely objections for each enterprise customer.

Risk Management

1. **Product** · 3/5 AI output generic. **Mitigation:** Use account-specific inputs.
2. **Customer** · 3/5 Strategy misses nuance. **Mitigation:** Require human review.
3. **Product** · 3/5 Implementation complexity. **Mitigation:** Start with templates.
4. **Commercial** · 3/5 Adoption is slower than expected. **Mitigation:** Embed in renewal workflow.
5. **Legal** · 4/5 Sensitive data risk. **Mitigation:** Control data access.

Speed	Effort	Cost	Revenue	Time to cash	Scalability
Medium (1-3 months)	**High**	**Medium**	**Very High**	**Medium**	**High**

Decision-flow: CFO → IT / Data → Customer Success

446. Create renewal milestones before formal renewal dates

Break renewals into smaller strategic checkpoints throughout the year instead of relying on one annual renewal conversation.

Why it works

Smaller ongoing alignment reduces surprise renewal risk and reveals dissatisfaction earlier.

Best for

SaaS, consulting, healthcare, education, logistics, subscriptions, B2B services, professional services

Execution Steps

1. Map the renewal calendar
2. Set quarterly or periodic renewal checkpoints
3. Review value, issues, and stakeholders
4. Document customer alignment
5. Resolve gaps before renewal window

Real-world example

A consulting firm replaces one annual renewal meeting with quarterly alignment checkpoints that prevent surprises.

Risk Management

1. **Customer** · 3/5 Checkpoints feel unnecessary. **Mitigation:** Make them useful.
2. **Operational** · 3/5 Team misses cadence. **Mitigation:** Automate reminders.
3. **Commercial** · 4/5 Issues still unresolved. **Mitigation:** Escalate gaps.
4. **Financial** · 2/5 Time cost high. **Mitigation:** Prioritize valuable accounts.
5. **Alignment** · 3/5 No renewal owner. **Mitigation:** Assign accountable lead.

Speed	Effort	Cost	Revenue	Time to cash	Scalability
Medium (1-3 months)	**Medium**	**Low**	**High**	**Medium**	**High**

Decision-flow: CFO → Customer Success → Sales

447. Use operational benchmarking to justify renewals

Compare customer operational performance against peers, baselines, or industry benchmarks to reinforce renewal value.

Why it works

Benchmark visibility helps customers see relative progress, strengthens perceived value, and increases switching hesitation.

Best for

SaaS, analytics, healthcare, logistics, HR tech, finance, consulting, B2B platforms

Execution Steps

1. Define relevant benchmarks
2. Compare customer performance to peers or baseline
3. Highlight improvement and gaps
4. Package benchmark insight for renewal
5. Review with customer before renewal

Real-world example

An HR platform shows a customer how their retention metrics improved relative to peer benchmarks before renewal.

Risk Management

1. **Product** · 4/5 Benchmark data weak. **Mitigation:** Use credible methodology.
2. **Customer** · 3/5 Comparison feels negative. **Mitigation:** Frame constructively.
3. **Legal** · 4/5 Customer data privacy is at risk if access, anonymisation. **Mitigation:** Aggregate data.
4. **Commercial** · 3/5 Benchmark not linked to value. **Mitigation:** Connect to outcomes.
5. **Financial** · 2/5 Low influence. **Mitigation:** Test in one controlled segment before expanding to the broader market.

Speed	Effort	Cost	Revenue	Time to cash	Scalability
Medium (1-3 months)	**Medium**	**Low**	**High**	**Medium**	**High**

Decision-flow: CFO → IT / Data → Customer Success

448. Create renewal save teams for strategic accounts

Build specialized cross-functional teams focused only on rescuing high-value renewals at risk.

Why it works

Strategic renewal losses deserve focused human intervention rather than generic account management.

Best for

Enterprise SaaS, consulting, telecom, healthcare, finance, logistics, B2B services, professional services

Execution Steps

1. Define strategic at-risk renewal criteria
2. Assemble cross-functional save team
3. Diagnose renewal risk quickly
4. Build save plan and owner map
5. Engage customer with clear recovery path

Real-world example

A SaaS company forms a renewal save team with customer success, product, finance, and executives for high-value accounts.

Risk Management

1. **Alignment** · 4/5 Team acts too late. **Mitigation:** Trigger earlier.
2. **Customer** · 3/5 Save effort feels desperate. **Mitigation:** Open every buyer conversation with the value delivered, not the price.
3. **Financial** · 4/5 Concessions too high. **Mitigation:** Require written manager approval for any deviation from standard terms.
4. **Operational** · 4/5 Root cause unresolved. **Mitigation:** Fix issue directly.
5. **Commercial** · 3/5 Too many accounts escalated. **Mitigation:** Define a minimum performance threshold before committing to scale.

Speed	Effort	Cost	Revenue	Time to cash	Scalability
Fast (0-30 days)	**Medium**	**Low**	**Very High**	**Medium**	**High**

Decision-flow: CFO → Customer Success → Cross-functional

449. Use hidden stakeholder analysis before renewals

Identify hidden influencers, blockers, budget holders, procurement pressures, and internal political dynamics before renewal periods.

Why it works

Many renewals fail because unseen stakeholders influence decisions silently.

Best for

Enterprise SaaS, consulting, healthcare, finance, logistics, education, B2B services, professional services

Execution Steps

1. Map formal and informal decision-makers
2. Identify blockers and budget pressures
3. Assess influence and renewal stance
4. Build stakeholder-specific action plan
5. Validate map with customer contacts

Real-world example

A consulting firm discovers procurement and finance are silent renewal blockers and engages them before renewal negotiation starts.

Risk Management

1. **Commercial** · 4/5 Hidden stakeholders missed. **Mitigation:** Ask multiple contacts.
2. **Customer** · 3/5 Mapping feels political. **Mitigation:** Keep professional.
3. **Commercial** · 3/5 Account owner assumes too much. **Mitigation:** Validate assumptions.
4. **Operational** · 3/5 No action follows mapping. **Mitigation:** Create stakeholder plan.
5. **Financial** · 4/5 Late discovery. **Mitigation:** Start months ahead.

Speed	Effort	Cost	Revenue	Time to cash	Scalability
Medium (1-3 months)	**Medium**	**Low**	**Very High**	**Medium**	**High**

Decision-flow: CFO → Sales → Customer Success

450. Create automated renewal readiness scoring

Score accounts continuously based on engagement, usage, support health, relationship depth, value proof, and commercial alignment before renewal windows.

Why it works

Renewal readiness scoring improves forecasting and helps teams prioritize preparation work before the formal renewal cycle.

Best for

SaaS, healthcare, logistics, fintech, education, subscriptions, B2B services, professional services

Execution Steps

1. Define readiness score inputs
2. Weight usage, value proof, relationships, and risks
3. Build automated scoring view
4. Review scores before renewal windows
5. Trigger readiness actions

Real-world example

A subscription platform scores each account's renewal readiness quarterly and triggers preparation actions for low-readiness accounts.

Risk Management

1. **Product** · 3/5 Score not predictive. **Mitigation:** Validate against renewals.
2. **Alignment** · 3/5 Teams ignore score. **Mitigation:** Tie to action.s
3. **Customer** · 4/5 Readiness gaps unresolved. **Mitigation:** Escalate risk signals early — do not wait for.
4. **Operational** · 3/5 Too many low scores. **Mitigation:** Prioritize value. at risk
5. **Financial** · 2/5 Low ROI. **Mitigation:** Track renewal lift.

Speed	Effort	Cost	Revenue	Time to cash	Scalability
Medium (1-3 months)	**Medium**	**Low**	**High**	**Medium**	**High**

Decision-flow: CFO → Revenue Operations → Customer Success

451. Use customer co-creation programs to strengthen

Invite strategic customers into advisory councils, beta programs, roadmap input, or innovation discussions before renewal periods.

Why it works

Customers are less likely to leave when they actively help shape future direction.

Best for

SaaS, technology, healthcare, fintech, education, B2B services, enterprise software, platforms

Execution Steps

1. Identify strategic renewal accounts
2. Invite them into co-creation forum
3. Capture roadmap or product input
4. Show how input influences direction
5. Connect participation to partnership value

Real-world example

A software company invites strategic customers into an advisory council before renewal windows to deepen commitment.

Risk Management

1. **Customer** · 3/5 Customer expects every request. **Mitigation:** Set expectations in writing before any engagement or commitment begins.
2. **Product** · 3/5 Input overload. **Mitigation:** Prioritize clearly.
3. **Commercial** · 2/5 Participation does not affect renewal. **Mitigation:** Track cohort outcomes.
4. **Operational** · 3/5 Program takes time. **Mitigation:** Limit group size.
5. **Market** · 3/5 Feels symbolic. **Mitigation:** Show visible action.

Speed	Effort	Cost	Revenue	Time to cash	Scalability
Medium (1-3 months)	**Medium**	**Low**	**High**	**Medium**	**High**

Decision-flow: CFO → Product → Customer Success

452. Build switching cost calculators for renewal defense

Quantify operational disruption, migration effort, retraining, downtime, integration loss, data transfer work, and hidden switching costs customers may underestimate.

Why it works

Customers often underestimate the true cost of switching providers. Clear switching economics strengthens renewal justification.

Best for

SaaS, enterprise software, logistics, healthcare, fintech, consulting, B2B services, platforms

Execution Steps

1. Identify real switching cost categories
2. Build calculator with conservative assumptions
3. Customize for renewal accounts
4. Review with customer transparently
5. Pair with value proof

Real-world example

An enterprise software company shows the migration, retraining, and integration cost of switching before renewal negotiations.

Risk Management

1. **Customer** · 4/5 Feels fear-based. **Mitigation:** Use factual tone.
2. **Legal** · 4/5 Claims overstated. **Mitigation:** Use conservative assumptions.
3. **Commercial** · 3/5 Customer challenges numbers. **Mitigation:** Show calculation logic.
4. **Commercial** · 3/5 Tool overused. **Mitigation:** Deploy only in high-confidence accounts before broadening the approach.
5. **Market** · 3/5 Looks defensive. **Mitigation:** Pair with future value.

Speed	Effort	Cost	Revenue	Time to cash	Scalability
Fast (0-30 days)	**Medium**	**Low**	**High**	**Medium**	**High**

Decision-flow: CFO → Finance → Sales

453. Use AI to detect renewal negotiation weakness signals

Analyze communication tone, response delays, stakeholder changes, procurement activity, meeting cancellations, and engagement patterns that indicate weakening renewal intent.

Why it works

Negotiation weakness signals often appear before direct objections are raised.

Best for

SaaS, enterprise software, consulting, telecom, healthcare, fintech, logistics, B2B services

Execution Steps

1. Define negotiation weakness indicators
2. Track communication and engagement patterns
3. Build risk alerts during renewal period
4. Escalate weakening accounts quickly
5. Adjust negotiation strategy

Real-world example

A SaaS company detects renewal risk when response delays, procurement involvement, and meeting cancellations increase together.

Risk Management

1. **Product** · 4/5 Signals misread. **Mitigation:** Validate with account context.
2. **Customer** · 3/5 Outreach feels reactive. **Mitigation:** Use relationship-first tone.
3. **Commercial** · 3/5 Alerts ignored. **Mitigation:** Assign escalation owner.
4. **Legal** · 4/5 Communication analysis concerns. **Mitigation:** Follow privacy rules.
5. **Commercial** · 3/5 Late escalation. **Mitigation:** Set low-threshold alerts.

Speed	Effort	Cost	Revenue	Time to cash	Scalability
Medium (1-3 months)	**Medium**	**Medium**	**Very High**	**Medium**	**High**

Decision-flow: CFO → IT / Data → Sales

454. Create future partnership renewal positioning

Position renewals around long-term strategic partnership, shared growth, innovation, and future operational alignment instead of transactional continuation.

Why it works

Strategic framing increases emotional and operational commitment beyond price comparison.

Best for

Consulting, SaaS, healthcare, logistics, finance, education, B2B services, professional services

Execution Steps

1. Identify strategic partnership themes
2. Reframe renewal messaging around future value
3. Prepare customer-specific partnership narrative
4. Train teams on language and proof
5. Use before commercial negotiation

Real-world example

A consulting firm frames renewal as a future operating partnership rather than continuing last year's service package.

Risk Management

1. **Customer** · 3/5 Message feels vague. **Mitigation:** Tie to concrete initiatives.
2. **Commercial** · 3/5 Price issue remains. **Mitigation:** Support with proof.
3. **Commercial** · 3/5 Overly fluffy language. **Mitigation:** Keep practical.
4. **Commercial** · 3/5 Team defaults to transaction. **Mitigation:** Train messaging.
5. **Financial** · 2/5 No measurable impact. **Mitigation:** Track renewal outcomes.

Speed	Effort	Cost	Revenue	Time to cash	Scalability
Fast (0-30 days)	**Low**	**Low**	**High**	**Medium**	**High**

Decision-flow: CFO → Marketing → Sales

455. *Use retention insurance incentives for long-term*

Offer strategic guarantees, dedicated support, performance protections, migration assistance, or operational safeguards tied to multi-year renewals.

Why it works

Risk-reduction mechanisms increase renewal confidence for larger commitments.

Best for

SaaS, healthcare, logistics, fintech, consulting, enterprise software, B2B services, subscriptions

Execution Steps

1. Identify risks blocking long-term renewal
2. Design protection or safeguard package
3. Tie benefits to longer renewal commitment
4. Set clear limits. and terms
5. Offer to suitable accounts

Real-world example

A SaaS company offers dedicated support and performance protections for customers signing multi-year renewals.

Risk Management

1. **Financial** · 4/5 Protection too costly. **Mitigation:** Cap support scope.
2. **Legal** · 4/5 Guarantee wording risky. **Mitigation:** Submit all commercial terms to legal review before customer presentation.
3. **Customer** · 3/5 Expectation expands. **Mitigation:** Define scope, access, and usage limits in writing before launch.
4. **Commercial** · 3/5 Used as discount substitute. **Mitigation:** Position as risk protection.
5. **Operational** · 3/5 Support capacity strained. **Mitigation:** Define and enforce eligibility criteria consistently from day one.

Speed	Effort	Cost	Revenue	Time to cash	Scalability
Medium (1-3 months)	**Medium**	**Low**	**High**	**Medium**	**High**

Decision-flow: CFO → Finance → Customer Success

456. Create live renewal command centers for enterprise

Build real-time renewal monitoring dashboards tracking account health, stakeholder engagement, negotiation risk, usage decline, competitor threats, and commercial exposure.

Why it works

Enterprise renewals involve many moving parts. Live visibility improves coordination and faster intervention.

Best for

Enterprise SaaS, telecom, fintech, healthcare, logistics, subscriptions, B2B platforms, enterprise services

Execution Steps

1. Define enterprise renewal signals
2. Integrate account, usage, support, and commercial data
3. Build renewal command dashboard
4. Assign a named owner to every action item before. to each risk signal
5. Review weekly during renewal window

Real-world example

An enterprise platform tracks usage, stakeholder engagement, procurement risk, and competitor activity in one live renewal dashboard.

Risk Management

1. **Operational** · 4/5 Dashboard creates noise. **Mitigation:** Prioritize critical signals.
2. **Alignment** · 3/5 Owners unclear. **Mitigation:** Assign actions. by signal.
3. **Product** · 3/5 Data latency. **Mitigation:** Invest in integration quality early to prevent downstream system failures.
4. **Product** · 3/5 Build complexity. **Mitigation:** Start with strategic accounts.
5. **Financial** · 2/5 Ongoing maintenance grows beyond the capacity planned at launch. **Mitigation:** Automate reporting to reduce manual effort and improve data reliability.

Speed	Effort	Cost	Revenue	Time to cash	Scalability
Medium (1-3 months)	**High**	**Medium**	**Very High**	**Medium**	**High**

Decision-flow: CFO → Revenue Operations → Customer Success

From Ideas to Action

Twenty ideas. Twenty ways to protect recurring revenue at the renewal moment — where the commercial relationship is most exposed.

Renewals are lost long before the renewal conversation. The account that renews easily has been actively managed — not chased at the last moment. Every idea here moves work earlier in the cycle, so the renewal is confirmed before it becomes a negotiation.

Before continuing, identify the single idea with the clearest commercial case right now. Name who owns it. Set a date for the first step. That is all that is required.

> ***A renewal that requires a fight was a relationship that was not managed. The work belongs in the months before, not the week of.***

What Comes Next

6.3 — Discount Control addresses businesses where gross margin is being eroded through undisciplined discounting in the field. If the pricing structure is sound but the actual transaction prices do not reflect it — the next chapter closes the leak.

6.3 — Discount Control

Protect revenue by reducing unnecessary discounting and preventing price leakage in live selling.

When These Strategies Work Best

Discount control strategies work best when the business has a solid pricing structure but margin is being eroded through undisciplined discount approvals, informal concessions, and habitual price reductions in the field.

- Discount rates vary significantly across deals of equivalent size and complexity
- Sales teams discount as a default response to any pricing objection
- Approval processes for discounts are slow, informal, or effectively bypassed in practice
- Average selling price is declining despite no change in list price or market conditions
- Gross margin reports show consistent erosion that does not correlate with volume growth

The Benefits

- Immediate margin improvement without changing pricing, products, or customers
- Healthier sales culture where value is defended rather than given away by default
- Better commercial data when actual transaction prices are recorded and visible
- Higher average deal value when the floor is enforced and visible to the sales team
- Stronger negotiation posture when discounts are earned rather than assumed

The Risks to Manage

- **Sales resistance** — controls that feel like bureaucracy will be worked around. Build process that is fast and commercial.
- **Lost deals** — some deals will not close at full price. Model the net impact before setting floors.
- **Inconsistent enforcement** — controls applied to some deals but not others create resentment and confusion. Apply uniformly.
- **Competitor exploitation** — tightening discounts without improving value story hands rivals an opening. Arm sales with value language.

457. Use AI to detect panic discounting by sales teams

Monitor deal behavior, negotiation timing, pipeline pressure, and rep behavior to identify emotional or unnecessary discounting patterns.

Why it works

Many discounts are driven by sales pressure rather than real customer need. Early detection protects margin before weak habits spread.

Best for

SaaS, consulting, logistics, healthcare, finance, B2B services, enterprise software, subscriptions

Execution Steps

1. Define panic discounting signals
2. Pull deal-stage and discount data
3. Build AI or rules-based alerts
4. Review patterns by rep and deal type
5. Coach high-risk behavior early

Real-world example

A B2B software company flags reps who discount heavily near quarter-end before customer objections are fully validated.

Risk Management

1. **Product** · 3/5 False positives. **Mitigation:** Validate with manager review.
2. **Commercial** · 3/5 Rep resistance. **Mitigation:** Frame as coaching not punishment.
3. **Commercial** · 3/5 Discounts may be justified. **Mitigation:** Add exception notes.
4. **Alignment** · 3/5 Managers ignore alerts. **Mitigation:** Tie to deal reviews.
5. **Financial** · 3/5 Margin impact unclear. **Mitigation:** Track discount leakage saved.

Speed	Effort	Cost	Revenue	Time to cash	Scalability
Medium (1-3 months)	**Medium**	**Medium**	**High**	**Medium**	**High**

Decision-flow: CFO → IT / Data → Sales

458. Create discount approval systems tied to margin impact

Require approval. workflows based on discount size, gross margin impact, deal quality, customer value, and strategic importance.

Why it works

Structured approval reduces uncontrolled price leakage and forces commercial discipline before concessions are granted.

Best for

SaaS, manufacturing, healthcare, logistics, professional services, retail, B2B services, enterprise software

Execution Steps

1. Define discount approval thresholds
2. Link thresholds to margin impact
3. Assign approval owners
4. Build approval workflow in CRM
5. Train sales. on rules

Real-world example

A services business requires CFO approval when discounts reduce deal margin below the agreed threshold.

Risk Management

1. **Commercial** · 3/5 Approval slows deals. **Mitigation:** Set fast SLA.
2. **Alignment** · 4/5 Teams bypass process. **Mitigation:** Enforce CRM controls.
3. **Financial** · 3/5 Thresholds too loose. **Mitigation:** Review margin impact.
4. **Commercial** · 2/5 Customer urgency ignored. **Mitigation:** Allow urgent escalation.
5. **Operational** · 3/5 Too many approvals. **Mitigation:** Tier by impact.

Speed	Effort	Cost	Revenue	Time to cash	Scalability
Fast (0-30 days)	**Medium**	**Low**	**High**	**Medium**	**High**

Decision-flow: CFO → Finance → Sales

459. Replace discounts with strategic value-add incentives

Offer onboarding, support, analytics, training, implementation help, faster delivery, or service enhancements instead of reducing price.

Why it works

Value-adds help customers justify buying while preserving headline price and protecting margin better than routine discounts.

Best for

SaaS, consulting, healthcare, education, logistics, retail, B2B services, professional services

Execution Steps

1. List common discount requests
2. Identify low-cost value-add alternatives
3. Build approved concession menu
4. Train sales. to offer value first
5. Track value-add acceptance

Real-world example

A consulting firm offers an extra workshop instead of reducing the project fee.

Risk Management

1. **Financial** · 3/5 Value-add cost underestimated. **Mitigation:** Cost each option.
2. **Commercial** · 3/5 Sales still discounts. **Mitigation:** Require value-first script.
3. **Customer** · 3/5 Customer only wants price cut. **Mitigation:** Trade value for commitment.
4. **Operational** · 3/5 Delivery burden rises. **Mitigation:** Define a strict scope boundary and enforce it from.
5. **Market** · 2/5 Value-add feels cheap. **Mitigation:** Make it relevant.

Speed	Effort	Cost	Revenue	Time to cash	Scalability
Fast (0-30 days)	**Low**	**Low**	**High**	**Medium**	**High**

Decision-flow: CFO → Sales → Customer Success

460. Use live pricing intelligence during negotiations

Give sales teams real-time pricing benchmarks, historical close ranges, competitor context, and deal guidance during active negotiation.

Why it works

Better pricing intelligence improves negotiation confidence and reduces reactive discounting based on guesswork.

Best for

SaaS, manufacturing, logistics, healthcare, fintech, B2B services, professional services, enterprise software

Execution Steps

1. Collect pricing and win-loss data
2. Add competitor and market context
3. Build live pricing guidance
4. Embed guidance in deal workflow
5. Train teams on interpretation

Real-world example

A sales team sees historical pricing ranges for similar deals before responding to a discount request.

Risk Management

1. **Product** · 4/5 Benchmark data weak. **Mitigation:** Use clean comparable deals.
2. **Commercial** · 3/5 Guidance ignored. **Mitigation:** Embed in CRM.
3. **Commercial** · 3/5 Competitor data inaccurate. **Mitigation:** Verify sources.
4. **Product** · 3/5 Tool complexity. **Mitigation:** Start with simple ranges.
5. **Financial** · 3/5 No margin improvement. **Mitigation:** Measure leakage reduction.

Speed	Effort	Cost	Revenue	Time to cash	Scalability
Medium (1-3 months)	**Medium**	**Medium**	**High**	**Medium**	**High**

Decision-flow: CFO → Revenue Operations → Sales

461. Create walk-away thresholds before negotiations begin

Define minimum acceptable pricing, margin levels, concession limits, and non-negotiable terms before customer discussions start.

Why it works

Predefined boundaries reduce emotional pricing decisions and prevent bad deals from being accepted under pressure.

Best for

SaaS, consulting, manufacturing, logistics, healthcare, B2B services, retail, professional services

Execution Steps

1. Define minimum margin rules
2. Set concession limits by deal type
3. Document walk-away triggers
4. Train sales. before negotiations
5. Review exceptions. after deals

Real-world example

A manufacturing firm defines minimum margin thresholds before negotiating with large distributors.

Risk Management

1. **Commercial** · 3/5 Reps fear losing deals. **Mitigation:** Coach value defense.
2. **Commercial** · 3/5 Thresholds too rigid. **Mitigation:** Allow exception review.
3. **Financial** · 4/5 Margins miscalculated. **Mitigation:** Use verified margin data.
4. **Customer** · 2/5 Customer pushes harder. **Mitigation:** Prepare alternatives.
5. **Alignment** · 3/5 Rules not followed. **Mitigation:** Require sign-off.

Speed	Effort	Cost	Revenue	Time to cash	Scalability
Fast (0-30 days)	**Low**	**Low**	**High**	**Medium**	**High**

Decision-flow: CFO → Finance → Sales

462. Use AI to benchmark discounting across sales teams

Analyze discount behavior by rep, region, product, customer type, industry, and deal size to identify recurring leakage patterns.

Why it works

Most companies lack visibility into where discounting is excessive. Benchmarking reveals coaching, policy, and pricing discipline gaps.

Best for

SaaS, retail, healthcare, logistics, manufacturing, fintech, B2B services, enterprise software

Execution Steps

1. Collect discount data across deals
2. Segment by rep, region, product, and customer type
3. Identify outliers and patterns
4. Review with sales leaders
5. Create targeted coaching or controls

Real-world example

A company discovers one region discounts twice as much as similar regions with no win-rate advantage.

Risk Management

1. **Product** · 4/5 Data inconsistent. **Mitigation:** Standardize discount fields.
2. **Commercial** · 3/5 Teams feel blamed. **Mitigation:** Use coaching framing.
3. **Commercial** · 3/5 Context ignored. **Mitigation:** Compare similar deals.
4. **Alignment** · 3/5 No follow-through. **Mitigation:** Assign a named owner to every action item before.
5. **Financial** · 3/5 Savings not measured. **Mitigation:** Track leakage reduction.

Speed	Effort	Cost	Revenue	Time to cash	Scalability
Medium (1-3 months)	**Medium**	**Medium**	**High**	**Medium**	**High**

Decision-flow: CFO → IT / Data → Sales

463. Create price confidence training systems for sales

Train teams to defend value, handle pricing objections, negotiate confidently, and avoid fear-based discounting behavior.

Why it works

Weak pricing confidence creates unnecessary concessions. Better negotiation discipline protects revenue already on the table.

Best for

SaaS, consulting, healthcare, education, logistics, B2B services, retail, professional services

Execution Steps

1. Identify common discount moments
2. Build price-objection scripts
3. Train reps through role-play
4. Add manager coaching
5. Track discount behavior by rep

Real-world example

A professional services firm trains sales teams to defend strategic value instead of cutting price at the first objection.

Risk Management

1. **Commercial** · 3/5 Training not applied. **Mitigation:** Use manager reinforcement.
2. **Commercial** · 2/5 Scripts sound robotic. **Mitigation:** Practice adaptive responses.
3. **Financial** · 3/5 No measured impact. **Mitigation:** Track discount change.
4. **Alignment** · 3/5 Managers not involved. **Mitigation:** Train managers.
5. **Customer** · 3/5 Poor handling harms trust. **Mitigation:** Use respectful language.

Speed	Effort	Cost	Revenue	Time to cash	Scalability
Medium (1-3 months)	**Medium**	**Low**	**High**	**Medium**	**High**

Decision-flow: CFO → Sales → HR / People

464. Use AI to predict deals likely to request discounts

Predict which deals are likely to face discount pressure based on customer behavior, deal timing, market conditions, and historical patterns.

Why it works

Early warning helps teams prepare value defense, alternatives, and approval plans before concession pressure arrives.

Best for

SaaS, B2B services, healthcare, logistics, manufacturing, fintech, enterprise software, subscriptions

Execution Steps

1. Identify past discount-request signals
2. Train model or rules on deal history
3. Flag high-pressure deals early
4. Prepare value defense and alternatives
5. Review with sales manager

Real-world example

A SaaS company predicts which late-stage deals will request discounts based on buyer timing and procurement involvement.

Risk Management

1. **Product** · 4/5 Prediction weak. **Mitigation:** Validate with history.
2. **Commercial** · 3/5 Alerts not used. **Mitigation:** Embed in deal review.
3. **Commercial** · 3/5 Pressure is legitimate. **Mitigation:** Prepare justified approach.
4. **Product** · 3/5 CRM data gaps. **Mitigation:** Improve fields.
5. **Financial** · 2/5 Low impact. **Mitigation:** Focus on large deals.

Speed	Effort	Cost	Revenue	Time to cash	Scalability
Medium (1-3 months)	**Medium**	**Medium**	**High**	**Medium**	**High**

Decision-flow: CFO → IT / Data → Sales

465. Create automatic discount expiration systems

Automatically expire temporary discounts, pricing exceptions, and promotional concessions unless formally renewed or reapproved.

Why it works

Temporary discounts often become permanent leakage. Expiration controls prevent accidental long-term margin erosion.

Best for

SaaS, subscriptions, retail, telecom, healthcare, logistics, B2B services, professional services

Execution Steps

1. Identify active temporary discounts
2. Add expiration dates to exceptions
3. Automate expiry alerts
4. Require reapproval to extend
5. Review expired exceptions monthly

Real-world example

A subscription company requires every temporary concession to expire unless reapproved by finance.

Risk Management

1. **Operational** · 4/5 Expiry not enforced. **Mitigation:** Automate controls.
2. **Customer** · 3/5 Customer surprised by price reset. **Mitigation:** Set clear expectations.
3. **Commercial** · 3/5 Reps create workarounds. **Mitigation:** Audit exceptions.
4. **Financial** · 3/5 Wrong expiry date. **Mitigation:** Review records.
5. **Legal** · 4/5 Contract terms conflict. **Mitigation:** Check agreements.

Speed	Effort	Cost	Revenue	Time to cash	Scalability
Fast (0-30 days)	**Low**	**Low**	**High**	**Medium**	**High**

Decision-flow: CFO → Finance → Revenue Operations

466. Use dynamic non-price negotiation levers

Negotiate using delivery speed, implementation timing, payment terms, exclusivity, support levels, training, or access instead of pure price cuts.

Why it works

Customers often value flexibility and operational benefits as much as discounts, allowing sellers to preserve price.

Best for

SaaS, consulting, logistics, healthcare, manufacturing, education, B2B services, professional services

Execution Steps

1. Build approved non-price lever menu
2. Cost each lever internally
3. Match levers to buyer needs
4. Train sales. to trade levers
5. Track concessions by type

Real-world example

A logistics provider offers faster onboarding rather than cutting monthly fees.

Risk Management

1. **Operational** · 3/5 Lever strains capacity. **Mitigation:** Cost before offering.
2. **Commercial** · 3/5 Reps default to discount. **Mitigation:** Use negotiation checklist.
3. **Customer** · 2/5 Lever lacks value. **Mitigation:** Match to buyer pain.
4. **Financial** · 3/5 Hidden costs rise. **Mitigation:** Track cost-to-serve.
5. **Commercial** · 3/5 Terms become complex. **Mitigation:** Keep menu simple.

Speed	Effort	Cost	Revenue	Time to cash	Scalability
Fast (0-30 days)	**Medium**	**Low**	**High**	**Medium**	**High**

Decision-flow: CFO → Sales → Operations

467. *Create margin visibility dashboards for live deals*

Show real-time gross margin, contribution margin, commission impact, and profitability impact during active negotiations.

Why it works

Sales teams often discount without seeing profitability damage. Live margin transparency improves commercial discipline.

Best for

SaaS, manufacturing, logistics, healthcare, retail, B2B services, enterprise software, professional services

Execution Steps

1. Define margin metrics for deals
2. Connect pricing and cost data
3. Build live deal margin view
4. Show margin effect of concessions
5. Train reps and managers

Real-world example

A sales rep sees how a proposed discount changes contribution margin before submitting a quote.

Risk Management

1. **Financial** · 4/5 Cost data inaccurate. **Mitigation:** Clean cost inputs.
2. **Commercial** · 3/5 Dashboard ignored. **Mitigation:** Embed in quote flow.
3. **Product** · 3/5 Integration difficult. **Mitigation:** Start with key products.
4. **Commercial** · 2/5 Margin not enough context. **Mitigation:** Add deal notes.
5. **Alignment** · 3/5 Finance and sales disagree. **Mitigation:** Define metrics.

Speed	Effort	Cost	Revenue	Time to cash	Scalability
Medium (1-3 months)	**Medium**	**Medium**	**High**	**Medium**	**High**

Decision-flow: CFO → Finance → Sales

468. Use concession trading instead of unilateral discounts

Require customers to give something in return whenever pricing concessions are granted, such as volume, term, case study, faster payment, or scope clarity.

Why it works

Mutual concessions reduce unnecessary discounting and improve negotiation balance.

Best for

SaaS, consulting, healthcare, manufacturing, logistics, B2B services, professional services, subscriptions

Execution Steps

1. Define acceptable customer give-backs
2. Create concession trading rules
3. Train sales. on exchange language
4. Require concession notes in CRM
5. Review deals for compliance

Real-world example

A company grants a small price concession only in exchange for a longer contract term and faster payment.

Risk Management

1. **Commercial** · 3/5 Reps give concessions for free. **Mitigation:** Require give-back field.
2. **Customer** · 2/5 Customer resists exchange. **Mitigation:** Explain fairness.
3. **Commercial** · 3/5 Give-back has low value. **Mitigation:** Define approved list.
4. **Financial** · 3/5 Trade not quantified. **Mitigation:** Estimate value.
5. **Alignment** · 3/5 Rules inconsistently applied. **Mitigation:** Audit deals.

Speed	Effort	Cost	Revenue	Time to cash	Scalability
Fast (0-30 days)	**Low**	**Low**	**High**	**Medium**	**High**

Decision-flow: CFO → Sales → Finance

469. Build pricing escalation alerts for leadership

Automatically alert leadership when discounts exceed thresholds, margins collapse, or pricing behavior deviates from policy.

Why it works

Real-time escalation improves oversight before severe price leakage spreads across teams or accounts.

Best for

SaaS, manufacturing, logistics, healthcare, retail, enterprise software, B2B services, professional services

Execution Steps

1. Define escalation thresholds
2. Connect alerts to CRM or quoting system
3. Route alerts to accountable leaders
4. Require documented response
5. Review repeated violations

Real-world example

A CFO receives alerts when a quote breaches approved discount thresholds or margin floors.

Risk Management

1. **Operational** · 3/5 Too many alerts. **Mitigation:** Set material thresholds.
2. **Alignment** · 3/5 Leaders ignore alerts. **Mitigation:** Assign response SLA.
3. **Commercial** · 3/5 Reps feel policed. **Mitigation:** Frame as governance.
4. **Product** · 3/5 False alerts. **Mitigation:** Validate inputs.
5. **Commercial** · 2/5 Deals slow down. **Mitigation:** Escalate only exceptions.

Speed	Effort	Cost	Revenue	Time to cash	Scalability
Fast (0-30 days)	**Low**	**Low**	**High**	**Medium**	**High**

Decision-flow: CFO → Revenue Operations → Cross-functional

470. Use AI to identify fake competitive pricing pressure

Analyze competitor behavior, market pricing, win-loss data, and negotiation patterns to detect exaggerated competitive discount claims.

Why it works

Customers sometimes use claimed competitor pressure to force unnecessary discounts. Validation protects pricing confidence.

Best for

SaaS, telecom, logistics, healthcare, manufacturing, B2B services, fintech, enterprise software

Execution Steps

1. Collect competitor pricing evidence
2. Track discount claims in CRM
3. Compare claims to market patterns
4. Flag suspicious pressure claims
5. Prepare evidence.-based responses

Real-world example

A sales team validates whether a competitor quote claim matches known market pricing before discounting.

Risk Management

1. **Product** · 4/5 Competitor data incomplete. **Mitigation:** Use multiple sources.
2. **Legal** · 4/5 Comparison claims risky. **Mitigation:** Avoid unsupported claims.
3. **Commercial** · 3/5 Reps distrust model. **Mitigation:** Provide rationale.
4. **Customer** · 2/5 Customer pushes harder. **Mitigation:** Stay factual.
5. **Commercial** · 3/5 True pressure missed. **Mitigation:** Allow manual review.

Speed	Effort	Cost	Revenue	Time to cash	Scalability
Medium (1-3 months)	**Medium**	**Medium**	**High**	**Medium**	**High**

Decision-flow: CFO → IT / Data → Sales

471. Create premium positioning defense playbooks

Build structured messaging, proof, differentiation, objection responses, and value stories that justify premium pricing consistently.

Why it works

Premium positioning weakens when sales teams improvise value defense inconsistently. Playbooks protect price perception.

Best for

SaaS, consulting, luxury, healthcare, education, professional services, premium products, B2B services

Execution Steps

1. Define premium value pillars
2. Gather proof and differentiation
3. Build objection response playbook
4. Train sales. and managers
5. Use in live deal reviews

Real-world example

A premium consulting firm arms sales with proof points and scripts that defend fees against cheaper alternatives.

Risk Management

1. **Commercial** · 3/5 Messaging too generic. **Mitigation:** Use specific proof.
2. **Commercial** · 3/5 Team does not use playbook. **Mitigation:** Embed in coaching.
3. **Customer** · 3/5 Value still unclear. **Mitigation:** Tailor by segment.
4. **Market** · 4/5 Premium claim unsupported. **Mitigation:** Use real evidence.
projections to build the commercial case.
5. **Financial** · 2/5 No margin lift. **Mitigation:** Measure discounts.

Speed	Effort	Cost	Revenue	Time to cash	Scalability
Fast (0-30 days)	**Medium**	**Low**	**High**	**Medium**	**High**

Decision-flow: CFO → Marketing → Sales

472. Use customer profitability scoring before discount

Evaluate long-term customer profitability, retention probability, support burden, payment behavior, and expansion potential before approving discounts.

Why it works

Not all revenue is equally valuable. Profitability visibility improves discount decisions and protects future margin.

Best for

SaaS, logistics, healthcare, manufacturing, consulting, fintech, B2B services, subscriptions

Execution Steps

1. Define customer profitability factors
2. Score customers before discount approval
3. Require written manager approval for any deviation from standard terms. by score
4. Review high-discount low-profit deals
5. Track profitability after approval

Real-world example

A company denies deep discounts for high-support, slow-paying customers with weak expansion potential.

Risk Management

1. **Product** · 4/5 Profitability data incomplete. **Mitigation:** Improve cost-to-serve tracking.
2. **Commercial** · 3/5 Sales disagrees with score. **Mitigation:** Show score logic.
3. **Commercial** · 3/5 Strategic value missed. **Mitigation:** Allow override notes.
4. **Financial** · 2/5 Scoring too complex. **Mitigation:** Launch with the simplest viable version and expand only after validation.
5. **Customer** · 3/5 Bias concerns. **Mitigation:** Use objective criteria.

Speed	Effort	Cost	Revenue	Time to cash	Scalability
Medium (1-3 months)	**Medium**	**Low**	**High**	**Medium**	**High**

Decision-flow: CFO → Finance → Sales

473. Create discount-free zones for strategic products

Protect flagship, premium, limited-capacity, or strategically important offers from routine discounting practices through formal policy.

Why it works

Frequent discounting weakens premium perception and damages long-term pricing power for strategic offers.

Best for

SaaS, luxury, consulting, healthcare, education, premium products, B2B services, professional services

Execution Steps

1. Identify strategic offers to protect
2. Define no-discount rules
3. Create approved alternative levers
4. Train sales. on rationale
5. Monitor compliance

Real-world example

A premium product line is protected from discounting while sales can offer implementation support instead.

Risk Management

1. **Commercial** · 3/5 Sales fears lower win rate. **Mitigation:** Provide alternatives.
2. **Customer** · 3/5 Customers expect discounts. **Mitigation:** Explain policy confidently.
3. **Commercial** · 3/5 Policy too rigid. **Mitigation:** Allow exceptional review.
4. **Market** · 3/5 Premium value unsupported. **Mitigation:** Strengthen proof.
5. **Alignment** · 4/5 Leadership grants exceptions. **Mitigation:** Require senior sign-off.

Speed	Effort	Cost	Revenue	Time to cash	Scalability
Fast (0-30 days)	**Low**	**Low**	**High**	**Medium**	**High**

Decision-flow: CFO → Finance → Sales

474. Use AI to simulate margin impact before concessions

Simulate the financial impact of discounts across profit, cash flow, commissions, operational load, support burden, and long-term customer economics before approval.

Why it works

Teams often evaluate discounts only on revenue. Full concession simulation reveals true economic cost before approval.

Best for

SaaS, manufacturing, logistics, healthcare, consulting, fintech, B2B services, enterprise software

Execution Steps

1. Define concession impact variables
2. Connect pricing, cost, commission, and support data
3. Build simulation model
4. Run before major concessions
5. Review results in approval workflow

Real-world example

A CFO simulates how a discount affects commission, support cost, cash flow, and lifetime margin before approving it.

Risk Management

1. **Product** · 4/5 Model assumptions wrong. **Mitigation:** Validate with actuals.
2. **Financial** · 4/5 Inputs incomplete. **Mitigation:** Start with core economics.
3. **Commercial** · 3/5 Approval process feels slow. **Mitigation:** Use for material deals only.
4. **Product** · 3/5 Build complexity. **Mitigation:** Pilot in spreadsheet first.
5. **Commercial** · 3/5 Model ignores strategy. **Mitigation:** Allow strategic notes.

Speed	Effort	Cost	Revenue	Time to cash	Scalability
Medium (1-3 months)	**High**	**Medium**	**Very High**	**Medium**	**High**

Decision-flow: CFO → IT / Data → Finance

475. Create deal review boards for high-risk pricing

Require cross-functional executive or commercial review for unusually large discounts, risky terms, or margin-threatening deals.

Why it works

Extreme pricing exceptions need shared oversight so isolated decisions do not damage pricing discipline or margin quality.

Best for

SaaS, enterprise software, healthcare, logistics, manufacturing, consulting, B2B services, professional services

Execution Steps

1. Define high-risk pricing exceptions
2. Create review board membership
3. Set submission template
4. Review deal economics and risks
5. Approve, reject, or modify terms

Real-world example

A strategic deal with deep discount and unusual terms requires CFO, sales, legal, and operations review before approval.

Risk Management

1. **Operational** · 3/5 Review slows urgent deals. **Mitigation:** Set fast cadence.
2. **Alignment** · 3/5 Board becomes political. **Mitigation:** Use clear criteria.
3. **Commercial** · 4/5 Sales avoids board. **Mitigation:** Require system control.
4. **Financial** · 3/5 Exceptions still leak. **Mitigation:** Audit outcomes.
5. **Commercial** · 3/5 Too many deals escalated. **Mitigation:** Raise threshold.

Speed	Effort	Cost	Revenue	Time to cash	Scalability
Medium (1-3 months)	**Medium**	**Low**	**High**	**Medium**	**High**

Decision-flow: CFO → Finance → Cross-functional

476. Use behavioral economics to reduce discount requests

Structure pricing presentation, anchoring, framing, options, fairness cues, and negotiation flow to reduce customer pressure for discounts.

Why it works

How pricing is presented strongly affects perceived fairness, comparison behavior, and willingness to pay.

Best for

SaaS, retail, consulting, healthcare, education, hospitality, B2B services, professional services

Execution Steps

1. Audit current pricing presentation
2. Improve anchoring and framing
3. Present options clearly
4. Add fairness and value cues
5. Train sales. on flow

Real-world example

A services firm reframes pricing into clear options with value anchors, reducing immediate discount requests.

Risk Management

1. **Commercial** · 3/5 Framing feels manipulative. **Mitigation:** Keep transparent.
2. **Commercial** · 3/5 Team uses inconsistently. **Mitigation:** Standardize materials.
3. **Customer** · 3/5 Options confuse buyer. **Mitigation:** Simplify choices.
4. **Legal** · 3/5 Pricing claims risky. **Mitigation:** Review all external-facing language with legal counsel before publishing.
5. **Financial** · 2/5 No measurable lift. **Mitigation:** Run an A/B test on a small cohort before deploying broadly. requests

Speed	Effort	Cost	Revenue	Time to cash	Scalability
Fast (0-30 days)	**Medium**	**Low**	**High**	**Medium**	**High**

Decision-flow: CFO → Marketing → Sales

From Ideas to Action

Twenty ideas. Twenty ways to protect margin from being eroded by undisciplined discounting and last-minute concessions.

Discounts are almost never a customer requirement. They are a sales habit — the path of least resistance when a conversation gets uncomfortable. These ideas build the structures that make that habit harder: approval rules, pricing floors, alternative responses. The margin is already there. These ideas protect it.

Before continuing, identify the single idea with the clearest commercial case right now. Name who owns it. Set a date for the first step. That is all that is required.

> ***Every unnecessary discount is a decision to work harder for less.***
> ***Build the guardrails before the next conversation.***

What Comes Next

6.4 — Deal & Margin Protection addresses businesses where deals are being won but the economic quality of those deals is deteriorating through poor scoping, weak contracts, and structural concessions. If revenue is growing but profit is not keeping pace — the next chapter is where that changes.

6.4 — Deal & Margin Protection

Protect revenue quality by defending deal economics, scope discipline, contract quality, and margin integrity.

When These Strategies Work Best

Deal and margin protection strategies work best when the business is winning business but the economic quality of deals is deteriorating through poor scoping, weak contract terms, or structural concessions that erode profitability.

- Gross margin varies significantly across deals of similar scope and value
- Scope creep is common and is absorbed by delivery teams without commercial consequence
- Contracts are weak on exclusions, change events, and protection against client behaviour
- Revenue is growing but profit is not keeping pace with it
- The business wins deals it later regrets because client behaviour was not qualified properly

The Benefits

- Higher profit on every deal without increasing prices or reducing delivery quality
- Fewer bad deals that consume delivery resource while destroying margin
- Cleaner commercial relationships when scope, obligations, and change are clearly defined
- Better delivery team experience when work is scoped honestly and charged appropriately
- Stronger long-term commercial health when the business selects clients as carefully as clients select the business

The Risks to Manage

- **Over-engineering** — deal protection processes that are too heavy slow good deals. Keep controls proportionate to deal size.
- **Sales conflict** — tighter deal requirements reduce short-term close rates. Align sales incentives with margin, not just revenue.
- **Client friction** — stronger contract terms require better communication of value. Do not tighten terms without improving the value story.
- **Delayed implementation** — scope controls that lack a fast change-event process create delivery bottlenecks. Build the mechanism before the policy.

477. Use AI to detect unbilled work automatically

Analyze tickets, emails, support logs, meetings, implementation activity, and operational tasks to identify work delivered without billing coverage.

Why it works

Many businesses quietly deliver large amounts of unpaid work that erodes margins over time.

Best for

Consulting, SaaS, agencies, healthcare, logistics, IT services, professional services, enterprise support

Execution Steps

1. Map billable vs non-billable activities
2. Connect operational systems and support data
3. Build AI or rules detection logic
4. Flag unbilled work automatically
5. Escalate repeated leakage patterns

Real-world example

An IT services company discovers large amounts of unpaid support work hidden inside email requests and informal tickets.

Risk Management

1. **Product** · 3/5 False-positive alerts. **Mitigation:** Validate with managers.
2. **Alignment** · 3/5 Team resistance. **Mitigation:** Explain profitability impact.
3. **Commercial** · 4/5 Billing disputes. **Mitigation:** Define scope clearly.
4. **Operational** · 3/5 Weak activity tracking. **Mitigation:** Improve workflows.
5. **Product** · 3/5 Data fragmentation. **Mitigation:** Centralize systems.

Speed	Effort	Cost	Revenue	Time to cash	Scalability
Medium (1-3 months)	**Medium**	**Medium**	**Very High**	**Medium**	**High**

Decision-flow: CFO → Operations → Finance

478. Create scope creep warning systems during delivery

Monitor project expansion, revisions, extra requests, support demands, and delivery deviations before uncontrolled scope growth damages margins.

Why it works

Scope creep often becomes normalized gradually before financial impact is recognized.

Best for

Consulting, agencies, construction, software projects, healthcare implementations, logistics, professional services

Execution Steps

1. Define original project scope clearly
2. Identify common expansion triggers
3. Create warning thresholds
4. Alert teams when scope expands
5. Escalate unapproved expansion

Real-world example

A software implementation firm detects excessive revision cycles before project profitability collapses.

Risk Management

1. **Commercial** · 4/5 Scope definitions unclear. **Mitigation:** Improve contracts.
2. **Alignment** · 3/5 Teams ignore warnings. **Mitigation:** Assign accountability.
3. **Customer** · 3/5 Customer pushback. **Mitigation:** Communicate early.
4. **Operational** · 2/5 Over-monitoring. **Mitigation:** Focus on high-risk projects.
5. **Operational** · 3/5 Slow escalation. **Mitigation:** Define escalation owners.

Speed	Effort	Cost	Revenue	Time to cash	Scalability
Fast (0-30 days)	**Medium**	**Low**	**High**	**Medium**	**High**

Decision-flow: CFO → Operations → PMO / Strategy

479. Use live cost-to-serve dashboards per customer

Track real-time servicing costs, support intensity, implementation effort, operational load, and delivery complexity by customer.

Why it works

Some customers consume far more resources than their revenue justifies.

Best for

SaaS, logistics, telecom, healthcare, B2B services, consulting, enterprise support

Execution Steps

1. Define servicing cost categories
2. Connect operational and financial data
3. Build customer-level dashboards
4. Monitor servicing intensity continuously
5. Escalate unprofitable accounts

Real-world example

A logistics company identifies customers generating excessive operational handling costs relative to contract value.

Risk Management

1. **Product** · 4/5 Cost allocation inaccurate. **Mitigation:** Improve methodology.
2. **Alignment** · 3/5 Teams reject visibility. **Mitigation:** Train managers.
3. **Financial** · 3/5 Profitability misunderstood. **Mitigation:** Combine financial and strategic views.
4. **Operational** · 2/5 Dashboard overload. **Mitigation:** Focus on key metrics.
5. **Commercial** · 3/5 Weak follow-up. **Mitigation:** Assign actions.

Speed	Effort	Cost	Revenue	Time to cash	Scalability
Medium (1-3 months)	**Medium**	**Medium**	**Very High**	**Medium**	**High**

Decision-flow: CFO → Finance → Operations

480. Create automatic over-servicing alerts

Trigger alerts when support, revisions, implementation hours, account management effort, or service requests exceed expected servicing thresholds.

Why it works

Over-servicing quietly destroys margins when teams continue delivering beyond viable economic limits.

Best for

Consulting, SaaS, agencies, healthcare, IT services, logistics, enterprise support

Execution Steps

1. Define expected servicing thresholds
2. Track service usage automatically
3. Trigger over-servicing alerts
4. Review root causes quickly
5. Escalate repeat offenders

Real-world example

A SaaS provider identifies accounts generating excessive support demand far above their subscription economics.

Risk Management

1. **Operational** · 3/5 Thresholds too aggressive. **Mitigation:** Run a controlled pilot with three to five accounts.
2. **Alignment** · 3/5 Teams ignore alerts. **Mitigation:** Assign accountability.
3. **Customer** · 3/5 Customer dissatisfaction. **Mitigation:** Communicate fairly.
4. **Product** · 2/5 Incomplete tracking. **Mitigation:** Improve system logging.
5. **Operational** · 2/5 False alarms. **Mitigation:** Refine triggers.

Speed	Effort	Cost	Revenue	Time to cash	Scalability
Fast (0-30 days)	**Low**	**Low**	**High**	**Medium**	**High**

Decision-flow: CFO → Customer Success → Operations

481. *Use AI to predict margin-risk accounts after sale*

Predict which customers, projects, or implementations are likely to become margin-destructive after contracts are signed.

Why it works

Margin risk often becomes predictable before major financial leakage fully appears.

Best for

Consulting, SaaS, healthcare, telecom, construction, logistics, enterprise projects

Execution Steps

1. Analyze historical margin failures
2. Identify predictive signals
3. Build AI or risk scoring logic
4. Flag risky accounts early
5. Trigger mitigation workflows

Real-world example

A consulting firm predicts which implementations are likely to exceed planned delivery economics before major overruns occur.

Risk Management

1. **Product** · 4/5 Weak prediction accuracy. **Mitigation:** Retrain models.
2. **Alignment** · 3/5 Teams distrust AI. **Mitigation:** Use explainable signals.
3. **Product** · 4/5 Data quality gaps. **Mitigation:** Clean historical data.
4. **Operational** · 3/5 False-positive escalations. **Mitigation:** Add a human review checkpoint for all high-value or high-risk outputs.
5. **Operational** · 3/5 Slow intervention. **Mitigation:** Define escalation owners.

Speed	Effort	Cost	Revenue	Time to cash	Scalability
Medium (1-3 months)	**High**	**Medium**	**Very High**	**Medium**	**High**

Decision-flow: CFO → IT / Data → Operations

482. Create profitability guardrails during delivery

Set operational, staffing, servicing, and implementation boundaries that prevent teams from unknowingly destroying delivery margins.

Why it works

Teams often optimize for customer satisfaction without visibility into profitability impact.

Best for

Consulting, agencies, SaaS, healthcare, construction, logistics, enterprise delivery

Execution Steps

1. Define minimum profitability targets
2. Build operational boundaries
3. Train delivery managers.
4. Monitor deviations continuously
5. Escalate breaches early

Real-world example

A consulting business creates staffing limits and revision controls to prevent margin erosion during projects.

Risk Management

1. **Operational** · 3/5 Guardrails too rigid. **Mitigation:** Allow exceptions.
2. **Alignment** · 3/5 Teams bypass controls. **Mitigation:** Audit compliance.
3. **Customer** · 2/5 Customer dissatisfaction. **Mitigation:** Communicate expectations.
4. **Product** · 3/5 Weak visibility. **Mitigation:** Improve reporting.
5. **Operational** · 3/5 Escalation delays. **Mitigation:** Define response rules.

Speed	Effort	Cost	Revenue	Time to cash	Scalability
Fast (0-30 days)	**Medium**	**Low**	**High**	**Medium**	**High**

Decision-flow: CFO → Operations → PMO / Strategy

483. Use dynamic service-tier enforcement

Automatically align support levels, response times, implementation access, and servicing intensity with the customer's purchased tier.

Why it works

Many businesses accidentally provide premium support to lower-margin customers.

Best for

SaaS, telecom, healthcare, enterprise software, logistics, managed services

Execution Steps

1. Define service tiers clearly
2. Map support entitlements
3. Automate service enforcement
4. Monitor exceptions continuously
5. Escalate repeated breaches

Real-world example

A SaaS provider stops providing enterprise-level support to standard subscription customers automatically.

Risk Management

1. **Customer** · 3/5 Customers are unclear on what is included, how to use it. **Mitigation:** Clarify entitlements.
2. **Alignment** · 3/5 Team inconsistency. **Mitigation:** Automate enforcement.
3. **Product** · 2/5 System complexity. **Mitigation:** Launch with the simplest viable version and expand only after validation.
4. **Customer** · 3/5 Support backlash. **Mitigation:** Provide upgrade paths.
5. **Product** · 2/5 Weak monitoring. **Mitigation:** Use dashboards.

Speed	Effort	Cost	Revenue	Time to cash	Scalability
Fast (0-30 days)	**Medium**	**Low**	**High**	**Medium**	**High**

Decision-flow: CFO → Customer Success → Operations

484. Create implementation margin tracking systems

Track profitability continuously during onboarding, deployment, setup, or implementation phases instead of only after completion.

Why it works

Implementation phases often create the largest hidden margin leakage.

Best for

Enterprise software, healthcare, telecom, consulting, logistics, construction, IT services

Execution Steps

1. Define implementation cost categories
2. Track delivery effort continuously
3. Compare planned vs actual economics
4. Escalate overruns early
5. Adjust staffing or scope

Real-world example

A healthcare software implementation team detects onboarding cost overruns halfway through deployment instead of after project closure.

Risk Management

1. **Product** · 4/5 Cost tracking weak. **Mitigation:** Improve time logging.
2. **Alignment** · 3/5 Teams underreport effort. **Mitigation:** Audit data.
3. **Operational** · 3/5 Delayed escalation. **Mitigation:** Create thresholds.
4. **Operational** · 2/5 Resistance from delivery teams. **Mitigation:** Train managers.
5. **Product** · 2/5 Visibility overload. **Mitigation:** Focus on core metrics.

Speed	Effort	Cost	Revenue	Time to cash	Scalability
Medium (1-3 months)	**Medium**	**Medium**	**Very High**	**Medium**	**High**

Decision-flow: CFO → Operations → Finance

485. Use AI to detect high-maintenance customer patterns

Identify behavioral, operational, and servicing patterns that consistently create disproportionate support and delivery costs.

Why it works

Some customers generate hidden operational drag that damages profitability repeatedly.

Best for

SaaS, managed services, consulting, healthcare, logistics, agencies, enterprise support

Execution Steps

1. Define high-maintenance behavior patterns
2. Analyze support and servicing history
3. Flag customers with repeated cost drag
4. Diagnose root causes
5. Adjust service model or expectations

Real-world example

A managed services firm identifies customers whose repeated urgent requests consume excessive support capacity.

Risk Management

1. **Product** · 3/5 Behavior labels feel subjective. **Mitigation:** Use measurable signals.
2. **Customer** · 3/5 Customer feels targeted. **Mitigation:** Frame around service fit.
3. **Alignment** · 3/5 Teams avoid action. **Mitigation:** Assign margin owner.
4. **Commercial** · 3/5 Strategic customers misclassified. **Mitigation:** Add a human review checkpoint for all high-value or high-risk outputs.
5. **Financial** · 2/5 Low impact. **Mitigation:** Prioritize high-cost patterns.

Speed	Effort	Cost	Revenue	Time to cash	Scalability
Medium (1-3 months)	**Medium**	**Medium**	**High**	**Medium**	**High**

Decision-flow: CFO → IT / Data → Customer Success

486. Create paid escalation pathways instead of free

Turn premium support escalation, urgent response, executive access, or accelerated delivery into monetized offerings instead of default free service.

Why it works

Businesses often provide expensive escalation support without recovering the operational cost.

Best for

SaaS, IT services, logistics, healthcare, consulting, managed services, enterprise platforms

Execution Steps

1. Identify costly escalation activities
2. Define paid escalation options
3. Set pricing and eligibility rules
4. Train teams to route requests
5. Communicate options transparently

Real-world example

A software company charges for premium emergency response instead of treating urgent escalation as default free support.

Risk Management

1. **Customer** · 3/5 Customer sees it as nickel-and-diming. **Mitigation:** Position as premium access.
2. **Commercial** · 3/5 Sales gives it away. **Mitigation:** Require written manager approval for any deviation from standard terms.
3. **Operational** · 3/5 Escalation capacity limited. **Mitigation:** Cap availability to protect quality and prevent over-commitment.
4. **Financial** · 3/5 Pricing is set too low to adequately cover the real cost. **Mitigation:** Model cost.
5. **Legal** · 2/5 Unclear terms create disputes and undermine trust in the commercial relationship.. **Mitigation:** Update service agreement.

Speed	Effort	Cost	Revenue	Time to cash	Scalability
Fast (0-30 days)	**Low**	**Low**	**High**	**Medium**	**High**

Decision-flow: CFO → Customer Success → Sales

487. Use delivery efficiency benchmarking across teams

Benchmark delivery speed, servicing efficiency, implementation cost, revision rates, and operational productivity across internal teams.

Why it works

Internal operational differences often create hidden profitability leakage.

Best for

Consulting, agencies, SaaS, logistics, healthcare, construction, IT services, professional services

Execution Steps

1. Define delivery efficiency metrics
2. Compare teams, projects, and service lines
3. Identify high-leakage patterns
4. Study best-performing teams
5. Standardize better practices

Real-world example

An agency finds one delivery team has far higher revision costs and uses best-practice benchmarking to reduce leakage.

Risk Management

1. **Alignment** · 3/5 Teams feel judged. **Mitigation:** Frame as improvement.
2. **Product** · 3/5 Metrics inconsistent. **Mitigation:** Standardize definitions.
3. **Operational** · 3/5 Best practices not adopted. **Mitigation:** Assign a named owner to every action item before.
4. **Financial** · 2/5 Savings not measured. **Mitigation:** Track margin impact.
5. **Customer** · 3/5 Quality drops from efficiency push. **Mitigation:** Protect outcome standards.

Speed	Effort	Cost	Revenue	Time to cash	Scalability
Medium (1-3 months)	**Medium**	**Low**	**High**	**Medium**	**High**

Decision-flow: CFO → Operations → Finance

488. Create AI-driven margin leakage heatmaps

Visualize where margin destruction occurs across customers, products, projects, geographies, service lines, and operational workflows.

Why it works

Margin leakage often hides inside operational complexity and fragmented reporting.

Best for

SaaS, consulting, logistics, healthcare, telecom, agencies, enterprise services

Execution Steps

1. Define leakage dimensions
2. Connect financial and operational data
3. Build heatmap views
4. Identify highest-leakage areas
5. Prioritize action by value at risk

Real-world example

A services company uses a heatmap to discover that one service line and customer segment drive most margin leakage.

Risk Management

1. **Product** · 4/5 Data too fragmented. **Mitigation:** Connect core systems first.
2. **Financial** · 3/5 Cost allocations disputed. **Mitigation:** Agree methodology.
3. **Alignment** · 3/5 Teams debate findings. **Mitigation:** Use transparent logic.
4. **Operational** · 2/5 Too many hotspots. **Mitigation:** Prioritize top leaks.
5. **Commercial** · 3/5 No action follows insight. **Mitigation:** Assign a named owner to every action item before.

Speed	Effort	Cost	Revenue	Time to cash	Scalability
Medium (1-3 months)	**Medium**	**Medium**	**Very High**	**Medium**	**High**

Decision-flow: CFO → IT / Data → Finance

489. Use operational friction scoring after the sale

Measure operational complexity, handoff friction, revision loops, servicing delays, and coordination inefficiencies tied to customer profitability.

Why it works

Operational friction increases hidden servicing costs and weakens margin quality.

Best for

SaaS, consulting, logistics, healthcare, agencies, construction, IT services, B2B services

Execution Steps

1. Define post-sale friction signals
2. Score projects or accounts by friction
3. Identify repeat friction drivers
4. Remove avoidable handoffs or delays
5. Escalate high-friction accounts

Real-world example

A consulting firm scores delivery friction and finds excessive client handoffs are increasing project cost.

Risk Management

1. **Operational** · 3/5 Friction score too vague. **Mitigation:** Use measurable inputs.
2. **Alignment** · 3/5 Teams ignore friction. **Mitigation:** Tie to margin reviews.
3. **Customer** · 3/5 Customer-side friction persists. **Mitigation:** Set expectations in writing before any engagement or commitment begins.
4. **Product** · 3/5 Incomplete workflow data. **Mitigation:** Improve tracking.
5. **Financial** · 2/5 Impact unclear. **Mitigation:** Link to cost-to-serve.

Speed	Effort	Cost	Revenue	Time to cash	Scalability
Medium (1-3 months)	**Medium**	**Low**	**High**	**Medium**	**High**

Decision-flow: CFO → Operations → Customer Success

490. Create profitability rescue workflows for projects

Intervene rapidly when projects, accounts, or implementations begin drifting toward low or negative profitability.

Why it works

Most businesses recognize margin destruction too late to recover profitability effectively.

Best for

Consulting, agencies, SaaS, construction, healthcare, logistics, IT services, enterprise projects

Execution Steps

1. Define margin drift triggers
2. Build rescue workflow steps
3. Assign rescue owner
4. Diagnose root cause quickly
5. Reset scope, staffing, or economics

Real-world example

A project team enters a rescue workflow when delivery hours exceed plan by 25 percent, forcing scope reset and executive review.

Risk Management

1. **Operational** · 4/5 Rescue starts too late. **Mitigation:** Use early triggers.
2. **Customer** · 3/5 Customer resists reset. **Mitigation:** Use contract and value logic.
3. **Alignment** · 4/5 No one owns recovery. **Mitigation:** Assign lead.
4. **Financial** · 3/5 Recovery actions too weak. **Mitigation:** Set hard options.
5. **Commercial** · 3/5 Relationship damage. **Mitigation:** Set clear expectations.

Speed	Effort	Cost	Revenue	Time to cash	Scalability
Fast (0-30 days)	**Medium**	**Low**	**Very High**	**Medium**	**High**

Decision-flow: CFO → Operations → Finance

491. Use AI to identify hidden fulfillment waste

Analyze operational processes, logistics, staffing patterns, service delivery, and fulfillment inefficiencies that reduce post-sale profitability.

Why it works

Many operational inefficiencies remain invisible without deep pattern analysis.

Best for

Logistics, healthcare, e-commerce, manufacturing, SaaS operations, field services, distribution

Execution Steps

1. Map fulfillment process data
2. Identify waste categories
3. Build AI pattern analysis
4. Prioritize waste by margin impact
5. Fix highest-value inefficiencies

Real-world example

A logistics business uses AI to identify routing and staffing patterns that create hidden fulfillment cost leakage.

Risk Management

1. **Product** · 4/5 Waste signals unclear. **Mitigation:** Define categories.
2. **Product** · 3/5 Complex implementation. **Mitigation:** Start with one workflow.
3. **Operational** · 3/5 Teams resist findings. **Mitigation:** Involve operators.
4. **Financial** · 3/5 Savings overstated. **Mitigation:** Validate with finance.
5. **Customer** · 3/5 Service quality affected. **Mitigation:** Protect delivery standards.

Speed	Effort	Cost	Revenue	Time to cash	Scalability
Medium (1-3 months)	**High**	**Medium**	**Very High**	**Medium**	**High**

Decision-flow: CFO → IT / Data → Operations

492. Create variable servicing models tied to profitability

Adjust servicing intensity, support allocation, account coverage, and operational resources based on customer profitability levels.

Why it works

Equal servicing across unequal profitability creates avoidable margin destruction.

Best for

SaaS, consulting, logistics, healthcare, managed services, professional services, enterprise support

Execution Steps

1. Segment customers by profitability
2. Define servicing model by segment
3. Align support and account coverage
4. Communicate boundaries internally
5. Monitor satisfaction and margin

Real-world example

A B2B services firm gives high-profit strategic accounts senior coverage while moving low-profit accounts to standardized support.

Risk Management

1. **Customer** · 3/5 Lower-service customers complain. **Mitigation:** Set clear expectations.
2. **Commercial** · 3/5 Strategic low-margin accounts under-served. **Mitigation:** Add strategic exception.
3. **Alignment** · 3/5 Teams apply rules inconsistently. **Mitigation:** Use clear tiers.
4. **Financial** · 4/5 Profitability data weak. **Mitigation:** Improve cost allocation.
5. **Market** · 3/5 Service perception drops. **Mitigation:** Maintain baseline. quality

Speed	Effort	Cost	Revenue	Time to cash	Scalability
Medium (1-3 months)	**Medium**	**Low**	**High**	**Medium**	**High**

Decision-flow: CFO → Finance → Customer Success

493. Use real-time delivery margin command centers

Build live dashboards tracking staffing efficiency, servicing costs, project profitability, operational risk, revisions, and fulfillment leakage continuously.

Why it works

Real-time visibility allows faster correction before margin erosion compounds.

Best for

Consulting, SaaS, logistics, healthcare, construction, IT services, enterprise delivery

Execution Steps

1. Define live delivery margin signals
2. Connect finance and delivery systems
3. Build command dashboard
4. Assign a named owner to every action item before. to risk signals
5. Review active margin risks weekly

Real-world example

An enterprise delivery firm monitors active project margin, delivery overruns, and revision load in one live control center.

Risk Management

1. **Operational** · 4/5 Dashboard creates noise. **Mitigation:** Prioritize critical signals.
2. **Product** · 3/5 Data latency issues. **Mitigation:** Invest in integration quality early to prevent downstream system failures.
3. **Alignment** · 3/5 Owners unclear. **Mitigation:** Assign action owners.
4. **Product** · 3/5 Build complexity. **Mitigation:** Start with major projects.
5. **Financial** · 2/5 Ongoing maintenance grows beyond the capacity planned at launch. **Mitigation:** Automate reporting to reduce manual effort and improve data reliability.

Speed	Effort	Cost	Revenue	Time to cash	Scalability
Medium (1-3 months)	**High**	**Medium**	**Very High**	**Medium**	**High**

Decision-flow: CFO → Revenue Operations → Operations

494. Create customer behavior clauses that protect margins

Build contractual protections around excessive revisions, delays, support abuse, implementation bottlenecks, or operational disruption caused by customers.

Why it works

Some margin leakage originates from customer-driven operational inefficiency.

Best for

Consulting, SaaS, agencies, construction, healthcare implementations, IT services, professional services

Execution Steps

1. Identify customer behaviors that create leakage
2. Translate them into fair contract clauses
3. Define scope, access, and usage limits in writing before launch., responsibilities, and fees
4. Train sales. and delivery teams
5. Enforce clauses consistently

Real-world example

A consulting firm adds revision and client-delay clauses to protect project margins from repeated customer-side delays.

Risk Management

1. **Legal** · 4/5 Clauses too aggressive. **Mitigation:** Use fair language.
2. **Customer** · 3/5 Customer pushes back. **Mitigation:** Explain mutual accountability.
3. **Commercial** · 3/5 Sales removes clauses. **Mitigation:** Require written manager approval for any deviation from standard terms.
4. **Operational** · 3/5 Clauses not enforced. **Mitigation:** Train delivery managers.
5. **Commercial** · 2/5 Deal friction increases. **Mitigation:** Use on high-risk work.

Speed	Effort	Cost	Revenue	Time to cash	Scalability
Medium (1-3 months)	**Medium**	**Low**	**High**	**Medium**	**High**

Decision-flow: CFO → Legal → Operations

495. Create margin kill-switches for bad economics

Set automatic stop, escalation, or renegotiation triggers when accounts, projects, or services cross agreed margin-loss thresholds.

Why it works

Companies keep serving margin-destroying work because no one is forced to stop and reset the economics.

Best for

Consulting, SaaS, agencies, construction, logistics, healthcare, managed services, enterprise support

Execution Steps

1. Define margin-loss thresholds
2. Set kill-switch actions
3. Assign escalation authority
4. Monitor active accounts and projects
5. Stop, renegotiate, or reset economics

Real-world example

A services firm automatically escalates any project projected below minimum margin for renegotiation or scope reset.

Risk Management

1. **Customer** · 3/5 Customer relationship strained. **Mitigation:** Communicate early.
2. **Alignment** · 4/5 Teams resist stopping work. **Mitigation:** Give finance authority.
3. **Commercial** · 3/5 Revenue loss fear. **Mitigation:** Show profit impact.
4. **Operational** · 3/5 Thresholds too rigid. **Mitigation:** Allow executive exceptions.
5. **Legal** · 3/5 Contract limits unclear. **Mitigation:** Submit all commercial terms to legal review before customer presentation.

Speed	Effort	Cost	Revenue	Time to cash	Scalability
Fast (0-30 days)	**Medium**	**Low**	**Very High**	**Medium**	**High**

Decision-flow: CFO → Finance → Operations

496. Turn hidden margin leakage into chargeable change

Convert repeated extra work, customer delays, additional revisions, emergency requests, and operational disruption into formal billable change events.

Why it works

Margin leakage often comes from small exceptions becoming free habits. Formal change events recover value without changing base pricing.

Best for

Consulting, agencies, SaaS implementation, construction, healthcare projects, IT services, professional services

Execution Steps

1. Define what qualifies as a chargeable change event
2. Train teams to identify events
3. Create simple change-order process
4. Communicate changes before extra work begins
5. Bill or approve exceptions formally

Real-world example

A software implementation firm converts extra customer-requested integrations into formal paid change orders.

Risk Management

1. **Customer** · 4/5 Customer resists extra charges. **Mitigation:** Explain scope clearly.
2. **Commercial** · 3/5 Team avoids difficult conversations. **Mitigation:** Provide scripts.
3. **Operational** · 3/5 Events not captured. **Mitigation:** Use change log.
4. **Legal** · 3/5 Contract support weak. **Mitigation:** Update terms.
5. **Financial** · 2/5 Charges too small to matter. **Mitigation:** Set minimum threshold.s

Speed	Effort	Cost	Revenue	Time to cash	Scalability
Fast (0-30 days)	**Medium**	**Low**	**Very High**	**Medium**	**High**

Decision-flow: CFO → Operations → Sales

From Ideas to Action

Twenty ideas. Twenty ways to protect the quality of deals being won — keeping margin intact from first conversation to final invoice.

Deals erode in the details. Scope expands informally. Payment terms drift. Contract language gets softened under closing pressure. The revenue number survives but the margin does not. These ideas build the discipline to protect deal quality from first conversation to final invoice.

Before continuing, identify the single idea with the clearest commercial case right now. Name who owns it. Set a date for the first step. That is all that is required.

> ***Revenue that arrives without margin is not a win. It is a different kind of loss.***

What Comes Next

6.5 — Delivery Reliability addresses businesses where operational or service failures are causing churn, refund exposure, and damaged commercial relationships. If the business wins customers well but delivery quality is the hidden leak in revenue retention — the final chapter in this section closes it.

6.5 — Delivery Reliability

Protect revenue by preventing operational or service failures that cause churn, refunds, lost renewals, or damaged commercial relationships.

When These Strategies Work Best

Delivery reliability strategies work best when operational failures are a recurring cause of customer loss, renewal risk, or commercial damage that is not being addressed systematically.

- Customer loss correlates with delivery failures or service quality issues
- The same operational problems recur without a root-cause resolution
- Delivery quality varies across the team without a consistent standard being enforced
- Commercial teams spend significant time managing the consequences of operational failures
- Reliability is becoming a competitive differentiator in the market the business operates in

The Benefits

- Revenue protection from the most preventable form of customer loss
- Lower commercial cost when sales teams are not spending time on failure recovery
- Stronger renewal rates from customers whose trust has not been eroded by poor delivery
- Premium pricing power when reliability becomes a demonstrable and visible competitive advantage
- Better team performance when delivery standards are clear, consistent, and enforced

The Risks to Manage

- **Measurement without action** — tracking reliability without fixing root causes produces data but no improvement.
- **Over-promising reliability** — commitments the business cannot consistently meet create worse commercial damage than no commitment at all.
- **Wrong investment priorities** — fixing the most visible failures rather than the most commercially damaging ones wastes resource.
- **Accountability gaps** — delivery reliability owned by no one improves for no one. Assign it explicitly before building process.

497. Sell Guaranteed Business Continuity subscriptions

Offer premium continuity packages guaranteeing operational fallback, priority recovery, backup fulfillment, and protected service continuity during disruptions.

Why it works

Customers will pay more when operational interruption creates major financial exposure.

Best for

Cloud infrastructure, SaaS, logistics, fintech, healthcare, telecom, enterprise platforms, managed services

Execution Steps

1. Identify continuity-sensitive customer segments
2. Define continuity guarantee scope
3. Build operational fallback capabilities
4. Price continuity subscriptions appropriately
5. Train sales. and operations teams

Real-world example

A cloud provider sells premium continuity subscriptions guaranteeing rapid failover and priority operational recovery.

Risk Management

1. **Legal** · 4/5 Guarantees too aggressive. **Mitigation:** Limit exposure clearly.
2. **Operational** · 4/5 Operational strain. **Mitigation:** Reserve continuity capacity.
3. **Customer** · 3/5 Customer misunderstanding. **Mitigation:** Clarify all terms in plain language before any customer-facing presentation.
4. **Financial** · 3/5 Underpricing risk. **Mitigation:** Model downtime economics.
5. **Commercial** · 2/5 Weak adoption. **Mitigation:** Target high-risk industries.

Speed	Effort	Cost	Revenue	Time to cash	Scalability
Medium (1-3 months)	**Medium**	**Medium**	**Very High**	**Medium**	**High**

Decision-flow: CFO → Operations → Sales

498. Create customer-controlled failover systems

Allow customers to activate backup delivery paths, secondary infrastructure, or emergency operating modes independently during disruptions.

Why it works

Giving customers operational control during incidents increases trust and reduces panic-driven churn.

Best for

Cloud services, SaaS, telecom, logistics, fintech, healthcare systems, enterprise infrastructure

Execution Steps

1. Identify failover-sensitive workflows
2. Build backup operating modes
3. Create customer activation controls
4. Test failover reliability
5. Train customers on activation

Real-world example

A logistics platform allows enterprise customers to switch automatically to backup fulfillment pathways during disruptions.

Risk Management

1. **Customer** · 3/5 Customer misuse. **Mitigation:** Add permission controls.
2. **Operational** · 4/5 Failover instability. **Mitigation:** Stress-test workflows.
3. **Product** · 3/5 Operational complexity increases faster than the team is resourced to manage.. **Mitigation:** Start with core systems.
4. **Operational** · 2/5 Post-launch support demand is higher than planned, straining the delivery team. **Mitigation:** Automate onboarding.
5. **Product** · 3/5 Integration gaps. **Mitigation:** Validate dependencies.

Speed	Effort	Cost	Revenue	Time to cash	Scalability
Medium (1-3 months)	**High**	**Medium**	**High**	**Medium**	**High**

Decision-flow: CFO → Product → Operations

499. Build operational trust scores customers can see live

Provide transparent real-time reliability scoring showing uptime stability, fulfillment quality, incident recovery performance, and operational consistency.

Why it works

Transparency builds commercial trust and differentiates against opaque competitors.

Best for

SaaS, fintech, logistics, telecom, healthcare, cloud infrastructure, managed services

Execution Steps

1. Define trust score methodology
2. Connect operational reliability data
3. Build customer-facing visibility layer
4. Validate score accuracy
5. Publish live operational trust metrics

Real-world example

A fintech platform displays live operational reliability scores to enterprise customers inside the customer portal.

Risk Management

1. **Customer** · 3/5 Score disputes. **Mitigation:** Use transparent methodology.
2. **Market** · 3/5 Weak reliability periods exposed. **Mitigation:** Improve recovery response.
3. **Product** · 3/5 Data inaccuracies. **Mitigation:** Audit calculations.
4. **Customer** · 2/5 Customers are unclear on what is included, how to use it. **Mitigation:** Explain metrics clearly.
5. **Market** · 2/5 Competitor scrutiny. **Mitigation:** Focus on consistency.

Speed	Effort	Cost	Revenue	Time to cash	Scalability
Medium (1-3 months)	**Medium**	**Low**	**High**	**Medium**	**High**

Decision-flow: CFO → Operations → Customer Success

500. Create reliability-backed premium pricing models

Charge premium pricing tied directly to operational consistency, uptime quality, fulfillment reliability, or continuity guarantees.

Why it works

Operational certainty becomes monetizable when downtime creates real business exposure for customers.

Best for

Cloud services, healthcare systems, logistics, telecom, SaaS, fintech, enterprise infrastructure

Execution Steps

1. Identify reliability-sensitive customers
2. Quantify continuity value economically
3. Create premium pricing structure
4. Link pricing to reliability guarantees
5. Train commercial teams

Real-world example

A cloud provider charges premium pricing for guaranteed uptime and continuity performance.

Risk Management

1. **Operational** · 4/5 Reliability underperformance. **Mitigation:** Improve operational controls.
2. **Customer** · 3/5 Customer skepticism. **Mitigation:** Provide proof metrics.
3. **Commercial** · 3/5 Weak pricing adoption. **Mitigation:** Target critical industries.
4. **Market** · 2/5 Competitive pressure. **Mitigation:** Differentiate strongly.
5. **Legal** · 4/5 Guarantee liability. **Mitigation:** Define exposure caps.

Speed	Effort	Cost	Revenue	Time to cash	Scalability
Medium (1-3 months)	**Medium**	**Low**	**Very High**	**Medium**	**High**

Decision-flow: CFO → Finance → Sales

501. *Build reliability escrow guarantees for enterprise*

Place financial penalties, credits, or recovery guarantees into structured agreements tied to operational continuity commitments.

Why it works

Financial accountability strengthens procurement trust and reinforces operational credibility.

Best for

Enterprise SaaS, cloud infrastructure, telecom, healthcare systems, fintech, logistics

Execution Steps

1. Define continuity commitment levels
2. Structure escrow or penalty mechanisms
3. Model financial exposure
4. Update enterprise agreements
5. Train commercial teams

Real-world example

An enterprise infrastructure provider offers contractual reliability guarantees tied to financial recovery commitments.

Risk Management

1. **Financial** · 5/5 Financial liability exposure. **Mitigation:** Cap penalties.
2. **Legal** · 4/5 Legal complexity. **Mitigation:** Use clear contract language.
3. **Operational** · 4/5 Operational inconsistency. **Mitigation:** Improve resilience.
4. **Commercial** · 3/5 Customer negotiation pressure. **Mitigation:** Standardize terms.
5. **Commercial** · 2/5 Thc offer lacks clear differentiation from what competitors or alternatives provide. **Mitigation:** Focus on high-value buyers.

Speed	Effort	Cost	Revenue	Time to cash	Scalability
Medium (1-3 months)	**Medium**	**Low**	**High**	**Medium**	**High**

Decision-flow: CFO → Legal → Sales

502. Create internal revenue penalties for reliability

Tie operational failure costs directly to departmental performance metrics, incentives, or accountability systems.

Why it works

Revenue-linked accountability changes reliability behavior faster than operational reporting alone.

Best for

SaaS, logistics, telecom, healthcare, fintech, enterprise services, managed services

Execution Steps

1. Identify reliability failures that damage revenue
2. Quantify revenue impact by failure type
3. Link impact to team performance metrics
4. Define fair accountability rules
5. Review incidents monthly

Real-world example

A logistics company links repeated delivery failures to operational team performance metrics and revenue-at-risk reporting.

Risk Management

1. **Alignment** · 4/5 Teams become defensive. **Mitigation:** Frame around shared revenue protection.
2. **Product** · 3/5 Revenue impact disputed. **Mitigation:** Use transparent calculation.
3. **Operational** · 3/5 Gaming behavior emerges. **Mitigation:** Audit reliability metrics.
4. **Alignment** · 4/5 Blame culture develops. **Mitigation:** Balance accountability with learning.
5. **Financial** · 3/5 Impact hard to isolate. **Mitigation:** Use conservative attribution.

Speed	Effort	Cost	Revenue	Time to cash	Scalability
Medium (1-3 months)	**Medium**	**Low**	**High**	**Medium**	**High**

Decision-flow: CFO → Finance → Operations

503. Use continuity simulation testing with customers

Run operational disruption simulations jointly with customers to test resilience, recovery readiness, and continuity planning.

Why it works

Customers trust providers more when continuity preparedness is visibly tested.

Best for

Cloud infrastructure, logistics, healthcare, fintech, telecom, enterprise SaaS, managed services

Execution Steps

1. Identify customers needing continuity confidence
2. Design realistic disruption scenarios
3. Run joint simulation sessions
4. Document gaps and recovery steps
5. Implement improvements

Real-world example

A healthcare platform runs continuity drills with hospital customers to test fallback workflows before real disruption occurs.

Risk Management

1. **Customer** · 2/5 Simulation creates anxiety. **Mitigation:** Position as preparedness.
2. **Operational** · 3/5 Gaps exposed publicly. **Mitigation:** Use controlled pilots.
3. **Alignment** · 3/5 Teams do not follow up. **Mitigation:** Assign remediation owners.
4. **Commercial** · 2/5 Low participation. **Mitigation:** Target strategic accounts.
5. **Financial** · 2/5 Time cost high. **Mitigation:** Use scalable templates.

Speed	Effort	Cost	Revenue	Time to cash	Scalability
Medium (1-3 months)	**Medium**	**Low**	**High**	**Medium**	**High**

Decision-flow: CFO → Operations → Customer Success

504. Create decentralized continuity networks

Build geographically distributed fulfillment, staffing, infrastructure, or delivery capabilities that reduce single-point operational failure risk.

Why it works

Centralized operations create concentrated reliability exposure that can damage revenue at scale.

Best for

Logistics, telecom, cloud infrastructure, healthcare, manufacturing, distribution, field services

Execution Steps

1. Map single-point failure risks
2. Identify distributed capacity options
3. Design decentralized continuity model
4. Build regional or functional backups
5. Test continuity handoffs

Real-world example

A fulfillment company distributes critical delivery capacity across regions to reduce dependency on one warehouse.

Risk Management

1. **Financial** · 4/5 Cost of redundancy too high. **Mitigation:** Prioritize revenue-critical operations.
2. **Operational** · 3/5 Network complexity rises. **Mitigation:** Build and enforce a standard process before any external deployment.es.
3. **Customer** · 3/5 Service inconsistency. **Mitigation:** Set uniform standards.
4. **Alignment** · 3/5 Ownership unclear. **Mitigation:** Assign continuity owner.
5. **Market** · 3/5 Partner availability limited. **Mitigation:** Build staged network.

Speed	Effort	Cost	Revenue	Time to cash	Scalability
Slow (3+ months)	**High**	**High**	**Very High**	**Medium**	**High**

Decision-flow: CFO → Operations → PMO / Strategy

505. Offer reliability insurance for mission-critical

Provide optional operational insurance packages covering downtime compensation, emergency support, rapid recovery, or continuity guarantees.

Why it works

Customers with high downtime costs value financial protection strongly.

Best for

Cloud infrastructure, telecom, fintech, logistics, healthcare, enterprise SaaS, managed services

Execution Steps

1. Identify mission-critical customer segments
2. Define insured reliability events
3. Model risk and payout exposure
4. Create insurance-style package terms
5. Sell as optional protection

Real-world example

A telecom provider offers mission-critical enterprise customers paid downtime protection and priority recovery coverage.

Risk Management

1. **Financial** · 5/5 Claims exceed pricing. **Mitigation:** Model downside carefully.
2. **Legal** · 5/5 Insurance-like structure regulated. **Mitigation:** Get legal review.
3. **Customer** · 3/5 Coverage misunderstood. **Mitigation:** Clarify exclusions.
4. **Operational** · 4/5 Recovery capacity inadequate. **Mitigation:** Reserve resources.
5. **Commercial** · 3/5 Customers resist premium. **Mitigation:** Target high-cost downtimc buyers.

Speed	Effort	Cost	Revenue	Time to cash	Scalability
Medium (1-3 months)	**Medium**	**Medium**	**Very High**	**Medium**	**High**

Decision-flow: CFO → Finance → Legal

506. Create public uptime reputation indexes

Publish transparent operational reliability performance over time to strengthen market trust and commercial differentiation.

Why it works

Operational transparency creates reputational pressure competitors may struggle to match.

Best for

SaaS, cloud infrastructure, telecom, logistics, fintech, healthcare platforms, managed services

Execution Steps

1. Define public reliability metrics
2. Verify data quality and methodology
3. Publish uptime or performance index
4. Add context for incidents and recovery
5. Use index in commercial materials

Real-world example

A SaaS infrastructure provider publishes a public uptime and recovery-performance index to strengthen procurement confidence.

Risk Management

1. **Market** · 4/5 Poor periods visible. **Mitigation:** Improve recovery communication.
2. **Legal** · 3/5 Claims challenged. **Mitigation:** Use verified data.
3. **Market** · 2/5 Competitors attack metrics. **Mitigation:** Show methodology.
4. **Customer** · 2/5 Misinterpretation. **Mitigation:** Provide context.
5. **Operational** · 2/5 Reporting burden. **Mitigation:** Automate publication.

Speed	Effort	Cost	Revenue	Time to cash	Scalability
Medium (1-3 months)	**Medium**	**Low**	**High**	**Medium**	**High**

Decision-flow: CFO → Marketing → Operations

507. *Use priority continuity rings for strategic revenue*

Create layered operational recovery priorities where the most revenue-sensitive customers receive accelerated continuity protection first.

Why it works

Not all operational failures carry equal commercial consequences, so reliability resources should protect the highest revenue exposure first.

Best for

SaaS, logistics, telecom, cloud infrastructure, healthcare, enterprise services, managed services

Execution Steps

1. Segment customers by revenue exposure and criticality
2. Define continuity rings
3. Align recovery priority rules
4. Communicate internally and selectively to customers
5. Test priority recovery workflow

Real-world example

An enterprise SaaS company assigns strategic accounts to a top continuity ring with faster incident recovery protocols.

Risk Management

1. **Customer** · 3/5 Customers feel neglected. **Mitigation:** Maintain baseline. service
2. **Alignment** · 3/5 Teams ignore ring rules. **Mitigation:** Embed in incident workflow.
3. **Legal** · 3/5 SLA conflicts. This creates friction that erodes delivery quality and margin. **Mitigation:** Review contracts.
4. **Operational** · 3/5 Priority overload. **Mitigation:** Limit top ring eligibility.
5. **Market** · 2/5 Perceived unfairness. This limits commercial impact if not addressed before launch. **Mitigation:** Position as enterprise tier.

Speed	Effort	Cost	Revenue	Time to cash	Scalability
Fast (0-30 days)	**Medium**	**Low**	**High**	**Medium**	**High**

Decision-flow: CFO → Operations → Customer Success

508. Build customer-side continuity toolkits

Provide customers with fallback procedures, emergency workflows, offline tools, contingency playbooks, and operational recovery kits.

Why it works

Prepared customers recover faster and maintain trust during disruptions.

Best for

SaaS, healthcare, logistics, fintech, cloud infrastructure, telecom, enterprise platforms

Execution Steps

1. Identify customer-side disruption pain points
2. Build fallback playbooks and tools
3. Train customers before incidents
4. Include emergency contact paths
5. Review toolkits after incidents

Real-world example

A SaaS provider gives enterprise customers an offline operating guide and emergency workflow checklist for service disruptions.

Risk Management

1. **Customer** · 3/5 Toolkits not used. **Mitigation:** Train users regularly.
2. **Operational** · 3/5 Content outdated. **Mitigation:** Review pricing, terms, and economics quarterly to maintain accuracy.
3. **Operational** · 2/5 Support burden increases. **Mitigation:** Use self-service format.
4. **Market** · 2/5 Toolkit implies failure risk **Mitigation:** Position as preparedness.
5. **Legal** · 3/5 Advice creates liability. This creates legal or compliance exposure that must be resolved before launch. **Mitigation:** Add clear boundaries.

Speed	Effort	Cost	Revenue	Time to cash	Scalability
Fast (0-30 days)	**Medium**	**Low**	**High**	**Medium**	**High**

Decision-flow: CFO → Customer Success → Operations

509. Create reliability reserve capacity exchanges

Build shared backup operational capacity pools across partners, suppliers, infrastructure providers, or fulfillment networks.

Why it works

Shared reserve capacity lowers catastrophic disruption risk economically.

Best for

Logistics, manufacturing, cloud infrastructure, telecom, healthcare, distribution, field services

Execution Steps

1. Identify capacity gaps during disruption
2. Find trusted reserve-capacity partners
3. Create shared activation rules
4. Set commercial terms for emergency use
5. Run activation drills

Real-world example

A fulfillment network creates shared emergency warehouse and delivery capacity with partner operators.

Risk Management

1. **Dependency** · 4/5 Partner reliability weak. **Mitigation:** Vet partners carefully.
2. **Operational** · 3/5 Activation delays. **Mitigation:** Run simulations.
3. **Financial** · 3/5 Reserve costs duplicate capacity. **Mitigation:** Use only for critical flows.
4. **Legal** · 3/5 Contract gaps. This creates legal or compliance exposure that must be resolved before launch. **Mitigation:** Standardize terms.
5. **Customer** · 3/5 Service inconsistency. **Mitigation:** Define quality standards.

Speed	Effort	Cost	Revenue	Time to cash	Scalability
Medium (1-3 months)	**High**	**Medium**	**Very High**	**Medium**	**High**

Decision-flow: CFO → Operations → Partnerships / BD

510. Use AI to recommend reliability investment priorities

Prioritize operational reliability investments based on potential revenue protection impact rather than purely technical severity.

Why it works

Many businesses allocate operational resources without understanding revenue exposure correctly.

Best for

SaaS, cloud infrastructure, logistics, telecom, healthcare, fintech, enterprise services

Execution Steps

1. Map reliability risks to revenue exposure
2. Score each risk by protected revenue
3. Use AI or analytics to rank investments
4. Prioritize reliability projects by commercial impact
5. Track revenue. protected after fixes

Real-world example

A SaaS company prioritizes reliability improvements based on ARR at risk rather than engineering severity alone.

Risk Management

1. **Product** · 4/5 Revenue exposure miscalculated. **Mitigation:** Validate with finance.
2. **Alignment** · 3/5 Technical teams disagree. **Mitigation:** Balance severity and revenue.
3. **Financial** · 3/5 Investment case unclear. **Mitigation:** Show protected revenue.
4. **Operational** · 2/5 Low-risk issues ignored. **Mitigation:** Set baseline standards.
5. **Product** · 3/5 Complex scoring. **Mitigation:** Start with simple model.

Speed	Effort	Cost	Revenue	Time to cash	Scalability
Medium (1-3 months)	**Medium**	**Medium**	**High**	**Medium**	**High**

Decision-flow: CFO → IT / Data → Operations

511. Create operational trust recovery guarantees after service failures

Offer structured recovery commitments including executive engagement, enhanced oversight, accelerated remediation, and continuity reinforcement after incidents.

Why it works

Strong recovery handling often determines whether customers stay or leave after failures.

Best for

SaaS, logistics, telecom, healthcare, fintech, cloud infrastructure, enterprise services

Execution Steps

1. Define failure events requiring trust recovery
2. Build recovery guarantee playbook
3. Assign executive and operational owners
4. Communicate recovery steps clearly
5. Reinforce continuity after resolution

Real-world example

A managed services provider commits to executive follow-up and enhanced monitoring for strategic customers after critical incidents.

Risk Management

1. **Customer** · 4/5 Recovery promise feels empty. **Mitigation:** Include concrete actions.
2. **Operational** · 4/5 Teams cannot deliver commitments. **Mitigation:** Align capacity first.
3. **Financial** · 3/5 Recovery costs escalate. **Mitigation:** Set eligibility.
4. **Market /** · 2/5 Over-apology weakens confidence. This limits market impact if not addressed before launch. **Mitigation:** Focus on control.
5. **Alignment** · 3/5 Owner unclear. **Mitigation:** Assign incident lead.

Speed	Effort	Cost	Revenue	Time to cash	Scalability
Fast (0-30 days)	**Medium**	**Low**	**High**	**Medium**	**High**

Decision-flow: CFO → Customer Success → Operations

512. Build reliability-backed procurement advantages

Position operational continuity, resilience, and reliability guarantees directly into enterprise procurement differentiation.

Why it works

Procurement teams increasingly evaluate operational reliability as a strategic buying factor.

Best for

Enterprise SaaS, logistics, healthcare, fintech, telecom, cloud infrastructure, managed services

Execution Steps

1. Identify procurement reliability criteria
2. Build procurement-ready reliability proof
3. Add continuity evidence to proposals
4. Train sales. to position reliability commercially
5. Use in competitive procurement processes

Real-world example

A healthcare technology provider uses continuity proof and recovery metrics as a procurement differentiator.

Risk Management

1. **Commercial** · 3/5 Reliability claims too vague. **Mitigation:** Use measurable proof.
2. **Legal** · 4/5 Claims overreach. This creates legal or compliance exposure that must be resolved before launch. **Mitigation:** Review all external-facing language with legal counsel before publishing.
3. **Commercial** · 3/5 Teams ignore reliability story. **Mitigation:** Add to proposal templates.
4. **Customer** · 2/5 Procurement does not value it. **Mitigation:** Target mission-critical buyers.
5. **Operational** · 2/5 Proof not updated. **Mitigation:** Refresh metrics regularly.

Speed	Effort	Cost	Revenue	Time to cash	Scalability
Fast (0-30 days)	**Low**	**Low**	**High**	**Medium**	**High**

Decision-flow: CFO → Sales → Marketing

513. Create self-healing operational workflows

Design workflows that automatically reroute, recover, rebalance, or stabilize operations when disruption signals appear.

Why it works

Automatic stabilization reduces failure escalation speed dramatically.

Best for

SaaS, logistics, telecom, cloud infrastructure, fintech, healthcare, operations platforms

Execution Steps

1. Identify workflows where failures escalate quickly
2. Define self-healing actions
3. Build automated rerouting or rebalancing logic
4. Test failure scenarios
5. Monitor stabilization performance

Real-world example

A logistics platform automatically reroutes orders when a fulfillment node becomes overloaded.

Risk Management

1. **Product** · 5/5 Automation fails incorrectly. **Mitigation:** Use controlled rollout.
2. **Operational** · 3/5 Workflow complexity rises. **Mitigation:** Start with one tightly defined use case and expand.
3. **Customer** · 3/5 Unexpected changes confuse users. **Mitigation:** Provide transparency.
4. **Financial** · 3/5 Build cost high. **Mitigation:** Prioritize high-exposure workflows.
5. **Legal** · 3/5 Automated decisions risky. This reduces product quality and undermines customer adoption. **Mitigation:** Review controls.

Speed	Effort	Cost	Revenue	Time to cash	Scalability
Slow (3+ months)	**High**	**High**	**Very High**	**Medium**	**High**

Decision-flow: CFO → Product → Operations

514. Offer continuity-certified delivery programs

Create independently verified operational reliability certifications proving resilience standards to customers and procurement teams.

Why it works

Third-party reliability validation strengthens commercial trust significantly.

Best for

Healthcare, logistics, cloud infrastructure, telecom, SaaS, fintech, enterprise services

Execution Steps

1. Define continuity standards to certify
2. Select internal or external certification path
3. Prepare evidence. and controls
4. Complete validation process
5. Use certification in sales and retention

Real-world example

A logistics provider earns continuity certification and uses it to support enterprise procurement and renewal discussions.

Risk Management

1. **Operational** · 2/5 Certification standard too weak. **Mitigation:** Choose credible standard.
2. **Financial** · 2/5 Certification cost. **Mitigation:** Target enterprise use cases.
3. **Market** · 2/5 Certification misunderstood. This limits commercial impact if not addressed before launch. **Mitigation:** Explain meaning clearly.
4. **Legal** · 3/5 Evidence gaps. This limits commercial impact if not addressed before launch. **Mitigation:** Prepare documentation.
5. **Commercial** · 2/5 Low customer impact. **Mitigation:** Use in reliability-sensitive segments.

Speed	Effort	Cost	Revenue	Time to cash	Scalability
Medium (1-3 months)	**Medium**	**Medium**	**High**	**Medium**	**High**

Decision-flow: CFO → Operations → Legal

515. Create customer-visible recovery countdown systems

Show live operational recovery timelines, recovery milestones, fallback activation status, and continuity progress during disruptions.

Why it works

Visibility reduces uncertainty and customer frustration during operational incidents.

Best for

SaaS, telecom, logistics, cloud infrastructure, healthcare platforms, managed services

Execution Steps

1. Identify disruption moments that create anxiety
2. Define recovery milestones
3. Build customer-facing countdown/status view
4. Connect operational updates
5. Train teams on communication standards

Real-world example

A telecom provider shows enterprise customers live recovery milestones during service disruption.

Risk Management

1. **Customer** · 4/5 Countdown misses target. **Mitigation:** Use ranges. not false precision
2. **Operational** · 3/5 Updates lag reality. **Mitigation:** Automate feeds.
3. **Market** · 3/5 Transparency backfires. This limits commercial impact if not addressed before launch. **Mitigation:** Use careful messaging.
4. **Product** · 3/5 Status integration complex. **Mitigation:** Start with major incidents.
5. **Legal** · 3/5 Commitment language risky. This creates legal or compliance exposure that must be resolved before launch. **Mitigation:** Review wording.

Speed	Effort	Cost	Revenue	Time to cash	Scalability
Medium (1-3 months)	**Medium**	**Low**	**High**	**Medium**	**High**

Decision-flow: CFO → Product → Customer Success

516. Build reliability-linked referral incentives

Reward customers for referrals tied specifically to operational reliability, continuity confidence, or service consistency experiences.

Why it works

Reliability-driven advocacy becomes a powerful trust-based acquisition channel.

Best for

SaaS, logistics, telecom, healthcare, cloud infrastructure, fintech, managed services

Execution Steps

1. Identify customers with strong reliability experiences
2. Ask for reliability-specific referrals
3. Create proof-led referral messaging
4. Reward qualified referrals
5. Track conversion from reliability advocacy

Real-world example

A logistics platform asks customers who experienced strong disruption recovery to refer peers with reliability-sensitive operations.

Risk Management

1. **Customer** · 3/5 Referral ask feels opportunistic. **Mitigation:** Ask after positive moments.
2. **Commercial** · 2/5 Proof too generic. **Mitigation:** Use specific reliability story.
3. **Legal** · 3/5 Claims not approved. This creates legal or compliance exposure that must be resolved before launch. **Mitigation:** Verify testimonials.
4. **Financial** · 2/5 Incentive too costly. **Mitigation:** Reward qualified outcomes.
5. **Commercial** · 3/5 Conversion from initial interest to completed purchase is lower than targeted.. **Mitigation:** Target similar buyers.

Speed	Effort	Cost	Revenue	Time to cash	Scalability
Fast (0-30 days)	**Low**	**Low**	**High**	**Medium**	**High**

Decision-flow: CFO → Marketing → Customer Success

517. *Create reliability-backed revenue sharing agreements*

Tie part of pricing or upside compensation directly to operational continuity performance, uptime achievement, or delivery consistency outcomes.

Why it works

Customers trust reliability claims more when the provider shares operational risk financially.

Best for

Cloud infrastructure, logistics, fintech, enterprise SaaS, telecom, healthcare systems, managed services

Execution Steps

1. Define measurable reliability KPIs
2. Structure shared upside/downside economics
3. Model exposure scenarios carefully
4. Create enterprise contract framework
5. Pilot with strategic customers

Real-world example

A logistics provider ties part of enterprise pricing to continuity performance during peak operational periods.

Risk Management

1. **Financial** · 5/5 Financial exposure too large. **Mitigation:** Cap downside liability.
2. **Legal** · 4/5 KPI disputes. This creates friction that erodes delivery quality and margin. **Mitigation:** Use objective measurements.
3. **Legal** · 4/5 Legal complexity. This creates legal or compliance exposure that must be resolved before launch. **Mitigation:** Standardize contract structures.
4. **Operational** · 4/5 Weak operational consistency. **Mitigation:** Improve resilience. first
5. **Customer** · 3/5 Customer misuse. **Mitigation:** Define exclusions clearly.

Speed	Effort	Cost	Revenue	Time to cash	Scalability
Medium (1-3 months)	**High**	**Medium**	**Very High**	**Medium**	**High**

Decision-flow: CFO → Legal → Sales

518. Build continuity partner ecosystems for emergency

Create pre-arranged emergency operational alliances with suppliers, distributors, infrastructure providers, staffing firms, or fulfillment partners.

Why it works

Operational resilience improves dramatically when recovery capacity already exists before disruption occurs.

Best for

Logistics, manufacturing, SaaS infrastructure, healthcare, telecom, distribution, field services

Execution Steps

1. Identify critical operational dependencies
2. Map continuity partner requirements
3. Build backup partner agreements
4. Test emergency activation workflows
5. Define escalation protocols

Real-world example

A fulfillment company creates backup warehousing partnerships across multiple regions to prevent delivery collapse during disruptions.

Risk Management

1. **Dependency** · 4/5 Partner reliability weak. **Mitigation:** Vet partners carefully.
2. **Operational** · 3/5 Activation delays. **Mitigation:** Run simulations. regularly
3. **Financial** · 3/5 Cost duplication. **Mitigation:** Prioritize critical areas.
4. **Operational** · 3/5 Coordination failures. **Mitigation:** Define ownership clearly.
5. **Legal**· 3/5 Contract gaps. This creates legal or compliance exposure that must be resolved before launch. **Mitigation:** Standardize agreements.

Speed	Effort	Cost	Revenue	Time to cash	Scalability
Medium (1-3 months)	**Medium**	**Medium**	**High**	**Medium**	**High**

Decision-flow: CFO → Operations → Partnerships / BD

519. Create zero-trust reliability audits across operations

Run aggressive internal reviews assuming systems, workflows, vendors, staffing, and infrastructure will fail under pressure.

Why it works

Most operational risk assessments are too optimistic and fail to expose hidden reliability weaknesses.

Best for

Cloud infrastructure, healthcare, telecom, logistics, SaaS, enterprise operations, manufacturing

Execution Steps

1. Identify revenue-critical operations
2. Stress-test assumptions aggressively
3. Simulate worst-case failures
4. Identify hidden weak points
5. Prioritize fixes by revenue exposure

Real-world example

A healthcare platform discovers hidden staffing and vendor dependencies that would have caused catastrophic downtime during demand spikes.

Risk Management

1. **Alignment** · 3/5 Teams become defensive. **Mitigation:** Frame as resilience improvement.
2. **Operational** · 2/5 Audit fatigue. **Mitigation:** Focus on critical systems.
3. **Alignment** · 4/5 Weak follow-through. **Mitigation:** Assign executive accountability.
4. **Operational** · 2/5 Overcomplication. **Mitigation:** Prioritize biggest exposures.
5. **Operational** · 3/5 Hidden issues ignored. **Mitigation:** Track remediation formally.

Speed	Effort	Cost	Revenue	Time to cash	Scalability
Fast (0-30 days)	**Medium**	**Low**	**High**	**Medium**	**High**

Decision-flow: CFO → PMO / Strategy → Operations

520. Create reliability moat marketing around operational

Turn operational consistency, uptime, fulfillment precision, recovery speed, and continuity capability into a visible market differentiation strategy.

Why it works

Most competitors market features. Few market operational trust as a strategic advantage.

Best for

SaaS, logistics, fintech, telecom, healthcare, infrastructure, enterprise services, managed services

Execution Steps

1. Identify strongest operational reliability strengths
2. Gather proof metrics and customer outcomes
3. Build reliability-focused messaging
4. Train sales.s on operational differentiation
5. Integrate into procurement and enterprise pitches

Real-world example

A logistics platform positions operational consistency and recovery speed as its primary enterprise differentiation strategy.

Risk Management

1. **Legal** · 4/5 Claims not supported. This creates legal or compliance exposure that must be resolved before launch. **Mitigation:** Use verified metrics.
2. **Market** · 2/5 Competitors challenge positioning. This limits market impact if not addressed before launch. **Mitigation:** Focus on proof.
3. **Operational** · 4/5 Reliability performance drops. **Mitigation:** Maintain standards.
4. **Commercial** · 3/5 Marketing overpromises. **Mitigation:** Align with operations.
5. **Customer** · 2/5 Weak customer resonance. **Mitigation:** Target reliability-sensitive buyers.

Speed	Effort	Cost	Revenue	Time to cash	Scalability
Fast (0-30 days)	**Low**	**Low**	**High**	**Medium**	**High**

Decision-flow: CFO → Marketing → Operations

From Ideas to Action

Twenty-four ideas. Twenty-four ways to protect revenue by ensuring what was sold is consistently delivered to the standard that retains customers.

Revenue protection does not end at the contract. It ends at delivery. A customer who buys well but receives poorly will not renew, will not refer, and will not stay quiet. Delivery reliability is the last line of commercial defence — and the most directly controllable one.

Before continuing, identify the single idea with the clearest commercial case right now. Name who owns it. Set a date for the first step. That is all that is required.

> ***The business that delivers what it promises does not need to fight for renewals. It earns them.***

What Comes Next

Part 7 — Build Playbook brings everything together. Parts 2 through 6 gave you 520 revenue moves across five commercial dimensions. Part 7 gives you the tools to prioritise them, audit where you stand, and build a 30-day action plan that turns the best ideas into revenue.

From 520 Ideas to One Clear Action

You have just read 520 revenue moves across five commercial dimensions. The ideas are practical, the formats are consistent, and the database is thorough.

The risk now is paralysis. Five hundred and twenty ideas is not a plan. It is a library. The value of the library depends entirely on your ability to select the right idea, at the right time, and act on it with enough focus to see a result.

Part 7 turns the library into a plan. Three tools. One outcome: revenue you can point to.

What This Part Covers

PART 7

Build Playbook & Sprint

7.1 — Revenue Prioritization Matrix — where to focus and which ideas to pursue first.

7.2 — Build Your Revenue Playbook — a sequenced set of revenue moves built around your situation.

7.3 — The 60-Day Revenue Sprint — a prescriptive week-by-week schedule with owners, milestones, and a single measurable outcome.

7.1 — Revenue Prioritization Matrix

This chapter tells you where to start.

Most people finish a book like this with ten ideas in mind and no clear first step. This matrix fixes that. It takes your business as it stands today, identifies the revenue theme with the most urgent opportunity, and points you to the specific ideas most worth acting on first.

It works in two stages. Stage 1 identifies the theme. Stage 2 selects the idea.

Stage 1 — Score Your Business

Read each row. Score it from 1 to 5 based on how well it describes your business right now.

1 = This does not sound like us. 5 = This is exactly our situation.

Score honestly. The output is only useful if the input is real.

Revenue Situation	Score (1–5)	Go to
We need new revenue sources that do not exist yet — new offers, products, or business lines		Part 2 — Create Revenue
Revenue is being left inside existing customer relationships — we are not capturing what we could		Part 3 — Unlock Revenue
Revenue is real but cash is consistently late — payment terms, slow invoices, long sales cycles		Part 4 — Accelerate Revenue
The core model works but we need to reach more customers — new channels, segments, geographies		Part 5 — Expand Revenue
We are losing revenue we should be keeping — churn, discounts, margin erosion, renewals slipping		Part 6 — Protect Revenue

Revenue theme	Score this if it sounds like your business	Score 1 – 5
Create Revenue	We have things we can do that we cannot easily sell.	
Unlock Revenue	We charge less than the value we actually deliver.	

Revenue theme	Score this if it sounds like your business	Score 1 – 5
Accelerate Revenue	Money takes too long to arrive after a deal is done.	
Expand Revenue	Not enough of the right customers are finding or buying.	
Protect Revenue	We are losing customers or margin we should be keeping	

Your highest score is your starting point. If two themes score equally, choose the one with the faster time to cash — this information is available in the metadata table on every idea page.

How to Read Your Score

Score	What it means
1–2	This is not your primary problem right now
3	Worth noting — may become your second sprint
4–5	This is where your revenue is being lost or left

Score	What it means	Next step
4 – 5	Your highest priority. Start here.	Go to the matching section of the book. Choose three ideas. Move to Stage 2.
2 – 3	Real opportunity. Second sprint.	Note the theme. Return to it after your first 60-day sprint is complete.
1	Low urgency right now.	Set aside. Revisit in 90 days.

Stage 2 — Filter Your Best Ideas

Go to the section of the book that matches your highest-scoring theme. Read the chapter opening. Review the ideas. Choose three that feel immediately actionable in your business. Then run each one through the Painkiller filter below.

Step	Question	Your number
1. Annual cost of the problem	What is this problem costing the business each year? Include direct cost, lost revenue, and compounding effects.	$ ________
2. All-in cost of the solution	What is the total cost to implement this idea — time, resource, any direct spend?	$ ________
3. Economic gap	Problem cost minus solution cost	$ ________
4. Value multiple	Economic gap ÷ solution cost = how many times bigger the value is than the cost	________ ×
5. Payback period	Solution cost ÷ annual value generated = months until the move pays for itself	________ months
6. Classification	Not buyable (<1×) · Vitamin (1–2×) · Supplement (2–4×) · Painkiller (4–6×) · Critical (6–8×) · No-Brainer (8×+)	____________

The Painkiller Model — Chapter 1.2

A revenue idea is only worth acting on if the problem it solves costs more than the solution. The model has two numbers: problem cost and solution cost. Divide them to get the value multiple. Any multiple above 3x is worth prioritising. Below 1x is not worth doing.

For each of your three ideas, estimate the annual cost of the problem it solves, the all-in cost of implementing it, and divide to get the value multiple. The idea with the highest multiple and the shortest payback is your first sprint priority.

Revenue idea	Problem cost per year ($)	Solution cost all-in ($)	Value multiple	Payback

The idea that scores highest is your first sprint priority. Write it in the box below before you continue.

Sprint Priority Commitment	
Sprint Priority (the one move)	
Why this one	
Named owner	
Measurable outcome at 60 days	

This is the one.

One idea. One owner. One measurable outcome. Everything in the next two chapters is built around what you write here.

My first sprint priority
The idea I am committing to for the next 60 days:

Value multiple: ________ **Payback:** ________ **Owner:** ____________________

This is your starting point. Take it to Chapter 7.2.

Clarity on one move is worth more than awareness of five hundred.

What Comes Next

7.2 — Build Your Revenue Playbook takes the priority you have just identified and places it inside a structured sequence of moves — a playbook designed to compound the first sprint into 90 days of compounding commercial momentum.

7.2 — Build Your Revenue Playbook

A playbook is a sequence. Not a list.

The Revenue Prioritization Matrix in Chapter 7.1 gave you a starting point. This chapter turns it into a structured sequence of moves, each taken from the idea chapters earlier in this book, each one creating the conditions for the next.

Four pre-built playbooks cover the most common commercial situations. Each one references the exact chapters you need. If none fits precisely, the custom framework at the end builds your own in six steps.

Which profile are you?

WHICH PROFILE ARE YOU?

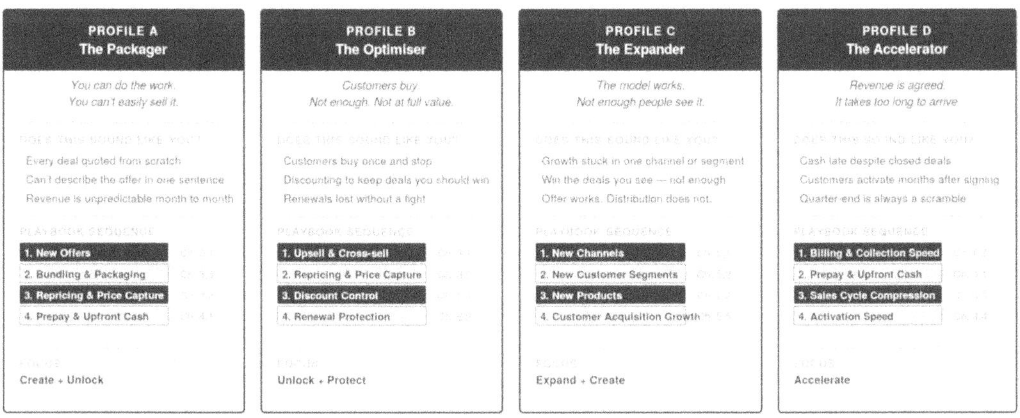

Read all four. The one that sounds most uncomfortable is usually right.

A — The Packager	**B — The Optimiser**	**C — The Expander**	**D — The Accelerator**
You can do the work. You can't easily sell it.	*Customers buy. Not enough. Not at full value.*	*The model works. Not enough people see it.*	*Revenue is agreed. It takes too long to arrive.*
□ Every deal quoted from scratch □ Can't describe the offer in one sentence □ Revenue is unpredictable month to month	□ Customers buy once and stop □ Discounting to win deals you should keep □ Renewals lost without a fight	□ Stuck in one channel or segment □ Win what you see — not enough of it □ Offer works. Distribution doesn't.	□ Cash late despite closed deals □ Customers activate months after signing □ Quarter-end is always a scramble
Create + Unlock	**Unlock + Protect**	**Expand + Create**	**Accelerate**

If two profiles feel equally accurate, your Chapter 7.1 diagnostic score determines the right one. Your highest-scoring revenue theme maps directly to the profile that addresses it.

Profile A **The Packager** *You can do the work. You can't easily sell it.* **FOCUS: Create + Unlock**	DOES THIS SOUND LIKE YOU? □ Every deal quoted from scratch □ Can't describe the offer in one sentence □ Revenue is unpredictable month to month	YOUR SEQUENCE **1.** New Offers **2.** Bundling & Packaging **3.** Repricing & Price Capture **4.** Prepay & Upfront Cash

The core problem is structural, not commercial. The business has genuine capability but no packaging. Every engagement is bespoke even when the work is largely the same. The sequence below builds commercial structure first, then uses it to capture more value from the customers already inside the business.

Your playbook — what to do and where to find it

Step	Move	Chapter	The pain this fixes
1	**New Offers**	Ch. 2.1	We quote the same work from scratch every time
2	**Bundling & Packaging**	Ch. 3.5	Buyers don't know what to choose or where to start
3	**Repricing & Price Capture**	Ch. 3.2	We charge less than the work is worth
4	**Prepay & Upfront Cash**	Ch. 4.1	Cash arrives late and unpredictably

90-Day Outcome The business has at least one named, priced, repeatable offer in market. Average deal value has increased. Revenue is measurably more predictable. A second offer is in development.

Decision-flow: CFO → Sales → Operations

Profile B **The Optimiser** *Customers buy. Not enough. Not at full value.* **FOCUS: Unlock + Protect**	DOES THIS SOUND LIKE YOU? □ Customers buy once and the relationship stops □ Discounting to win deals you should keep anyway □ Renewals lost without a commercial fight	YOUR SEQUENCE **1.** Upsell & Cross-sell **2.** Repricing & Price Capture **3.** Discount Control **4.** Renewal Protection

The core problem is value leakage. The customers exist. The relationships are real. But revenue per customer is below what it should be. Discounts are given away without discipline. Renewals are lost without a fight. The sequence below recovers value already inside the commercial relationship before looking elsewhere.

Your playbook — what to do and where to find it

Step	Move	Chapter	The pain this fixes
1	**Upsell & Cross-sell**	Ch. 3.1	Customers buy one thing when they could buy three
2	**Repricing & Price Capture**	Ch. 3.2	We deliver more than we charge for
3	**Discount Control**	Ch. 6.3	We give away margin to close deals we should win anyway
4	**Renewal Protection**	Ch. 6.2	Renewals are being lost without a commercial fight

90-Day Outcome

Revenue per customer has increased. Discount rates have fallen. Renewal rates are above the pre-playbook baseline. Every renewal now has a proactive commercial motion behind it.

Decision-flow: CFO → Customer Success → Sales

Profile C **The Expander** *The model works. Not enough people see it.* **FOCUS: Expand + Create**	DOES THIS SOUND LIKE YOU? □ Growth stuck in one channel or one segment □ Win the deals you see — not enough of them □ Offer works. Distribution does not.	YOUR SEQUENCE **1.** New Channels **2.** New Customer Segments **3.** New Products **4.** Customer Acquisition Growth

The core problem is distribution, not delivery. The offer has been validated. The unit economics are solid. The business is not reaching all the buyers who would buy from it. The sequence below builds reach first, then drives volume through it.

Your playbook — what to do and where to find it

Step	Move	Chapter	The pain this fixes
1	**New Channels**	Ch. 5.1	We only reach buyers who find us directly
2	**New Customer Segments**	Ch. 5.2	We serve one type of buyer when others have the same problem
3	**New Products**	Ch. 2.2	Growth requires hiring more people every time
4	**Customer Acquisition Growth**	Ch. 5.5	Not enough qualified buyers are entering the funnel

90-Day Outcome

The business generates revenue through at least one new channel or segment. A second revenue stream is producing measurable output. Customer acquisition volume is above the pre-playbook baseline.

Decision-flow: CFO → Sales → Marketing

Profile D **The Accelerator** *Revenue is agreed. It takes too long to arrive.* **FOCUS: Accelerate**	DOES THIS SOUND LIKE YOU? □ Cash is late despite deals being closed □ Customers activate months after signing □ Quarter-end is always a scramble	YOUR SEQUENCE **1.** Billing & Collection Speed **2.** Prepay & Upfront Cash **3.** Sales Cycle Compression **4.** Activation Speed

The core problem is speed, not volume. The deals are closing. The customers are real. But cash is consistently late, activations are slow, and the quarter always ends in a scramble. The sequence below removes the friction between agreement and cash.

Your playbook — what to do and where to find it

Step	Move	Chapter	The pain this fixes
1	**Billing & Collection Speed**	Ch. 4.2	We invoice late and chase payment for weeks
2	**Prepay & Upfront Cash**	Ch. 4.1	We deliver first and get paid months later

Step	Move	Chapter	The pain this fixes
3	**Sales Cycle Compression**	Ch. 4.3	Deals take far longer to close than they should
4	**Activation Speed**	Ch. 4.4	Customers who signed are not using what they bought

> 90-Day Outcome
> Cash flow is materially ahead of where it was before the playbook began. Customer activation time has reduced. Sales cycle length is shorter and close date predictability has improved.

Decision-flow: CFO → Finance → Operations

Build Your Own Playbook

BUILD YOUR OWN PLAYBOOK — 6 STEPS

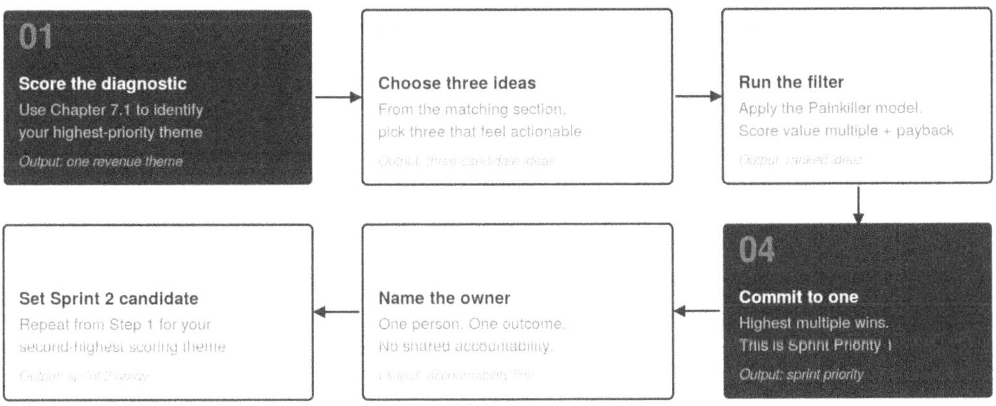

None of the four profiles fits precisely? Build your own.

The six steps below use your Chapter 7.1 diagnostic output as the input and produce a custom playbook ready for the sprint. The process is the same logic the four pre-built profiles were constructed from.

01 Score the diagnostic → **02 Choose 3 ideas** → **03 Run the Painkiller filter** → **04 Commit to one** → **05 Name the owner** → **06 Set Sprint 2 candidate**

How each step works

The table below summarises each step. The descriptions that follow give you the detail needed to execute each one.

Step	Action	Your input
1	Score the Chapter 7.1 diagnostic — your highest theme is your starting point	Highest theme: _________
2	Choose three ideas from that theme's chapter — most executable, not most ambitious	Idea 1: _____ / Idea 2: _____ / Idea 3: _____
3	Run the Painkiller filter (Chapter 7.1) for each idea — highest multiple wins	Sprint Priority: _________
4	Commit to one move — write your Sprint Priority in Chapter 7.1's commitment box	Committed: _________
5	Name the owner and measurable outcome	Owner: _________ / Outcome: _________
6	Set your Sprint 2 candidate (second-highest theme — activate only after Sprint 1 delivers)	Sprint 2 candidate: _________

Step	Action	Output
01	**Score the diagnostic**	One prioritised revenue theme
02	**Choose three ideas**	Three candidate ideas from that section of the book
03	**Run the Painkiller filter**	Ranked list of three ideas with value multiples and payback
04	**Commit to one**	Your confirmed sprint priority — the highest value multiple
05	**Name the owner**	One named individual accountable for execution + one measurable outcome
06	**Set Sprint 2 candidate**	Sprint 2 move ready to activate when Sprint 1 delivers a result

Step 01 — Score the diagnostic. Open Chapter 7.1 and complete the five-statement scoring table. Score your business honestly against each revenue theme. Your highest-scoring theme is your starting point for this playbook. If two themes score equally, choose the one with the faster time to cash — this is visible in the metadata table on every idea page throughout the book.

Step 02 — Choose three ideas. Go to the section of the book that matches your highest-scoring theme. Read the chapter opening to confirm it fits your situation. Then select three ideas from that chapter that feel immediately actionable — not the most ambitious ones, the most executable ones. You are looking for ideas you could start within the next two weeks, not ideas that require months of preparation.

Step 03 — Run the Painkiller filter. For each of the three ideas, complete the filter table in Chapter 7.1. Estimate the annual cost of the problem the idea solves. Estimate the all-in cost of implementing it. Divide to get the value multiple. The idea with the highest multiple and the shortest payback is your Sprint Priority. If two ideas score similarly, the one with the faster time to cash wins.

Step 04 — Commit to one. Write your Sprint Priority in the commitment box at the end of Chapter 7.1. This is the one move that gets the next 60 days. Not three moves. Not two. One. The discipline of committing to a single move is what separates a playbook from a list of good intentions. Everything in Chapter 7.3 is built around the single move you write here.

Step 05 — Name the owner. Every move in the playbook needs a single named individual who is accountable for the result. Not a team. Not a function. One person. Define one measurable outcome they are responsible for delivering. Write both the name and the outcome down before the sprint begins. Without this step, the playbook has no one behind it.

Step 06 — Set the Sprint 2 candidate. Once your Sprint Priority and owner are confirmed, repeat Steps 1 through 5 for your second-highest scoring theme from the Chapter 7.1 diagnostic. This becomes your Sprint 2 candidate — the move waiting to activate when Sprint 1 delivers a result. Do not start Sprint 2 until Sprint 1 has a confirmed and measurable outcome. Running two sprints simultaneously splits the focus the first sprint requires.

- **Maximum four moves in any 90-day sequence.** Each move must create the conditions for the next. More than four is a list, not a playbook.
- **One named owner per move.** Shared accountability is no accountability.

A good playbook is not the one with the most ideas. It is the one that gets executed.

What Comes Next

7.3 — The 60-Day Revenue Sprint takes your confirmed Sprint Priority from Step 4 above and turns it into a prescriptive day-by-day execution plan. What to do on Day 1. Who to involve in Week 2. What to measure by Week 8. One move. One owner. One outcome.

7.3 — The 60-Day Revenue Sprint

A playbook tells you what to do. A sprint tells you when.

Chapter 7.2 gave you a sequenced playbook — a set of moves in the right order drawn from the chapters of this book. This chapter takes the first move in that playbook and turns it into a day-by-day execution plan with a named owner, specific actions, and a single measurable outcome.

The sprint runs for 60 days. The first two weeks are day-by-day — this is where most sprints succeed or fail. From Week 3 onward the sprint moves to weekly milestones. One focal point throughout: the outcome written in the mandate.

The Sprint at a Glance

Five phases. Two weeks of daily precision. Four weeks of weekly discipline. One outcome.

WEEK 1	WEEK 2	WKS 3–4	WKS 5–6	WKS 7–8
Diagnose	Design	Launch	Measure	Scale

The Sprint Mandate

Complete this before Day 1. The sprint has no formal start until the priority, owner, measurable outcome, and dates are agreed. A sprint without a mandate is a list of good intentions.

Sprint Mandate	
Sprint Priority	
Named owner	
Measurable outcome	
Revenue or cash target	$ __________
Sprint start date	
Sprint end date (Day 60)	
Week 8 review date	
Who approves the outcome	

Sprint Mandate

Complete before Day 1. The sprint does not start until this is signed off.

Sprint priority:

Owner: **Outcome:**

Start date: **End date:**

Week 1 — Diagnose

One purpose: confirm the opportunity is real, quantify the value, and align the people who will deliver it. Do not start designing the solution this week. Start by proving the problem is as significant as the Painkiller filter suggested.

Day 1 — Mandate briefing

Brief the sprint owner on the full mandate. Confirm they are available and committed for 60 days. Walk through the value multiple, the measurable outcome, and what success looks like at Week 8. This conversation sets the standard for everything that follows.

Output: Signed mandate. Owner is committed.

Day 2 — Stakeholder map

Identify every person whose buy-in or input is needed for this sprint to succeed. Name them individually, note their role, and schedule a brief for each before the end of Week 1. No stakeholder should be surprised by the sprint in Week 3.

Output: Named list with brief scheduled for each.

Day 3 — Problem validation

Validate the problem cost in real numbers. Pull data: lost revenue, late invoices, stalled deals, churn events — whatever the sprint priority addresses. Make the cost of inaction visible. If the data does not support the value multiple, rerun the Painkiller filter before continuing.

Output: Problem cost confirmed in actual numbers.

Day 4 — Sales and delivery brief

Brief the sales lead and delivery lead. Explain what is being tested, what they need to do differently, and what feedback is needed from them in the first two weeks. A conversation, not a presentation. Their input shapes the design in Week 2.

Output: Sales and delivery teams aligned on the sprint.

Day 5 — Pilot customer identification

Identify three to five existing customers best placed to be the first test of the sprint move. They should know and trust the business, have the problem the sprint addresses, and be willing to give honest feedback before any commitment.

Output: Three to five pilot customers named and ready to contact.

End of Week 1 checkpoint

Mandate confirmed. Problem cost quantified. Teams briefed. Pilot customers named. If any of these are not complete, do not start Week 2.

Week 2 — Design

One purpose: build what is needed to make the first sale or execute the first instance of the sprint move. No perfection required. The goal is a version good enough to test with the pilot customers named on Day 5.

Day 6 — Offer or action design

Define exactly what the sprint move looks like in practice. If it is a new offer, write the scope, price, and a one-line pitch. If it is a process change, define the new steps. Write it down. Unwritten offers do not sell.

Output: Draft offer, process, or pricing defined in writing.

Day 7 — Pricing and terms

Set the price, commercial terms, and any qualifying conditions. Confirm the floor price and get CFO sign-off before the first sales conversation. A pricing decision made under deal pressure is not a pricing decision. Make it now.

Output: Pricing confirmed. CFO sign-off received.

Day 8 — Sales brief and materials

Build the minimum materials needed to sell or execute. One-page summary, one talking-points document. Then brief the sales team. Walk through the offer, the pitch, the price, and the qualifying criteria. Answer every question before the first customer conversation.

Output: Materials ready. Sales team briefed.

Day 9 — Pilot customer outreach

Contact the pilot customers from Day 5. Confirm the problem exists for them. Share what you are testing. Ask for honest feedback before any commitment. A pilot customer who gives difficult feedback in Week 2 saves a failed launch in Week 3.

Output: Pilot conversations held. Feedback documented.

Day 10 — Launch readiness check

Review everything. Offer defined, pricing confirmed, materials ready, sales team briefed, at least one pilot customer ready to move forward. If yes to all, the sprint launches on Day 11. If not, identify the single blocker and remove it.

Output: Launch confirmed. Sprint begins Week 3.

End of Week 2 checkpoint

Offer or action defined. Pricing confirmed. Materials exist. At least one pilot customer is ready. The sprint launches on Day 11.

Weeks 3–8 — Launch, Measure, Scale

From Week 3 onward the sprint moves to weekly milestones. A 30-minute review every Monday. One question: are we on track for the outcome in the mandate? If yes, continue. If not, one adjustment. Do not change the mandate. Adjust the execution.

Weeks 3–4 — Launch

Make the first sale or execute the first sprint instance. Progress pilot customers. Collect feedback after every interaction. Fix delivery or process issues before broadening. A problem discovered with three customers is a learning. With thirty it is a crisis.

Output: First revenue event confirmed. Three or more active opportunities in pipeline.

Weeks 5–6 — Measure

The pilot has run. Measure it honestly. What is the conversion rate? What does the actual value multiple look like against the model? Make one adjustment based on real data, not speculation. Document what changed and why. If the value multiple is confirmed, the case for scaling is made.

Output: Revenue versus target at midpoint. Value multiple confirmed in live data.

Weeks 7–8 — Scale

Broaden beyond the pilot cohort. Document the repeatable process so it can run without daily oversight. In the final week, measure the full result against the mandate. Then decide: continue and scale, adjust and run again, or conclude and move to Sprint 2.

Output: Sprint outcome measured against mandate target. Next decision confirmed.

Sprint 2 starts when Sprint 1 delivers a confirmed result. Not when it looks like it is working. Running two sprints simultaneously splits the focus both require.

Who to Involve and When

A sprint fails when the right people are brought in too late.

- **Brief leadership early and briefly.** A 10-minute update in Week 1 prevents a 60-minute intervention in Week 5.
- **Treat pilot customers as partners, not prospects.** Early involvement means better feedback and faster decisions.
- **Protect the sprint owner's focus.** Every non-sprint request for their time is a threat to the outcome. The CFO owns this boundary.

Role	When	Action
CFO	Day 1	Approve the mandate. Confirm budget and commercial sign-off.
Sprint owner	Pre Day 1	Confirm commitment. Accept the 60-day accountability for the outcome.
Sales lead	Day 2	Brief on the sprint. Ask for pilot willingness and early feedback.
Delivery / Ops	Day 3	Brief on operational requirements. Confirm capacity.
Pilot customer	Week 2	Introduce the sprint move. Request honest feedback before any commitment.
Leadership	Wk 1 + Wk 4	Brief on mandate at start. Share headline result at Week 4.

The Sprint Rules

These are not guidelines. They are the conditions under which the sprint works.

1. **One move at a time**
   The sprint has one priority. Starting a second move before the first delivers a measurable result splits the focus the first move requires. If something else feels urgent, write it down for Sprint 2.

2. **One named owner**
   The sprint owner is named in the mandate. They are accountable for the outcome — not the team, not the function, not a committee. If something goes wrong, there is one person to call.

3. **No scope changes during the sprint**
   The mandate is fixed at Day 1. Changes to scope, pricing, or objective during the sprint signal the mandate was not clear enough. Note the change for next time. Do not act on it now.

4. **Weekly review without exception**
   Thirty minutes every Monday. Same question every week: are we on track? If not, one adjustment. Not a redesign. One adjustment. Reviews that are skipped are sprints that drift.

5. **Measure the actual outcome**
   The outcome in the mandate is what gets measured at Week 8. Not effort. Not activity. Not intent. Revenue received, conversion rate achieved, or cash received.

Three to five customers before broader rollout. Proving the move works in a controlled group is faster and cheaper than fixing it after a full launch.

The Sprint Is the Start

Sixty days is not enough time to transform a business. It is enough time to prove a move works — and proof is what everything else is built on.
The sprint ends with a result. That result tells you one of three things: the move works and should scale, the move works with one adjustment and should run again, or the move does not work here and Sprint 2 should start with the next priority from the playbook.
None of these outcomes is a failure. All of them are information. The only failure is finishing the sprint without measuring the outcome.

> ***Sixty days. One move. One owner. One result. That is how revenue changes.***

Closing

This is the final chapter of the book's core content. You have read 520 revenue moves across six parts, identified your highest-priority opportunity, built a structured playbook, and now have a 60-day sprint plan ready to execute.
The only remaining question is whether Day 1 gets started.

About the Author

Nader Sabry is a growth scientist. He has spent two decades working at the point where growth strategy meets commercial execution — not as a theorist, but as someone who builds, tests, and deploys growth systems in real organisations facing real constraints. CEOs, boards, and governments across the GCC, MENA region, and globally have brought him in for one reason: to find the growth that was sitting in plain sight but going uncaptured.

His background cuts across deep-tech commercialisation, foreign direct investment, capital raising, and organisational growth strategy. He has raised $120 million, facilitated $3 billion in FDI across the GCC and MENA region, and led the commercialisation of $36 million worth of NASA technology. These are not background credentials. They are the commercial proving grounds where the Growth Science framework was built and tested.

He is a practitioner first. Every methodology, every tool, and every framework in his body of work was developed in the field before it was written down. The books came after the results. The programmes came after the methodology worked at scale. That sequence matters. It is the difference between a framework that looks good on paper and one that holds up when a CFO needs to answer for the next quarter.

Between 2020 and 2023 he delivered 52 tier-one keynotes on growth and innovation to senior leaders across global and regional stages. As a contributor to **Harvard Business Review Arabia** from 2021 to 2024, he brought the Growth Science lens to the most consequential growth challenges facing leaders in the region.

He is known, in the words of those who have worked with him, as the person you never want your competition to hire.

The Growth Science Mission

GROWTH SCIENCE MISSION

- Ready Set Growth Hack
- Growth Thinking
- Growth Thinking School
- 10-Day Growth Hacking Challenge
- Growth Analytics
- Harvard Business Review Arabia
- Hire Me If You Can
- **More Revenue, Please** — *This book*

Every major business discipline has been codified, taught, and institutionalised. Finance has a framework. Marketing has a framework. Operations, strategy, technology — all of them have structured bodies of knowledge that can be learned, applied, and built upon. Growth does not. It has been left to instinct, imitation, and trial and error.

This is not an accident. Growth is treated as an outcome — a number to be chased — rather than a discipline to be mastered. Business education teaches all the surrounding disciplines but leaves growth itself as something practitioners are expected to figure out on their own. The result is a fragmented, reactive, and deeply inconsistent approach to the most important commercial question any organisation faces.

Growth Science exists to correct that. It treats growth as what it actually is: a science. A discipline with its own methodology, its own tools, its own language, and its own body of evidence. One that can be learned systematically, applied deliberately, and improved over time.

The mission is to structurally enable growth through four dimensions. Education that builds growth thinking as a durable capability. Tools that give practitioners the means to measure and act. Practice that closes the gap between knowing and doing. And cutting-edge technology that disrupts the future of how growth is built, sustained, and compounded.

The books, the programmes, the analytics platform, and the challenge are not separate products. They are different expressions of the same mission — each one addressing a different barrier between where growth currently sits and where it should be: a core organisational capability that every business builds deliberately.

The Books

Ready Set Growth Hack was the entry point — a practical, accessible framework for anyone who wanted to start thinking and acting like a growth practitioner. It became a bestseller because it treated growth as something learnable, not reserved for a specific type of organisation or a specific budget.

Growth Thinking went deeper. It gave practitioners a design methodology for how growth thinkers approach problems — how they frame a challenge, run experiments, and turn outputs into repeatable systems. The methodology is now used by more than 5,000 practitioners, 150+ Fortune 1000 companies, and over 100 unicorns.

Hire Me If You Can addressed the talent dimension. Knowing how to grow is only half the problem. Building and hiring teams with genuine growth capability is the other half. The book gives leaders the tools to identify, develop, and hire people who bring real growth capability with them.

More Revenue, Please — the book you are holding — is the commercial application. 520 specific moves across five commercial dimensions, focused entirely on generating more revenue from what a business already has. Not theory. A system with a 60-day sprint attached.

Order the books at nadersabry.com

Ready Set Growth Hack	Growth Thinking	Hire Me If You Can
Scan to order	Scan to order	Scan to order

Beyond the Books

The Growth Thinking School has trained more than 12,300 students in the Growth Thinking methodology — practitioners at every level building growth as a durable personal and organisational capability.

The 10-Day Growth Hacking Challenge is the methodology in action. In ten days, contenders apply the Growth Thinking framework to their own business, generating real results with measurable commercial impact. Collectively, challenge contenders have generated $124 million in revenue and a 634 percent return on investment against a $1 million scholarship mandate.

Growth Analytics is the data and AI layer of the ecosystem. More than 150 tools built to help practitioners measure, track, and act on growth signals in real time — extending the framework from strategic insight into daily operational execution.

The Track Record

The work is grounded in commercial reality. Nader has raised $120 million, facilitated $3 billion in FDI across the GCC and MENA region, and led $36 million in NASA technology commercialisation. He has worked directly with organisations building growth at national and regional scale across some of the world's most growth-focused economies.

$120M	$3B	$36M	52
Raised	FDI · GCC/MENA	NASA Tech Commercialisation	Tier-1 Keynotes · 2020–2023

More Revenue, Please is the latest expression of the Growth Science mission — the most commercially direct, the most immediately executable, and the most explicitly focused on the revenue dimension of what growth science delivers.
The mission is not finished. The next book, programme, and tool are already in development.

Growth is not an event. It is a system. Build it deliberately.

To follow the work and access the full Growth Science ecosystem:
nadersabry.com · mygrowththinking.com

www.ingramcontent.com/pod-product-compliance
Lightning Source LLC
LaVergne TN
LVHW060012210926
848481LV00013B/3689
* 9 7 8 1 7 3 8 0 5 4 3 2 9 *